Sourcebook
for Modern Catechetics

VOLUME 2

Sourcebook for Modern Catechetics

VOLUME 2

Edited by
Michael Warren

Saint Mary's Press
Christian Brothers Publications
Winona, Minnesota

This book is for Berard Marthaler,
to honor his contribution to catechetical thought,
marked by his scholarly energy,
pastoral insight, and uncommon wisdom.

Genuine recycled paper with 10% post-consumer waste.
Printed with soy-based ink.

The publishing team for this book included Robert P. Stamschror, development editor; Jacqueline M. Captain, manuscript editor; Holly Storkel and Alan S. Hanson, typesetters; Maurine R. Twait, art director; Rick Korab, Punch Design, Inc., cover designer; pre-press, printing, and binding by the graphics division of Saint Mary's Press.

Printed in the United States of America

Printing: 9 8 7 6 5 4 3 2 1

Year: 2005 04 03 02 01 00 99 98 97

ISBN 0-88489-392-8

Contents

Part D. Evaluating Catechetical Structures and Developments

Part E. Catechism and Catechesis

Part F. Church (Catholic) Schools

Part G. Ecclesial Documents

Preface

Since the publication of the first *Sourcebook for Modern Catechetics* in 1983, the situation of catechetics has changed, in some ways, for the good. The first volume of *Sourcebook* contributed to that positive direction. It made available to students doing advanced study important source material of the catechetical renewal. These same students made the material available to catechists at the diocesan and parish level. As a result, the foundations of the renewal have now come to be more widely understood and appreciated. This incremental nature of volume 1's influence was quite unforeseen in the days when I made my rounds with publishers, seeking a hearing for my project. Another happy result—possibly a coincidence—is that publishers now seem to be more ready to risk publishing similar sets of source material in other pastorally related fields. Volumes of liturgical source documents have been published, and at least one scholar is planning a collection of source documents in pastoral ministry. Having such documents gathered in one place is also nurturing interdenominational ferment in Christian education, as Protestants and Catholics have access to formative elements in one another's traditions.

Far more than for volume 1, selecting the materials for a second volume of the *Sourcebook for Modern Catechetics* has been an eclectic process. Establishing connections among various published materials and making decisions about what to include and what to omit were even more difficult for this volume. Additionally, increased publishing costs set a limit on the number of selections. In the end, the materials I chose for this volume were those that shed light on the catechetical questions I was asking and on what I sense will be the key catechetical issues in the future.

Now that the material is assembled, those questions and issues seem more clear. The end of the twentieth century is a time marked with a colonization of the human spirit by those who control electronic communications. The unifying link among the disparate materials here is the problem of maintaining, in such a time, a vibrant Gospel commitment in local churches. Without the human activities of naming, judging, deciding, and acting—behind all of which is the more basic activity of speaking—

the local church will not be able to develop itself as a distinctive Christian cultural zone within a wider culture. To name, judge, decide, act—and speak—in keeping with the Spirit of Jesus can only be done gradually and as a struggle toward fidelity, especially because it involves taking a Gospel stance toward the earth, toward the distribution and uses of wealth, toward the resolution of conflict, and toward those who are social outsiders.

The unifying link, then, among the disparate materials in this volume is their attention to this overriding issue of ecclesial fidelity and the insights they offer into the kind of catechetical enterprise that will address it.

The material included here indicates the kind of sound scholarship that has become a feature of catechetical theory and research worldwide. This scholarship is not the "ivory tower" variety, insulated from this-world concerns. Though this volume is too small to indicate the extent of such scholarship, its essays cross varied disciplines: theology, religion, history, sociology, education, cultural studies, social and institutional analysis, hermeneutics, and pastoral reflection. Catechetics is as solidly interdisciplinary as any field of study I know.

What is lacking here, due to the limited number of selections, are catechetical materials from Asia, Africa, and Latin America, scenes of creative catechetical ferment. From these sources will surely come other volumes of catechetical materials and documents.

Grateful acknowledgments are in order. Though it is true that I edited this volume, I did not do so by myself. Without the time awarded me by colleagues and administrators at Saint John's University, who supported my applications for a reduced teaching load, this volume would have remained a fervent dream.

The one who helped most with my selections and organization for this volume was Berard Marthaler of Catholic University, repeating the indispensable help he had given for volume 1. Ironically, when the size of the book became a problem, he convinced me to leave out several writings of his own that I had originally selected, and called my attention instead to the important "Guide for Catechists." Through his astute essays in this volume, readers will get a sense of his contribution to catechesis.

Thanks are also due to Saint Mary's Press, who took a financial risk in publishing volume 1 and are doing so again with this volume. I owe particular thanks to Father Bob Stamschror of Saint Mary's Press, who showed indefatigable patience in the back and forth of thirteen different versions of this volume and at least a hundred letters.

MICHAEL WARREN

PART A
Initiation and Worship

Introduction

MICHAEL WARREN

My claim is that the ministry of catechesis is not so much a ministry to the Gospel understandings of the local community as it is to the *practice* of those Gospel understandings. If there is merit in my claim, the focus of catechesis shifts from the communication of ideas to concern for the sacramentality of group life of a particular ecclesia. Catechesis, as an aspect of the ministry of the word, is not responsible for all dimensions of ministry. Yet it cannot succeed without concern for how all ministerial efforts coalesce to form a particular kind of congregation.

Through his study of the North African Christian communities, Thomas Finn reminds us in reading 1 how thoroughly attention to the restructuring of behavior ("demonstrated reform of conduct") marked all the early Christian churches. In several places in this essay, Finn relates how habits of seeking entertainment in the spectacles of theater, racetrack, and boxing ring were reversed in favor of a new set of spectacles—Christian spectacles involving communal rituals celebrating an alternative set of perceptions, convictions, and values. With behavior thus restructured, so was desire. Finn's description of this process of restructuring has powerful implications for our own time, when marketeers have mastered techniques for orchestrating desire.

Finn also highlights the close connection between *aversio,* or turning away, and *conversio,* or turning toward. Conversion is impossible without a corresponding aversion. Conversion and aversion represent the two sides of the coin of discipleship. At issue was whether one's primary allegiance was to the empire or to the Reign of God. The rites of Christian initiation involved a process of choosing on which side to stand and of testing the quality of one's allegiance. In the initiation process, the individual's efforts were bolstered by "the capacity of ritual to elicit the restorative powers inherent in the community" (page 27). Here the ongoing conversion of the community was even more important than the conversion of the individual. To paraphrase P. L. Berger and Thomas Luckmann, conversion is not a big deal; it is the maintenance of conversion at the communal level that is the big deal.

"The restorative powers of the community" cannot be taken for granted, however. The community could well have, as its unspoken but lived allegiance, a primal commitment to the empire. That commitment to civil power could be masked by an oft-spoken but unlived commitment to the Gospel. Reading 2 attempts to surface this danger.

When people stroll into the zone of worship, their lived commitments stroll in with them and may possibly belie what they say and do around the altar. What is written in the texts they read from during the worship ritual may not at all be written in their life, either individually or corporately. A major crisis for Christian faith in our time may be the disconnection between what we intone around the altar and what we say and do in our everyday business. Part of the ongoing task of catechesis is to reconnect and make integral these two zones.

Reading 2 claims that the highest form of catechesis is the teaching embodied in the church's practice. "The preoccupation of catechesis is not the condition of the community's understanding of the Christian message but rather the condition of the community's practice of that understanding." An embodiment, an enfleshing of Jesus' teaching, is what makes the local church an effective sacrament of God's living presence. Achieving this goal is, in Finn's words, "arduous beyond words," demanding, I would add, a lifelong struggle for fidelity.

Further Reading

Finn, Thomas M. "Ritual Process and the Survival of Early Christianity: A Study of the Apostolic Tradition of Hippolytus." *Ritual Studies* 3, no. 1 (1989): 69–89.

It Happened One Saturday Night: Ritual and Conversion in Augustine's North Africa

THOMAS M. FINN

That people express in ritual what moves them most is an anthropological axiom (Wilson 1954:230). The importance of the axiom for the historian of religion is that rituals disclose what most moves a people and, in the process, open up a broad new avenue into their inner history.[1]

Consider the study of early Christianity, bound as it has been largely by the Scriptures (canonical and non-canonical) on the one hand and the writings of the church fathers on the other.[2] With ritual as a way of seeing what was there once, early Christian liturgy becomes an invaluable source for the study of early Christianity: one is enabled to see and feel things as they saw and felt them. Nowhere is this more evident than in the ritual process that made Christians of Jews and others. Known as the "catechumenate" (De Puniet 1910, Dujarier 1979), the process began with formally registered interest, ended with baptism, and could take from several years to a lifetime. Elsewhere I have explored the importance of the catechumenate for the survival and spread of early Christianity (Finn 1989). Here I explore pivotal rites in the North African catechumenate to determine what moved the early Christians most about conversion.

The rites in question consisted of a solemn exorcism, its dénouement the renunciation of Satan, and its concomitant, the recitation of the creed. Together they formed the pivot around which the ritual process of conversion turned, at least in the Western Empire. Already deeply planted in second-century soil (Finn 1989), these rites achieved their most distinctive development by the end of the fourth century in North Africa. To understand what they disclose about the early Christian and conver-

Reprinted from the *Journal of the American Academy of Religion* 58, no. 4 (1990): 589–616. Copyright © 1990 by the American Academy of Religion Scholars Press. Used with permission.

sion, however, an overview of the whole ritual process of conversion in North Africa is in order. With the catechumenate as context, we can then consider the pivotal rites in detail, and, finally, attempt to understand their function and what they disclose.

The North African Catechumenate[3]

When North Africans became seriously interested in the church, they sought preliminary instruction given either in private or in small groups.[4] If interest quickened, the next step was entry into the catechumenate, signaled by inscription. The rite consisted of a formal interrogation about the state of the inquirer's belief and commitment, tracing the sign of the cross on the forehead (consignation), exorcism, the imposition of hands, and the ingestion of salt (Aug. *De cat. rud.* 26:50). From that point on the candidate was a *catechumenos* or *auditor,* traditional terms for those who, though not yet Christians, could, nonetheless, "hear" the scriptural readings and the interpretive homilies at the Eucharist. Dismissed at the end of the homily, the catechumens were thereby excluded from the Eucharist proper. But since they bore the mark of Christ's ownership (the sign of the cross imprinted at inscription), they were counted as his and were gradually initiated into the community, normally over a two-year period.[5]

Although their role was largely learning by listening, what they learned was intended to shape both mind and heart. Indeed, the test of whether conversion was taking hold lay in demonstrated reform of conduct (Burghardt 1964). However slowly, one's values and conduct had to change. Thus the connotation of the Greek-based term "catechumen," the root of which was *echo:* the catechumens were to "echo" in their conduct what they heard in church (Finn 1967:60). Augustine, for instance, expresses horror at the prospect of a catechumen of unbridled sexuality entering the baptismal font (*De adult. coniug.* 2:16), and his younger Carthaginian contemporary, Quodvultdeus,[6] chides both catechumen and Christian who want to embrace the saving scriptural "spectacles" of mystery and miracle and the withering far-from-scriptural spectacles of theatre, racetrack, and the fights (*SI* 2:1–17). In an earthy play on a passage about Elijah (1 Kgs. 18:21), he describes them as people who limp about as if "with two swollen testicles" (*SIII* 1:14).

Those catechumens who clearly did not "limp" and appeared ready for baptism were encouraged to hand in their names at the start of Lent, as Augustine himself did at Milan in 387 (*Conf.* IX, 6:14). The rite (appropriately called *nomen dare*) included a homily and the chanting of Ps. 41(42): "As the hart longs for flowing streams. . . ."[7] At that point the catechumens became *competentes*, because, as Augustine puts it (*S* 216:1), they seek baptism at the same time (*petentes simul*). From then on their daily fare was the instructional part of the Eucharist (*missa catechumenorum, S* 49:8) and the strict observance of Lent: no wine, no meat, no baths, no public entertainment, and no use of marriage.[8] Although intended for faithful, competents, and catechumens alike, the homilies often featured the competents prominently, intent especially on their final prebaptismal moral formation.

"Competency" was especially a time for probing and testing. As a result, exorcism was a frequent part of the competents' experience. As Augustine puts it, the purpose was to grind the competents as grain into flour for the bread that he calls *corpus mysticum Christi* and thinks of as both the church and the Eucharist (*S* 229). In the rite[9] the ministers imposed their hands on the competents, invoked the power of Christ and the Trinity, and voiced angry biblical rebukes of the devil, peremptorily commanding his instant expulsion. The striking finale was "exsufflation": grasping the competents, the exorcist hissed in their faces. Were exsufflation done to a statue of the emperor, according to Augustine, the offence would have been the capital crime of denigrating majesty (*Sec. Jul. resp.* 3:199).[10] As for the competents themselves, they may have been dressed in coarse leather outer garments (*tunicae pelliciae*) and stood barefoot, with necks bent (Busch 1938:439–440). Although we will return to the subject shortly, one can sense that exorcism could be a terrifying experience. *Caveat competens!*

Prayer, exorcism, catechetical homily, and strict Lenten observance, then, were the regular diet of the competents. As baptism approached, the preparations intensified. On Saturday, fifteen days before Easter, the bishop confided the baptismal creed to them (Poque 1966:27, n. 2) in a rite (*traditio symboli*) which required him to present the creed orally article by article in the course of a homily.[11] The competents were asked to repeat it several times during the homily, thus initiating the work of memorizing the creed. During the week following, their sponsors took charge of recitation practice (Aug. *S* 214, and *S 1 Guelf.* 1:11).[12]

Next came what I consider the pivotal rites in the process of conversion. Since their reconstruction is the subject of the next section, here I indicate only setting and sequence. On Saturday, eight days after the *traditio*, when the rite of lamplighting (*lucernarium*) signaled the arrival of evening, competents and community gathered in a solemn vigil comprised of prayers, psalmody, and homiletic instruction. Well after darkness set in, two of three related rites were celebrated: the scrutiny and the renunciation of Satan, followed on Sunday morning by the recitation of the creed.[13] They were accompanied by homilies which first dwelt on the challenge of conversion built into the rites and then explored the articles of the creed.

Later in the day, the competents returned for another *traditio*, this time the confiding of the Lord's Prayer (*traditio orationis dominicae*), which the competents, having learned it by heart, would recite on Easter either as they emerged from the baptismal font or at their first Eucharist or both: as newborn members of the family of God they could rightly pray "Our Father."[14] Prominent in the rite was a homily on the prayer organized petition by petition (Aug. *S* 56–59).

On Wednesday of "Great" Week,[15] the Lenten liturgy turned toward the passion of Christ, with the lessons at the Eucharist devoted to the Lamentations of Jeremiah (Jer. 9) and to Matthew's account of the unknown woman who anointed Jesus for his burial (Mt. 26:1–13). The psalm of the day was Ps. 21 (22): "My God, my God, why hast thou forsaken me. . . ."

On Thursday, bathing was permitted and the fast relaxed for a special evening meal and the Eucharist, both in commemoration of the Last Supper (Aug. *Ep. ad Jan.* 54:4–5). The foot-washing recounted in the Gospels (Jn. 13:1–11; cf Lk. 22:24–27) appears to have been part of the rite.[16]

Friday initiated what Augustine calls "the most holy triduum of the crucifixion, burial, and resurrection" (*Ep. ad Jan.* [55] 14). The day was devoted to the remembrance of Christ's crucifixion, with rites that included the reading of the passion according to Matthew and a homily on the passion. The order of the day also called for fasting in solidarity with the competents as they approached the end of their long and exacting journey (Aug. *S* 210:1).

And so the stage was set for Saturday and the "sublime nightwatch" (Aug. *S. Guelf.* 5). Devoted to biblical lessons, responsive prayers (largely psalms), meditation, and biblical homilies, the vigil lasted from sunset, when the paschal candle was lit,[17] to cockcrow Easter morning, when baptism was celebrated. A central event of vigil was the second recitation of the creed—as in the earlier vigil, an extremely solemn public moment.[18]

At cockcrow the process of conversion reached its climax in the rites of baptism proper: 1) baptismal water was consecrated; 2) the competents processed to the font while chanting the now familiar Ps. 41 (42); 3) they removed their garments (the coarse leather penitential tunic); 4) they responded to a final inquiry into their faith and firm will as they stood waist-deep in the font; and 5) they were immersed three times in the name of the Father, of the Son, and of the Holy Spirit. When they emerged the bishop imposed his hand on them, anointed their heads with chrism, and traced the sign of the cross on their foreheads, probably also with chrism. The newly baptized then dressed in white, including a linen head cover. They then received a baptismal candle and the embrace of the congregation. Finally, they celebrated their first Eucharist, which included a cup of mixed milk and honey and a homily on the resurrection. As newly-baptized, they would return later Easter morning for a second Eucharist (and perhaps in the afternoon for a third), hearing a homily devoted to the meaning of the Eucharist.[19]

White-robed, they returned each day for the rest of the week to celebrate the Eucharist and hear homilies on the resurrection accounts in the Gospels and the Acts of the Apostles.[20] They sat prominently in the chancel of the city's basilica, resplendent in their "garments of resurrection"; the only thing to cloud their horizons, as Augustine saw it, was how to keep unstained the inner renovation symbolized by their garb, which they would wear for the last time on the octave day of their baptism: would they also put away what had been accomplished in baptism (S 259, 260)?

The Pivotal Rites[21]

Holy Week and Easter Week were official holidays (*dies feriati*), during which the newly-baptized (*infantes*, Aug. S 228) occupied center stage. They had come from every station of life: rich, poor, masters, and slaves. And they had come from the surrounding villages and town as well as from the episcopal city.[22] Their diversity added to the drama, as did the fact that the non-resident competents were accustomed to take up residence in the city for the whole of Lent and Easter Week; their families, encouraged by the holidays, would swell the congregation for the climactic rites. Indeed, an important function of the Easter holidays was to focus public attention on those new-born, who, in their long and taxing journey, had moved from unbeliever to catechumen to competent to newly-baptized and, finally, to faithful, when, as Augustine notes, they shed their prominence, mingled with the rest of the congregation, and wore their white no longer (S 260).

When infant baptism came to be the norm toward the end of the fifth century (Whitaker 1981:38–39), the charged ambience would change. But here in Roman Africa at the end of the fourth century and in the early fifth the ritual drama of baptism and its Lenten preparations were the *spectacula christiana*—the new theatre, the new racetrack, and the new boxing ring.[23] It is difficult to overestimate the impact of this long-extended ritual drama on convert and community alike. But one need not simply imagine. In the celebrated diary of her pilgrimage, the fourth-century Spanish nun and contemporary of Augustine, Egeria, speaks of Jerusalem's churches and streets, which, she says, mourned with weeping and rang with applause (*Itin. Aeth.:* 37, 47).

Clearly the events of Holy Week and Easter Week marked the ritual climax of conversion. But the pivotal rites, hardly less intense, are our direct concern, and they anticipated Easter by a week. As we have already seen, the rites were scrutiny (*scrutatio, examen*), the renunciation of the devil (*renunciatio*), and the recitation of the creed (*redditio symboli*). However striking Augustine's personal drama of conversion in the garden at Cassiciacum, the even more striking ritual drama, which he calls the "stages of curative treatment" (*ordo curationis*), began in earnest on Saturday evening before what would come to be called Palm Sunday.[24]

With the rite of lamp-lighting (*lucernarium;* Weller 1959:36–38) the ritual moment of conversion was at hand. Competents and community gathered in vigil for a night devoted to prayer, psalms, biblical readings, and instruction. In the dead of night the competents—naked, heads bowed, and barefoot—were led out before the assembled community, there to stand on coarse animal hides (goat skin, *cilicium*).[25]

Such was the setting for the first rite, a solemn exorcism, or as Augustine puts it, *sacramentum exorcismi* (*S* 227). As in their Lenten exorcisms, the competents heard the invocations of Christ and the Trinity and the biblical condemnations of the devil and his legions, and they felt the rough hands and hot breath of the exorcist. But this exorcism was not like the others. Called "scrutiny," it involved a physical exam to determine whether any competent had a disease that would disqualify from baptism.[26] While the exam was conducted, the congregation chanted an interpretive psalm.[27] Quodvultdeus has provided the only firsthand account of the rite. In a homily the following morning he asks:

> Beloved, what is it that was celebrated among you? What is it that was done this past night that we have not done on previous nights? From a secret place you were each presented before the entire church, and then with your head bowed, which was proudly upright before, and standing barefoot on goat skin, the scrutiny was performed on you, and while the humble and most noble Christ was invoked, the proud devil was rooted out of you. All of you were humble of demeanor and humbly you pleaded by praying, chanting, and saying: "Probe me, Lord, and know my heart" (Ps 138:3). He has probed, he has weighed, he has touched the hearts of his servants with his fear, by his power he has caused the devil to flee, and he has freed his household from the devil's way. (*SI:*1, 4–7)

The scrutiny culminated in the rite of the renunciation of the devil, long a critical rite in baptismal preparation.[28] Still naked and barefoot on goat skin but standing upright, the competent professed for all to hear: "I renounce the devil, his pomps, and his angels" (Aug. *S* 215:1; Quod. *SI*:1,11). Before Constantine, the monster which loomed behind the ancient words was a hostile Roman state (Finn 1989); after Constantine, it was the omnipresent culture of the Greco-Roman "world" (*saeculum, mundum*).[29] For Augustine the world was inward, made up of desire gone awry (*S* 116:2); for Quodvultdeus it was the outer, cultural world of the racetrack, the theatre, and the arena (*SI*, 2:1–28; *SIII*, 1:15–21).[30] But both agreed that fear and desire unleashed by the "world," be it inner or outer, were the weapons the devil used with cunning to capture and break the spectators.

Scrutiny and renunciation were parts of a whole: scrutiny had made renunciation possible, and renunciation had given scrutiny meaning. Augustine called the two rites *aversio;* the competents had "turned away" from the devil and his world, declaring before the packed assembly "a glorious strife" against them (*S* 216:6). Quodvultdeus saw the rites as a public profession, the words of which were recorded by God and his angels (*SIII:* 1, 10–12). For both, however, the critical result was that the competents, in Augustine's words, were "free from their former master (*immunis*) and healthy (*sanitas*) in body and heart" (*S* 216:11). Suzanne Poque highlights the impact of the two rites: "Naked, overcome with lack of sleep, stomachs empty, unwashed, barefoot, head bowed, the candidate for baptism felt the insulting breath of the exorcist, heard the curses hurled at the mysterious occupant of his being, and professed to renounce the baggage of the world: his pride was put to the test and 'the old man' began to die in him" (1966:27).

The final rite of the three awaited the arrival of morning and the (Palm) Sunday Eucharist (Aug. *S* 215:1; Quod. *SI:* 1, 1–4). The heart of it was the recitation of the creed, for which, as we have seen, the competents had been preparing all week, followed by a homily based on its articles (Aug. *S* 215; Quod. *SI, SII, SIII*). At Hippo the chant on the occasion was Ps. 26 (27): "The Lord is my light and my salvation; whom should I fear . . . ?" (Poque 1966:31). Individually the competents came forward, now not to renounce the devil but to profess their faith, which Augustine implies was a cry of the heart (*S* 216:5). The awe of the occasion and the strain of the previous night's ordeal, however, apparently caused many a heart to clutch with fear and many a memory to go blank. But all was not lost, for one had a second chance to make a creedal recitation at the Easter Vigil (Aug. *S* 58:1). Augustine has preserved something of the drama of the rite in his account of the conversion of the celebrated Neoplatonic philosopher, Marius Victorinus, at Rome about 360:

> Finally, when the hour arrived for him to make a public profession of his faith—which at Rome those who are about to enter into thy grace make from a platform in the full sight of the faithful people, in a set form of words learned by heart—the presbyters offered Victorinus the chance to make his profession more privately, for this was the custom for some who were likely to be afraid through bashfulness. But Victorinus chose rather to profess his salvation in the presence of the holy congregation. . . . So, then, when he ascended the platform to make his profession, everyone, as they recognized him, whispered his name one to the other, in tones of jubilation. Who was there among them that did not know him? And a low murmur ran through the mouths of all the rejoicing multitude: "Victorinus! Victorinus!" There was a sudden burst of exaltation at the sight of him. He pronounced the true faith with an excellent boldness, and all desired to take him to their very heart—indeed, by their love and joy they did take him to their heart. And they received him with loving and joyful hands. (*Conf.* VIII: 2:5)[31]

What had started the night before with *aversio* now reached that moment which Augustine calls *conversio* and identifies as this public profession of faith (*redditio symboli*). In the stages of "curative treatment" recitation was the counterpart of renunciation, which in turn was the counterpart of scrutiny.[32]

The cure had begun to take, and conversion was in evidence. The competents, upright and on their own, had turned from the devil to Christ and made with him a "pact" (*pactum*), the terms of which were spelled out in the creed (Aug. *S* 216:2). But conversion was as yet embryonic. Quodvultdeus regards the newly-professed as in the womb of "holy mother church" who carries them joyfully to the day of rebirth and on the way feeds them with the rites, especially scrutiny, renunciation, and recitation (*SIII:* 1, 1–4). Rebirth awaited the "rite of the font and of baptism" (Aug. *S* 228:3)—which is another story, beyond the scope of this study.

Function and Meaning

I take the axiom that people express in ritual what moves them most to be a fair formulation of the ancient liturgical principle, *lex orandi, lex credendi:* rituals do indeed reveal the deep convictions and experiences of a community. From start to finish the rituals of the catechumenate had deeply etched in them what most moved early Christians about conversion. This is especially the case with the pivotal rites just reconstructed. They at once expressed and shaped the North African Christian experience of self, other, community, the world at hand, and the world beyond.

At the outset, however, one is faced with a difficult problem. The rites speak in the many voices of poetry and drama.[33] Like biblical texts, they require exegesis, with this difference, that the method of the ancients was mystagogy (Finn 1967:59–73), controlled on the one hand by a common tradition and on the other by typology and allegory—an exacting enterprise for even the giants among the ancient mystagogues like Origen, Cyril of Jerusalem, Ephrem Syrus, and Augustine. For the modern interpreter, who sits astride the shoulders of the ancients, the enterprise must include liturgical and social history as well. In short, an even more exacting task, which prompts me to confine my attention in this section largely to the competents and my observations to four themes: 1) a threshold people, 2) ritual combat, 3) culture and the convert, and 4) the power of ritual.

1. A Threshold People

The most obvious thing about the competents is their anonymity: they were faceless, naked, head bowed, barefoot, wholly passive, and without identity, personality, or sexuality. Not even "nobodies," they were just bodies. Indeed, they were not even the exorcists' primary object: the devil who inhabited them was. Except as *competentes*—those about to be baptized—they had no status. Whether rich or poor, master or slave, they were treated the same (Quod. *SI*, 1:7). As they stood abjectly before the congregation they evoked the familiar image of the slave auction (Aug. *S* 116:3), and Augustine and Quodvultdeus repeatedly depict them as enslaved captives.

How had they come to their present plight? Quodvultdeus answers that their "ancient and begrimed enemy," the devil, captured them in the mad fury of the racetrack or through the lewd desires unleashed in the theatre or by the savagery of the arena (*SI*, 2:1–10). Augustine offered his competents a less colorful reason: in as much as they have sinned they languish under the deadly, everlasting, and accursed fault destined for punishment (*S* 215:5). Although Quodvultdeus explained that already in Adam they had been ensnared by the devil (*SII*, 10:2), and Augustine also intimated that descent from Adam was the cause of their condition (*S* 228:1; 233:3, 246:5), neither homilist has much to say to the competents about Adam and the Fall. Rather they reflect the traditional understanding built into the rites and first made explicit by Origen: sin is a contract with the devil, to whom the sinner sells her- or himself, becoming his debtor and slave in the bargain (Lukken 1973:185–187).

Nonetheless, in spite of their condition, the competents were neither hopeless aliens nor outcasts. From the moment of inscription they were of the church. As such they attended the *missa catechumenorum,* heard the scriptures read and explained, and, from the beginning of Lent on, were very much a presence in the congregation. Recall that for Quodvultdeus they were in the womb of holy mother church (*SIII,* 1:3); according to Augustine, they were in the throes of birth to the faith (*S* 216:7). Yet the competents were not insiders either: they stood in the dark on the edges of the congregation, on the boundaries of the church as slaves, and were treated as enemy territory, if not the enemy himself.

Anonymity involved ambiguity: they were neither insiders nor outsiders but people in between. In transition, they stood on the no-man's land between the world which they sought to leave and the church which they sought to enter. Of both but in neither, they were in a state which anthropologists call "liminal," that is, they were a "threshold people" who elude the positions assigned by law, custom, convention, and even ceremonial (Turner 1969:95). Characteristic of "liminars," whether modern or ancient, is the fact that two worlds meet in them, the world from which they are being separated and the world into which they are being initiated. What intrigues me about the liminars of Augustine's North Africa is a fact not often enough acknowledged: one hundred years or more after Theodosius proclaimed orthodox Christianity (392) the religion of the empire, the imperial world and the ecclesial world still stood poles apart.[34] In the values proclaimed by the rites of scrutiny and renunciation and in the mystagogy of Augustine and Quodvultdeus (and countless others homilists; Finn 1967:99–103) there was no union of church and state, no "establishment" of Christianity. As will be clear shortly, they were two mutually opposed worlds—the *ecclesia* and the *saeculum*—embodied in the competents, who were liminal in both worlds, and their liminality dramatically reminded the church of its own stance on the threshold positioned between the here and now and the hereafter. Granted that Ambrose and Augustine could invoke the martial power of the Roman world, the rites on which they commented continued to despise that world.

2. Ritual Combat

Indeed, the controlling metaphor in the rites is struggle (*agonista, certamen*) between church and world. Recall for a moment the physical circumstances of the scrutiny: the dead of night, the procession of the naked candidates and their arraignment before the community, the goat skin, their empty, sleepless, grimy bodies, imposition of the exorcist's hands and his insulting breath, the imprecations, the physical inspection. Surveying the scene which had just been enacted, Augustine cried out: "Behold where the stadium is; behold where the wrestling grounds are; behold where the racetrack is; behold where the boxing ring is!" (*S* 216:6).

A contest of Olympic proportions was at hand: a cosmic struggle between the world embodied in the competents and the world embodied in the exorcist. About the competents' world, as we have seen, it was devil's. The conviction behind this *exorcismus solemnis* was that the devil inhabited the competents. The dead of night, for instance, prompted Augustine to alert his competents: "For you are still in darkness and darkness is in you. . . . Now at last be weary of the Babylonian Captivity! Behold Jerusalem. . . ." (*S* 216:4). Long before Augustine, doubtless from the time that the exorcismal aspects of baptism came to be enacted in separate rites, liturgical tradition rested on two coordinate convictions: just as the Holy Spirit dwelled in the baptized, so the evil spirit dwelled in the unbaptized.[35]

About the exorcist's world, which Augustine calls the "full assembly of a new people" (Aug. *S* 216:7), the exorcist spoke and acted on behalf of the church for the "Savior" and the "mighty Trinity."[36] What unfolded was a ritual combat. The place of combat, the arena, was at once the church as building[37] (doubtless in the *consignatorium* attached to the city's basilica; Marrou 1938:115, 148–149), and the church as community, signified by the encircling congregation (Quod. *SI:*1, 4). The subject of the drama was the competent, with the exorcist in the leading role. The stage directions and script were the rites of the scrutiny. Very likely, however, competent and exorcist stood face to face, more accurately, bowed head to face. The hands of the exorcist were imposed, perhaps roughly, on the competent's shoulder, and the congregation as chorus chanted an interpretive psalm.[38] In a stentorian voice and biblical language the exorcist assaulted the devil in the competent and sought to drive him out in the name of Christ, the Redeemer, and of the Trinity.[39] The contemptuous hissing of exsufflation brought the assault to a climax.

The physical exam, however, which gave this solemn exorcism the name "scrutiny," brought the assault (one may be permitted to think of it as the drama's first act) to a close. Augustine says about the rite that whatever the devil has wrought in the competents by dangerous entrapments and seductive solicitations "will now be publicly revealed and done away with" (*S* 216:7); he concludes his comments about scrutiny by assuring the competents that they are now free from evil spirits and "healthy in their bodies" (*S* 216:11). And we know from Ambrose that a physical exam (*inquisitum*) was made to determine whether any uncleanness "might still cling to the body" of any competent (*Epl. symb.* 1:1). It seems certain that scrutiny was designed to uncover contagious diseases like leprosy and venereal disease, which, as the symptoms of sinfulness, disclosed the continuing presence of the devil, rendering the competent unfit for baptism (Busch 1939:71). In the process, the rite put to the test their psychological mettle for evidence of diabolic possession.[40]

By design, then, scrutiny was an ordeal at once physical and psychological. Quodvultdeus actually calls it "the trembling *(pavor)* endured for the gift of full peace of mind" (*SIII*:1:3), and Augustine implies as much. Did any competents fall in combat? Neither homilist provides an answer. But the antecedent probability is that some, at least, did not pass scrutiny and were set aside. In addition, the document which must be regarded as the seed bed from which these pivotal rites sprang, the *Apostolic Tradition* of Hippolytus, makes the probability more than antecedent. Close to baptism the competents (called the "elect" in the *AT*) underwent a final searching exorcism to determine whether they were "pure"—very likely a physical exam to determine ritual purity. Those found to be "impure" were rejected: they had not "heard the instructions with faith," and the "alien" continued to cling to them (*AT* 20). Compiled as a jural document to record existing practice, the *Apostolic Tradition* concerns itself with the actual rather that the hypothetical and points to the fact that some competents did not pass scrutiny (Finn 1989:69–70). For them the struggle was over, at least for that year, perhaps forever.

3. Culture and the Convert

Granted the ritual combat in scrutiny, who exactly were the combatants? The underlying principle in ritual is that two worlds intersect, the visible world of every day and the world of perception, conviction, and values that lies beyond the visible yet shapes and is shaped by it (Turner 1969:25). As a result, what is made perceptible to the participant (and observer) through symbolic enactment is made accessible to the action of the community. We have considered the visible world of the pivotal rites in detail, and to some extent, the invisible world disclosed by them. As we have just seen, for instance, the two worlds which intersected in the scrutiny were the visible showdown between competent and exorcist on the one hand and the invisible showdown between the divine and diabolic on the other. Clearly revealed is the radical opposition between the two.

Scrutiny, thus, reveals the nature of the struggle. The second and third rites—renunciation and recitation—reveal the underlying identity of the contestants. First, the investing evil one. Recall the formula of renunciation: "I renounce the devil, his pomps, and his angels" (Aug. *S* 215:1; Quod. *SI*:1, 11).[41] The devil, his pomps, and his angels may have been invisible, but they were far from abstractions in early Christianity.

For the pre-Constantinian Christians of Rome, for instance, the object of renunciation was the devil and his agents embodied in the social and legal system of a hostile Roman state and society (Finn 1989:70–72). Among their contemporary North African brethren the object was the devil and his agents resident in the heart of Greco-Roman religion and strikingly epitomized in the processions that took place at the amphitheater and racetrack, where the gods were carried about, and with the cultic activities associated with them (Kelly 1985:96–98).

For Augustine, as we have seen, the object renounced was the "armed enemy" who ruled the inner world (*saeculum, mundum*) of desire gone awry in the hearts of both the competents and humankind. From one perspective he saw it as the world they had created by a life "lived for so many evil years in sins" (*S* 216:4); from another, as the world of the "old man" (216:2); from still another, as the "land of the dying" (216:5); from still another, as a life of "eternal punishment because of longstanding guilt" (216:8); and from still another, as a world made dangerous "from the sins of others" (216:10). In summary, however, Augustine insisted that his competents renounce their former life lived in the fallen world of North Africa's largely urban culture.[42]

Quodvultdeus, however, stood more directly in the tradition of his African predecessors. He trained his competents to see that the "ancient and begrimed enemy" was embodied in their cultural institutions, especially in the centers of entertainment that exerted such fascination in Greco-Roman urban life: the racetrack with its savage competition and ferocious crowds; the theatre, with its lewd trivializing of the divine and human; and the amphitheater, with its inhuman contests and spilt blood (*SI*, 2:2–28). He regards them as the "devil's dens" and intimates that they provide the opium of the people: "There," he states, "smoke is breathed in, so that a person, under the influence of some strong power, when he thinks about what it means to be a man, does not realize that he is one himself" (*SII*, 1:5).

To this heavily-snared world the homilist opposes what he calls the "wholesome and worthy spectacles" designed to attract, delight, and to preserve rather than to destroy them (*SI*, 1:2–28): there in the Christian arena is the greatest of all charioteers, Elijah (2 Kgs. 2:9–12), who drove with such speed and skill that he reached the very boundaries of heaven; there on the Christian stage is the biblical drama which presents Mary, at once virgin and mother, chaste Joseph (Gen. 39:7, 20), Peter walking on water (Mk. 14:29), virtuous Susannah (Dan. 13:8, 45), and holy hymns and canticles; there in the church's amphitheater are featured Daniel and the lions, a battle fought without steel or killing (Dan. 14:3–42).

How extensive was the rejection of the competents' cultural world to be? Clearly, it embraced those traditional bastions of the entertainment industry: the racetrack, the theatre, and the amphitheater. Even shorn of their Greco-Roman religious heritage they inculcated values and cultivated habits and actions wholly unacceptable to the church; Quodvultdeus is eloquent on the subject.[43] Unfortunately, the homilists do not divulge what other institutions of culture, popular or otherwise, proved to be battlegrounds between the ecclesiastical and secular worlds. The focus was on the forums of leisure, because, above all others, they attracted the allegiance of the city's people—that, at least, is the message between the lines of every post-Constantinian mystagogical homily of the fourth and fifth centuries delivered on renunciation within the boundaries of the empire. Whether it be racetrack, theatre, or amphitheater, such was the arena where God and devil fought for the soul of competent and faithful alike.[44] To be sure, with drama, conviction, and feeling the competents renounced the devil, his pomps, and his angels, but their victory was fragile. If the repeated denunciations of these "dens of the devil" are any index, the instances of recidivism were high (Finn 1967:99–104). All of which brings me to what the pivotal rites accomplished and how they worked.

4. The Power of Ritual

Later ages speak of function or of cause and effect. The rites, however, speak of symbolic action. When competents passed scrutiny, the rite considered them freed from diabolic possession in all its manifestations: such was the message whether in Ambrose's Milan, Hippolytus' Rome, Augustine's Hippo, or Quodvultdeus's Carthage. No longer with head bowed but standing upright before the entire congregation, each competent proclaimed the words of renunciation, the intent of which was to break the devil's hold. The rite testified to the renunciants' newfound freedom to break and cast off the shackles of captivity. They could turn away from the devil, however powerful the pomps and angels. And, as the searching light of morning revealed, the renunciants could go on to proclaim allegiance to Christ before the assembled congregation (as Marius Victorinus once did):

> I believe in God, the Father almighty, creator of the universes, king of the worlds, immortal and invisible. I believe in his son Jesus Christ our Lord, born of the Holy Spirit and the Virgin Mary. He was crucified under Pontius Pilate and was buried. On the third day he rose from the dead, ascended to the heavens, sits at the right hand of the Father, from which he will come to judge the living and the dead. I believe in the Holy Spirit, in the remission of sins, the resurrection of the flesh, and life eternal in the holy church (Aug. *S* 215: *passim*).[45]

In two words—both Augustine's as we have seen—the rites accomplished *aversio* and *conversio*.[46] The process of conversion was complete; the competents were now ready for baptism. But did the rites bring about the conversion they signified? The North African Christianity we have explored insists on an affirmative answer, the rites themselves demand it, and Augustine and Quodvultdeus affirm it. To be sure, conversion was the result of long and exacting collaborative effort that involved the congregation, the competents, the ministerial church, and the unseen world of the Redeemer and the Trinity (Aug. *S* 216:5–6, 11). But the nexus was the rites; there is where the action was. So convinced was Augustine that he required even of infants that they be subject to scrutiny and participate in renunciation and recitation through their sponsors.[47] Nor was the requirement a formality, for in a letter to an episcopal colleague, Augustine insists that, although infants do not have the voluntary faith of the adult believer, the rite of recitation confers on them "fidelity" (*fidelem*); indeed, he even calls the rite *sacramentum fidei* (*Ep. ad Bon.* [98]:9).[48]

Conditioned, then, by what the rites proclaimed of themselves, and following in the footsteps of their older North African contemporary, Optatus of Milevis, Augustine and Quodvultdeus seem quite convinced that the rites effect what they signify (Finn 1990:813).[49] But how did the rites do so? Augustine's answer to his competents' unspoken question is theological: "Run to [Christ] and be converted, for it is he who brings back those who have turned away; who searches after the fugitives; who finds those who have been lost; who humbles the proud; who feeds the hungry; who releases those who are in chains; who gives light to the blind; who cleanses the unclean; who refreshes the weary; who raises the dead; and who rescues those who are possessed and held by the spirits of iniquity (*S* 116:11). For all three, it is Christ who acts in the rites and nothing, in their view, can brook his action.

From the physical and psychological standpoint, the state of the competents, Suzanne Poque concluded that the "old man" had truly begun to die.[50] From the perspective of ritual's dynamics, it is clear to anthropologists that symbolic action evokes powers inherent in both community and subjects, especially in curative rites like scrutiny, renunciation, and recitation.[51] After all, what is made perceptible to the senses in the form of symbolic action is by that fact made accessible to the purposive action of the community (Turner 1969:25).[52]

A temptation that sorely tries the student of ritual is reductionism, whether one reduces the effect of ritual to grounds theological, medicinal, psychological, social, or economic. Augustine, for instance, without further consideration, ascribes the liberation of his competents to the grace-giving Redeemer "who rescues those who are possessed and held by the spirits of iniquity" (*S* 216:11). Someone else, untutored by Augustine's insistence that unless "you believe you will not understand" (*S* 212), may well see the effect of the rite in a physically induced psychological therapy. Still another may conclude that wholeness lies in the capacity of ritual to elicit the restorative powers inherent in the community. However, what the rites of scrutiny, renunciation, and recitation themselves insist is that the invisible world of perceptions, convictions, and values intersects with the visible world of words, gestures, things of nature, and enactment to restore *sanitas* and to bring about *conversio*. To put asunder the two worlds, whether among the Christians of ancient Roman Africa or among the modern pre-industrial tribes of Sub-Saharan Africa or is to shut oneself off from a vital human reality. In short, they "worked," and in the process revealed the underlying world of ancient North African Christianity.

Conclusion

Between 300 and 400 C.E., the Christian population of the empire increased from five to thirty million. How were so many won over? It hardly needs to be said that what made the difference was Constantine and the preferred status for Christianity that came in his train. Before Constantine the church kept pretty much to itself, drawing fairly sharp boundaries, largely in reaction to hostility from its Greco-Roman world. The people who crossed those boundaries were initially led by the desire for blessings, the fear of physical pain, and credence in miracles (in that ascending order); with the arrival of Constantine, the added inducements which made the difference were the desire for a blend of social and material rewards that Christian status could bring, coupled with actual and potential coercion (MacMullen 1984:102–119).

The catechetical homilies of the fourth and fifth centuries lend a good deal of credence to this profile, not because they yield the same picture, but because their pervasive insistence on reformation of character and life gives every evidence that conversion, which the homilists see as the coming to birth of *homo novus*, was an arduous task for all concerned. In fact, it was arduous beyond words, as the drama of the North African catechumenate and its pivotal rituals underscore.

The low estate of the motives which brought the inquirers to basic instruction as beginners (*rudes*) was not particularly relevant, for the first thing the rites disclosed is that task of conversion was to reshape an entire way of living and system of values. To be sure, conversion was a personal process; from what we have seen in Augustine's North Africa, however, at bottom conversion was a ritual process. The garden at Cassiciacum inevitably led Augustine himself to the baptismal font. In a

striking confirmation of this ritual fact, the Second Council of Orange
(529 C.E.) responded to the aftermath of the Augustine-Pelagius controversy by re-orienting the entire discussion about the first stirrings of
conversion (*initium fidei*) by shifting the focus from the interplay between God and the individual soul to the interaction between God, the
community, and the baptismal candidates (Mansi 8:718).

The process (even in the infant, Augustine's case) truly began with
inscription, which normally took place at the end of initial instruction.
What the catechumenate reveals, however, is that the process was ever
so gradual, a slow weaning through extensive exposure to homiletic instruction, to the community, and to ritual. The early stages with their accompanying rites are stamped with the conviction that conversion was
a long process requiring extensive socialization, normally for several
years, but often, as in the case of Augustine and most of the leading
post-Constantinian churchmen, for half a lifetime.

Pace and intensity accelerated dramatically when a catechumen determined to seek baptism and entered the group of competents through
the rite of inscription at the beginning of Lent. The critical period of conversion had arrived. And the rites confirm what Augustine and Quodvultdeus make abundantly clear in their Lenten homilies, namely, that
the conversion of competents and community alike was the issue. Indeed, each of the rites which characterized the Lenten catechumenate
makes the point in its own distinctive voice that conversion was a communal enterprise designed to change both catechumen and community.
Thus, the community, as we have also seen, was an encircling presence
in all the rites, and dramatically so in the pivotal rites: if the competents
were to be reborn by the rites, then the community was to be renewed
in the rites. The holidays which marked the Easter season celebrated
both rebirth *and* renewal. The fact is that rites of initiation can and do
"through brief revelation 'burn out' or 'wash away'—whatever metaphor
of purification is used—the sins and sunderings of the community"
(Turner 1969:185). But granted that conversion of competent and community alike is the object, what do the pivotal rites say about conversion?

The stentorian voice of the scrutiny called attention to the central
theme of the rites: conversion was a matter of mortal combat with a
range of unseen forces. The divine and the diabolic were locked in combat within and over the competents. Either they would die to the "old
man" and live to the "new" or be listed as casualties, even though they
were not the principal combatants. Enslaved to the culture and values of
the world—the *pompa diaboli* (Rahner 1931)—from which they were
coming, the competents alone and unaided had no inherent capacity to
fight, much less to break away. Others with commanding authority had
to fight for them, specifically, Christ and the Trinity embodied in the

church and acting through its ministers, especially, the instructor and the exorcist. The competents' contribution was passive obedience and the strict adherence to Lenten asceticism (not exactly a small matter!).

A very different voice, the still voice of fear, was there for the hearing also, lurking largely in the setting: the darkness, the undress and demeanor of the competents, the impact of the exorcist, the physical exam and its outcome. All these pointed to the liminality of the competents, who stood anonymous on the boundaries of the congregation, betwixt and between. And their liminality generated fear: the world from which the competents sought to flee had penetrated through them to the very hearth of the church. Nor was the successful outcome of the ensuing combat a given: there would be casualties. In addition, the congregation had compelling reason to be afraid, for the world they had renounced, if we can believe Augustine and his colleagues, was too much with them.[53] In the liminality of the competents they encountered their own continuing liminality, for as members of the church they nonetheless stood on the boundaries of the world subject to its enchantments, or, in Quodvultdeus's image, its opium. Competent and Christian alike had learned from basic instruction that there was no conversion through hope, only through fear.[54]

Still another voice, in fact, many different voices, disclosed that, however enslaved to and by their past the competents might be, the possibility of making a break and new start was within reach. Stripped of everything but the grime, hunger, and exhaustion of the struggle, yet standing upright, they stepped forward into the half light of dawn, each in her or his own voice, publicly to renounce the devil, his pomps, and his angels. If modern weddings are any index, the sound of one's own voice doubtless made some renunciants tremulous, but each formally announced the break, which, according to Quodvultdeus, a scribe recorded in the hidden world of the Carthaginian Christian archives. In the morning those same voices, perhaps fortified by some sleep (but not much) and with the *sanitas* restored the night before, affirmed a new allegiance by professing the North African baptismal creed—also a daunting experience for some. Nonetheless, nourished by the rites, as Quodvultdeus put it, they could and did embrace publicly their own conversion.

Were it possible to draw a profile of the newly-professed as they left the basilica of Hippo or Carthage on Palm Sunday would it be markedly different from the profile they bore to their initial instruction? A final voice spoke of accomplishment. The rites we have explored and Augustine and Quodvultdeus, to whom we have listened, answered a ringing yes. But the rites spoke performative not prophetic language; they declared the present but did not address the future. Would these new converts stay converted? They themselves went away to their homes at the end of Easter Week with the answer, for in an Easter Wednesday homily Augustine exclaimed: "There are penitents here in great numbers. When the blessing is given, the line is very long, indeed. . . . I examine penitents and find them living badly. If they are repentant, let them not commit these sins; if sins continue to be committed, their name is a mistake; their guilt remains. . . . Change yourselves, change yourselves. The end of life is uncertain" (S 232:7–8).

The newly-professed might soon join the long line of penitents, indeed, might fall away altogether. Although effective, this rich, complex, and "trembling" ritual process of conversion was neither infallible nor invincible.

NOTES

1. For an account of the rise and thrust of symbolic anthropology and ritual studies, see Douglas 1970, 1984, Turner 1969, and Grimes 1985. Particularly helpful in situating the work of Turner and Douglas in relation to liturgical studies is Farwell 1976.

2. Archaeological studies, of course, have long been important, producing the monumental DACL; more recently, the social sciences have been harnessed to the study of early Christianity; for an up-to-date account see Osiek 1989.

3. The key studies are Busch 1938, and Poque 1966:13–115. But see also Weller 1959. The primary sources are principally Augustine's Lenten and Easter homilies (PL 38) and the three homilies De symbolo of Quodvultdeus (CCL 60:305–378). I am unaware of any studies of the North African catechumenate beyond Tertullian (Evans 1964).

4. Augustine's De catechizanis rudibus was composed for just such preliminary instruction and contains two model instructions (chs. 16–25, 26:51–57) and the rite of inscription (26:50).

5. The period could vary from a few weeks, as in the case of Marius Victorinus (for whom see below, p. 19), to years, as in the case of Augustine.

6. For Quodvultdeus see the entry in DS 15:282–290 by René Braun, who has done the critical edition of Quodvultdeus's work (Quod. CCL 60). He holds that the three homilies De symbolo, originally attributed to Augustine, are Quodvultdeus's. The homilies are abbreviated in this article as follows: SI, SII, SIII. Quodvultdeus was the last pre-Vandal Catholic bishop of Carthage.

7. Muldowney has collected and translated five of Augustine's nomen dare homilies (1959:83–115); see also Aug., En. in pss. 41:1. His enumeration is that of the Vulgate, which is the first number given in this study; the RSV number is added in parentheses.

8. See Aug. De fid. et op. 6:8; Poque discusses Lent (23–25) and the appropriate liturgical psalms (31–33).

9. See Poque (24–29). Although she gives these details in connection with the scrutiny, they were the normal part of Lenten exorcism. See also Leclercq 1922.

10. Augustine notes that exsufflation was performed also on infants, showing that even they, who are not capable of personal sin, are under the devil's sway.

11. See below, pp. 18–19 and 25, for the Hippo baptismal creed. For examples of homilies see *S* 212–214.

12. Guelf. abbreviates Codex Guelferbytanus. The texts for homilies thus abbreviated can be found in the entry under Augustine *Sermo Guelferbytanus*.

13. Poque 1966:26–27 thinks of them as successive, but the homilies of Quodvultdeus assign the scrutiny and renunciation to the vigil and the recitation to the morning of Palm Sunday.

14. There is some dispute about just when the prayer was first recited; for discussion see Poque 1966:65–69. Tertullian is the first to write a commentary on the Lord's Prayer, followed by Cyprian and Origen. At some point between Tertullian (ca. 200) and the Jerusalem liturgy as Cyril comments on it (ca. 350) the custom entered the baptismal liturgy. In my opinion it has already done so in Tertullian's Carthage, since the Lord's Prayer was the preparatory prayer Christians said before receiving the eucharistic bread they had brought home and kept in what they called *arca* for daily communion.

15. The term is in Egeria's diary, where *major* and *paschale septimana* are used (*Itin. Aeth.* 30). See Poque 1966:69–77, and Busch 1932:446–449, for discussion of the Holy Week liturgy.

16. Poque thinks it was a postbaptismal rite as at Milan (1966:37–38), while Busch thinks it was Holy Thursday (1938:447). But see Aug., *Ep. ad Jan* [55] 35. Given the commemorative thrust of the day, Thursday seems best. Ambrose considered the evangelical rite as the institution of baptism.

17. For the psalms and Augustine's surviving 15 vigil homilies see Poque 1966:31–33, 73–78. For the Paschal candle and the *Praeconium paschale* see Weller 1959:34–38, and Leclercq 1938. Although Augustine composed a metrical eulogy on the candle (see *De civ. dei* XV:22) as a result of which some have thought him author of the celebrated *Exsultet* hymn, it first appears in the *Gregorian Sacramentary* (ca. 800 C.E.). Ambrose is thought by some to be the author, and Jerome by others. Whoever authored the hymn, the blessing of the paschal candle was a rite which had already taken hold in the west by Augustine's time.

18. Busch thinks it may have come at the beginning (1938:449).

19. Muldowney 1959 and Weller 1959 have both collected and translated into English Augustine's Easter homilies; about Weller, however, see Poque 1966:10–11, n. 3.

20. Muldowney and Weller have also collected and translated Augustine's Easter Week homilies.

21. For discussion see Busch 1938:434–440, 449–453, and Poque 1966:26–33. Busch separates scrutiny and renunciation, which he places just before baptism, whereas Poque (correctly, I think) joins them. Unfortunately, she links them chronologically with the recitation of the creed during the vigil, which disregards the evidence of Quodvultdeus, who places recitation on Sunday morning.

22. See Aug. *De cur. pro mort. ger.* 15; *S* 259:4; Quod. *SI*:1, 18.

23. See Quod. *SI*:1–28 for the origin of the notion of the "new spectacles."

24. See *De Fid. et op. 36*, and Poque 1966:36. Technically, they began at inscription. For the "curative cult" in an anthropological perspective, see Turner 1969:13–15. "Palm" Sunday seems to have originated in the Frankish kingdom with the rite of blessing the palms.

25. For discussion, see Quasten 1942. See also Quod. *SI*:1, 4–7; Aug. *S* 216:11.

26. Ambrose is the first to name the rite and give its function: *Expl. symb.* 1:1. Augustine uses the term sparingly (*S* 216:6, 10). Quodvultdeus uses the term

*examen (SI:*1, 5). For the origin and development of the rite see Leclercq 1950, and Dondeyne 1932, and for Augustine and North Africa, Busch 1938:434–440, and Poque 1966:26–33.

27. In Hippo, Ps. 33(34): ". . . let the afflicted hear and be glad . . ."; and 138(139) in Carthage: "Probe me Lord and know my heart." See Aug., *S* 116, Quod. *SI:*1, 6–7, and Poque 1966:32–33.

28. See Rahner 1931, Boismard 1964, and Finn 1967:86–118. Hints of the rite are present in the early second century, rooted in the exodus typology. Satan is Pharaoh, his service is Egyptian slavery, and the work or burden imposed is pagan cult. The term *pompa diaboli* is first used by Tertullian.

29. Augustine uses the terms interchangeably; Quodvultdeus uses *mundum* exclusively in his three homilies.

30. For similar attitudes in the East see Finn 1967:99–102.

31. His profession seems to have been made just before baptism, perhaps during the Easter Vigil. The event antedated Augustine by some 30 years. The translation is Outler 1955:161.

32. For discussion, see Poque 1966:29–30. She comments that the term in Augustine appears so frequently and is so often associated with *credere* that it must be a liturgical formula. She regards the renunciation-conversion as a single rite with two moments. One should note, however, that both temporally and logically renunciation belongs to the scrutiny. In my view, scrutiny, renunciation, and conversion are a single complex rite with three moments.

33. For discussion of the multivocality or "polysemy" of symbols in early Christianity see Daniélou 1956 and 1960; for an anthropological approach see Turner 1969:1–93, espec. 14–15, 37–43.

34. But see MacMullen 1984:74–85, and Wilken 1983:29–33. Orthodox here means that of the Nicaea and Constantinople councils.

35. See Lukken 1973:185–187, 228–229, and n. 272.

36. This is the tenor of Aug. *S* 216: 6, 7, 10. For the role of the "adept" in curative cults, see Turner 1969:20–38.

37. For discussion of the building history of Hippo's basilica of the "Three Naves," see Marrou 1960:115–117, 123–133, 143–154. He concludes that the basilica of the second stage was built by the Catholics between 347 and 361, but he reviews the counter-evidence that it was the Donatist basilica and agrees that a cloud of doubt hangs over the whole question (148–150). For a review of recent archaeological work on baptisteries in Carthage, see Duval 1988.

38. As noted above p. 17 and n. 27: in Hippo, Ps. 33(34); in Carthage, Ps. 138(139).

39. For discussion of baptismal exorcism in the fourth century, see Finn 1967:73–81, compare Aug. *S* 216:6, 10.

40. John Chrysostom tells his competents that possession, like drunkenness, is often accompanied by foaming at the mouth, passing out, rolling of the eyes, and vomiting; *Ad il. cat. alt.* See also Poque 1966:32, including notes.

41. For a recent historical survey, see Kelly 1985:94–105; for the fourth century east, see Finn 1967:86–117.

42. See *S* 215:1, a homily he delivered at the *redditio symboli.* Augustine equates the devil, his pomps, and his angels with the past and their former life and insists, doubtless tutored by his own experience, that they withdraw their mind and soul from that former world.

43. The attitude was widespread: see Finn 1967:99–102. The idolatrous aspect, so prominent in Tertullian, receded by the fourth century.

44. See Wilken 1983: "The full impact of paganism, however, can be seen not in popular amusements or pagan holidays; its most significant impact was on the upper classes, on the way they educated their children, in the web of traditional values and behaviour. . . . Paganism and Christianity were not on equal footing in Antioch. Hellenism set the tone, undergirded the institutions, inspirited the art and literature" (30).

45. In *S* 214, composed toward the end of his career, Augustine records a creed text closer to the Nicene Creed. It is thought that he did so to propose a model for priests at the start of their ministry. The text in *S* 215 is that of the church at Hippo and, doubtless, the rest of Roman North Africa. See Poque 1966:61–64. The formula in Antioch paralleled the renunciation (called *apotaxis,* "breaking ranks"): "And I enter into your service, O Christ" (the rite was called *syntaxis,* "entering the ranks"), for which see Finn 1967:105–110. The recitation may have followed immediately.

46. See above p. 19 and n. 32.

47. Aug. *Sec. Jul. resp. imp. op.* IV:7 (PL 45:1343).

48. In the same letter, he calls the rite of renunciation *sacramentum conversionis.* Augustine appears to use the term *sacramentum* as the rough equivalent of *mysterium;* I think it best translated "rite," when he deals with the rites which compose the baptismal liturgy, as here. The term first appears in Tertullian, who may well have gotten it from Old Latin Version of the Scriptures. See Finn 1990:811–815.

49. In *Against Parmenian the Donatist* V:4, Optatus isolates three "elements" which make up the body of the sacrament: the action of the Trinity, the faith of the recipient, and the action of the minister. He regards only the first two as indispensable; the third, the minister, is only instrumentally necessary, and his moral condition, of no effect. Augustine, in his similarly anti-Donatist work, *On Baptism, Against the Donatists,* turns his attention from the "unholy" minister to the "deceitful" candidate for baptism, and argues that, irrespective of his unworthiness, the sacrament gives him the seal or character of Christ in virtue of which the "benefit" of the sacrament revives when he is contrite and reconciled (1.7:10–13; PL 43:115–122). It is very likely that his teaching about the seal or character was derived from the postbaptismal rite of chrismation in Hippo and elsewhere. In any case, it proved to be the foundation of the medieval teaching that the sacraments effect what they signify *ex opere operato.*

50. See above pp. 14–15 and for full discussion her 1966:26–33.

51. See Douglas 1970 and 1984, who tends to see rituals as a response (not always beneficent) to social determinants, especially social structure. Turner explores in detail the curative function of rites (1969:18–43). In the rites he studies they are effective for the restoration of the right relation between matrilinity and marriage, the reconstruction of the conjugal relations between wife and husband, and making the woman, and hence the marriage and lineage, fruitful (18). See also Douglas 1984:7–28, 58–72. She argues that Frazier, whose influence she sees as baneful as it is widespread, did not understand symbolic action.

52. See above p. 12. On the subject of magic, Douglas has an extensive and valuable discussion of its rise and inadequacy as a tool of analysis (1966:7–28, 58–72). She traces its prominence back to Frazier.

53. See especially Augustine's postbaptismal Easter season homilies (*S* 229–260).

54. Aug. *De cat. rud.* 5:9; see MacMullen 1984:64–65.

Abbreviations

AA	*American Anthropologist*
CCL	*Corpus Christianorum, series Latina*
CSEL	*Corpus Scriptorum Ecclesiasticorum Latinorum*
DACL	*Dictionnaire d'archéologie chrétienne et de liturgie*
DS	*Dictionnaire de spiritualité*
EEC	*Encyclopedia of Early Christianity*
ELA	*Ephemerides Liturgicae Analecta*
FC	*Fathers of the Church*
Guel	*Sermo Guelferbytanus* (see Augustine)
HTR	*Harvard Theological Review*
LQF	*Liturgiewissenschaftliche Quellen und Forschungen*
Mansi	*Sacrororum conciliorum nova et amplissima collectio*
PG	*Patrologia Graeca*
PL	*Patrologia Latina*
REA	*Revue des études Augustiniennes*
RHE	*Revue d'histoire ecclésiastique*
SC	*Sources chrétiennes*
SCA	*Studies in Christian Antiquity*
TS	*Theological Studies*
ZKT	*Zeitschrift für Katholische Theologie*

Source References

Ambrose:

Expl. symb.	*Explanatio symboli.* SC 25bis. 1961

Augustine:

Conf.	*Confessiones libri XIII.* CCL 27:1–273
De adult. coniug.	*De adulterinis coniugiis.* CSEL 41:347–410
De cat. rud.	*De catechizandis rudibus.* CCL 41:121–178
De civ. dei	*De civitate dei.* CCL 48:452–497
De cur. pro mort. ger.	*De cura pro mortuis gerenda.* PL 40:591–610
De fid. oper.	*De fide et operibus.* CSEL 41:37–97
Enn. in pss.	*Ennarationes in psalmos XLI.* CCL 38:459–474
Ep. ad Bon. [98]	*Epistularum XCVIII.* CSEL 34:520–533
Ep. ad Jan.	*Epistola ad inquisitiones Januarius [54–55].* CSEL 34:158–213.
S	*Sermones.* 1–340. PL 38:23–1484
S. Guelf.	*Sermo Guelferbytanus,* G. Morin, ed. 1930 *Sancti Augustinni sermones post Maurinos reperti,* in *Miscellanea Agostiniana I.* Rome: Vatican (SeT)
Sec. Jul. resp. imp. op.	*Secundam Juliani responsionem imperfectum opus.* PL 45:1049–1608.

Chrysostom:

Ad il. cat. I, II	*Ad illuminandos catechesis prima et altera.* PG 49:221–240

Egeria:

Itin. Aeth.	*Itinerarium Aetheriae.* SC 21, 1948.

Quodvultdeus:

SI, SII, SIII	*Sermones de symbolo.* CCL 60:305–378

Tertullian:

De bapt.	*De baptismo.* Evans 1964.
TA	*Traditio apostolica.* Münster: LQF 39, 1963.

References

Boismard, M. E.
1964   "'I Renounce Satan, His Pomps, and His Works.'" In *Baptism in the New Testament: A Symposium,* 107–112. Ed. A. George, et al. Baltimore: Helicon.

Burghardt, Walter J.
1964   "Catechetics in the Early Church," *The Living Light* 1, 100–118.

Busch, Benedictus
1938   "De initiatione christiana secundum sanctum Augustinum," ELA 52, 159–167 (pre-Aug. N. Africa), 385–483 (Aug. N. Africa).

Daniélou, Jean
1956   *The Bible and the Liturgy.* Notre Dame: University of Notre Dame Press.
1960   *From Shadows to Reality.* London: Burns and Oates.

De Puniet, P.
1925   "Catéchuménat," DACL 2,2:2579–2621.

Dondeyne, A.
1932   "La discipline des scrutins dans l'église latine avant Charlemagne," RHE 28:5–33, 751–787.

Douglas, Mary
1970   *Natural Symbols: Explorations in Cosmology.* New York: Pantheon Books.
1984   *Purity and Danger: An Analysis of the Concepts of Pollution and Taboo.* London: Routledge & Kegan Paul (Ark edition).

Dujarier, Michel
1979   *A History of the Catechumenate: The First Six Hundred Years.* New York: Sadlier.

Duval, Noel
1988   "Un nouveau baptistère de Carthage," *REA* 34:86–92.

Evans, Ernest, ed.
1964   *Tertullian's Homily on Baptism.* London: SPCK.

Farwell, Lyndon I.

1976   "Betwixt and Between: The Anthropological Contributions of Mary Douglas and Victor Turner Toward a Renewal of Roman Catholic Ritual." Claremont, CA. Dissert.

Finn, Thomas M.

1967   *The Liturgy of Baptism in the Baptismal Instructions of St. John Chrysostom.* Washington, D.C.: Catholic University of America Press. SCA 15.

1989   "Ritual Process and the Survival of Early Christianity: A Study of the Apostolic Tradition of Hippolytus," *Ritual Studies* 3, 1:69–89.

1990   "Sacraments," EEC, 811–815.

Grimes, Ronald L.

1985   *Research in Ritual Studies: A Programmatic's Essay and Bibliography.* Metuchen, NJ: American Theological Library and Scarecrow Press.

Kelly, Henry Ansgar

1985   *The Devil at Baptism: Ritual, Theology, and Drama.* Ithaca: Cornell.

Leclercq, Henri

1922   "Exorcisme, Exorciste," DACL 5/1:964–978

1938   "Pâques," DACL 13/2:1559–1571.

1950   "Scrutin," DACL 15/1:1038–1052.

Lukken, G. M.

1973   *Original Sin in the Roman Liturgy.* Leiden: Brill.

MacMullen, Ramsay

1984   *Christianizing the Roman Empire, A.D. 100–400.* New Haven, CT: Yale.

Mansi

See Abbreviations.

Marrou, Henri I.

1960   "La basilique chrétienne d'Hippone d'après le résultat des dernières fouilles," REA 6 109–154.

Muldowney, Sarah, trans.

1959   *Saint Augustine: Sermons on the Liturgical Seasons.* New York: FC 38.

Osiek, Carolyn
1989   "The New Handmaid: The Bible and the Social Sciences." TS 50:260–278.

Outler, Albert, trans.
1955   *Augustine: Confessions and Enchiridion.* Philadelphia: Westminster.

Poque, Suzanne, ed.
1966   *Augustin d'Hippone: Sermons pour la Pâque.* Paris. SC 116.

Quasten, Johannes
1942   "Theodore of Mopsuestia on the Exorcism of the Cilicium," HTR 35:209–219.

Rahner, Hugo
1931   "Pompa Diaboli," ZKT: 239–273.

Russell, Jeffrey Burton
1981   *Satan: The Early Christian Tradition.* Ithaca, NY: Cornell.

Turner, Victor
1969   *The Ritual Process: Structure and Antistructure.* Chicago: Aldine.

Weller, Philip T.
1959   *Selected Easter Sermons of Saint Augustine.* Saint Louis: B. Herder.

Whitaker, E. C.
1981   *The Baptismal Liturgy.* London: SPCK, 2nd ed.

Wilken, Robert L.
1983   *John Chrysostom and the Jews: Rhetoric and Reality in the Fourth Century.* Berkeley: University of California Press.

Wilson, Monica
1954   "Nyakyusa Ritual and Symbolism," AA 56:228–241.

The Worshiping Assembly: Possible Zone of Cultural Contestation

MICHAEL WARREN

What sort of transformative power does liturgy possess? This is the question I wish to address in this essay. Although the question might seem to be an outmoded one, having been settled in the Reformation controversies about the efficacy of sacraments in a sinful church,[1] I wish to raise it again for its implications for the place of Christian education or catechesis in the local church. More than ever, the question of ritual's transformative power brings with it further unsettling questions about the more deeply transformative, yet unrecognized power of the life structure of particular communities.

Many Christian thinkers would claim that the "enacted word" has the ability to move those assembled into the mystery being celebrated and also toward the Christian way, and do it using powerful communicative means that transcend logic. They hold that the various sensual signs offered in ritual—gesture, ritual movement, sung prayer, bread and wine, water, oil, incense—all these work to bring subtle realities to vivid awareness. After all, as part of a centuries-old tradition, the ritual itself has been crafted as a classic way of expressing the tradition's core. Such convictions put great confidence in the liturgy's directive and corrective power in a worshiping community.[2]

However, the actual functioning of worship is not so simple. While the meanings expressed in liturgical ritual are embedded in a tradition, those using them may not be embedded there at all, but may be much more securely embedded in the signification system of a culture having little in common with the religious tradition. The key question for liturgy today is whether the meaning intended by the tradition to be ritualized in worship is capable of being an authentic expression of the life of this community. The possibility exists that the highly patterned ritual "language" could function as a historical artifact only, a kind of museum

Reprinted from *Worship* 63, no. 1 (January 1989): 2–16. Copyright © 1989 by Michael Warren.

piece expressing meanings once significant to people of an earlier time but now quaint and not expressive of the life of any community.

One might think that when a ritual became a historical curiosity, it would no longer be used to express religious meaning. True, but the process by which a ritual ceases to signify is gradual, not immediate. Sri Lankan theologian Aloysius Pieris chooses the word "fade" to get at the gradualness of this process: "A religion fades out of history when its symbols and institutions lose their capacity to evoke among its followers the distinctive salvific experience that defines its essence. Did not this happen to the great religions of Ancient Egypt, Rome, Greece, and Mesopotamia?"[3]

It is important to note another aspect of Pieris' nuance here. It is not that the ritual loses its life. After all, ritual is no more nor less than an expressive medium. What becomes defective is a relationship: the one between the ritual and the believers. Among the assembled worshipers, the "distinctive salvific experience" ceases to be compelling and thus cannot be expressed or evoked in ritual. The life, understanding, and commitments of the followers are the key component in this dialectic. When a religion loses its communicative capacity for religious seekers, it dies, as do the rituals that allowed it to express its religious insight. When religious seekers halt their search or find "salvation" in something other than God, a religion, along with its ritual media, perishes. In a sense, ritual has no meaning in itself apart from the intention of some actual person or group; when that group is totally in the past, the ritual has become a museum piece.

Vision and Intention in Worship

The point I highlight here: the centrality of the intention of the worshipers in any liturgical assembly may initially seem too obvious to be stated, but this obviousness conceals a problem needing attention. The importance of worshipers' intention is a standard point emphasized in the literature of worship. Liturgiologist Geoffrey Wainwright notes that a Christian worshiping assembly, and by extension any group following a religious way, embodies a "vision" and a version of reality. I want to stress his use of the word "vision" because it suggests a way of imagining the possibilities of human life. The religious group inhabits this vision and makes it tangible to itself and accessible to others. "A historical community . . . can transmit a vision of reality which helps decisively in the interpretation of life and the world. . . . It is the Christian community that transmits the vision which the theologian, as an individual human being, has seen and believed. . . . *Worship* is the place in which that vision comes to a sharp focus, a concentrated expression, and it is here that the vision has often been found to be at its most appealing."[4]

Seeing ritual as "regular patterns of behavior *invested with symbolic significance* and efficacy"[5] by a particular group of persons puts special emphasis on the subjectivity of the worshipers. They must find in a particular ritual, though often patterned according to ancient prescription, an authentic and meaningful way of expressing their religious vision. Of course, once entered for the purpose of expressing faith, ritual expresses for a community the dimensions of faith beyond discursive speech. In this way ritual's own symbolic patterning contains the possibility of carrying a group (or individuals in the group) to a grasp of religious mystery beyond words. The diversity of rituals used among the Christian churches suggests great variety in the possible ways this religious vision can be symbolized. However, lacking that vision none of these ways has any significance beyond that of a museum artifact. The underlying issue in worship is religious vision, subjectivity, and intentionality. The liturgical document issued by Vatican II makes this point clear. "In order that the sacred liturgy may produce its full effect, it is necessary that the faithful come to it with proper dispositions, that their thoughts match their words, and that they cooperate with divine grace lest they receive it in vain (cf. 2 Cor 6:1). Pastors of souls must therefore realize that, when the liturgy is celebrated, more is required than the mere observance of the laws governing valid and licit celebration. It is their duty to ensure that the faithful take part knowingly, actively, and fruitfully."[6] Neither now nor in the past has having the proper dispositions been automatic or easy.

The history of Christianity shows that concern for the proper dispositions was an intense one for early Christians. For any person to be invited to worship, he or she had to engage first in a relatively intense period of preparation involving instruction, initiatory steps, scrutiny of life patterns, clarification, change, further instruction, and so forth. Such preparation, called the catechumenate, was a period of significant change lasting up to three years. Such change or conversion remains the norm of the church: "Before persons can come to the liturgy, they must be called to faith and to conversion."[7] Liturgical ritual does not invest nonbelievers or even beginners with understanding; instead, they must first come to an understanding authenticated by living and then express that vision in worship.

Vision and Life Structure

A vision of life is not verified so much by its truth claims as in the life practice it fosters or produces. A key feature of the early procedure for preparing neophytes for full participation was the correction of life practice. Understanding was not sufficient; correct practice of that understanding was a more important requirement. In the third century, Origen wrote, "The profound and secret mysteries must not be given, at first, to disciples, but they must be first instructed in the correction of their lifestyle." In another place, Origen is more explicit: "When it becomes evident that the disciples are purified and *have begun, as far as possible, to live better* only then are they invited to know our mysteries"[8] (emphasis added). Regis Duffy, who has examined the catechumenate as the shaper of life structure, emphasizes that before being admitted to the community of worshipers the candidate had to have succeeded, beyond any merely stated desire, in transforming his or her way of life. "One major characteristic of the catechumenal process . . . [was]: God's Word leads to commitments long before it leads to initiation. . . . Three years 'hearing the word' in the catechumenate of Hippolytus at Rome might seem long until we reflect on the quality of commitment that was expected of any Christian at the time. Hippolytus tells us that the first time inquirers came 'in order to hear the word,' the teachers questioned them on their motivation, their life situation, and their willingness to change work that might hinder the practice of God's word."[9]

Unfortunately, the implications for worship of the early communities' preoccupation with life structure has not been explored sufficiently. If we accept that worship is no "pure" realm of activity independent of the lived vision of the worshipers, and if we further accept that the actual vision of life brought to worship is influenced by the pattern of commitment worked out in one's life practice, then everyday life practices of both individuals and of the local church itself need examination. That the way of worship is also the way of believing has come to be widely accepted, as in the formula, *lex orandi, lex credendi.* This formula needs, if not a corrective, then at least an addendum, to avoid the kind of liturgical overstatement I described above. My addendum would be the formula: *lex vivendi, lex credendi* or even: *lex vivendi, lex orandi.*[10] As life structure goes, so go the *enacted* beliefs of the community; the quality of the community's worship is determined more by the quality of the community's life structure than by the quality of the words spoken or the rituals enacted during worship. For a credible Christian life, the proper relationship among all three elements—life structure, worship, and belief—is crucial. In appreciating this relationship, the position of philosopher C. S. Pierce is helpful. "Belief consists mainly in being deliberately prepared to adopt the formula believed in as the guide to action; the essence of belief is the establishment of a habit; and different beliefs are distinguished by the different modes of action to which they give rise."[11] According to this understanding of belief, where the behavior consonant with the belief is lacking, one has grounds for doubting whether there is in fact a belief.

The centrality of life structure has been getting more and more detailed attention in recent years. Jacques Ellul, for example, points out that concern for the actual practice of truth is something Christians and Marxists have in common. "In one respect there is . . . an obvious point of similarity between what takes place in Marxism and in Christianity. Both have made practice the touchstone of truth or authenticity. In other words, it is by practice that we have to appreciate or not the intentions or purity of the doctrine, of the truth of the origin or source. The link between praxis and theory in Marx is well known. One should not forget, however, that it is a circular link. This means finally that false practice inevitably engenders false theory, and one can see the falsity of practice not only from its effects . . . but also by the new theory to which it gives birth. . . . Christianity too, judges itself by practice. We thus confront a constant challenge in this regard."[12]

The Problem of Practice

If we accept that the material conditions of our life create the mindset and perceptions that direct our lives, we may be as close to the convictions of the early Christians as to those of Marx. The choices we make and follow become our embodied commitments, and they include our choice of work, of residence, of mode of transportation, of friends, of patterns of eating and interacting with family and friends, of our way of using finances, of our way of getting information about the world we live in, and of our use of leisure time. Note that all these matters are for most people choices that then become structure in our life pattern. These choices-become-patterns-of-action shape our consciousness, our values and biases about the world, our concerns. Whenever we walk into a place of worship, these patterned commitments walk in with us. Whatever word or hymn of praise we utter has them as its horizon.

Earlier in this essay, I noted that ritual is a patterned way of expressing, and here I point out that life structure is a patterned way of acting. These two patterned ways are either coherent or incoherent one to the other. One whose life structure is alien to the Gospel may come to the ritual and join in speaking its patterned responses, but these belie, and not necessarily in the awareness of the "worshiper," the lived commitments. One could say that worship is a zone of contestation that puts the question of credibility to the lived commitments of the worshipers—but only if the worshipers are in search of greater credibility and coherence in their faith lives. Unfortunately, the pattern of expression in ritual may possibly be casual and routine. The pattern of acting in life structure also tends to be routine, but infinitely more difficult to change. Most worshipers serious about the call to discipleship do not engage in worship glibly. Ritual puts them in a struggle for coherence between the two patterns, and that struggle is never glib or routine.

The situation of Christians today in many parts of the world brings out the importance of the struggle for greater coherence between worship and life structure. When Roman Catholics from the wealthy elite families in Guatemala attend the Eucharist, they say the same words in the same ritual as those whose friends and relatives are being killed by the death squads for announcing the good news of justice. In each case, the same ritual is not being invested with the same meaning. Because of such situations, this matter of life structure and practice calls for more attention and study, and two modern thinkers have offered helpful understanding of the ways life structure is shaped. They are Raymond Williams and Pierre Bourdieu.

Raymond Williams claimed in a lifetime of writing that one could understand society through studying its forms of communication. The means of communication are a key part of the material conditions of a society's life, which ultimately shape consciousness.[13] In our century a communications revolution is still underway, and its power to shape the way we perceive and what we value is still not adequately assessed. Film and television, with their penchant for narrative, offer vivid imaginations of the purpose and possibilities of the human project. Those who imagine the meaning of life for others hold great power in those others' lives. The power of such narratives cannot be appreciated until we recognize how tightly bound they are to consumer capitalism and the production of consumption. Advertising's strategic use of the persistent image tied to a persistent slogan shapes the consciousness of even those who think they resist. Advertising has perfected in this century the orchestration of desire as the foundation of its production of consumption. Person becomes defined as consumer, perhaps not in formal definition but more in one's basic assumptions, in patterns of purchasing, and in modes of possession.

Intense religious issues are at stake here. Consumerism is a religion promising salvation through the wisdom of the right purchase and with goods as its sacramental signs. When worshipers who have ingested the religion of consumerism bring it unnamed and unrecognized into the place of worship, we have a radical conflict between two claims of ultimacy: the overt one of a formal religion and the covert one of the consumerist faith. The conflict and the issues at stake in it have been expressed well by John Kavanaugh. "The great paradox of finding one's identity in wealth is ultimately the paradox of all idolatries: entrusting ourselves to our products, our silver and golden gods, *we become fashioned—re-created—in their image and likeness.* Bereft of personhood and human sensibility, we lose our vision. We become voiceless, unable to utter words of life and love. . . . To make wealth one's god, is to become brittle and cold, to become like unto a thing, to become invulnerable, impenetrable, unloving."[14] Embracing a religion involves embracing the vision of human life proposed by its gods. At this point it should be clearly stated that when a community enters worship in touch with the message of Jesus and its deep contestation of the consumer ethos, the act of worship celebrates the Gospel in a way that itself radically contests that ethos.

While Raymond Williams is interested in how communications structures influence thought and ultimately action, French sociologist Pierre Bourdieu's concern is with the relation of social structure and action. Bourdieu claims that economies produce in people the dispositions demanded by the economy and by the position people have in that economy.[15] To a religiously committed person this claim at first appears startling, since it says something about the shaping of a person's spirit, here termed "dispositions." Bourdieu is talking about the shaping of a spirituality. Religious persons, preferring to think that religious values shape one's dispositions, might resist Bourdieu's position. Indeed the cogency of his claim only gradually emerges from the data that undergird this theory. The theory and the data are worth study.

In Bourdieu's view, two histories intersect in each person. One is the habitat or objectified history that has accumulated over time in objects like machines, buildings, monuments, books, theories, customs, law, and so forth. The second is the habitus, the embodied history, which is a matrix of perceptions, appreciations and actions functioning as an "imminent law laid down in each agent by his or her earliest upbringing."[16] Habitus functions as "durably acquired schemes of perception, thought, and action engendered by objective conditions but tending to persist even after an alteration of those conditions."[17] While the habitus gives "regularity, unity and systematicity to the practices of a group or class,"[18] the fact of its hold on one's attitudes and action tends to be unconscious. Bourdieu uses subtle religious imagery to explain this process. "The principles em-bodied in [the habitus] . . . are placed beyond the grasp of consciousness, and hence cannot be touched by voluntary deliberate transformation, cannot even be made explicit; nothing seems more ineffable, more incommunicable, more inimitable, and, therefore, more precious, than the values given body, *made* body by the transubstantiation achieved by the hidden persuasion of an implicit pedagogy, capable of instilling a whole cosmology, an ethic, a metaphysics, a political philosophy, through injunctions as insignificant as 'stand up straight,' as 'don't hold your knife in your hand.'"[19]

Bourdieu also insists that the orchestration of attitude and action is "conductorless." There is no conspiracy on any individual's part to instill these attitudes; the functioning of the social and economic order is the agent at work. Habitus is not a matter of individual influences. "Thus, when we speak of class habitus, we are insisting . . . that 'interpersonal' relations are never, except in appearance, *individual-to-individual* relationships . . . [emphasis his]. In fact it is their present and past positions in the social structure that biological individuals carry with them, at all times and in all places, in the form of dispositions which are so many marks of *social position.* . . ."[20] In another place Bourdieu emphasizes this influence of social class. "Though it is impossible for *all* members of the same class (or even two of them) to have had the same experiences, in the same order, *it is certain that each member of the same class is more likely than any member of another class to have been confronted with the situations most frequent for the members of that class* [emphasis added]. The objective structures which science apprehends in the form of statistical regularities (e.g., employment rates, income curves, probabilities of access to secondary education, frequency of holidays, etc.) inculcate, through the direct or indirect but always convergent experiences which give a social environment its *physiognomy*, with . . . the sense of reality or realities which is perhaps the best-concealed principle of their efficacy."[21]

I warn readers not to put Bourdieu's ideas too neatly into the pigeonhole of "socialization." He brings to his study of social structures an economic critique that certainly complements that of Berger and Luckmann but has significant differences. To describe adequately the matter of influences so important to it, religious education theory needs more, not less, nuance. What Bourdieu invites us to ponder is not the condition of religious understanding but the condition of life practice that exists along with, and sometimes belies, religious understanding. Robert Coles has almost intuited Bourdieu's insight in the following description of worship in the churches of the well-to-do.

> There is more order [than in the churches of the poor], but order of a different kind, more self regard in the way in which one worships. Attention is paid, and in a certain way: to what one sees and what one hears and what one reads, yes, but also, significantly, to one-

self. You enter the churches of the privileged full of yourself. You are well dressed, pleased to be in a place where you are treated well, with great respect and personal attention, and where there will be—and this is important—no surprises. The format is fixed, and the words and music are modulated, no extremes either from church or from those who are at worship. Without having been told, you understand that if anything happens to you of a spiritual nature, you are to keep it to yourself. Just as there are certain words used in certain ways in rural services, these privileged places of worship have theirs, and time moves along here in a measured (but pleasant) fashion. By contrast [with the worship of the poor] there are no unplanned stops at this word, no responses or outbreaks to that moment of sound; in these places of worship there are no abrupt moves forward or doubling back, either in response to the minister or to those at worship. As I said, the privileged ones do not like to be surprised; they have not come to be confronted or to be put into situations where they are not in control.[22]

While illustrating Bourdieu's habitus, this passage brings us back to the matter of worship and how life practice, here seen from the angle of class, influences the ways of the liturgical assembly.

The Role of Catechesis and Christian Education

Bourdieu's approach to social conditioning seems to be deterministic. Though I have found little in his writings about ways of contesting a particular habitus, let alone becoming aware of it,[23] I assume he would see that extreme economic shift would dislocate habitus. Raymond Williams, however, is more sanguine about the possibilities of demystifying the ways communications work in a social structure, thus putting the means of cultural analysis into the hands of ordinary persons. I myself believe that the problem I have tried to set forth here—the maintenance of a community's religious vision so that its life practice and its practice of worship are coherent—offers a special challenge to Christian education, which I prefer to name catechesis.

The preoccupation of catechesis is not the condition of the community's understanding of the Christian message but rather *the condition of the community's practice of that understanding.* Aloysius Pieris has noted how early in Christianity, especially in Irenaeus' writings, there was a shift in emphasis from its being a way of acting to being a way of understanding. According to Pieris, it was the monastic movement, strongly influenced by non-Christian monastic movements, that in its move to the desert or to enclaves of rigorous practice maintained the early emphasis on Christianity as an art of living.[24] In highlighting the persistent attempts of the church to find the correct lived way, Pieris never underestimates—and neither should we—the difficulties of finding and living that way. We do well to avoid naive claims, such as G. A. Coe's, made earlier this century, that religious education could foster a revolution in U.S. society at large. Still I believe that local churches can be, though not easily, zones of contestation of the class habitus and of the dominant culture.

One of the reasons I have in my own studies gone back again and again to C. Ellis Nelson's *Where Faith Begins* is for its emphasis on the connection between the faith understood and the faith lived. Other works have claimed to be concerned about practice, though few exhibit the focused concern for the lived way that Nelson's does. His convictions behind the book are close to my own. In Nelson's words, "It is an assumption of this book that America is increasingly becoming a secular, pluralistic, urban society and that the Protestant ethos which dominated when the Constitution was written is no longer the ethos of the country generally. It is further assumed that the Christian faith is based on a revelation from God which transcends culture and comes into human life for the purpose of directing human culture. It is essential, therefore, that we explore what culture communicates in order to separate *to some extent* the Christian tradition from culture."[25]

Nelson's concern consistently is with the worshiping, believing community as the zone where the Christian tradition lives to some extent separated from the wider culture. Though he does not use the exact language, Nelson's intent is to propose the local church as a zone of cultural contestation. In their living faithful practice people find the most cogent and coherent expression of what that faith means for our time. In a passage I have often cited, Nelson expresses this conviction in a compelling way.

> After seeing that the group of believers is the unity with which we must work, we must then see that whatever is done or said, or not done or not said, is teaching. There is no such thing as postponing the solution to a problem. The decision to postpone is a decision; it teaches that the issue is too hot to handle, that such issues are not appropriate for the church, or that the tactic of postponement is more important at this point than a resolution to settle the matter. People learn from the way events are handled. There is no neutrality. If a congregation attempts to be neutral, it teaches that on the issues at hand it can't make up its mind, it is fearful of the result of a

decision, or it is confused about how to proceed. There is no avoidance of an issue. Not to see an issue is to teach that Christians do not see issues. Christians who avoid problems in social ethics—such as involvement in racial relations, war, or the distribution of wealth—are saying that the Christian faith does not operate in these areas. . . . What the congregation as a group says and does in the community is the meaning they give to their faith.[26]

From this view, Christian education and catechesis is a ministry to the condition of the community's practice of its understandings. In this view, also, the community must in some sense be a school of practice, not of practice imposed on those too young to resist but of practice sought after by those who seek to be disciples. If the community is to be a zone of contestation, then its members can together discover how to embody the contesting values in their life structure. Congregations adept at setting up schools of doctrine, to ensure a proper understanding of its tenets, must also become schools of practice, with a ministry to practice.

Competence in the living practice of discipleship is learned in situations. Like language, it is learned, inextricably, as the mastery of practice but also as the practical mastery of situations, in which one becomes able to act in a way adequate to the Gospel. Discipleship is not a "thought" art but a lived-out one. The churches' interest in the verbal mastery of doctrinal tenets and in the spoken language of discipleship has generally not been matched by adequate attention to the living practice of fidelity, except perhaps in matters of sexual morality. As one form of practice having to do with Gospel values, ritual behavior in worship is not sufficient to show a full range of competence. Competence in discipleship must also, and characteristically, exhibit competent practice in a variety of situations.[27]

The Problem of Vision

There is need here to deal with the large question of which religious vision we are talking about. In the religious climate of the United States, Christians are aware that they all do not espouse the same faith. They claim to espouse the same sacred writings, but they apply their writings in very different ways, with different implications for the political and economic orders. In a country of perhaps four percent of the world's population holding the rest of the world hostage to its globally destructive weapons' systems, some Christians seek to find a stance that will radically contest the dominant culture. My own view is that in a consumerist culture, no Gospel stance so radically contests the dominant ethos as does solidarity with the poor. Similar stances might include solidarity with victims and bonding with the disenfranchised. Such stances load Christianity with important economic and political agendas that have deep implications for life structure and practice in local communities. Perhaps the difficulty of actually taking such stances verifies Bourdieu's claims about the priority of economic status in fostering habits of the heart and of action. In the context of lived out commitments to the poor and victims, worship becomes a coherent celebration of dangerous memories. Lacking them, worship becomes, if not an actual celebration of class privilege, then a celebration of its being overlooked and ignored.

NOTES

1. Among Roman Catholics, this question has taken the form of the distinction between sacrament as *opus operatum* and as *opus operantis*. The first, literally, the deed done or the work worked, is the unambiguous and efficacious word of God present and available in ritual; the second, literally, the work of the one doing the work, involves the subjective dispositions of those who worship. This distinction was a way of disavowing Reformists' claims that sacraments were magical rites, seeking in a sense to control God, and at the same time to assert that God's power worked in sacraments beyond the holiness or lack of it in the chief celebrant. Although Karl Rahner implies that few worshipers see sacraments as magical: "*In individual instances of personally unenlightened people* (emphasis added) a concrete Christian can misunderstand the sacraments in a magical way and also does in fact misunderstand them," I believe that many Christian people, including leaders, have what might be called a "nuanced misunderstanding" of the power of sacraments that overstates their efficacy. Not so bald as the magical misunderstanding possessed by Rahner's odd, misinformed person, such a misunderstanding tends to be unwilling to situate worship in the total life of the church. See Karl Rahner, *Foundations of Christian Faith: An Introduction to the Idea of Christianity* (New York: Seabury, 1978), 413–415.

2. It is possible to find clues to this overstated sacramental efficacy in some passages of Vatican Council II's liturgical document, but only if these passages are taken out of their context in a well-nuanced treatise. For example, the following passage:

> For it is through the liturgy, especially the divine Eucharistic Sacrifice, that "the work of our redemption is exercised." The liturgy is thus the outstanding means by which the faithful can express in their lives, and manifest to others, the mystery of Christ and the real nature of the true Church. . . . Day by day the liturgy builds up those within the Church into the Lord's holy temple, into a spiritual dwelling for God. . . . At the same time the liturgy marvelously fortifies the faithful in their capacity to preach Christ.
>   . . . The liturgy is considered as an exercise of the priestly office of Jesus Christ. In the liturgy the sanctification of man is manifested by signs perceptible to the senses, and is effected in a way which is proper to each

of these signs; in the liturgy full public worship is performed by the Mystical Body of Jesus Christ, that is, by the Head and His members.

From this it follows that every liturgical celebration, because it is an action of Christ the priest and of His Body the Church, is a sacred action surpassing all others. *No other action of the Church can match its claim to efficacy nor equal the degree of it* (emphasis added). *Constitution of the Sacred Liturgy*, nos. 2 and 7, in W. M. Abbott and J. Gallagher, eds., *The Documents of Vatican II* (New York: Association Press, 1966), 137–138, 141.

3. Aloysius Pieris, "Christianity and Buddhism in Core-to-Core Dialogue," *Cross Currents* 37, no. 1 (Spring 1987): 47–75, at 57. In the same passage Pieris expresses optimism about Christianity's ability to perdure. "Both Buddhism and Christianity are vibrant with life because each has developed its own religious system—doctrines, rites, and institutions—which make the original experience available to contemporary society."

4. Geoffrey Wainwright, *Doxology: The Praise of God in Worship, Doctrine and Life: A Systematic Theology* (New York: Oxford University Press, 1980), 2–3.

5. Ibid., 8.

6. Ibid., no. 11; Abbott, 143.

7. Ibid., no. 9; Abbott, 142. Notice that the previous passage cited calls for the matching of thoughts and words. This passage, which actually comes earlier in the document, suggests a necessary (and prior) correlative: that words must be matched by lived commitments.

8. Both quotes are found in D. Capelle, "L'Introduction du catechumenat à Rome," *Recherches de théologie ancienne et medievale* 5 (1933): 151, notes 38 and 39. Capelle gives the original references as: 1) Hom. V, 6 in lud., 2) C. Cels. 3, 59. Regis Duffy first called my attention to this source.

9. Regis Duffy, *On Becoming a Catholic: The Challenge of Christian Initiation* (San Francisco: Harper and Row, 1984), 44.

10. As I understand it, *lex vivendi* was the whole point of the literature on the ascetical life that goes back to early Christianity but which assumed almost a literary form in the eighteenth and nineteenth centuries. On this point, see Sandra Schneiders, "Theology and Spirituality: Strangers, Rivals, or Partners?" *Horizons* 13, no. 2 (1986): 253–274.

11. Cited in Thomas McCarthy, *The Critical Theory of Jurgen Habermas* (Cambridge: MIT Press, 1978), 63.

12. Jacques Ellul, *The Subversion of Christianity* (Grand Rapids, MI: Eerdmans, 1986), 4.

13. Most of Williams' corpus deals with this question. For a brief statement, see "Means of Communication as Means of Production," in *Problems in Materialism and Culture* (London: Verso Editions, 1980), 50–63.

14. John Kavanaugh, "The World of Wealth and the Gods of Wealth," in L. Boff and V. Elizondo, *Option for the Poor: Challenge to the Rich Countries*, in *Concilium* 187, no. 5 (1986): 17.

15. See Pierre Bourdieu, *Distinction: A Social Critique of the Judgment of Taste*, trans. Richard Nice (Cambridge: Harvard University Press, 1984), 101. Here I paraphrase the sense of his argument, found in so many of his writings.

16. Pierre Bourdieu, *Outline of a Theory of Practice* (New York: Cambridge University Press, 1977), 80.

17. Cited in Henry A. Giroux, "Theories of Reproduction and Resistance in the New Sociology of Education: A Critical Analysis," *Harvard Educational Review* 53, no. 3 (1985): 257–293. Giroux's essay gave me several leads in studying Bourdieu's work.

18. Ibid.

19. Bourdieu, *Outline*, 94.

20. Ibid., 81–82.

21. Ibid., 85–86.

22. Robert Coles and George Abbott White, "The Religion of the Privileged Ones," *Cross Currents* 31, no. 1 (1981): 1–14 esp. 7.

23. See, for example, his essay, "Intellectual Field and Creative Project," in Michael F. D. Young, *Knowledge and Control* (London: Collier-Macmillan, 1971), 161–188. At one point he explains what he calls the necessity of the "cultural unconscious," which tacitly assumes its very foundations.

24. Aloysius Pieris, "Christianity and Buddhism in Core-to-Core Dialogue," *Cross Currents* 37, no. 1 (Spring 1987): 47–75.

25. C. Ellis Nelson, *Where Faith Begins* (Atlanta: John Knox, 1967), 43. Nowhere in the book do I find Nelson lamenting the loss of the "Protestant ethos," which has led to a greater pluralism in U.S. life.

26. Ibid., 184–185. This is one of many such passages in the work.

27. Here I have paraphrased in the language of discipleship a passage from the following essay of Pierre Bourdieu, "The Economics of Linguistic Exchanges," *Social Science Information* 16 (1977): 645–668 esp. 647.

PART B
Culture and Inculturation

Introduction

MICHAEL WARREN

Some will be surprised to find a detailed section on inculturation in a book of catechetical sources intended for the United States and other English-speaking nations. Such people may understand inculturation to be a matter only for "young churches" in lands where the people are new and have a decidedly minority status. Inculturation, seen this way, is about bringing the Gospel to "mission countries" where it has not yet been heard. Yet, inculturation is a process that must go on in any place where the church is struggling to be authentic. Every religious truth the church is trying to live or communicate has been inculturated sometime, someplace. No thought, religious or otherwise, can be expressed except in a cultural mode.

The question of inculturation for Christians is, How can the Gospel find an expression that is authentic for the people of a particular time and place? The model of inculturation is Jesus himself, the Galilean Jew of the first century, fully a Jewish faithful one of his time and place.

The famous Jesuit catechist Alfonso Nebreda once commented that it was easier for Jesus and his message to get the attention of a Japanese person who had never before heard of him than the attention of a French person who had heard of Jesus since infancy. In France, with its long Christian tradition, many might assume they already *knew* what Jesus was all about and that therefore there was nothing here to be learned. In this comment, Nebreda alerts us that inculturation might be far more difficult in the so-called Christian lands where rote repetition has lost communicative vibrancy than in the "mission" lands.

A Perspective on Culture

To understand inculturation well, one best begins with the word embedded in it: *culture*. In our own time, this word seems to be on almost everyone's tongue. However, not all who use this commonplace word have a common meaning for it. Some use it to mean the general "ways" of a particular society, found in its language, music, various customs, and rituals. Such a use has value for helping us think about how a people's way of life functions and works. Anthropologists use culture with this meaning to chart the life of particular peoples, whom they study through the lens of nonjudgmental, descriptive social science. However, such an approach may not be sufficient for religious people who must evaluate a way of life using religious norms. Religious norms prompt judgments about what in a culture fosters or diminishes the process of humanization.

For religious purposes, in this case, catechetical ones, I describe culture as the signifying system communicating a social order. From this angle, culture is a system of signs—by their very nature visible and accessible—that become the channels through which a particular social order is communicated. From this angle, too, culture cannot only be described but critiqued for whether the social order serves the well-being of all members and for the extent to which the system of sign is humanizing or not. This description is valuable in a time of electronic communications, when a dizzying diversity of signs—all communicating a social order—come tumbling at us with the speed of light. Seeing culture this way invites us to ponder the messages latent in all signs. It also invites us to step back and consider that these signs are some person's communication trying to convince me of a particular rendition of the world and of a particular social order. If, as a human construct, that social order is open to human questioning and critique, so are the signs communicating that social order.

Church as Culture

Seeing culture as a signifying system is also a useful way of understanding the meaning of the communities of people we call the church. The church, with some qualifications, is a signifying system by which the new social order proclaimed by Jesus—God's Reign or sacred commonwealth—is communicated, experienced, explored, and reproduced. God's Reign is not realized the way the civic social order is; neither is it synonymous with the church's own civic social order. The Reign of God is in process the way yeast hidden in dough is in process. It works gradually with a quiet leavening effect. As a norm of the social order, God's Reign gives all social arrangements critical scrutiny. The ideal of God's Reign—and the sacred texts that support it—provides norms by which to make judgments about all reality, though not easily.

Of course the way of life of the church, as an embodied system of meaning, may confound and contradict Jesus' message in various ways. If so, the church moves into a conflict between its verbal signifying system and the signifying system of its living. The conditions of the dough may so impair the yeast that the dough becomes inert or even infected with harmful bacteria. In such a situation, the church as a culture loses coherence and even credibility.

Another useful example for inculturation is language. In this context, the word of God is meant to be on the lips of people in their own tongue, in their own idiom. Via inculturation the signifying system of the Christian assemblies translates God's holy commonwealth into the idiom native to a particular place and a particular culture. By going native in a culture, the Christian Way can be lived out by those of the culture who espouse God's coming Reign. Just as yeast is not an alien element in the dough, but infuses and enlivens it, so the Gospel through the process of inculturation becomes a source of life and enrichment in a particular society. Whatever the actual process of coming to sacred Word in this tongue, inculturation is a work, not of simple translation, but of allowing the energy of religious insight present in people to find authentic expression in their own ways of speaking.

In my view catechesis cannot function properly unless it works from a sound understanding of culture, its various forms and institutions, and how they influence people. The current catechetical renewal shows catechesis to be more than communicating a system of doctrines or dogmas. It is a lifelong process of influencing people toward the practice of the Jesus-Way. In that work, catechesis must examine, sometimes confront, and sometimes use, the great influencer, culture.

Each of the following essays brings the issue of inculturation and its many facets to *catechetical* significance. The literature that gave rise to the catechetical renewal of the twentieth century, going back to the 1930's writings by Rahner and Jungmann, deals again and again with the matter of inculturation, though under varied headings: kerygma, adaptation, correlation, indigenization, localization, contextualization, evangelization, and renewal.[1] To use Arrupe's words found in the first of these essays, these terms all were ways of striving to "save the proposition of the neighbour . . . where authentic dialogue begins."

1. For an examination of some of these terms see Congregation for Worship and Sacraments, "Instruction: Inculturation and the Roman Liturgy," *Origins* 23, no. 43 (14 April 1994): 745, 747–756.

Further Reading

Warren, Michael. *Communications and Cultural Analysis: A Religious View.* Valley Forge, PA: Trinity Press International, 1997.

READING 3
Introduction

Decades after being written, Arrupe's letter to the Society of Jesus still brims with important principles of inculturation, a word coined by the Thirty-second General Congregation of the Society of Jesus. Readers will find his oft-cited description of inculturation (section 1) repeated and amplified in Peter Schineller's later essay. Arrupe highlights the need for inculturation in countries where the Gospel has been preached for centuries. The issue is the stance the church takes in the face of the wider culture within which it functions. In regard to the wider culture, re-inculturation of the faith is an ongoing, indeed endless, process, as is the related work of the evangelization of cultures. Arrupe's sketch of necessary attitudes for a love marked by delicacy could be easily compared with the attitudes set forth by Augustine in his fifth-century catechetical classic, *De Rudibus Catechizandus*. In Arrupe's letter, sections 3 and 4 provide principles with notable implications for all levels of cate-chetical work.

Letter on Inculturation to the Whole Society

PEDRO ARRUPE, SJ

*The Decree on Inculturation—Fr. Parmananda Divarkar wrote once—
is one of the shortest and most pedestrian products of the Thirty-second
General Congregation, but the interest it soon aroused is an indication of the importance of the issues it raises and of the urgency of the
task it imposes on the Society and the individual Jesuit.*

*Inculturation—at least the term—was born in the Congregation.
It was the experience of a deep-rooted oneness at the heart of a wide-
ranging variety: never had there been such diversity in a Jesuit assembly before, never such a problem of language—and yet there was
real communication, seemingly effortless because of the overwhelming
consciousness of belonging together, of having very much to share. It
was even said that the tensions that some members reported as existing in various quarters seemed so trifling, and paradoxically so serious, in the light of their own felt unity. Old timers who had attended
previous Congregations could not help remarking that though this was
the first time that they had no common tongue—for Latin was in general use even at the Thirty-first—yet there was greater mutual acceptance and understanding than before, in spite of a greater variety of
backgrounds—with, of course, differences of opinions.*

*It was only three years after the Thirty-second General Congrega-
tion, after much study, consultations and experience, that Father Arrupe addressed the Society on this complex subject. He also wrote a
special letter on the subject to the Jesuits in India and Sri Lanka.*

Dear Brothers in Christ:
The Thirty-second General Congregation in its decree on inculturation
entrusted Father General with the task of "further development and promotion of this work throughout the Society" (decr. 5, n. 2).

Reprinted from *Selected Letters and Address III: Other Apostolates Today*, edited by
Jerome Aixala, SJ (Saint Louis: Institute of Jesuit Sources, 1981), 171–180. Copyright
© 1981 by the Institute of Jesuit Sources. Used with permission.

I accepted this mandate of the Congregation with all the greater interest because my experience both before and after my election as General has profoundly convinced me of the importance of this problem.

Taking "culture" in the same sense in which it is understood by the Pastoral Constitution *Gaudium et Spes* (53), and subsequently by the Apostolic Exhortation *Evangelii Nuntiandi* (20), and by the recent Synod of 1977 in its final message (n. 5), the problem of inculturation presents itself on such a large scale, in situations of such wide diversity and with such profound and varied implications, that it is not at all easy to settle on concrete lines of approach that are universally valid.

For this reason, I have decided to limit myself in this letter to a few considerations that may serve as a stimulus for you not only to promote this process of inculturation but to be actively involved in it. I want to tell you how I see this problem as it touches the Society.

In a separate document, attached to this letter, some reflections are offered, and various issues raised; questions are formulated that are intended to focus our efforts to find solutions. For, in spite of the progress we have made, this is a subject that still requires much study, consultation, and discernment.

1. The Notion of Inculturation and Its Universal Relevance Today

Inculturation can be looked at from many viewpoints and seen at different levels, which must be distinguished but cannot be separated. Yet, amid the multiple formulations of the problem that we have to reckon with, the fundamental and constantly valid principle is that inculturation is the incarnation of Christian life and of the Christian message in a particular cultural context, in such a way that this experience not only finds expression through elements proper to the culture in question (this alone would be no more than a superficial adaptation), but becomes a principle that animates, directs, and unifies the culture, transforming and remaking it so as to bring about "a new creation."

In every case, this Christian experience is that of the People of God, who live in a definite cultural space and have assimilated the traditional values of their own culture, but are open to other cultures. In other words, it is the experience of a local Church that, accepting the past with discernment, constructs the future with its present resources.

I believe that we are much more conscious nowadays than we were before of the urgent importance and the deep implications of this process.

It is clear that the need for inculturation is universal. Until a few years ago one might have thought that it was a concern only of countries or continents that were different from those in which the Gospel was assumed to have been inculturated for centuries. But the galloping pace of change in these latter areas—and change has already become a permanent situation—persuades us that today there is need of a new and continuous inculturation of the faith everywhere if we want the Gospel message to reach modern man and the new "sub-cultural" groups. It would be a dangerous error to deny that these areas need a re-inculturation of the faith.

So you should not think that this document I am sending you has reference only to what have been called "mission countries" until now. It finds application everywhere, perhaps all the more so where people think they do not have this need. The concepts, "Missions," "Third World," "East/West," etc., are relative and we should get beyond them, considering the whole world as one single family whose members are beset by the same varied problems.

The Christian experience in a given culture has an influence that transforms and renews and, perhaps after a crisis of confrontation, leads to a fresh wholeness in that culture. Further, Christian experience helps a culture to assimilate universal values that no one culture can exhaustively realize. Christian experience invites us to enter into a new and profound communion with other cultures, inasmuch as all the nations are called to form, with mutual enrichment and complementarity, the "robe of many colours" of the cultural reality of the one pilgrim People of God. In today's world, a large contact between cultures is inevitable, and this provides a providential opportunity for inculturation. The problem lies in a wise channeling of this intercultural influence. It is here that Christianity can play a most important role: its mission is that of searching the depths of the past with lucid discernment, whilst it opens a culture both to values that are universal and common to all human beings, and to the particular values of other cultures; it must ease tensions and conflicts, and create genuine communion.

Surely this is one of the great contributions that we should be making.

2. Inculturation and the Society of Jesus

As Jesuits we should feel especially challenged by this problem. It is one we have confronted throughout the history of the Society, and unless we solve it, great obstacles to our work of evangelization will block our path.

Ignatian spirituality, with its unifying vision of Salvation History, and its ideal of service to the whole human race ("with such diversity . . . of dress and behavior; . . . some white, others black . . ." Sp.Ex., 106), was a stroke of genius that, according to some experts, channeled the sensibilities and the cultural characteristics of the sixteenth century into the steady stream of Christian spirituality; nevertheless, it did not confine itself to its own age, but in the course of history has been able to promote both the dynamism of the Spirit and human creativity, in a never ending process of adaptation to all peoples and times.

Quite obviously, Saint Ignatius never used the word *inculturation.* But the theological content of this term is present in his writings, including the Constitutions.

The *Presupposition* of the Exercises demands a basic disposition at the outset of the retreat that is of immense value in inculturation: to be ready to "save the proposition of the neighbour" (22). This is where authentic dialogue begins.

The Exercises ask us to reflect on the one beginning and end for all human beings (23), their solidarity in sin (51, 71), the call of the King addressed to the whole world (102). Furthermore, they recall that everything comes to us as a token of God's love, as gifts that descend from above (234, 235, 257).

The personal experience of Christ and his message that we live in the Exercises, the interior knowledge of the Lord (104), helps us to discern correctly what is inalienable in Christian faith and what might be merely its cultural wrappings.

Concern for the concrete situation is a constant in the thought of Saint Ignatius and in his government. It appears in more than twenty passages of the Constitutions. He keeps insisting that attention be paid to the circumstances of country, place, language, different mentalities, and personal temperaments (Cfr. Constitutions, 301, 508, 581, 747, 395, 458, 462, 671, 64, 66, 71, 136, 211, 238, 449, etc.).

Along the same line are the words of advice he gives in various instructions: "They should make themselves approachable by humility and love, becoming all things for the sake of all (I Cor 9,22); let them clearly adopt, as far as the Institute of the Society allows, the customs of those peoples" (to the Fathers and Brothers sent on ministries: Rome, 24 September 1549; MI Epp XII, 239–242). He orders that penances be given to those who do not learn the local language (to the Superiors of the Society: Rome, 1 January 1556).

The tradition of the Society has always been faithful to this principle of adaptation. This is the way our great missionaries acted—Xavier, Ricci, de Nobili, and so many others, each according to the mentality of his time—when they launched bravely and creatively on an effort at pastoral adjustment to a given situation.

The task of evangelization of cultures, which is one aspect of the total problem, cannot be ignored in our days, and it calls for Jesuits who make a similar creative effort. Paul VI invites us to take up this responsibility, so much in keeping with the tradition of the Society, when he encourages messengers of the Gospel to make every effort and give serious attention to the evangelization of cultures (Cf. *Evangelii Nuntiandi*, 20).

This is surely one of those difficult and yet very important areas mentioned by the Pope, in which there has been or now is a tension between pressing human needs and the Christian message, and where Jesuits have always been ready to work (Cf. Allocution to the members of GC 32, 3.xii.74).

The ignatian spirit was once summed up in this sentence: *"Non cohiberi a maximo, contineri tamen a minimo, divinum est."* In our context, this maxim challenges us to hold on to the concrete and the particular, even to the last cultural detail, but without renouncing the breadth and universality of those human values that no culture, nor the totality of them all, can assimilate and incarnate in a perfect and exhaustive way.

3. Necessary Attitudes

Many factors contribute to achieve a successful inculturation, and these demand from whomever is involved in the process a fine sensibility and some definite attitudes.

Beyond the fundamental attitude already mentioned, that is, of the *unifying vision* of Salvation History, one needs in the first place *docility to the Spirit,* who is the real *"causa agens"* of all new inculturation of the faith. This docility demands a continuous and attentive listening in prayer, so that the action of the Spirit is effective in the midst of all our studies and projects. This docility guards against preconceived conclusions. Putting it in ignatian language, it presupposes *indifference,* adopting a stance that is open both to receive and to give.

Genuine inculturation also supposes an attitude of ignatian *discernment,* which is ruled by evangelical principles that give to human values a transcendental dimension, so that we neither overestimate the elements of our own culture nor underestimate elements that can be found in other cultures. Discernment leads to readiness to learn from others and makes one cautious in the face of misleading appearances or superficial judgments; otherwise one might accept indiscriminately values of secondary importance while sacrificing fundamentals—for example, one might overstress technical development at the cost of destroying basic values of the person such as freedom and justice. This kind of "discretion" is vital today when all around us we see a tendency toward extremes.

Objective authenticity, which is fostered by this discretion, leads to an *interior humility* that makes us recognize our own errors and helps us to be understanding toward those of others. The countries with a long Christian tradition have certainly made mistakes in their work of evangelization, but today these are openly admitted and should be forgiven and forgotten. Likewise, the new nations who have received the Gospel from others, have made mistakes that they recognize; and these too should be forgiven and forgotten. Thus the way is open for a collaboration in which there is mutual acceptance in the creation of a present and a future, without prejudice or reservations, without limits set on the power of the Spirit.

Inculturation also requires a *persevering patience*, which is indispensable for studies in depth (psychological, anthropological, sociological, etc.) and for the unhurried experimental projects that will surely have to be undertaken. We must also steer clear of sterile polemics and, still more, of easy bargains with error.

On the contrary, it is necessary patiently to search for the *"semina Verbi,"* those *"pierres d'attente"* predestined by Providence for the building up of truth.

Caritas discreta is another requirement for inculturation, so that prophetic boldness and the fearlessness of apostolic zeal are blended with the prudence of the Spirit. Thus we can avoid extreme positions and counterproductive imprudence without restricting the impulses of a sound prophetic sense that can inspire us to take calculated risks.

Above all, we need the ignatian *sensus Ecclesiae*. In a process that is so important and full of implications, one cannot remain on the fringe of the Church—and we understand the Church as does Vatican Council II, that is, in its twofold aspect of People of God and of Hierarchy. Neither of these elements can be overlooked. It is evident that final responsibility rests with the Hierarchy. But we have to avoid two extremes: the excess *"non secundum scientiam"* (Rom 10:2) that would have us proceed regardless of the Hierarchy, and the small-mindedness that would keep us timid and passive, inhibited in our creativity. As in all else, so too in this process of inculturation, the love that we profess for the "Spouse of Christ" must lead us to think "with the Church" and "in the Church," submitting our activities and experiments in this delicate matter to the Church's direction.

These dispositions should awaken in the members of the Society that *universal charity* that urges them to outstanding efforts as creators of communion, not only at the level of the local Church, but with concern for the communion of the entire pilgrim People of God.

4. Internal Consequences

The effect this process would have on the inner life of the Society should be obvious. The changes that have taken place and that will keep on taking place in the future, as we try to adapt ourselves to contemporary cultural changes, have their origin in the criteria of Vatican Council II and in the priorities and directives of the Thirty-first and Thirty-second General Congregations. But these changes will have no practical effect if we do not allow the transforming power of the Spirit to modify our personal life from within. We might call this "the personal interior inculturation," which must necessarily precede, or at least accompany, the external task of inculturation. All changes arising from Vatican Council II and from our last two General Congregations have precisely this objective: to make us effective agents of a genuine inculturation of the Gospel.

In order to understand our charism in contemporary terms and to discern in apostolic spirit our service to the Church today, we have to rethink our way of applying ignatian criteria to the concrete situations that face us. This is a kind of inculturation that is personal and *"intra Societatem"* and it is not easy. Although we admit in theory the necessity of inculturation, when it comes to practice and touches us personally, demanding of us profound changes in our attitudes and scale of values, often there is insensibility and resistance. This shows up our lack of inner disposition for "personal inculturation."

If we want to let ourselves be caught up in the process of inculturation, theory and study are not enough. We need the "shock" of a deep personal experience. For those called to live in another culture, it will mean being integrated in a new country, a new language, a whole new life. For those who remain in their own country, it will mean experiencing the new styles of our changing contemporary world—not the mere theoretical knowledge of the new mentalities, but the experiential assimilation of the way of life of the groups with which we must work, the outcasts, Chicanos, slum dwellers, intellectuals, students, artists, etc.

Take, for example, the wide world of the young people whom we serve in our schools, parishes, Christian Life Communities, Centres of Spirituality, etc. They belong to a culture that is quite different from that of many Jesuits, with mental structures, scales of value, and language (especially religious language) not always easily intelligible. Communication is difficult. In a certain sense, we are "foreigners" in their world. I think that many Jesuits, especially in the developed countries, have no idea of the abyss that separates faith and culture; and for that very reason they are less well equipped servants of the Word.

The experience of what is called insertion into another culture should free us from so much that keeps us shackled: class prejudice and narrow loyalties, cultural and racial discrimination, etc.

The total inculturation required of a Jesuit should never turn him into a hidebound nationalist or regionalist. Our universalism, the sense of belonging to the "universal body" of the Society, must be kept inviolate, "lest diversity damage the bond of charity," as Saint Ignatius notes in the Constitutions (672). So too, we have to maintain in full vigour the disposition of availability, a fundamental attitude of every Jesuit, which makes him ready to go wherever there is hope of greater service of the Church, if he is sent on mission by obedience.

It is in keeping alive this availability that we feel more personally and intimately the tension between the particular and the universal, between the sense of being identified with the culture of a particular people and, at the same time, keeping ourselves free and ready to be sent to any part of the world where our apostolic service is required.

Authentic inculturation, with the above-mentioned characteristics of particularity and universality, has an obvious importance in the *formation of our young men*. They are called to become agents of inculturation and must, therefore, be formed in its spirit and in its concrete expression.

In line with the desire of the Thirty-second General Congregation that we "continue with even greater intensity today" the work of inculturation, I would like that a persevering effort in this area become the object of "ever growing concern on the part of the Society" (Decree 5, n. 1). I want us to be vitally aware of the capital importance of inculturation for our mission of defence and propagation of the faith, conscious that we belong at one and the same time to the local Church and to the Universal Church.

But this will not come about without personal and profound convictions—so whoever does not have these should strive for them—and without the well-ordered collaboration of all, in study, in reflection, and in concrete experiences. Only in that way will we discover those living channels of communication and expression that will enable the Christian message to reach the individuals and the peoples with whom we work, opening them up at the same time to the riches of other cultures.

A delicate task this, to be sure; but indispensable. It is one of the best services which the Society of today can render in the cause of evangelization. All of us, sons of the Society, should be conscious of being sent as heralds and agents of a communion that not only gathers together people of our own countries, but brings to unity, whilst respecting distinct identity, "all God's children scattered far and wide" (John 11:52).

I am sending you this letter on the Solemnity of Pentecost, and I invoke upon all of you the light and grace of God's Spirit.

Feast of Pentecost, Rome, 14 May 1978
Pedro Arrupe,
Superior General of the Society of Jesus

READING 4
Introduction

This essay is actually about the production of meaning (cultural production) by a people in their own local church assemblies. I put the matter this way to highlight the connection Schreiter's essay has with the other essays in this section of the *Sourcebook* dealing with culture and inculturation. Schreiter's essay is broken down into four topical issues, followed by important reflections on method. The significance of Schreiter's issues and his methodological reflections for catechesis will become evident to those who understand catechesis as a ministry to the practice of the community's understandings rather than as a work of imposing doctrinal positions produced outside the community. Schreiter is examining the conditions under which a local assembly becomes a coproducer of Gospel insight and practice, instead of being simply a consumer of religious insight produced elsewhere. From concern for this issue arose the initial objections against the proposal for a new universal catechism, later published as the *Catechism of the Catholic Church*.

Schreiter's first issue is that of starting with the needs (problems, issues, conflicts, obstacles) of the local community, as these lead to an analysis and evaluation (that is, norm-based judgments) of the local situation by the local assembly. Instead of a translation approach of bringing the Gospel to a local situation, he advocates a contextualization approach of discerning the ways the Gospel is already present.

The second issue presents local theology as being more concerned with the practice of a local assembly than with the concerns of the "academy." Here theology (like catechesis, a form of the ministry of the Word) is reflection on the struggle to bring the Gospel into local practice, but measured against the practice of the tradition. "The common reflection of the community itself . . . provides the base out of which a theology is to emerge." To repeat: the community becomes a producer of Gospel insight, and is not only a reproducer or consumer of it.

The third issue has to do with balancing the value of both the local theology and the various dimensions of the wider tradition. For example, the Scriptures come to the local situation as a normative text endowed by the tradition with a long history of interpretation. As Schreiter notes, this matter of local theology has to be addressed with great care. Catechists will understand these tensions as ones they have faced squarely since Vatican Council II, as, for example, in the conflicts over the age of first confession and the sequence of communion and penance for children.

The fourth issue revolves around the questions: How does local theology know if it has, on the one hand, fallen into "a dogmatic fundamentalism imposing itself upon the culture" or, on the other hand, into "a kind of cultural romanticism which attentuates the Christian message in an accommodationism to every value or whim of the culture?" What are the criteria for authentic Christian identity? I suspect the answer to this dilemma is for the churches to become simultaneously truly local and truly global, analogous to the ways great art is both particular and universal.

Schreiter goes on to propose the norm by which local churches can judge their fidelity—the practice of other local churches, current ones and those of the past. I consider this point of great significance in a time when local churches are slow to recognize (and celebrate) the communities among them living virtuoso discipleship. Schreiter wisely asks for local theology both the latitude to find its voice and an openness to critique from other local communities.

His section on the analysis of culture is astute, meriting the close study of all concerned with the major influences on people's imaginations and how these influences determine what people actually live in their daily lives. If the church is the great foundational sacrament of the secret of Jesus, and if its life is the great catechizer, then the matters Schreiter raises here are indeed catechetical ones.

Local Theologies in the Local Church: Issues and Methods

ROBERT J. SCHREITER, CPPS

The shift in interest to the reality of the local church has raised important ecclesial questions for the whole Church. So, too, will an interest in local theologies. The purpose of this paper is to examine some of the issues that talking about local theologies is bound to raise (and, indeed, has already done so). I intend to concentrate here on four such basic issues that recur in discussions about developing local theologies. Through the last number of years, these issues have become more clear in the minds of those working in such theologies. However, a second area, the methods needed to address these issues, is less clearly worked out. I will try to raise some questions in this area as well by discussing three methodological areas that become important in a developing local theology. Between the presentations on issues and methods there will be a short interlude that will try to set out what is going on in the creation of a local theology.

Issue One: Translation or Contextualization?

If one were to ask for some preliminary definition of local theology, it might run something like this: Local theology is the result of a continuing adaptation or translation of the Gospel message and ensuing Christian tradition in local, concrete contexts. The purpose of this adaptation is to make the Gospel message more intelligible and lively within the local church, and to make the larger church tradition and practice a better vehicle for responding to the Gospel in the local situation. So defined, local theology can be seen to be part of a long history of historical development within the church.

Reprinted from *CTSA Proceedings* (1981): 96–112. Copyright © 1981 by the Catholic Theological Society of America (CTSA). Used with permission.

But this commonsense definition of local theology begins almost immediately to run into all sorts of problems. The most obvious question that arises is: How far is one to go in such adaptations? To what extent is one bound to forms and formulae that have been part and parcel of the Christian Tradition? For example, may one abandon the use of wine and bread as eucharistic elements in those parts of the world where these mid-Eastern staples are unknown, or where (as in some Muslim countries) the importation of wine is forbidden? Or, to take another case of problems of form, what is one to do when the symbol has an opposite effect of the one intended? Among the Masai of Eastern Africa, to pour water on a woman's head is to curse her with infertility. Should the local church continue then to administer baptism in the traditional fashion? How should one communicate the meaning of metaphors of shepherd and sheep to peoples who have no acquaintance with such things? Formulations of doctrine can cause something of the same problem. The doctrine of the Real Presence has caused genuine problems in some parts of Papua New Guinea among peoples whose neighbors practiced cannibalism. They considered Christianity an inferior religion because of this.

The question of how far one is to go in adaptation usually prompts a response in which the task of theology is seen as undoing a husk of cultural accretions from the core Christian message, and then rewrapping that core in a new set of cultural symbols and values. Most liturgical adaptation follows this pattern, and many official Vatican documents encourage this kind of approach.

While this response can sometimes ease the difficulties in a situation, seldom does a core-and-husk approach work so easily. Christianity was not put together in that fashion in the first place, and core and husk have tended to become co-constitutive over a period of time. It is for this reason that such projects as the "dehellenization" of Christianity proposed by Harnack and more recently by Dewart seldom work out as well as their proponents would anticipate. Second, there is the problem of who will determine what may be adapted. This is an increasingly difficult problem.

These adaptation or translation approaches, while laudable in their intent, suffer from a basic weakness. Despite their avowed concern with the local situation, they do not take the local church seriously enough. What happens in translation approaches is that people are busy adapting answers before the questions have been asked by the local situation. Solutions are provided before problems are adequately defined.

For this reason, there is a need to try to begin from the other side; namely, the needs of the local community. One needs to begin with an analysis and evaluation of the local situation, and only then turn to the Gospel and the larger church Tradition. This is what is generally understood as the contextualization approach; that is, an approach that emphasizes sensitivity to the context of the situation before presuming to be able to understand how the Gospel might best find its voice there. To put it another way: in the matter of evangelization, it becomes the difference between evangelization as bringing Christ to a situation (translation approach) or finding him already there in the life, values, and symbols of the culture (contextualization approach).

The main reason why the translation approach has seemed so commonsense and has so often been used is that we have developed a custom in our Church whereby the leaders of the local church are often not from that community, but have come there from another place. Since the development of the idea of absolute ordination, leaders are often no longer called by and for a local community in our tradition.[1] The translation approach becomes the most usable approach for such leaders. It can be developed more rapidly, and allows for a good deal more control on the part of the leaders than does the contextualization approach, where the emphasis is laid upon the discerning processes of the community. Such considerations bring me to the second issue in the development of local theologies.

Issue Two:
Theology—Its Audience, Intent, and Author

When one begins to speak of local church, and then of local theology in a local church, one has to become more highly sensitive about the audience to whom this theology is addressed. Indeed, because of the growing call for local theology, we have become much more aware of the audiences to whom we have been addressing most of our theology.

While theologians are aware of the rootedness of their work in a confessional tradition, and their responsibility to address members of the Church (or to address world issues as members of the Church), I would hazard to say that most of what we theologians write is ultimately addressed to other colleagues in the academy.[2]

This is not surprising, since we receive our legitimation to be considered theologians from the academy,[3] and maintain our standing primarily, though not exclusively, by being held accountable to other members of the academy. All of this is not surprising, since the academy has been the locus for theologians *par excellence* since the thirteenth century. The fact that the academy has formed our primary audience has also affected our intent. The classical definition of theology as *fides quaerens intellectum* has meant for us a clarification of the revelation received from God, especially in terms of other attempts at such knowledge. The best kinds of theology have presented faith in clear terms, especially as it would relate to other forms of knowledge, be that rationality as such (in the Middle Ages and in the post-Cartesian period), or the natural and social sciences (in the nineteenth and twentieth centuries). This kind of theology has a two-fold purpose: locating faith within a given world view, and providing the basis for an apologetic in dialogue with competing forms of knowledge.[4]

Moreover, the kind of theology most of us engage in has become so complex that only such "experts" as ourselves are genuinely good at it. Theology has become a full-time profession, whereas for much of the first twelve hundred years of the Church's existence, it was an occasional enterprise, engaged in as the need for such reflections arose.

If local theology in local churches has done anything, it has made us much more aware of theology's context and intent. Local theology is addressed in the first instance to a local believing community, where it tries to answer its questions and struggles, and to illuminate its concerns and values on the basis of the experience of the Gospel and the ensuing Tradition of the larger Church. Much of the theology that is now coming from local churches resembles more closely the older wisdom tradition of theology that predominated in the patristic period, and continues today in the Christian East. In that tradition, how one is to live provides the focus for the *intellectus* that faith seeks. Despite some of the polemics against the wisdom tradition put forward by liberation theologians as to its introverted and individualized focus, I think it is fair to characterize liberation theology as a wisdom theology turned outward, concerned as it is with a lifestyle and with the crucible of praxis.[5]

Second, the fact that such theology is addressed primarily to believers and those struggling with belief within their communities means that the academy becomes a secondary audience. Thus many of the questions with which we busy ourselves (e.g., the status of the truth-claims of Christianity) do not take on the same importance. Others of our questions (e.g., whether one has to be a believer to do Christian theology in the university context) become well-nigh superfluous.

Third, local theology heralds the return of theology to a much more occasional exercise. While many theologians today would admit that the pluralist situation in which we now live does not make system-building as possible as it once was, we still tend to address ourselves to many system-generated questions. Such activity tends to be looked upon as a luxurious enterprise within local communities. Theological expression becomes tied more closely to genuine need and questions of a community, rather than what can be safely and adequately said within the confines of a journal article or a dissertation.

Finally, local theology in local churches redefines the authorship of theology. To use Marxian categories here: the mode and means of production change hands. Whereas in the more common situation today it is the professional theologian who, by dint of extended education and ownership of the amount of time needed for such reflection, controls the means of theological production, in the situations emerging in local churches it is the common reflection of the community itself that provides the base out of which a theology is to emerge. It is for this reason that models of theological reflection have become the focus of so much attention. To be sure, the professional theologian continues to be an important resource in the theological process. The theologian is the bearer of knowledge of the larger church Tradition, and as such is indispensable to the theological process. The point here, however, is that the solitary role of theologians is significantly reduced.

In sum, then, local theology heightens our awareness of the process whereby theology is created, the conditions under which this happens, and the actors involved in the process. The development of this kind of theology does not make forms of theology emerging from the academy obsolete; such continue to be needed. Most local theologies lose in comprehensiveness what they gain in particularity, and a balance needs to be struck here. This brings me to the third issue.

Issue Three: Particularity and Universality

If one can legitimately ask what is the relation between the local church and the universal Church—an important question for Roman Catholics—then one can also ask what is the relation between local theology and more universal manifestations of the Gospel.

There are actually two different concerns here. The first has to do with the relation between the theology produced in and for a local situation, and the theology that is not produced in such circumstances. Those coming from the more universal perspective will ask: What are the limits of the legitimacy of local theology? Those coming from the local perspective will ask: Is there any theology that is *not* local; that is, produced as a response to some local context? Is the so-called more universal theology actually imposed on other local circumstances for the sake of uniformity and control? Is this concern for universality masking a deeper interest in such ecclesiastical control on a centralized basis? While some theologies may have more transcultural appeal than others, what this reflection prompts is the idea that perhaps all theology is ultimately local theology—arising out of a particular context and most suited to that context. In view of this concern, the matter of particularity and universality needs to be addressed with great care. While the local church may see the criterion of universality as a way of imposing hegemony, the universalists feel they may be seeing nothing more than sectarian growth under the aegis of local church and local theology.

A second concern has to do with the relation of local theology to the sources of theology shared by all local churches: the Scriptures, the ensuing Tradition, and (for Roman Catholics) the Magisterium in the variety of dimensions in which it can be construed. How are these relations to be understood and legitimated? How is a local church called to task if other local churches deem its theological expression inadequate or even wrong? What kind of normativity do the traditional sources of theology just named exercise in the local church when we realize that they, too, grew up in a concrete context and as responses to concrete situations?

In regard to both of these questions, there is a strong sense in the Roman Catholic heritage that, while the fullness of Christ may dwell in the local church, the local church cannot be genuinely church in isolation from the worldwide community of Christ. There has always been a history of dialectic between local and universal manifestations of church, and how the current realities of being church today will influence this dialectic still remains to be seen. After some encouragement of the development of local communities, there are signs that this process is beginning to contract. From a theological perspective, the questions of legitimacy arising out of the local-universal dialectic brings me to the fourth issue.

Issue Four: Criteria for Christian Identity

Much of the concern about the ultimate legitimacy of local theology centers around what, in the last analysis, constitute the criteria by which genuine Christian identity is to be measured. This becomes especially important when the theology that emerges from the local church does not resemble anything achieved in theology heretofore, or when the results look like what at one time may have been considered heresy. In other instances, the interaction between Christianity and culture may come up with a result that some would call syncretistic. In developing local theologies, how do we know if our desire to escape a dogmatic fundamentalism imposing itself upon the culture has led us instead into a kind of cultural romanticism that attenuates the Christian message in an accommodationism to every value or whim of the culture?

This matter of criteria for Christian identity is one of the major concerns of the theologies developing in local churches. In situations where the categories of thought and expression do not correspond to those more familiar to us in the West, the adequate translation from the one world to the other becomes extremely difficult. In view of the fact that the Euro-American churches are only gradually coming to terms with the impact of historicity upon the classic *loci theologici*, what does this mean for situations where we understand the context, as outsiders, even less than we do the historical circumstances surrounding certain pronouncements and statements within our own culture? To not be willing to come to terms with this question condemns local churches throughout the world, whose membership is rapidly approaching the majority of those who profess the Christian faith, to becoming Western in order to be Christian. Certainly this could be considered the most urgent of the tasks facing theology.

The Multiplicity of Roots of Local Theology

From what has been said about the major issues facing the development of local theologies, it becomes clear that any such development depends upon a multiplicity of contributing factors. It is for this reason that any one-directional method or application of principles will be unsuccessful. Rather, some dialogal, or even dialectical, approach will be necessary to hold all the factors together.

For this reason I would say that the process of developing a local theology involves a multiplicity of roots or sources. I would see such theology as characterized by dialectical movements between Gospel, church, and culture.

Gospel here means more than the Scriptures, although it certainly includes them. It refers to the Word of God as an event needing proclaimer, message, and hearer for its proper enactment. The Word of the Gospel, the living presence of the Risen Lord in the local community, needs all three of these elements for its efficacy. We are often concerned about the preparation of the proclaimer and the purity of the message. But without hearers, and indeed hearers who can hear in such a way as to have the message transform their lives, can we really say that the Gospel has been fully enacted?

It goes without saying that without the Gospel being alive and present in this sense, there is quite simply no theology to be done.

Yet our faith is a *fides ex auditu*, brought to us or identified for us by members from another local church in a network of such communities encircling our planet and reaching back in time. The proclaimer represents a tradition of understanding and response to the Word which colors the proclamation (and therefore the response) given to us. Without church, the Gospel cannot come to full flower. It becomes prone to being but the echo of the ego of the proclaimer. Moreover, against what will the local church test the veracity of its own response to the Gospel but that of other local churches, alive now or part of the Christian past? To think of some proclamation of the Gospel apart from a church Tradition is sociologically, and theologically, naïve.

Finally, culture is the context in which all of this happens. Culture provides the hearers. Culture represents its own network of traditions, values, symbols, meanings, and ways of life for a people in a given time and space. To abstract from these realities in order to establish a "universal" church or a *theologia perennis* leads to a paternalist and oppressive situation. To ignore cultural realities is to engage in a kind of theological docetism that ultimately undermines our belief in the reality of the Incarnation. At the same time, an undialectical relationship that grants the culture anything and everything and does not offer a challenge to transformation is cultural romanticism. One would wonder why one would want to see the Gospel proclaimed in the first place in such instances where this romanticism may have taken hold.[6]

There needs to be a continuing movement, then, between church and culture in the light of the Gospel for a genuine local theology to develop. Local theology needs the latitude to find its own voice, but also needs the critique of other local communities, both present and past. And the larger church Tradition needs the challenge of the theology of the local churches to come to a deeper and more textured understanding of the meaning of the Gospel of Jesus Christ for the world. To understand this movement, we need to turn to the methodological questions that give direction to the dialectical process. Most of these are familiar to anyone who has been engaged before in the theological process. But there are specific considerations that bear some treatment here.

Methods: The Analysis of Culture

When people begin to be concerned about local teleology, they usually find themselves already in the midst of the process. Ideally, however, the process should begin with listening to the culture and analyzing the results of what is heard. Put another way, the process should begin with an analysis of the situation in which the local church finds itself.

This may seem to be a truism, but in practice it is seldom observed. More often than not, the culture gets a half-hearing as the theologian rushes to the Tradition to begin what was called above a translation process. Many theologians recognize the importance of listening to the culture,[7] but it still seems to receive secondary attention.

"Culture" here is used in the broad, anthropological sense, encompassing the values, beliefs, habits, customs, behaviors, and institutions that make up a way of life for a people. It includes the phenomena to which the social sciences—sociology, economics, psychology, anthropology—address themselves.

There are many modes of cultural and social analysis, depending upon what one wishes to examine the most closely. And indeed, theology has always assumed at least some of this kind of analysis, at least on a philosophical level. Whatever kind may be used—functional, structural, semiotic, Marxian, or other forms—three things need to be kept in mind from the methodological perspective necessary for developing local theologies.

First, the mode of analysis must be holistic; that is, it must be capable to some extent of embracing the totality of the culture. Often our analyses have restricted themselves to one area, such as the rational or the intellectual, as was the case in much of the theology in the Western Church. The analysis cannot be complete if it stays on one such level, be that intellectual, socioeconomic, or even the patently religious. The reason for this is that religion is not only a view of life, it is also a way of life, and so any analysis must be able to embrace a wide variety of manifestations. This is particularly important because much of what happens to be religious may not on the surface look religious in nature, or is rejected as irreligious too quickly. In pluralist and tolerant settings such as North America, where religion is a voluntary undertaking, much religious behavior takes place not in churches, but in domed stadiums or on psychoanalytic couches. Another example of this would be the once-disdained *religiosidad popular* of the peoples of Latin America. It is now clear that one cannot understand the reality of the culture in those settings without a more sympathetic and positive valuation of this phenomenon. At the same time, phenomena not genuinely religious may be presented under the guise of religious behavior. Need for esteem and belonging has a profound effect on church attendance in the United States. Also, one must realize how much religious forms, even within the same denomination or church, can be influenced by considerations of class, race, and economic or educational status. To ignore these realities is to impoverish the response to the Gospel.

Second, the mode of analysis must be able to address the question of identity—what it is that gives the local church definition. What are the values, the relationships, the ideals, and the ills of a people, and what are the symbolic expressions given to them? The sense of identity, given in establishment of group boundary and agreement upon common world view, is a deep human need. Certainly one of the ultimate intents of local theology is to give identity to a local church, to help it find its own distinctiveness and its place with the larger mosaic of the Christian Church. And one could read much of church history, especially the history of heresy, as an attempt to establish such boundaries for communities. It is interesting to note that some of the most dramatic heretical movements or schismatic developments were often ostensibly about doctrine, but were responded to with great vigor because of their implications for group identity. In retrospect, the doctrinal differences may seem small. Some dimensions of Arianism, the Albigensian crisis, and the sixteenth century Reformation all come to mind here.

What are the best methods to analyze culture in a holistic fashion so as to discover the underlying roots of identity? Each mode of analysis has its particular strengths. I prefer some of the methods developed in symbolic anthropology, especially the "thick description" of culture proposed by Clifford Geertz.[8] I also use some of the semiotic modes of description, which see cultural forms as a network transmitting messages of meaning via a system of signifiers.[9] Some of these methods can be quite complicated, and are being adapted for use by non-expert people in local situations. But both of these approaches raise questions important enough to the theological enterprise about the dominant values guiding a culture and their symbolic expression, and how ill will and dissonance are coped with in a community.

Third, the mode of analysis must be able to address the issue of social change. Often the very need for theology arises from changes that need to be identified, analyzed, and integrated into the network of meaning in the community. In situations of culture contact, urbanization, and sudden economic and social shifts, the need to deal with what change does to a community is obvious. Often change is a threatening reality to a local community and for that reason alone needs to be addressed.

There are a variety of models for analyzing social change. Some are based on a model that sees change as the attempt to restore equilibrium in a community. In this regard, many of the models proposed by Talcott Parsons and others in American sociology come to mind. Other models, such as the Marxian models, are based upon notions of conflict and the resolution of conflict. The latter kind of models have been used especially in liberation theology, a kind of local theology that addresses especially the need for social change. Some may question whether using a model with assumptions about conflict is compatible with Christian theology. This debate is too complex to take up here; suffice it to say that some model for analyzing change needs to be part of the tool kit for theology in a local church.

In summary, any process for developing local theology will need to employ methods that address these three areas in adequate fashion for that local church. To center in upon one to the exclusion of the others will result in a weakening of the emergent theology at best, and alienating ideology at worst.

Methods: The Question of Church Tradition

A comment was made above that, from the perspective of the local church, all theology is really a series of local theologies. Such a view is important for local theologies since it allows for a more even-handed dialectic to be set up between the larger Tradition and the local church. Without it, a struggling local church would be confronted with a monolithic presence.

The Tradition of response to the Gospel of Jesus Christ is essential for the development of the self-understanding of the local church. It provides the touchstone against which it can measure its own responses. But this does not mean that all that has happened in that tradition is of equal value, nor that it need be emulated. Yet it does represent a history of responses to a variety of different circumstances that both enrich and limit the results of reflection.

One task that needs to be given more attention is a study of the tradition that allows it to re-emerge as a series of local theologies. I have suggested elsewhere that a judicious use of the sociology of knowledge, which studies the relation of forms of thought to social contexts, might be a profitable way of going about this.[10] What needs to be done is an identification of the various forms of theology (that is, the genres of expression), and then an investigation of their relations to specific contexts. In other words, does theology shaped in certain fashions fit some circumstances better than others? For example, the kinds of theology that emerge from the academy can be shown to be particularly useful in university and urban settings, and where Christian belief needs to be legitimated in the face of competing forms of knowledge. Much of patristic theology could be characterized as variations on a sacred text (hymns, homilies, commentaries). The Tradition has also seen theology as *sapientia* (wisdom), as *scientia* (sure knowledge), and as liberative praxis. These distinctions become important in the local context when one wants to discover just what kind or form of theology is best suited to a circumstance. The patristic forms, for example, are often quite usable today in predominantly oral cultures. The *scientia* approach with which we are most familiar works best in pluralist situations where that pluralism needs to be acknowledged and confronted. The *sapientia* approach works best when the concern is for spirituality. Liberative praxis is important in situations of conflict and oppression. Such identification of different forms for different situations allows us to retrieve segments of the Tradition otherwise lost to us, and prevents one kind of theology from exercising an hegemony whereby it is considered the sole, legitimate form.

A second task for method in the matter of church Tradition is the development of a more adequate theory of tradition itself. This has been recognized for some time already as a problem in cultures such as those of Europe and North America where the impact of Enlightenment thought has been to denigrate the role and authority of tradition in life. The questions that have been with us for some time—how does a tradition legitimately develop, what is the authority of a tradition (the issue of Magisterium, normativity of documents marking key moments in the tradition), what constitutes departure (heresy) from a tradition—become even more pressing under the matter of developing local theologies. To my knowledge, such a theory of tradition has not yet been developed that deals with these questions, especially in light of the needs of local churches and their theologies. The concept of tradition itself has been critiqued much in recent years, and some more positive valuations of its role in post-Enlightenment societies are beginning to appear.[11] But much work needs to be done here. Without such work, the dialogue envisioned for the building up of local theologies will be impeded in its progress.

Methods: Criteria for Christian Identity

The whole issue of the development of local theologies devolves finally upon one point: are the results faithful to the Gospel and consonant with church Tradition? And how is this fidelity and consonance to be ascertained?

Just as the development of local theologies makes us more sensitive to the multiplicity of roots in any theology, and the dialectical relationship that needs to obtain between them, so too the criteria for ascertaining Christian identity will share in that complexity.

The Tradition has always used a variety of different ways of establishing the Christian nature of the identity of a local church and its theology. We know from history that whenever the dialogue is complicated by cultural pluralism (as in the Christological controversies of the fourth and fifth centuries), difficulties increase exponentially. With that in mind, I want to make a proposal for consideration in this matter.

It seems to me that history has taught us that there is no single criterion that in itself can guarantee the continuity of a new response with the Gospel and the ensuing Christian Tradition. What we perhaps need, for our own safety, is a set of multiple criteria that, taken together, might come closer to achieving that desired end. For that reason I would like to suggest here five such criteria. The idea would be that for a theological development to pass but one, or even two or three of these would not be sufficient. All five would have to be taken into consideration. The five are as follows:

1. Cohesiveness of the Christian symbolic network. Close study of the Tradition indicates that there is a remarkable cohesion among the symbolic assertions that we as a Church have tried to make. This consistency, which involves the scriptural witness, major conciliar, and magisterial statements, and the mainstream of the theological endeavor, do not form an airtight and fully rigorous system, yet do provide certain key assertions that need to be taken into consideration if any symbolic statement is to be considered complete, and also some limits on the range that reflection may undertake. To get at these assertions and the expressive range involves a delicate hermeneutical operation, sensitive not only to the historical context and the language used, but also to the intent of the statements and how those intentions have been perceived in history. This is a complex area, and the details of it cannot be gone into here. But nonetheless I cannot imagine any assertion coming from a local church that can forego this kind of test for ascertaining Christian identity.

2. The worshiping context of the community. The worshiping community recognizes the presence of its Lord in a subtle blend of *pneuma* and *anamnesis*, of the Spirit present and the memory treasured of Jesus Christ. It is this blend that through the centuries has made the *lex orandi, lex credendi* such a powerful yet elusive criterion of Christian identity. It has often been evoked in the past (as in the Arian controversy by Athanasius and in the Pelagian controversy by Augustine), and continues to be a major source of theology for the Eastern Church today. One can test new theological formulations in the worshiping context by asking: do they find a genuine home there? How are they experienced in this context? Can they be "prayed"? There is a dictum from Medieval times about good theology leading to good preaching; that can still be a guideline for us today.

3. The praxis of the community. The scriptural admonition, "By their fruits shall you know them," has long been used to characterize and to anathematize certain practices. It still remains a powerful resource for ascertaining Christian identity. It works in a twofold fashion. On the one hand, the behavioral result of certain theological stances can be examined. Does an advocacy of direct use of violence by Christians extirpate the structural violence of a situation, or does it simply reverse roles, with the oppressed becoming the new oppressors? On the other hand, new formulations can be brought forward that do not seem to be accepted by the community. If this happens, one has to ask whether they are indeed part of Christian identity in any necessary sense. The reception of the injunctions of *Humanae vitae* by what seems to be a majority of Christians in the world Church might be considered an example of this.

4. Openness to the judgment of other churches. A local church that closes in upon itself and refuses dialogue and judgment from its sister communities has been considered traditionally as being in schism, outside the pale of the Church universal. This judgment, provided mutually by sister churches, is part of the voice of the Lord. This dialogue is to be held not only with contemporaneous communities, but also with the experience of the local churches of the past as well. In such mutuality, the possibility of genuine fidelity to the Lord is increased. At the same time, it should be remembered that the exercise of this criterion is incumbent not only on newer churches, but on the older ones as well. The example of what has been coming from the base communities of Latin America, and how their commitment to justice has been a word of judgment upon churches in North America, is an example of how this might work.

5. Prophetic challenge to other churches and to the world. New theology should provide new insight into Christian discipleship, and new formulations should challenge other local churches and the larger social context to a deeper fidelity to the Lord. If a community closes in upon itself, and really has nothing to say to other churches; if it settles into a comfortable non-dialectical relationship with its cultural context; if it can only speak comfort and not justice; then one has to wonder about the fullness of the Christian character of such a community.

To sum up, no single criterion in isolation from the others can be considered adequate. And there may be others that should be added to this list. In times past, the Tradition has tended to use the first and fourth of these criteria more than the others. But this combination seems to me to offer a better guarantee of Christian identity and fidelity in view of the welter of cultural and linguistic differences that mark a universal Church which takes its local churches seriously.

Conclusion

There are, of course, many other issues important to the formation of local theologies in local churches. There are other methods emerging that deserve our consideration as well. But these were chosen as issues that reach beyond any one local situation, and in one way or another affect much if not most of what is going on now in these areas. Even these could not be developed here in any detail.[12]

But one thing is certain: it will take communal effort and reflection on the part of more than a few individuals to achieve the desired goals in this area. It seems to me that professional theologians such as ourselves have a special responsibility and task in both thinking through the methodological issues and in reflecting upon our tradition in a way that will aid in this process. While the task of the professional theologian is changed in such a theological process, it is in no way diminished. And this needs to be kept in mind as we respond to the task of helping shape a theology in a local church which is true both to the local situation and to the Gospel of Jesus Christ.

NOTES

1. The Council of Chalcedon (canon 6) condemned absolute ordination: the Third and Fourth Lateran Councils restored it. For a discussion of this, see Edward Schillebeeckx, *Ministry: Leadership in the Community of Christ* (New York: Crossroad, 1981).

2. David Tracy's book *The Analogical Imagination* (New York: Crossroad, 1981) speaks of the three "publics" of theology: the academy, the church, and society, and urges theologians to strike a proper balance between them. It would seem at the same time fair to say that the theologian's own social context will heavily determine how he or she sees the proportion among these three publics.

3. The recent outcry (and puzzlement) over a theologian like Hans Küng's being declared as no longer being a "Catholic theologian" points up the ambiguity about who constitutes whom as a theologian. The discussions going on around the *"missio canonica"* proposed as part of the revised code of Canon Law can point to attempts to rearrange relationships in this matter.

4. Perhaps one of the best statements on this kind of theology is still Thomas Aquinas, *Summa Theologiae*, la, q. 1, aa. 2–10.

5. I develop this point in "Theologie in context: Naar een sociologie van de theologie," *Tijdschrift voor Theologie* 17 (1977), 3–23.

6. Local theologies, in their concern for the cultural context, stand open to the accusation of repeating some of the worst mistakes of the nineteenth century, such as a Ritschlian Kulturprotestantismus, if they allow that attention to culture to become undialectical, and see the local culture as some prelapsarian state inhabited by noble savages. Any good local theology will also raise questions about what is wrong with the culture, but only on the basis of an understanding of the culture that has developed in a patient and thorough fashion.

7. To cite a fairly recent example: Tracy, op. cit., 339–370, devotes a well-presented section on the Euro-American cultural situation. A local theologian would ask how a systematic theology can be developed (in Tracy's case, a Christology) when these considerations follow, rather than precede, the interpretation of Christian theological classics.

8. See the essays in Clifford Geertz *The Interpretation of Cultures* (New York: Basic Books, 1973).

9. Semiotics (the study of signs) is a burgeoning field. One introduction that can be helpful for its use in the study of culture is Edmund Leach, *Culture and Communication* (Cambridge, England: Cambridge University Press, 1976).

10. Schreiter, op. cit.

11. The Frankfurt School of Social Criticism (Habermas, Wellmer, et al.) developed an extended critique of the role of tradition (and especially Hans Georg Gadamer's interpretation of it in *Truth and Method*) in the early 1970s. They stressed the oppressive nature of tradition. A more recent positive approach to tradition can be found in Edward Shils, *Tradition* (Chicago: University of Chicago Press, 1981).

12. I develop these and other points in *Constructing Local Theologies* (Maryknoll, NY: Orbis Books, 1985).

READING 5
Introduction

When editing the three essays in this section, I passed Peter Schineller's "Ten Summary Statements" to a colleague interested in and well read in inculturation. She confessed she had never considered the issue from Schineller's angle: What are the conditions under which the Gospel can take root in the United States? For her, inculturation was a matter of bringing the Gospel to life in places where it had not taken root, not in places like the United States where churches mark every street corner. Lurking behind the ten statements posed and commented on by Schineller, she found the important question: To what extent is inculturation in the United States possible at all without some wrenching kind of physical or psychic dislocation? Though many Christians in North America would find this question distasteful, it becomes unavoidable in this essay.

Essential to Schineller's thesis are two matters set out at the start. The first is the circle of interpretation, a process of entering a situation to understand its various features and then bringing that situation under the scrutiny of the Gospel. The Gospel confirms the good and challenges the evil in the situation. Ways of challenging the evil are always there in the situation itself and can be teased out by careful noticing. This noticing carries a new awareness of the situation's possibilities back into the situation itself, and the process goes on. Another way of describing this pastoral circle is: see, judge, act. The seeing influences the judging, which in turn influences the acting, but the acting in turn brings a new way of seeing, which is then brought to the judging, and so forth. The matter is crucial, since a catechesis without an interpretation of the social situation is dead. Lacking such interpretation, catechesis speaks only to the past, not to the present or the future.

Schineller's second underlying issue is modernization. He is saying that the church cannot undertake inculturation suitably unless it deals with modernization, that is, "the profound qualitative and quantitative changes that have taken place in human society, changes affecting the political, economic, ecological and cultural spheres." Based on this insight, Schineller's work is a cousin to Herman Lombaerts' writings found in this *Sourcebook*. My own way of stating the matter is this: To have nothing to say to the political, economic, ecological, and cultural forces shaping our lives is to have nothing to say catechetically. A catechesis that avoids these matters is, to say the least, inept.

However, reflection on these matters is admittedly complex, and Schineller points to the reason why: the ambiguity of most social shifts. They merit neither outright applause nor condemnation but instead need to be evaluated for the ways they enhance or diminish the humanity of those affected by them. Schineller's claim that "modernization . . . wishes to rule and dominate all cultures" leads him to claim that dialog with this force is more important than any other church-initiated dialog. Instead of postures of optimism or pessimism, Schineller proposes scrutiny and analysis.

His essay moves on to offer a lens through which modernization might be evaluated in a Gospel mode: how modernization affects weak people and poor people in both the long range and the short range. Sections 7–10 of Schineller's essay have clear implications for catechesis at national, regional, diocesan, and local levels. Sadly, the matters he raises here are still those most easily overlooked in the chief form of catechesis—adult catechesis.

Now working in Nigeria directing Jesuit ministries, Peter Schineller explained to the editor in a 1995 letter the background of his essay ("one of my favorites; . . . much or most of it still stands up today"). Teaching at the Jesuit School of Theology in Chicago until its demise in 1981, he met many missionaries, who influenced his thinking. As he stated:

> I myself wanted to see a different church—either in Africa or Latin America. Eventually, in 1981, I went to Africa. But even before that, several influences struck me. One was Fr. Arrupe, and his letter and working paper on inculturation. Another was Bob Schreiter, and his work on inculturation, which I had in manuscript form. A third was the Jesuit priest from Brazil, Fr. Marcello Azevedo, who has also published in the Gregorian series. His particular focus at one point was on modernity, modernization. He studied this in New York, where I met him. We shared reflections, and I learned much from him.

Further reading

Schineller, Peter. *A Handbook on Inculturation.* New York: Paulist Press, 1990.

World Catechism or Inculturation? Concilium Series. Edited by Johann-Baptist Metz and Edward Schillebeeckx. Edinburgh: T. and T. Clark, 1989.

Ten Summary Statements on the Meaning, Challenge and Significance of Inculturation as Applied to the Church and Society of Jesus in the United States, in Light of the Global Processes of Modernization

PETER SCHINELLER, SJ

Introduction

My own expertise has been in systematic theology, especially Christology. Having taught this for about six years, I came to the insight that new creativity, input must come not from further study in systematic theology, but in the correlation or inculturation of theology and Christian values into the modern world. I have led a seminar on "Inculturation" on two occasions, and took the opportunity of a five-month sabbatical to begin to study and understand the processes of modernization that have occurred in the United States and are affecting the entire earth. My goal was to study how the Church must inculturate Gospel values into this modern world.

This paper flows from that sabbatical study. It is the beginning of a long-range project and thus suffers from all the inadequacies of an unfinished project. It is written under the outline of ten summary statements, moving from the more general methodological considerations of inculturation, through more specific descriptions of the process and results of modernization, to the difficult task of bringing a theological and Christological perspective to bear on this phenomenon of modernization. It concludes with more specific strategies and emphasizes the indispensable role of the laity in the process of inculturation with modernization.

Reprinted from *On Being a Church in a Modern Society*, edited by Theodore F. Zuern, SJ, Joseph A. Tetlow, SJ, and Peter Schineller, SJ (Rome: Gregorian University, 1983), 51–87.

Since many parts of the paper are highly compressed and compact, the notes refer to further exploration and grounding of some of the perspectives and positions given in the text.

Ten Summary Statements

1. The basic ingredients, methods, and attitudes of inculturation can be seen in the employment of the pastoral or hermeneutical circle.
2. The inculturation of Gospel values into the process of modernization is the most challenging and important place for inculturation to occur, more significant than Roman Catholic dialogue with other Christian Churches, with non-Christian religions, with traditional cultures, and with atheism.
3. A key strategic concept in evaluating modernization is "ambiguity" whereby both positive and negative elements of modernization are attended to. This allows genuine dialogue and inculturation, and not an overly one-sided, or one-directional prophetic denunciation.
4. Aspects of the modern world that are intertwined with modernization, and that call for critical Christian, theological response include the growing gap of rich and poor, world hunger, technological society, nuclear power and weapons, transnational corporations, ecology and the limits to growth, and the changing role of women in modernized society.
5. God is not neutral, but involved and on the side of the weak and the poor. Thus the theological response (God's word and viewpoint) to modernization, the viewpoint from which to evaluate it theologically, must be on how it affects the weak and the poor in both the long range and the short range.
6. The Roman Catholic Church (and the Society of Jesus) as an international body, can surface and speak for the concerns of all, especially the poor, in the evaluation of modernization.
7. Specific vices or forms of sin in a modernized society would include those of (1) failure to transcend one's limited perspective in both time and space, (2) passivity and complicity before complex systems, and (3) consumerism.
8. Specific virtues called for in light of inculturation with modernization would include (1) simplification of lifestyle, (2) enlarging one's sympathies toward global awareness and responsibility, and (3) wisdom as the integrating understanding that leads to responsible action.
9. To succeed in the task of inculturating Gospel values in modern society, the Church itself must be modernized in structure, style of operation, and language.

10. Only through the Christian laity can the Gospel be inculturated in the modern world.

1. The basic ingredients, method, and attitudes of inculturation can be seen in the employment of the pastoral or hermeneutical circle.

Inculturation is one of many concepts to describe the process by which Gospel and Christian values come to bear on a particular culture, context, or situation. Of the varied concepts to describe this process, each with its own nuances, words such as indigenization, localization, strategic theology, correlation, contextualization, the two most helpful, and of growing import, seem to be inculturation and contextualization.[1] The possible advantage of contextualization is that it points to the ongoing, never-ending nature of the project. So too the generic meaning of the word *context* allows the process to be applied to a variety of different cultures or contexts.

The process of inculturation or contextualization can be understood as putting into operation the hermeneutical or pastoral circle.[2] The pastoral agent, or minister, or theologian immersed or inserted into the situation listens, studies that situation, with its problems and possibilities, facilitates the self-understanding of those in the situation, engages the resources of social sciences, and then brings to bear the Christian upon that situation, culture, or context. The comfort and challenge of the Christian message leads to action that confirms the good and challenges the evil of the situation. Movement around the circle is in both directions; elements of the solution (*semina verbi*) are already or always found in the situation; the pastoral agent functions as facilitator or catalyst to those persons in the situation.

In this paper, in terms of the pastoral circle, I as pastoral agent, will begin to look at the situation or culture of modernity and the process of modernization, and begin the process of inculturating the Christian message in this situation of modernity. In so doing, I am echoing the Pastoral Constitution of Vatican Council II, the *Church in the Modern World*, in its method and in its goal that the Gospel come to bear upon the specifically modern world.

2. The inculturation of Gospel values into the process of modernization is the most challenging and important place for inculturation to occur, more significant than Roman Catholic dialogue with other Christian Churches, with non-Christian religions, with traditional cultures and with atheism.

The usual image of inculturation is in the context of the missionary activity in a distant village, telling the Good News to those who may never have heard of Christianity. But as Father Arrupe reminds us, it must be a more encompassing concept, and each Jesuit is called to be an "agent of inculturation," wherever he is engaged in mission.[3] My thesis is that in the present world situation, the dialogue with modernization must rate as most significant for the mission of the Church. To show how this dialogue can be viewed as a process of inculturation, I will present general definitions of (1) culture, (2) inculturation, and (3) modernization.

Culture has been defined in more than one hundred ways. For our purpose we might view it as "a set of symbols, stories (myths), and norms for conduct that orient a society or group cognitively, affectively, and behaviorally to the world in which it lives."[4] Culture points to how humans have reshaped the world, created a human environment. It becomes the horizon or context within which and under the influence of which we live, move, decide, act. *Inculturation*, as in Arrupe, is "the incarnation of Christian life and of the Christian message in a particular cultural context, in such a way that this experience not only finds expression through elements proper to the culture in question but becomes a principle that animates, directs, and unifies the culture transforming it and remaking it so as to bring about a new 'creation.'"[5]

In the attempt to show that *modernization* can and must be considered as a culture, and hence the object of the process of inculturation, I will present several descriptions of modernization. Cyril Black states that modernization "may be defined as the process by which historically evolved institutions are adapted to the rapidly changing functions that reflect the unprecedented increase in man's knowledge, permitting control over his environment, that accompanied the scientific revolution."[6] Peter Berger echoes this emphasis upon the institutionalized aspect holding that "modernization consists of the growth and diffusion of a set of institutions rooted in the transformation of the economy by means of technology."[7] Berger also calls it the universalization of heresy, meaning the need and ability of persons today in a modernized society to choose among options, the movement from fate to choice amid a pluralization of worldviews.[8] Marion Levy looks more to the technological center of modernization, suggesting that modernization be "directly and simply defined as the growing ratio between inanimate and animate sources of power."[9] James O'Connell repeats the thrust of Black, but emphasizes the mental attitude at the base of modernization, namely that of a creative rationality, or the development of an inquiring and inventive attitude of mind that lies behind the use of techniques and machines. Greater control over the environment (natural and social) is based upon the expansion of scientific and technological knowledge.[10]

Modernization thus points to the new world that is emerging, and describes the profound qualitative and quantitative changes that have taken place in human society, changes affecting the political, economic, ecological and cultural spheres.

Precisely because modernization is a reality that must be approached from a variety of disciplines, (such as political science, sociology, psychology, anthropology, philosophy, history, history of science) it is difficult to define. In any case, it is a reality that encompasses differences between east and west, between capitalism and socialism. Hence it cannot be equated with westernization, even if that is the form it appears under for the most part. And while modernization is in its most advanced forms in the so-called First World countries, the north rather than the south, it is a phenomenon that on the one hand effects all peoples and nations, and secondly, a phenomenon that seems to be an irreprehensible movement, something desirable by all peoples. Some thus speak of modernization as a systemic, global, progressive, and irreversible process.[11]

Modernization can thus be considered as a process or way of thinking and acting; it can also be considered in its effects, as modernity. To understand this aspect of modernization, namely modernity or the modern world, we can only at this point refer to several books that precisely attempt to delineate the modern world. These would include, *North-South*, edited by Willy Brandt; *World Without Borders*, by Lester Brown; *The Lean Years*, by Richard Barnet; *Only One Earth*, by Barbara Ward; *Limits to Growth*, edited by Donella Meadows; *An Inquiry into the Human Prospect*, by Robert Heilbroner. We will rely upon these and similar works in our unfolding of that culture that we have called modernization.[12]

Finally, and most important for this section, I would argue that the dialogue of Christianity with modernization—as a process and in its results—is a more significant dialogue than that with other religions, with traditional cultures, and with atheism. Modernization is not simply one culture among others, but one that wishes to rule and dominate all cultures. Traditional religious and political values are shaken when modernization enters. In contrast to religion (Christian and non-Christian) modernization is in no way a superstructure or ideology apart from human lives, but a force that more and more affects all persons, physically as well as spiritually. It is a more inclusive concept than secularization, which is a subset of modernization, pointing to its challenge to traditional Christian and non-Christian religions. And while inculturation of Christian values with traditional cultures remains important, there is the clear danger that these traditional cultures will be swept up and torn apart by the all pervading forces of modernization. Even the traditional contrast of socialist and capitalist ideologies is relativized by modernization, as is demonstrated by the fact that all the major countries, the United States, Russia, and China, regardless of their political and economic ideologies are united in their common process of modernization (as attested to in cooperation between transnational corporations, the international business and communications communities). Finally, the dialogue between theism and atheism becomes relativized as both believers and non-believers can and must join in the common human concern to assure that we do not destroy or ruin our earth, but hand it on to our children's children. The enemy of the Christian or theist is not so much the atheist, but the potential exploitive and evil forces and affects of modernization.

3. A key strategic concept in evaluating modernization is "ambiguity" whereby both positive and negative elements of modernization are attended to. This allows genuine dialogue and inculturation, and not an overly one-sided or one-directional prophetic denunciation.

Before setting forth some characteristics of the modernized world, I wish to set forth the category of ambiguity as a way to critically evaluate the culture of modernization. We will see that modernization is a truly ambiguous process, one bringing forth good and evil, benefits and harm to the human community. Unless it is seen as such, we are in danger of being captured and overwhelmed by it. The use of the word ambiguity is, I admit, not as strong as many might like; they would prefer a more wholesale condemnation of modernization or at least certain aspects of it. But my strategy is different. In light of the complexity of the modern world, I intend to alert Christians to critically examine modernization. While torture, for example, is always and everywhere wrong, the process of modernization is too complex for such general prophetic denunciation.

The term ambiguity is used extensively by Paul Tillich to signify that in all the processes of life "positive and negative elements are mixed in such a way that a definite separation of the negative from the positive is impossible."[13] The human condition as such has an inseparable mixture of true and false, good and evil, creative and destructive forces, both individual and social. In Tillich's system and in my reflections, the category of ambiguity is held forth to assure a self-critical attitude to what one sees as one's highest achievements, including religious, political, social, and economic achievements. As Tillich notes, "He who is not aware of the ambiguity of his perfection as a person and in his work is not yet mature; and a nation that is not aware of the ambiguity of its greatness also lacks maturity."[14]

Thus, for example, modernization brings increased mobility but also rootlessness; the machine eases the work load but also can make us into automatons; the higher standard of living of First-World peoples is often achieved at the expense and exploitation of Third-World peoples. In place of an overly optimistic or pessimistic interpretation of modernization, we prefer to analyze it under the category of ambiguity, that is, as leading to, and involving both positive and negative effects.

4. Aspects of the modern world that are intertwined with modernization, and that call for critical Christian, theological response include the growing gap of rich and poor, world hunger, technological society, nuclear power and weapons, transnational corporations, ecology and the limits to growth, and the changing role of women in modernized society.

This rather long section aims at beginning the process of analysis of the modern world under the category of ambiguity. It is the most incomplete section of the paper, and points to an ongoing agenda for Christian ministers and laity. We will highlight here some of the main characteristics of the modern age, all of which result from the process of modernization. To assist in the ongoing reflection on these realities, we will add bibliographical references in the notes.

Growing gap of rich/poor. The most glaring characteristic of the modern world is the growing, rather than lessening gap between rich and poor, north and south, powerful and powerless, privileged and underprivileged, elite and marginated, underdeveloped and overdeveloped, dominating and dependent, center and periphery. Countries, persons at the periphery are subservient to the interests of the center; everything of import is treated with reference to the interests, plans, and wishes of the center. What appears from the center as a state of equilibrium, is in reality a struggle to maintain the imbalances. This occurs both within a rich country, where the rich are rich at the expense of the poor; it also occurs between rich and poor countries, where the poorer nation feeds the overdevelopment of the rich.

Even an optimistic futurist such as Herman Kahn admits that this gap will not become smaller for decades. In his projections, he says that it will at best decrease only very slowly in the next few decades, and at worst will increase for forty years.[15] The gap is not only a statistical, factual gap in regard to income, quality of life, health, basic human needs, but also a psychological gap of rising expectations on the part of the poor, expectations and possibilities that are receding rather than beginning to be realized. In addition, it is argued that the rich are becoming richer precisely at the expense of the poor. The economies of the north can only sustain their increasing use of energy, raw materials, and labor by exploiting the poor nations and poor people.

Such a description immediately calls into question, or at least raises the category of ambiguity as applicable to the process of modernization in terms of the overall development of peoples. While some, namely the few rich, benefit from modernization and technological advances, the majority, the poor seem to be falling further behind.

Hunger. A further specification of ambiguity is seen in the case of world hunger. The UN World Food Conference states that on a conservative estimate, there are well over 460 million people (40 percent of them children) who are permanently hungry and whose capacity for living a normal life cannot be realized. The tragic irony or ambiguity lies precisely in the fact that in the time when we have the technology, tools, and means to feed the entire world, we are in fact losing the battle against world hunger, and more persons are going to bed hungry than ever before in human history, in terms of absolute numbers. When we can send men to the moon, and can arm the world with nuclear weapons supposedly to save and protect life, millions are dying of starvation.

The troubles of the rich nations, of unemployment, inflation, volcanoes, and so on, pale before the reality of world hunger, a major scandal of our so-called modern world. The reality and horror of world hunger calls into question the progress of modernization. In fact, it points squarely to the corruption, decadence, blind-sightedness of the technological, industrial, or post-industrial age if the power and promise of this age fails to alleviate this ongoing holocaust. Finally, technological progress of radio and television brings the faces of the starving into our homes. Yet we must ask if we are becoming less sensitive rather than more sensitive to their plight. It almost seems that the reverse of what might be expected is occurring, namely, a hardening, insulation, and isolation of the rich in our homes from the reality of poverty and hunger, both in the developed nations and especially in the poorer nations.[16]

Technology. The key to modernization, according to Ellul and others, is technology. Without entering into this debate, we obviously see it as one key factor. Ellul refers to the technological society, the technological system, and the technological environment, or milieu, in which we live and act.[17] Ellul, more than any, reminds us that equally as significant as the advances, and potential of technology for good is its danger and potential for evil. It is truly ambiguous, involving negative and positive potentialities. The influence and effect of technology is clearly two-faced, two-edged; with every sign of progress, there is an attendant danger. The automobile, radio, television have not been unmixed blessings for human welfare. These extensions of the human body (our brain, via the computer; eyes, via television; arms, via machines and weapons; feet, via cars and planes, etc.) truly result in a new milieu in which we live. The very definition of the human today must include reference to this human-created environment of technology, otherwise one is defining the human in abstraction.

Another characteristic of technology is efficiency, which becomes almost an end in itself. The multiplication of the possible rather than the necessary becomes the rule and end. When this occurs, technology begins to function not only as one factor in human life, but as a totalizing factor, that is, as autonomous, its own absolute, with a dynamism of its own, shaping and controlling rather than under the control of human persons and freedom. The universal applicability of technology makes it too, like modernization, a reality that encompasses the differences between east and west, socialism and capitalism. In this sense, it is a force more powerful in the long run than political ideologies, hence of obvious concern to Christian theology.

Through its use of inanimate sources of energy, technology is making us, ironically, more rather than less dependent upon nature. To maintain our growing technological way of life, we need increasing sources of energy—at this point nonrenewable. Problems of pollution result, as well as the already mentioned exploitation of the poorer nations to allow the rich to maintain their state of overdevelopment. The imbalance of rich and poor grows greater. In addition, when technology makes its way into the less modernized cultures, it often enters as an intruder and disrupter of the traditional culture, offering false gods and destroying traditional ways of living. It creates gaps in the poorer countries between the ruling elite and the common folk, it thrusts them into a world they are ill-prepared to enter, and equally unable to resist.

Television and mass media. In the United States there has been concern recently over the potential of television for religious broadcasting. Evangelical communities (followed by Roman Catholics) are utilizing the TV channel for their message. While this is significant, it is equally important to think of television itself functioning as a religion, a culture, or force that is shaping our way of thinking and acting. It is a key symbol and value carrier in our day. When children spend more time in front of the TV than in school, when the average household has its TV set on for 6.5 hours per day, there should be cause for concern, even in the light of tremendous benefits that TV can bring in the way of education, art, information.

The danger consists in thinking that the world of TV is reality. Rather than encounter the world or the neighbor we are victims of the cyclops or one-eyed monster for our interpretation of reality. Television, in light of its commercialism, as well as the very nature of the medium, is highly selective, presenting too often the Hollywood story, the successes more than the failures, the surface rather than the depth and connections. Above all, it tends to reduce reality to manageable and salable packets, to make reality thus fit into the consumerist structure of the medium. As a result, we can speak of a new alienation from reality brought about by this medium, a distancing of the human from the depths of nature and the interpersonal. The technical triumphs over the ecological. While we may be growing in factual information about reality, our wisdom and understanding are less.

Nuclear power and weaponry. The extreme case of technology in relation to modernization is the growing reliance upon nuclear weapons as the way to maintain peace. Nowhere is the ambiguity of modernization seen more clearly than in our use and misuse of nuclear energy. For the first time in human history, humankind has the capability to destroy all human life of planet Earth. Expenses for nuclear swords far outweigh expenses for ploughshares of education, food, health—to meet basic minimum human needs. More than one billion dollars is spent daily for military efforts. The United States has more than ten thousand nuclear warheads, each far more destructive than the bomb that destroyed Hiroshima. One Poseidon submarine carries sixteen missiles, 160 warheads each having three times the power of a Hiroshima weapon. Twenty million persons could be killed by this one submarine. The equivalent of four tons of explosive power in TNT hangs over the head of every human alive today.

The direction is toward increased spending, more powerful and sophisticated weapons, all of which result in inflation, result in the rich nations exploiting the poor nations for raw materials and for energy sources. Nuclear weapons point to the poverty of our way of thinking, living, and relating in the modern world, where the secure way to peace turns to the way of fear and threat. The true image of the world is of the loaded gun, armed, poised, aimed at one out of every four persons alive. We have learned to live with this absurdity, taking it for granted, as if normal. Our creativity and technology, our budgets are askew, unbalanced, and ultimately irrational and inhuman.[18]

Transnational corporations. A particularly complex phenomenon that again demonstrates the ambiguity of modernization is the multinational or transnational corporation. It can be defined as a company that produces and markets goods and services in more than one country, looks at the entire world as its area of operation, and acts accordingly. Transnational corporations (TNC) are possible only in the light of modern technology, such as communication systems, computers, and jet plane travel. They show the intertwining of economics, politics, and technology in such a way that they constitute a cultural, global reality new in human history. As a matter of fact, many TNC's are more powerful than most of the individual nations of the world, in terms of influence over human lives. But precisely as such, they bear within themselves all the ambiguities of modernization, and manifest great potential for both good and evil.

Positively, the TNC has been called the most powerful agent for the internationalization of human society.[19] It points to the global context of all decision making in the everyday world of business. No nation, indeed, no person, is an island unaffected by global business enterprises. The TNC can become a force for peace between nations by linking nations that might be enemies through economic, business, and communication ties. Such companies seek peace and stability in order that trade and commerce can flourish. They act as counterforce to a nationalism that seeks isolation from the international community. Products of such companies, goods, technical and health services, educational opportunities are made available for more people than ever before; capital is made available for local projects.

But in reality, it would seem that very little of the potential mentioned above is being realized. Viewed from the perspective of the poorer nations, the TNC is seen not merely as ambiguous, but as destructive and exploitative. Each of the above-mentioned points has a negative side to it, and all too often this outweighs the positive contribution. Thus while they remind us of the global village, in their actual operation they often result in loss of control at the local level of decisions affecting that level. Decisions made in New York affect the lives and welfare of workers in the Philippines; local people become the cogs in the wheels of big business. Truly free competition is often undercut by monopolies or trade agreements imposed by the haves over the have-nots. Rather than a true spirit of internationalism to replace a narrow nationalism, we have the interests of the rich exploiting the resources (labor, natural resources) that belong to the poor. Thus Nestlé Company, in place of meeting the real need for milk, ends up creating a false need for artificial powdered milk, and the last is worst than the first. While it may be true that TNC's can best operate in conditions of peace rather than war or hostility, they often serve to preserve the peace by causing, backing, allowing rightist governments to rule. An indication of this is the resistance of TNC's to the efforts of the United Nations at international trade agreements.[20]

A final and important example of the ambiguity of the TNC is seen in raising the question of who has control over the TNC. There are three possible control mechanisms, but each is subject to ambiguity. First, economic control from the market, the competition, the consumer; but this is often (due to the size of the TNC) not a free market, but monopolistic in reality. Second, control from internal management, from the conscience of the executives; but this is subject to forces of greed, to self-interest rather than the good of those one intends to serve. Third, governmental control on the local, national, and international level; but here again, due to their size and power, TNC's begin to dictate to small nations, and even exert political and economic power over the strongest and richest of nations. Thus, as with so much of modernization, as the potentiality for good increase, so does the potentiality for evil. Unless we are aware of this ambiguity, we are blind to the reality of the TNC.

Ecology and the limits to growth. Modernization, especially in its technological aspects, requires increased and increasing uses of energy. As scientists inform us, and as the oil crisis of 1973 made apparent, we are talking of limited sources of energy, and limited natural resources. The average person in the United States, at the forefront of modernization, uses fifty times the amount of energy as a citizen of India, and nine times that of a Mexican. With 6 percent of the world's population we use a third of the energy now expended by humankind. Two problems result. First, unless new and renewable sources of energy are discovered, eventually our lifestyle and the benefits of modernization must be changed. Second, if other nations seek to follow in the steps of the United States, the energy crisis will strike home all the more quickly. In other words, it is impossible to conceive of a world where even 40 percent of the population lives at the standard and high level of energy use that we in the United States have grown accustomed to.

Neither capitalism nor socialism fares much better in this impending crisis. Both are based upon modernized, expanding economics; neither has an economic theory that allows for the needs of future generations. It seems only a matter of time before nature becomes literally exhausted. Coal, oil, gas are finite in quality; nuclear energy is both expensive and far from guaranteed safe for large-scale usage. Thus again we face the ambiguity of modernization. It seems to be running a course that is a dead end. Unless we can convert and live within limits, we will leave to our children's children a desolate, exploited, rather than life- and energy-giving planet. To continue at present rates of energy usage, with consequent pollution and exhaustion of natural resources, is the supreme exemplification of irresponsibility to nature and to future generations.[21]

Changing role of women in modernized society. Technological advances in modern industrial and post-industrial society have made it possible for men and women to do the same kind of work. No longer is physical power and ability a criterion for employment in the technological society. As in the work world, so in the family, the home, there are signs of more shared responsibility by husband and wife in raising children. Greater opportunities are thus available for women in terms of education, careers, areas of employment. Yet discrimination remains, and it is felt more deeply by women in modernized society. Hence movements for women's liberation and the anxiety and anger of many women.

In this search for a new equality of male and female, there are tensions in both the home and marketplace, and finally too in the area of Church and theology. This is to be expected, if the Church is inserted, inculturated into particular cultures. Unless the forces of modernization are reversed, and the advances (and legitimate expectations) of women in the modern world are denied, the church will not be able to resolve the question of women in ministry and indeed in the priesthood by a simple appeal to tradition. That is to say, the issue of women in ministry and priesthood must be seen as a question of the inculturation of the Gospel in the modern, postindustrial age. If the Church tries to fight against this current and culture, it will do so only at great peril to the credibility of its Gospel or good news to women of today and tomorrow. It will cease to be a Church in the modern world, but a ghetto Church of the past, clinging to traditions and cultural values of the past.

5. God is not neutral, but involved and on the side of the weak and the poor. Thus the theological response (God's word and viewpoint) to modernization, the viewpoint from which to evaluate it theologically, must be on how it affects the weak and the poor in both the long range and the short range.

We have already begun to offer some evaluative comments on modernization, under the rubric of its ambiguities—its beneficial and destructive effects. Our goal now is to deepen and broaden this critical response by bringing to bear a theological perspective. Thus we are shifting from the pole of the pastoral or hermeneutical circle, toward the pole of the Christian message. We will proceed in three stages, first, indicating a theological (and Christological) perspective, second, an ecclesial perceptive, and finally, offer some more strategic suggestions on how the Church and Church community might dialogue, respond to, and criticize the culture of modernization.

A key task of theology is to discover or uncover God's word in and for a particular situation. When we say God, we do this as Christians, and therefore the God and Father of Jesus Christ, and not the God of the philosophers. The Christian God is the God of Incarnation who in that event weds heaven to earth, joins the highest to the lowest, the universal and particular, the divine and the human in a way that can never again be separated. In that powerful phrase used to describe the Ignatian spirit and spirituality, *"non coerceri maximo, contineri tamen a minimo, divinum est."* "To suffer no restriction from anything, however great, and yet to be contained in the smallest of things, that is divine."[22] If this joining of the universal perspective to the smallest of details is the divine outlook, then the Christian, the theologian who tries to find and express the word or viewpoint of God, must take this perspective on earthly realities. That is to say, we must try to bring the long run, widest, most universal perspective to bear upon, focus upon the particular present. Truth, hence theological truth, is precisely this joining of opposites, of the universal with the particular, the long range with the present focus. The divine input, therefore in the process of inculturation with modernization, is the perspective that safeguards the present and the particular, by keeping it always in relation to the values of the past, future, and the general.

But the Christian perspective goes even further in specifying the concrete and the particular. The God of the Old and New Testament is the God on the side of the weakest and the poor, rather than as one might expect, with the strong and the rich. God identifies his cause with the person in the greatest need, material and spiritual need. While he is the God of all, this is specified in favor of those on the margin of society. The Christian theological perspective must echo (and incarnate) this viewpoint, this non-neutrality of God in its judgments and its actions. Several principles or strategic moral priorities could be shown to flow from this interpretation of where God stands: (1) the needs of the poor take priority over the wants of the rich; (2) the freedom of the dominated takes priority over the liberty of the powerful; (3) the participation of marginalized groups takes priority over the preservation of an order that excludes them; (4) the production of survival goods must take priority over the production of enhancement and luxury goods.[23] These are strong statements, but they can be shown to follow from belief in the Christian God. Evaluation of modernization, therefore, must take principles such as these into account and ask whether the effects of modernization are helping or hurting the weakest of the weak, the marginated and poor. If any results or aspects of modernization go against this universal concern of God for the poor, then they are to be criticized as not being in tune with the call or word of God for today.[24]

As an example of how this theological perspective comes to bear on modernization, we might look briefly at the beginnings of an evaluation of a transnational corporation. In accord with the Ignatian motto, the incarnational principle, with God on the side of the poor, the test of the TNC would be whether its operations, effects are improving the quality of life of the poorest of the poor (in the South Bronx, the favelas of Rio, etc.) or are they contributing to their plight. By helping the South Bronx, I do not mean through charitable donations, foundations, but through structural and depth impact upon the socioeconomic conditions of the poor. Are they part of the problem, or of the solution to the poverty and unemployment in the South Bronx or Rio.

Thus the first part of the Ignatian motto, *"non coerceri maximo,"* would give encouragement to the TNC to be global and universal in its scope, to build bridges between nations and peoples, to share the good effects of science, medicine, technology with as wide a range of persons as possible. Here, the great potential of the TNC for good is underlined. The second part of the maxim, *"contineri tamen a minimo,"* would add the critical perspective. Globality is not the only goal, but is always in function of helping the individual, and that individual is specified in the Christian Gospel as the poor or weak. Are the resources, potential of the TNC brought to bear upon the needs of the poor—material and spiritual? Or is the TNC in effect enlarging the gap between rich and poor, in fact not only enlarging but systematizing and institutionalizing it? The conclusion of the maxim, *"divinum est,"* would say that only if the unique resources of the TNC, with its global power and perspective, are brought to focus upon quality of life of the lowest individual, only then can this institution, this aspect of modernization be in tune with God's word and will.

This incarnational and Ignatian perspective can also come to bear upon any group or institution that is global in intent or actuality, such as the United States government, the United Nations, the International Monetary Fund, the World Bank, the Roman Catholic Church, the Society of Jesus. Universality and globality are always to be at the service of the weak, not at their expense. It also applies on the more local level; a particular parish or local church must be evaluated by asking whether it touches, supports, gives life and hope to the poorest, neediest in its area of influence. Does the parish reach out to the marginated, elderly, imprisoned, sick, unemployed, etc.

In this section, without focusing upon Jesus Christ, we have in reality been setting forth the incarnational perspective. That is to say, Jesus Christ is precisely the focusing of the universal love of God upon the particular time, place, persons of Palestine two thousand years ago. Inculturation of Christic, Gospel values in today's complex world including its culture of modernization imitates that pattern of God in Jesus Christ. The universal, all-inclusive, long-range viewpoint of God (the divine) is focused and incarnated, brought to bear upon the particular human and earthly reality under discussion.

6. The Roman Catholic Church (and the Society of Jesus) as an international body, can surface and speak for the concerns of all, especially the poor in the evaluation or modernization.

From the more universal perspective of theology, and of Christology, we turn now to the more historical and concrete involvement of the Christian, and especially the Catholic Church in the effort to inculturate Gospel values in the process and culture of modernization. With all Christian Churches, the Catholic Church has the resource of God's word and Gospel. But the specific Roman Catholic input is precisely the universal or catholic perspective from which the Roman Church can stand and speak. Included in the membership of the RCC are persons of every nation, and in her communion the voices of the poor can be heard. The RCC can and must assure that their plight and viewpoint is heard by the more wealthy nations and peoples. Thus within her membership, the Church can begin to model the unity and pluralism, the mutual concern and sharing that must begin to take place in the world at large, so that the gap between rich and poor lessens rather than increases.

Second, the RCC should realize that her catholicity and universality are now a given, but a goal to be strived for. Rather than an established fact, the universality is precisely the task and point of Church mission. Inculturation in the modern world is the equivalent of the traditional understanding of Church mission in relation to non-Christian peoples. This means that the Church see herself not as a shelter or sanctuary, but as ec-centric, that is, centered not in herself, but in her mission in and for the modern world.[25] Rather than an ecclesiocentric attitude, she must profess and live as a serving Church in and for the world. In light of its universality, the Church therefore, should stand as a sign of God's universal and all-inclusive love, reaching from the strong to touch especially the poor and the weak. She should be a sign of community in a world all too often impersonal and technological. In this way, the Church will echo and represent to the world the theological and incarnational viewpoint we outlined in the previous thesis.

As a subset of the RCC, we mention briefly the input of the Society of Jesus in this enterprise. We have a tradition of theological expertise, intellectual excellence, and a universal scope and mission. Recent documents on faith and justice put our mission and ministry on the side of the poor and oppressed. Thus a special responsibility and opportunity lies upon the Society in the task of inculturating Gospel values in the complex, modern world.

7. Specific vices or forms of sin in a modernized society would include those of (1) failure to transcend one's limited perspective in both time and space, (2) passivity and complicity before complex systems, and (3) consumerism.

We now move toward more specific responses of the Christian community to the process of modernization. We proceed under two areas, virtues and vices, trying to retrieve the strong Roman Catholic Tradition on these, and make them pertinent to our problematic. By vices I refer to attitude, ways of thinking and living that are prevalent in modernized society but which are ultimately destructive and unsustainable in the light of a vision of humanity as God's people. While these vices have been present throughout human history, they receive special form today, arising from and feeding into the destructive aspects or modernization. While the vices most readily apply to individuals, they are also characteristic of social systems and social groupings, hence participating in the nature of social sin.

1. The most encompassing fault or sin is the inability of the individual (and the society) to transcend itself and its narrow interests. This echoes the powerful image of sin as the person or heart *"incurvatus in se."* This inability to move out in sympathy and love is concretized in two directions, both space and time. In regard to *space*, we view our family, our community, our nation as the center and are unable to see or judge from the perspective of the foreigner or outsider: yet our actions affect and often destructively affect the lives of others. Thus the First World lives in ignorance of the plight of the Third World. We fail to act out of the needed global consciousness. In terms of *time* we become so intent upon the present with its needs, wants, opportunities, that we are unable to conserve the resources, good things of the earth for future generations. We are short sighted and self-centered in our decision-making processes as well as in their consequent lifestyle and live with unbased and phantom hopes for the welfare of future generations. This inability to transcend our limited vision of time and space corresponds and correlates with our all too narrow view of God. He becomes *our* God rather than the God of all times and all places, and the God especially of the weak and the poor as is revealed in the Scriptures. Our narrow image of God mutually interacts with our narrow perception of the world.

2. Related to the previous vice is the failure to see the consequences and implications of our modernized lifestyle for the entire world. Admittedly this is ever more difficult in the light of growing complexity by which society is organized. Yet we can speak of the sin of knowing or lazy ignorance, which prefers selfishly to avoid the effort to inform oneself and rather live from an uncritical and unconscientizied viewpoint?[26] This results in a passivity before the forces and powers of modernization, or an unwillingness to accept responsibility for one's actions under the excuse of ignorance because of the complexity of the issues. As a result, we let others direct and run one's world. This attitude of neutrality really reinforces the status quo and in fact gives more power to the

ruling and controlling powers of government and business. One last consequence of this attitude of passivity is that it increases the ease with which power and violence are seen as the way to solve differences between peoples. We hand over personal responsibility to impersonal and technological forces—military solutions take a priority over solutions based on social justice.

3. A final area of concern is captured under the concepts consumerism, concupiscence, and curiosity.[27] I take consumerism to be the modern equivalent to what Augustine called *vane* curiosity, an insatiable fascination or itch for spectacles, that parades as a desire for knowledge. This desire for sensate experience, and for material things can become the whole, rather than an integrated part of life. Consumerism also corresponds to concupiscence as defined by Tillich or Gilkey for example. They take it to be the desire to draw the whole of the world into oneself, the desire to reach unlimited abundance.[28] It refers to physical hunger as well as sex, to knowledge as well as power, to material wealth as well as spiritual values. This greed is never satisfied, but is the drive to possess and devour more and more objects.

Consumerism stands for the attitude of aggressive grasping for more and more, the measuring of success and happiness through one's possessions. The consumption and accumulation of good and services becomes the central purpose of life, a meaning and end, rather than a means. Luxuries become necessities, while much of the world goes without basic needs. Every good becomes a fashion; the latest is the best, the pacesetter becomes the ideal; we live in the throwaway society, blind to the exploiting of the earth and its limited resources. This attitude of consumerism is fostered through the advertising media, which fuels the imagination toward curiosity and concupiscence. The capitalism economy runs on this psychology of moreness, where the acquisitive impulse is recklessly indulged.

8. Specific virtues called for in light of inculturation with modernization would include (1) simplification of lifestyle, (2) enlarging one's sympathies toward global awareness and responsibility, and (3) wisdom as the integrating understanding that leads to responsible action.

Virtues in essence are the power and presence of God operative in and through human persons, concretizing the call of God to this age. Thus in setting forth these virtues, we are specifying the word of God for this age, seeking those attitudes that are needed not only for the well being of society, but even for the survival of humankind.

1. The author, Saul Bellow, in accepting the Nobel prize for literature, viewed the present age as one of confusion and obscurity, with the human spirit struggling for survival. There is a need to lighten ourselves, to dump encumbrances, to reconsider, and finally to simplify. In light of the prevailing consumerist mentality, conversion to a style of simplicity, austerity, and frugality becomes a necessity if humanity is to hand on the gifts of earth to future generations. This involves a refocusing upon what is important and essential, rather than what is accidental and superfluous. Interpersonal values take precedence over material, impersonal values, character over possessions. Human life must be celebrated, and not the externalities of a technological age. We must cut through the various screens that cut us off from reality of persons, nature; we cannot afford to lose our spirit in the intermediary objects or things that separate us from a fresh relationship to our deepest self as well as to the world, especially the world of persons. Involved in this conversion to simplicity and a modest lifestyle is an abhorrence for violence and for a mechanized solution to the problems of human existence. The appeal to persuasion and personal freedom takes priority over the appeal to solutions through physical power.

2. In contrast to an attitude of self-centeredness is the virtue or power of self-transcendence, the ability to transcend one's narrow interests in the dimensions of both space and time. In regard to time, this involves a sense of stewardship for the earth and its resources, in contrast with an attitude of exploitation at the expense of future generations.[29] The finite earth can sustain our needs but not our greed. Based upon a theology of creation, the world is viewed as gift to be shared by all; care for persons is seen as inseparable from care or stewardship toward the earth. In regard to space we must grow in the capacity to feel the pain and the joy of those who live at a great distance. We must see that their concerns are ours, that our standard and way of life affects everyone on this earth. Without wiping out our local allegiances, we must enlarge them to include concern for all, especially the weak. Global responsibility must grow with global awareness, which modernization makes not only possible but necessary.

This broadened range of sympathy, this wider loyalty is at its deepest reality the grace and love of God in us, calling and enabling us toward self-transcendence. It involves a dying to oneself and one's narrow interests, and living in light of the global community.

This is only possible if one enlarges one's view of God. God cannot be a household or family God, not the God of the clan or nation, but the God of all people, especially of the weak and marginated. God is the God of male and female, rich and poor—and if we are to hear his voice we must listen to the voice and call of the poor. Otherwise we are believing in a false God, living in idolatry of gods made in our own narrow image. The struggle against atheism might be considered not so much a struggle against belief in no God, but belief in narrow and inadequate gods.

3. Modernization results in increased specialization, differentiation, and hence in alienation, fragmentation of persons from each other, from nature. It is more and more difficult to see the whole, the unity of the parts in this increasingly complexified society. There is therefore crying need for the virtue of wisdom, which I take to be the ability to integrate and see the relations and connections between finite realities, as well as see them in relation to transcendent value and reality. In contrast to the specialist, one-track mind, the wise person has an integrating imagination that is not satisfied with partial explanations, with surface understandings. With a probing and questioning intelligence, the wise person constantly asks *why*, until the partial explanations fit together into a coherent whole. Wisdom therefore, is the ability to see events and realities in their interconnectedness, the ability to trace to root causes and adequate rationales.

This is needed in particular spheres of life, such as law, medicine, polities, economics, theology, but is needed above all in the relationship between disciplines. The coherent vision, the unifying understanding is demanded in an age of increased differentiation. More focus upon integration of what we already know, rather than increased specialization may become essential if we are to maintain human community.

The wise person lives the truth of John Donne, "No man is an island unto himself." There is a structural link between the cup of coffee I drink in the United States and the condition of the peasant worker in Brazil. Automobile travel, and even more so, jet travel must be seen as part of our assault upon the limited, finite energy resources of earth. But wisdom is not only an integrated understanding: it must move toward action based upon a priority of values, the understanding of finite values in relation to infinite good and value. From an integrated understanding of the situation of modernity should come conviction, determination, and persuasiveness—effective strategies to build the human and eliminate the inhuman and dehumanizing.

9. To succeed in the task of inculturating Gospel values in modern society, the Church itself must be modernized in structure, style of operation, and language.

Most attention thus far has been on how the Church must understand and relate to the modern world. But a further step must be taken, namely, the modernization of the Church herself. If the Church is not to be a ghetto church, or reactionary, she must be not only in dialogue with, but in tune with the positive aspects of modernization. In a world that values democracy, the church cannot be authoritarian or strictly monarchical; some form of participation, shared leadership is demanded. In a pluralistic religious culture, or a secular culture where one values individual freedom highly, church authority must be a moral authority and never simply external. In a culture marked by a sense of relativity and historical consciousness, the church should recognize the historicity of its own institutions, and work at adapting them to the structure of the modern world. In an empirical-minded world, distrustful of abstractions, the church should translate its doctrines and beliefs and preaching into programs of action. In a culture where hope in the future becomes a universal expectation, the church should collaborate in the effort of building a better society. In a culture in which values of justice and equality are prized, the church should look carefully at its criteria for leadership and ordination.[30]

Most importantly, in a rapidly changing world, the church must be open to new meanings, implications, and formulations of its basic doctrines in faith and morals. Such a church must be an open and experimenting church, creative and forward looking. This *"ecclesia semper reformanda"* will prove itself credible not by simply repeating the traditions of the past, but by contributing to the human enterprise in the present with the aid of its rich Tradition. The entire church might well envision itself as a community of disciples, acknowledging that the truth is greater than any one member can fathom, and indeed greater than the entirety of the church. The way ahead to this ever greater truth is the way of shared, mutual dialogue among all members of the Christian community, and the way of dialogue with the culture in which the Church exists.[31]

If we can speak of three revolutions in human history, namely the agricultural, the scientific and industrial, and finally the technotronic, then it is in dialogue with this latter age that the Church must form its message today.[32] The point of insertion for Gospel values can no longer be based upon a view of the human as living on farms or in villages, but must take into account urbanization and suburbanization. The dreams, hopes, and fears of modernized, technologized humanity become the point of contact with the Gospel message of life. In this urbanized society, metaphors from nature have less impact and effectiveness. While we live in a service-oriented society in terms of employment percentages, we do not have familiarity with shepherds and farmers. The concrete forms of the city, its skyscrapers and transit systems, its electric network of communication must be seen as providing imagery/metaphor for the word of God to come alive today. In cities where the physical building of the church is no longer the outstanding center, the visible point of unity for the culture as it once was for the village, the very function of religions shifts. Government, business, university personnel, doctors and lawyers are turned to for advice rather than the clergy. The priest is no longer the expert in this complex society. Religion in the technotronic age takes on a less direct and more mediated function in the fabric of society. Its message and Gospel must be mediated through other institutions such as government, school, and business. This, as we will see, can best, indeed only, be done through the laity.

10. Only through the Christian laity can the Gospel be inculturated in the modern world.

A comparison of modern and pre-modern cultures would show that the Church had a much greater influence upon the currents of culture and society in the pre-modern period. The clergy, the bishop, for example exercised much authority and power over people's lives and destinies. The process of modernization, especially under the aspect or secularization, means precisely the loss of this Church power, with the corresponding increase of secular powers over lives. The world turns more by banks, governments, corporations, than by the Church.

In other words, the non-cleric, the laity have more influence over lives than in the age where the Church was at the center. In light of this shift, in light of the complexity of the modernized society, in light of the expertise needed simply to begin to understand this culture, the balance of responsibility must shift toward the Christian laity in this process of inculturating Gospel values in society. Laity are already inserted, involved in positions of power and thus can and must bring Christian values to bear on seemingly secular decisions, but decisions which affect the lives of many. A basic principle of inculturation is at stake here, namely that the process involves competence, knowledge of the situation, dialogue with those in place—and not a word coming from outside, over against the culture that has not first listened and tried to understand that culture.

This shift toward a laity-centered Church in the modern world seems to be one of the major insights of Vatican II, in its document on the *Church in the Modern World,* and its *Decree on the Apostolate of the Laity.* So too, many of the other decrees on education, communication, missionary activity can be implemented only through the laity. Thus the decree on the laity gives a quite accurate description of inculturation when it states that "they (the laity) exercise a genuine apostolate by their activity on behalf of bringing the Gospel and holiness to men, and on behalf of penetrating and perfecting the temporal sphere of things through the spirit of the Gospel." (no. 2) In fact, many have argued that the chief failure of renewal since Vatican II has precisely been the failure to incorporate, empower the laity in this challenge of inculturation. As the Chicago Declaration maintains, there has been a new clericalism, of priest and deacon, rather than a calling forth of the laity as laity, an enlisting of the laity in bringing Christian values to bear on politics, economics, government, business, and communications. for example.[33]

In light or this needed shift, the role of the clergy, religious minister shifts too, toward one of being a catalyst, empower of the laity, calling them together for their mission in the modern world–rather than substituting clerically for what they can best, and must do. The example of the transnational corporation illustrates this point. Priests, bishops, theologians have little or no direct experience with the TNC—how they operate, what options are possible, what results are achieved. But if the Gospel values are to touch the TNC, this can only be done by one knowledgeable and in place, hence the Christian laity. Just as the laity have little expertise in the intricacies or canon and Church law, so the clergy and theologian are unfamiliar with the rules and dynamism of the TNC. As we sent forth missionaries to foreign lands, so the Church should equivalently commission the laity to their task in the market place. The laity in business and government should feel that the entire Church is empowering, entrusting them to their vocation in the seemingly secular world. Obviously there is need here for knowledge of Christian values, and the Church should provide this through adult education programs, and through providing the opportunity for basic Christian communities within or at times apart from the parish structures. At stake is the realization and challenge that every Christian is called upon to be on agent of inculturation in family, home, business and community. Every Christian, according to Vatican II, shares in the priestly, prophetic and kingly (or servant) role of Jesus Christ (*Decree on the Laity*, no. 10). If this process of incorporating the laity as the prime movers in the task of inculturation in the modern world does not occur, the Church will only become more and more an irrelevant, ghetto Church, speaking a Word that will not be listened to, a Word that does not address the culture of modernity. The gap between Gospel and life, church and world, will grow ever wider.

With this, we return to the overall theme of inculturation, and the key of who does theology. The theology of inculturation of Gospel values in the modernized world is too complex and important to be left to theologians. It must become the task of those involved more directly in the working, the creativity of the modern world. If we believe with Rahner, that grace is hidden in the depth of all reality, or with Pope Paul VI that the *semina Verbi* are generously given, then theology must turn more and more to the laity to discover, uncover the truth and call of God

in the complexity of the modern world. This turn to the laity is obviously no magic solution, but rather points to the difficult task ahead, a task
which involves a conversion to a new vision of Church, a new role of the
minister as catalyst or facilitator in calling forth the talents and gifts of
the laity for the process of inculturation in the modern world.

Bibliography

Apter, David E. *The Politics of Modernization.* Chicago: University of
    Chicago Press, 1967.
Azevedo, Marcello de Carvalho. "Humanity Today: Its Formative Process
    and Fundamental Traits," in *Women Religious at the Service of a
    New Humanity,* UISG Bulletin, Number 49, 1979.
Barnet, Richard, and Ronald Müller. *Global Reach.* New York: Simon and
    Schuster, 1974.
Barnet, Richard. *The Lean Years.* New York: Simon and Schuster, 1980.
Barta, Russell, ed. *Challenge to the Laity.* Notre Dame, IN: Our Sunday
    Visitor, 1980.
Bennett, John. *The Radical Imperative.* Philadelphia: Westminster Press,
    1975.
Berger, Peter. *Facing up to Modernity.* New York: Basic Books, 1977.
———. *The Homeless Mind.* New York: Vintage Books, 1974.
———. *The Heretical Imperative.* New York: Doubleday, 1979.
Black, Cyril, ed. *Comparative Modernization.* New York: Free Press,
    1976.
———. *The Dynamics of Modernization.* New York: Harper, 1966.
Brandt, Willy, ed. *North-South.* Cambridge, MA: MIT Press, 1980.
Brown, Lester. *World Without Borders.* New York: Vintage Books, 1973.
Brzezinski, Zbigniew. *Between Two Ages.* New York: Viking Press, 1970.
Camilleri, Joseph. *Civilization in Crisis.* Cambridge, England: Cam-
    bridge University Press, 1976.
Commoner, Barry. *The Poverty of Power.* New York: Knopf, 1976.
Dulles, Avery. "The Church as a Community of Disciples," to be pub-
    lished in *Catholic Mind.*
Ellul, Jacques. *The Technological Society.* New York: Vintage Books,
    1964.
———. *The Technological System.* New York: Continuum, 1980.
Falk, Richard. *A Global Approach to National Policy.* Cambridge, MA:
    Harvard University Press, 1975.
———. *A Study of Future Worlds.* New York: Free Press, 1975.
Ferkiss, Victor. *The Future of Technological Civilization.* New York:
    Braziller, 1974.

————. *Technological Man.* New York: New American Library, 1969.

Gibbs, Mark. *Christians with Secular Power.* Philadelphia: Fortress, 1981.

————. *God's Frozen People.* London: Collins Press, 1964.

————. *God's Lively People.* Philadelphia: Westminster, 1971.

Gilkey, Langdon. *Naming the Whirlwind.* Indianapolis: Bobbs-Merrill, 1969.

————. *Reaping the Whirlwind.* New York: Seabury, 1976.

Global 2000 Report to the President. vol. 1. Washington, DC: U.S. Government Printing Office, 1980.

Greeley, Andrew. "Sociology and Theology: Some Methodological Questions," *Proceedings of the Catholic Theological Society of America,* Vol. 32 (1977): 31–54.

Haight, Roger. "The Established Church as Mission." *The Jurist,* 1980.

Heilbroner, Robert. *An Inquiry into the Human Prospect.* New York: W. W. Norton, 1974.

Holland, Joe, and Peter Henriot. *Social Analysis: Linking Faith and Justice.* Center for Concern publication, Washington, D.C., October 1980.

Hollenbach, David. *Claims in Conflict.* New York: Paulist Press, 1979.

Idris-Soven, Ahamed et al. *The World as a Company Town.* The Hague: Mouton Press, 1978.

Jegen, Mary Evelyn, ed. *The Earth Is the Lord's.* New York: Paulist Press, 1978.

————. *Growth with Equity.* New York: Paulist Press, 1979.

Kahn, Herman. "The Economic Present and Future," in *The Futurist* (June 1979): 202–222.

Laszlo, Ervin et al. *Goals for Mankind.* New York: Dutton, 1977.

————. *The Inner Limits of Mankind.* London: Pergamon, 1978.

Levy, Marion. *Modernization: Latecomers and Survivors.* New York: Basic Books, 1972.

Luzbetak, Louis. *The Church and Cultures.* California: William Carey Library (reprint), 1976.

Martin, David. *A General Theory of Secularization.* New York: Harper, 1978.

McGinnis, James B. *Bread and Justice.* New York: Paulist, 1980.

Meadows, Donella et al. *The Limits to Growth.* New York: Universe Books, 1976.

Miles, Rufus E. *Awakening from the American Dream.* New York: Universe Books, 1976.

————. "Energy Obesity," *The Futurist* (December 1980): 34–44.

Poggie, John, and Robert Lynch, eds. *Rethinking Modernization.* Westport, CT: Greenwood Press, 1974.

Schillebeeckx, Edward. "The Christian Community and its Office-Bearers," in *Concilium*, 133, *The Right of the Community to a Priest*. New York: Seabury, 1980.

Schineller, Peter. "A Method for Christian Ministry," *Emmanuel* vol. 87, no. 3 (March 1981): 137–144.

Schreiter, Robert. *Constructing Local Theolgies*. Unpublished manuscript, Chicago, 1977.

————. "Issues Facing Contextual Theologies Today," *Verbum SVD* 21 (1980): 267–278.

Schumacher, E. F. *Small Is Beautiful*. New York: Harper, 1973.

Segundo, Juan Luis. *The Hidden Motives of Pastoral Action*. New York: Orbis, 1978.

————. *The Liberation of Theology*. New York: Orbis, 1976.

Shinn, Roger, and Paul Abrecht, eds. *Faith and Science in an Unjust World*. 2 vols. Philadelphia: Fortress, 1980.

Tillich, Paul. *Systematic Theology*. 3 vols. Chicago: University of Chicago Press, 1963.

Vernon, Raymond. *Sovereignty at Bay*. New York: Basic Books, 1971.

————. *Storm over the Multinationals*. Cambridge, MA: Harvard University Press, 1977.

Ward, Barbara. *Only One Earth*. New York: Norton, 1972.

————. *Progress for a Small Planet*. New York: Norton, 1979.

Whitehead, James, and Evelyn Whitehead. *Method in Ministry*. New York: Seabury, 1980.

Woodward, Irene, ed. *The Catholic Church: The United States Experience*. New York: Paulist Press, 1979.

NOTES

1. The literature on inculturation is growing rapidly. Most important for me has been Robert Schreiter, *Constructing Local Theologies*, an unpublished manuscript. He favors the language of contextualization over inculturation. Tillich introduces the word correlation into mainstream systematic theology in his *Systematic Theology*, I, 59–66. John Bennett speaks of strategic theology in his *The Radical Imperative*. Luzbetak's *The Church and Cultures* remains a rich resource. Also from Schreiter, see "Issues Facing Contextual Theologies Today," *Verbum SVD* 21 (1980): 267–278.

2. For my own fuller explanation of the hermeneutical, or pastoral, circle, see "A Method for Christian Ministry, in *Emmanuel*, vol. 87, no. 3 (March 1981): 137–144. Additional writings on method employing some form of circle would include *Method in Ministry*, by James Whitehead, and Evelyn Whitehead; *Social Analysis: Linking Faith and Justice*, by Joe Holland, and Peter Henriot; *The Liberation of Theology* and *The Hidden Motives of Pastoral Action*, by J. L. Segundo.

3. Arrupe, *Studies in the International Apostolate of Jesuits*, 8–9.

4. Don Browning, *The Moral Context of Pastoral Care*, 73. Luzbetak, Schreiter, and Roest Crollius also discuss the different understanding of culture.

5. Arrupe, *Studies in the International Apostolate of Jesuits*, 2.

6. Cyril Black, *The Dynamics of Modernization*, 7. This book, and the book Black edited, *Comparative Modernization*, are two of the most helpful on the topic of modernization.

7. Peter Berger, *The Homeless Mind*, 9. Berger, a sociologist, has several works of interest on secularization, modernization. See also his *Facing up to Modernity* and *The Heretical Imperative*.

8. See *The Heretical Imperative*, where Berger's sociology of religion most closely intersects with modernization.

9. Marion Levy, *Modernization: Latecomers and Survivors*, 3. While very brief, this book is very powerful in its message on the upsetting, disrupting aspects of modernization.

10. James O'Connell, *Comparative Modernization*, 13–24.

11. Further reading on modernization would include Apter, *The Politics of Modernization*, from a political scientist perspective; Poggie and Lynch, *Rethinking Modernization*, especially the concluding summary comments and evaluation. See also Greeley, "Sociology and Theology: Some Methodological Questions," in Proceedings of the Catholic Theological Society of America, vol. 32 (1977): 31–54. There is also a whole area of literature on secularization, which obviously intersects with modernization. In general, I prefer the term or concept modernization over secularization, since it is more neutral or positive, and since it is approached from a variety of disciplines, rather than the more sociological perspective on secularization. One central book on secularization would be David Martin's *A General Theory of Secularization*.

12. See also *The Global 2000 Report to the President*, vol. 1 (1980); Barry Commoner, *The Closing Circle*; Jeremy Rifkin, *Entropy*; Richard Falk, *A Global Approach to National Policy*, and *A Study of Future Worlds*; Richard Camilleri, *Civilization in Crisis*; and Barry Commoner, *The Poverty of Power*.

13. Tillich, *Systematic Theology*, III, 32. The entire third volume of the Systematics develops different levels and aspects of ambiguity in human lives and institutions.

14. *Time* (17 May 1963): 69, from a lecture by Tillich on "The Ambiguity of Perfection."

15. In addition to his many books and reports projecting into the future, see Kahn's summary report in *The Futurist*, June 1979, "The Economic Present and Future," 202–222, which includes bibliographic references. He is a decided optimist on the future. Brandt's report, *North-South*, presents a different picture, since it includes much more of the South, Third-World perspective.

16. The best way into the hunger crisis is through the work and publications of organizations such as Bread for the World and Oxfam. These, for example, would combine up-to-date statistics on hunger, as well as projects and strategies to combat hunger in the light of research and study into its causes, and so on.

17. The central figure here is Jacques Ellul from his early writing, *The Technological Society*, to his recent *The Technological System*. Both are pessimistic, but he promises another book that will point the way forward. See also the writings of V. Ferkiss, the World Council of Churches Conference and reports, *Faith and Science in an Unjust World*, 2 vols. For an interesting theological response

to technology and even to the more general problems of modernity, see L. Gilkey, *Reaping the Whirlwind.*

18. As with world hunger, often the best way into the question of nuclear power and weaponry is through one of the many organizations focusing on these issues, such as Fellowship of Reconciliation, World Without War, Pax Christi U.S.A., Clergy and Laity Concerned, Institute for Policy Studies, Sojourners.

19. "Multinational Corporations, Hope for the Poorest Nations," Freeman and Persen, in *The Futurist,* December 1980.

20. For a discussion of the ambiguity of the TNC, see Falk, *A Study of Future Worlds,* 390ff. There is a growing amount of literature on the TNC. See Idris-Soven, *The World as a Company Town;* Richard Barnet, *The Global Reach;* Raymond Vernon, *Sovereignty at Bay* and *Storm Over the Multinationals.* Chapters in the books by McGinnis, *Bread and Justice;* and Jegen and Wilber, *Growth with Equity,* also treat the TNC. Here again, information, bibliography, newsletters from various organizations studying the TNC's are most helpful, for example, Center for Global Perspectives, Interfaith Center for Corporate Responsibility, Institute for World Order.

21. There is a growing amount of literature on this subject too. A recent and comprehensive work is that of Richard Barnet, *The Lean Years.* A more popular account is that of Rifkin, *Entropy.*

22. For further explanation of this maxim, see Hugo Rahner, *Ignatius the Theologian,* 23ff. Also his earlier essay in *Stimmen der Zeit,* 1947 on this maxim.

23. For this I am indebted to David Hollenbach, *Claims in Conflict,* 54.

24. This, I believe, adds an interesting, creative perspective to the Jesuit mission or task to combat atheism. What is often at stake is a false, inadequate notion of God, which Christians themselves all too easily fall prey to.

25. For these views of ecclesiology—of Church as mission—I am indebted to Segundo, and especially to Roger Haight, for his essay "The Established Church as Mission: The Relation of the Church to the Modern World," in the *Jurist* (1980).

26. On this aspect of sin, and on the more general area of social sin and sinful social structures, see Kerans, *Sinful Social Structures.* Much more research has to be given to this topic, as explored in *Soundings,* from the Center of Concern, several years ago. An example of the retrieval of the traditional virtues in the light of modernization is found briefly in the epilogue to Schumacher, *Small Is Beautiful.*

27. Sölle, a theologian, treats consumerism in several essays. So too, Arrupe in an address in Montreal, 1977, where he speaks against consumerism and for simplicity of lifestyle. See also Rufus E. Miles, "Energy Obesity—The Deadly Disease of a High-Consumption Society," in *The Futurist,* December 1980, as well as his book *Awakening from the American Dream: The Social and Political Limits to Growth.*

28. Tillich, *Systematic Theology* II, 52. Gilkey echoes Tillich in his *Naming the Whirlwind,* and *Reaping the Whirlwind.*

29. On stewardship, see Jegen, *The Earth Is the Lord's: Essays on Stewardship.* Also, Falk, *A Study of Future Worlds* lists values, attitudes needed for survival. So too, Laszlo's *Goals for Mankind* and *The Inner Limits of Mankind* indicate the personal values or virtues called for today.

30. I rely heavily upon Haight, op. cit., for this section.

31. Dulles has an essay to be published in *Catholic Mind* on "The Church as a Community of Disciples," pointing to the continual search for truth by the

entire church—hierarchy and laity, and therefore dialogue as key to this search. See also the challenging essay of Schillebeeckx, "The Christian Community and its Office-Bearers," in *Concilium* 133. The last section of this essay points to the need of the Church to allow and foster experimentation as the only way to keep alive and moving into an unknown future.

32. Brzezinski, *Between Two Ages*, employs this terminology in pointing to shifts in history. See Azevedo, "Humanity Today: Its Formative Process and Fundamental Traits," to whom I am most indebted in my studies and in this essay. He indicates the levels of human cultural evolution that have led to the modern world.

33. Pope Paul VI, *Evangelii Nuntiandi*, no. 70 points to the task of the laity. "Their primary and immediate task is not to establish and develop the ecclesial community, but to put to use every Christian and evangelical possibility latent but already present and active in the affairs of the world." He then points to the areas of politics, economics, culture, science, art, media, education, family, etc. For this emphasis upon the laity, there is a growing body of literature. I have found most helpful Mark Gibbs, *God's Frozen People; God's Lively People;* and *Christians with Secular Power*. Also, the essays in *Challenge to the Laity*, edited by Russell Barta. Finally, the essay of John Coleman "American Catholicism and Strategic Social Theology," in *The Catholic Church: The United States Experience*, ed. Irene Woodward, gives a historical overview of options or models of church-society relationship, including reflections on the Catholic Action model, which focuses heavily upon Catholic laity.

PART C
The Ecclesial Zone of Catechesis

Introduction

MICHAEL WARREN

Readers of the following essays will see a close connection between them and those of the preceding two sections. The essays in this section focus in various ways on the practice of the local assembly as the primal catechetical form and on how the social and cultural climate of a time influences our faith perceptions. Though "the teaching act" is necessary, even finely crafted pedagogy is in itself an insufficient means of fostering the kind of life stance and commitments called for by discipleship.

READING 6
Introduction

At the time when Berard Marthaler published his much-quoted essay on the use-fulness of socialization theory for catechesis, theoretical debates had already erupt-ed about whether catechesis should fall within the broader category of ministry or within that of education. Some of these debates are documented in the first volume of the *Sourcebook*. Marthaler begins his essay by alluding to this controversy and explaining his desire to create a model allowing conversation among people who use various kinds of language to speak about imparting and maintaining religious traditions.

As Marthaler's essay unfolds, it become clear that in the range of influences on religious persons—social, cultural, and religious—the influence of the religion teacher or catechist is both more complex and more diminished than the one ordi-narily set forth in educational models. Thus, "the success of catechesis . . . is not judged by how much information, even information about religion and church, that one imbibes." Catechesis is rooted in the sacramental insight that any reality can symbolically disclose ultimate meaning and thus can transform individuals and communities. Jesus himself is the great sacrament of God's love; the church is the sacrament of Jesus-faith. The process of adopting a faith stance and then living it is much more complex than can be disclosed in an analysis of the activities of teaching. "In the framework of a faith community, catechesis becomes community education."

Readers will want to give special attention to the final section of Marthaler's essay, which deals with socialization's implications for catechesis. In various ways, all the essays in this *Sourcebook* volume provide added support for Marthaler's claims here.

Socialization as a Model for Catechetics

BERARD L. MARTHALER, OFM CONV

Recent literature in religious education journals of one kind or another indicates some confusion over terminology. If it were simply a matter of semantics, a glossary could straighten out the matter. The terminological differences reflect diverse views about the nature of religious education, its goals, objectives, and methods. Sometimes—in my view, most often—it is a matter of emphasis and priorities; at other times it is a question of defining the discipline. It is the latter question that most interests me, but I realize that one cannot proceed to that point without first entering into the thicket of definitions and technical terms.

The way one defines the discipline has practical ramifications in every area. It affects one's visions as well as one's strategies for religious education at the local level. It shapes the design of the graduate programs in which the professionals in the field are trained. It defines the relationship of religious education to other disciplines—theology, liturgics, the social sciences, education, and so forth. The need to have a clearer identity was made evident not long ago at a meeting on the catechesis of children and youth sponsored by the department of education of the United States Catholic Conference.[1] The meeting presented an unusual opportunity to carry on interdisciplinary discussions among men and women interested in various dimensions of religious education. While the participants were predominantly Catholic, there were a few Protestants and one Jew. Religious educators and social scientists confronted one another. They were broadly representative of the field: They came from schools and CCD programs; the social sciences; they were publishers, researchers, and administrators. But many participants felt that the full potential of the meeting was never realized for want of some common understanding of the goals, objectives, and methods of religious education. The group did not speak a common language nor operate with commonly shared assumptions. In a sense the meeting simply mirrored the actual conditions of the field.

Reprinted from *Foundations of Religious Education*, by Padraic O'Hare (New York: Paulist Press, 1978), 64–92. Copyright © 1978 by The Missionary of St. Paul the Apostle in the State of New York. Used by permission of Paulist Press.

It is the purpose of this paper to sketch a model that will elucidate the nature of religious education and provide a basis for interdisciplinary discourse. I use "model" as a heuristic device to disclose the way selected phenomena interact and relate to one another. Models of their nature focus on selected sectors of reality, but some models are more comprehensive than others.[2] The adequacy of a model is measured in pragmatic terms, that is, by its usefulness in interpreting data and establishing patterns of meaning. It is my contention that a socialization model is useful for explaining and interpreting many of the varied activities that are carried on in the name of religious education.

Although the word may have a strange ring in church circles, the socialization process has been operative in the Christian community since two or three first gathered together in Jesus' name. Insofar as it was an intentional process, socialization was traditionally called *catechesis*. Nor is religious education as socialization unknown among modern authors. It was the model underlying Horace Bushnell's idea of "Christian nurture." While C. Ellis Nelson does not use the idiom of social science, he in fact describes socialization into the church community in *Where Faith Begins*. John Westerhoff uses both the term "socialization" and the socialization model to explain the dynamics of religious education in *Generation to Generation* and most recently in his *Will Our Children Have Faith?* It is a model that social scientists like Herve Carrier, Andrew Greeley, and Merton Strommen understand and, more often than not, operate from when they undertake research in the field of religious education.

In the following pages I first explore what is involved in the notion of socialization in general, drawing heavily on the social sciences. Second, I show how various activities, formal and informal, associated with religious education are illuminated in themselves and in their relationship to one another by the socialization model. Third, I briefly sketch some of the implications in this approach to religious education.

I. Socialization

Though philosophers and pedagogues as far back as Plato carried on sophisticated discussions about various phenomena of socialization, the term itself is relatively new. It began to appear with some frequency in the writings of social scientists less than a century ago, and according to Clausen it was not until 1939 that it came to be at all widely used in its present sense.[3] Although the definitions of socialization are as numerous as the authors who write on the subject, there is a common denominator in all the descriptions and theories, namely, the interaction of an individual with a collective. The collective may be the nuclear family, a voluntary society, a cultural tradition, or any kind of community of humans. The individual may be a child or an adult, a normal person or a deviant, a willing agent or an unwitting participant. In short, every human being, except perhaps the feral child, is consciously or unconsciously a product of socialization. It must be stressed, however, that socialization is interaction: The individual is not simply a bit of clay to be molded by society, but rather an actor who while acquiring personal and social identity influences the group. A child is not simply a tabula rasa that mysteriously responds to the stimuli of adults. Nor are adults fixed and stable factors in a child's world, but are themselves likely to change under the impact of their offspring's challenge.[4]

The number and variety of definitions of socialization reflect the different concerns and foci within the social sciences themselves. Psychologists and psychoanalysts discuss socialization in terms of personality theory, impulse control, ego identity, and the many other factors that contribute to tension or compatibility between the individual and the social environment in which he or she is situated. The sociologist concentrates more on institutional structures, the societal apparatuses that shape the roles expected of the members of a particular group. The anthropologist focusing on cultural traits of one kind or another studies the means by which traditions, customs, and behavioral patterns are transmitted from one generation to another.

Modern psychology is in reality a galaxy of subfields. It incorporates theories of learning and personality as well as stage theories that seek to explain cognitive and moral development. It deals with ego identity and motivation and other aspects of the human psyche. Psychology studies the influence of every imaginable stimulus on human behavior. Psychology understands socialization in a general sense as the development of the individual as a social being with emphasis on the consciousness of self in relationship to other selves. While many psychologists operate within a socialization model, socialization is not a principal focus of research in child psychology, social psychology, and some personality theories. Even in these subfields, however, researchers and theorists have not shown "major interest in the larger process by which an individual is prepared for full participation in adult life."[5] Thus for all the contributions made by the different branches of developmental psychology with its concentration on conditioning experiments, learning theory, and the measurement of attributes of the child, it has for the most part neglected the crucial influence of social interaction and the transmission of culture. One noted exception is Erik Erikson, who, while concerned with the development of one's self-concept, recognizes the importance of the interplay of psychosocial phenomena.

By way of contrast, relatively few sociologists regard small children as proper subjects for study except as members of a family, peer group, or some other social unit. Sociology focuses on group relationships and the ways in which they influence the individual. It is concerned with social control and such agents of socialization as the family, school, church, mass media, and so forth. It sees socialization as the process whereby individuals are assimilated into and brought to conform to the ways of the social group to which they belong.

While psychology and anthropology, emphasizing as they do personality and cultural transmission, concentrate more heavily on the study of childhood socialization, sociologists show greater interest in adult socialization. Sociology studies the processes whereby personnel are recruited and trained to fill positions in the societal structures: how one acquires and is influenced by his or her role of parent; how one assumes a professional identity and finds that his or her attitudes and behavior are shaped by the role of doctor or lawyer; how sex roles are assigned, and so forth. In fact, sociologists in the classic tradition generally understand adult socialization in a restricted sense so that it means little more than the acquisition of social and occupational roles.

Anthropologists, however, understand socialization in a more basic sense. They see it in terms of culture and even use "enculturation" and "acculturization" as synonyms for socialization. (The former describes the initiation of a "cultureless" person into the patterns of meaning and expected behavior of a particular adult society; the latter describes the transition of an adult from one culture to another.) Culture is the key word. It comprehends the explicit and implicit values and patterns of meaning embodied in configurations of behavior, social institutions, and all the traits and artifacts that give a particular group its distinctive identity. They are the symbols that constitute and give expression to a culture. Thus culture is understood as a comprehensive symbol system that gives meaning and value to every aspect of social living. The anthropologist who is interested in the socialization process studies how the culture is transmitted from generation to generation by means of the symbols.

These three approaches are delineated for purposes of study and research. Even though psychologists, sociologists, and anthropologists focus on different aspects of the process and use different methods, they complement one another. In the concrete, socialization is all of a piece. If one takes a phenomenological approach socialization is seen as a dialectic, an interaction between the objective world in which one finds him or herself and the subjective world of the individual with his or her particular angles of vision. Both worlds are very real. They shape one another. Society exists, write Berger and Luckmann, "only as individuals are conscious of it" while, on the other hand, "individual consciousness is socially determined."[6] It is in the interplay of the objective and subjective worlds that groups and individuals construct their symbol systems, grow to self-awareness, and take on their particular identities. It is through this "symbolic interaction" that an individual comes to recognize him/herself as a male or female, as an American in the twentieth century, perhaps as a Catholic Christian, and in all the secondary roles that one acquires by reason of state of life, occupation, and situation in time and place.

Socialization as Dialectic

Social scientists generally recognize that socialization takes place in a fundamental dialectic. Berger and Luckmann, who use a phenomenological rather than an empirical method, describe the dynamics of the process as three "major moments": (1) externalization, (2) objectification, and (3) internalization.[7]

Externalization is an anthropological necessity. A human being cannot but pour him/herself out into the world in which he/she is situated. While the relationship of the human being to a specific environment is a given, it is not permanently fixed. Humans struggle to shape the world in their own image and to fit it with their own needs. Building on the physical universe, societies construct a human world we call culture. Although culture becomes "second nature" to humans, it can still be distinguished from them in the sense that it is the product of their own activity and ingenuity. The preservation and transmission of culture depend upon the ability of peoples to maintain specific social structures and ideals. Seen in this light the world as it is known by human beings is not a static, fixed entity, but the product of the interaction between the physical universe, the culture, and the drive on the part of human beings to externalize their inner needs and desires.

Objectification is a corollary of externalization. When we speak of externalized products of mental and physical activity, we imply that they have attained a distinctive existence apart from their producers. They are like works of art, the painting that exists after the painter dies, the music that continues to be played in a different way from what the composer intended. Thus the socially constructed reality takes on a facticity of its own, it is something "out there." It consists of objects, patterns of behavior, social structures, meanings, and so forth, that are capable of resisting the desires and designs of their creators. "Although all culture originates and is rooted in the subjective consciousness of human beings," note Berger and Luckmann, "once formed it cannot be reabsorbed into consciousness at will."[8]

A special case of objectification is the human production of signs, the carriers of meaning. All objectifications are susceptible to use as signs even though they were not produced with this intention (for example, a weapon made for hunting animals may become in certain circumstances a sign for violence and aggressiveness). Language, however, is a system of verbal and/or nonverbal signs for the avowed purpose of self-expression—of transmitting thoughts, information, and meaning. Language possesses an inherent quality of reciprocity that distinguishes it from all other sign systems. As a network of words, grammatical constructions, and gestures it is external to the individuals who use it while at the same time it has a formative effect on their thinking and manner of expression. Language forces one into patterns of meaning, but it also opens the possibility of transcending the concrete and particular. Language objectifies the shared experiences of a community, making them available to all the members present and future. Sophisticated practitioners of the language arts can construct extensive edifices of symbolic representations that interpret the objectifications of everyday life and form them into configurations that bring out their significance. It is an axiom of modern sociological tradition "that human action is never simply behavior, but behavior plus meaning. Meaning is constitutive of the human world in which we live."[9] Historically, religion, philosophy, and art have provided the most important symbol systems in the social construction of reality.

Internalization is the term used to describe the reassimilation into consciousness of the objectified world of meanings. It occurs in such a way that the structures of the external world come to determine the subjective structures of consciousness itself. Although individuals are born with a proclivity, even a need, to be socialized, it is only to the extent that they internalize the values and attitudes of the milieu in which they find themselves that they are considered full-fledged members of society. In the sense that socialization connotes a sharing of common meanings and values it is the basis that permits the members of a particular group to understand and communicate with one another.

Identity Formation

Cultural patterns and social institutions function as formative agents of an individual's self-image and world view. Or to put it another way, identity is a phenomenon that emerges from the dialectic between the individual and society. In the course of appropriating the language, institutionalized values, and objectified meanings of a culture or society one acquires a sense of belonging. As one becomes older and gains some degree of autonomy, one becomes more or less free to filter the values and attitudes of the group, but much continues to be dictated by the accident of birth. (A college education, for example, does not have the same importance for the ghetto child that it does for the son or daughter of a university professor.) Society assigns a name and sometimes a fixed role in life. These designations define the individual's place in the world. As one accepts (or rejects) the identification and the roles assigned by the culture and society, one acquires a social identity. To the extent that a person internalizes and consciously appropriates this social identity, it becomes inseparable from his/her self-image.

Every society instinctively, if not deliberately, seeks to form its young and its proselytes according to a predetermined archetype of what a loyal member should be. It inducts new members not by a mechanical process that would stamp an image on them as in minting coins or religious medals. Even a totalitarian society wants to win minds and hearts. The convergence of one's social identity and personal self-image emerges more from a dialogical process in which the socializee is an active participant. The conversation usually begins at home and continues in school with the "significant others" in one's life. An individual's social identity reflects the attitudes taken by the mother, the father, the teacher, and later by one's peer group. In time an individual may come to have a different self-image from the one adults tried to impose on him or her as a child but these initial experiences leave a lasting imprint.

Society carries on this dialogue at various levels and in a number of ways. Two of the principal ones have already been discussed. One way is to assign a social identity to an individual with the expectation that he or she will internalize it. A person becomes what he or she is named. A child consistently described as an Orthodox Jew learns to regard himself or herself as an Orthodox Jew and comes to know in a preconceptual way what is expected of one who would be an Orthodox Jew. A second way in which a group socializes its members is by encouraging the socializees to appropriate as their own the symbol system that embodies the meanings it shares and gives expression to its values and attitudes. The Orthodox Jew learns of the temple, the Torah, and the Talmud, of the Sabbath, Yom Kippur, and Passover, of kosher food, of the Holocaust, and of the many other practices and sacramentals that constitute Jewish tradition. The self-image of a Jew is inseparable from these symbols. They define his/her social identity and give meaning and purpose to his/her world. A Jew writing an autobiography cannot tell his or her story without at least some reference to the history of the Jewish people.

Socialization, at least in the case of the young, begins before the socializees are capable of normal reasoning, and in every case involves more than purely cognitive learning. Even the adult learner and, *a fortiori*, the child, identifies with the significant other in a variety of emotional ways.

Berger and Luckmann go so far as to say "there is good reason to believe that without such emotional attachment to the significant others the learning process would be difficult if not impossible."[10] Furthermore, the symbols that are the carriers of traditions and meanings have rich connotations that speak to the whole person, not just the mind. They evoke what no concept can, namely, the polyvalent meanings that a person attributes to a particular act or event. Religious symbols in particular seek to disclose the ultimate meaning of human existence. They are not simply incidental to one's social identity but are so interwoven with one's self-image that an individual who has internalized them has no personal identity without them.

Gregory Baum sums up the function of religious symbols in the socialization process as follows:

> Ever since we are little children, we are exposed to values, norms, meanings and purposes, through our parents and the social institutions (including language) of which they are part, so that we assimilate a system of symbols long before we achieve the rational maturity to be critical and search for our own values. Even when we reach this stage of maturity, we are never empty subjects in search of new meaning, for woven into our personal, intellectual, and emotional structure are the meaning and values in which we participated as we grew up. We are able to re-educate ourselves, but our deep conviction or doubts about love, trust, fidelity, and the orientation to grow are so deeply tied into our personal being that it is only on these and through these that we modify our conscious purposes. Man's relationship to the deepest dimension of his life remains inevitably implicit; it can never be conceptualized; it can only be spoken of in symbols.
>
> The symbol, then, expresses man's relationship to the ultimate in his life. The symbol makes this relationship more conscious and communicable and thus intensifies man's involvement in it.[11]

Before moving from this discussion of socialization in general to a consideration of the specialized form of religious socialization we call catechesis, it might be well to add that the socialization process is never completed. The dynamics of externalization, objectification, and internalization continue through one's lifetime. Erik Erikson's well-known "eight ages of man," each with its successive crisis, illustrates that a person continues to grope for identity. In every stage of life one restructures past identity images in the light of an anticipated future.

II. Catechesis[12]

The socialization model brackets out aetiological, theological, and epistemological considerations. It takes the present realities of everyday life as its starting point. In dealing with the Christian religion it begins with the phenomena at hand. It asks why and how the members of the first Christian community came to believe and act as they did only insofar as these questions throw light on why and how modern men and women come to believe and act as they do.[13]

The modern Christian neophyte, child or adult, confronts a world of organized religion, with its buildings, social institutions, sacred texts, creedal statements, moral norms, authority figures, canonized heroes and heroines, and a bewildering fabric of sacramental practices (e.g., devotions, fasting) and artifacts (images, the rosary, etc.). They constitute the symbol system that embodies the Church's meanings and values, expresses its attitudes and priorities, and, taken together, give it identity. In other words, the modern Christian finds a world already externalized by previous generations who shared a common faith. The modern Christian comes to know it as an objectified world of structured meanings and patterned behaviors that he/she is expected to internalize.

Social scientists, students of world religions, and, under the influence of the previously named groups, Christian theologians have come to make a distinction between faith and beliefs. Faith is understood as a basic orientation, a fundamental attitude, described by David Tracy as "primal and often non-conceptual."[14] It is an act of the whole person; it engages the totality of one's being, conscious and unconscious. When communities reflect upon and attempt to express faith—their belief stance vis-à-vis the transcendent, the numinous or limit situations—in concrete terms, they fall back on a variety of verbal and nonverbal symbols. In this framework beliefs are symbols that explicate particular historical, moral, or cognitive claims implicit in a particular faith stance. Religious beliefs are thematized in doctrines, moral codes, rituals, prayer formulas, and countless other commonly shared symbols. They interpret the way individuals and communities apprehend transcendent reality and at the same time provide purpose and patterns for organizing the realities of everyday living. Beliefs disclose the meanings and values implicit in the primal faith of particular communities and their members. Beliefs, grounded as they are in faith values, identify the good and evil. Faith is the primal orientation of individuals and communities in their living and feeling; specific beliefs mediate its meaning. To be socialized into a particular religious tradition, therefore, is more a matter of belief than faith.

Beliefs are expressed in symbols that explicate faith and bring it to consciousness. There are foundational symbols and second-order symbols. For Roman Catholics (and probably for all Christians), examples of foundational symbols are Jesus Christ, Church, Eucharist, and Scripture. Second-level symbols can be as diverse as Canon Law and the parish church, the Vatican and religious orders, Gregorian chant and infant baptism. Though a specific symbol may be peculiar to Catholic practice—the rosary, for example—it does not have a religious meaning apart from the whole system wherein certain moments (mysteries) in Christ's life are understood to have special significance and Mary is accorded a singular place. The pope is another distinctively Catholic symbol. The unique authority associated with the papacy, however, can be understood only in the broader context of ecclesiology. Roman Catholics and Anglo-Catholics thus see the role of the pope in the church in a different light because they see church structure in a different light. The Roman Catholic takes his/her identity from the network of interlocking and mutually supportive beliefs, values, attitudes, and patterns of behavior that distinguishes that particular Christian tradition.

"Education in Faith"

"Faith," says John Westerhoff, "cannot be taught by any method of instruction; we can only teach religion."[15] Richard McBrien seems to agree that faith cannot be taught. "When all is said and done," he writes, "religious educators, bishops, preachers, and the Church at large do not transmit 'the faith.' They transmit particular interpretations or understandings of faith. In direct words: they transmit theologies."[16] Catechesis, which is here taken to be synonymous with "education in faith," assumes much the same thing. Faith is at once a gift of grace and the free response of the person to God's call. Because it is a grace, no human expedient can pretend to instill and increase faith, and even less to program its growth and development from the outside. "Catechetical training," in the words of Vatican II, "is intended to make men's faith become living, conscious, and active, through the light of instruction."[17] Catechesis cannot engender faith, but only awaken, nourish, and develop what is already there.

Catechesis begins as an exercise in hermeneutics. Education in faith becomes a lesson in interpreting one's personal experiences as well as historical events in the light of faith—*lumen fidei*. "There are not two sorts of human experiences," writes Peter Hebblethwaite, "one Christian and the other secularist. There is only one reality called human experience, but there are two different interpretations of it."[18] Simply to reflect, therefore, on one's own experience, to narrate historical incidents, or even to discuss current events in which the Church is involved is not enough. Catechesis is a matter of consciousness-raising, of uncovering the mysteries hidden beneath the surface of everyday life. It is an introduction to reading and interpreting signs—"the signs of the times," biblical signs, ecclesial signs (creedal symbols and lifestyles), and liturgical signs. "Faith," says Karl Rahner, "is never awakened by someone having something communicated to him purely from the outside, addressed solely to his naked understanding as such. . . ." Education in faith—catechesis—therefore means "to assist understanding of what has already been experienced in the depth of human reality as grace (that is, as in absolutely direct relation to God)."[19]

The success of catechesis, therefore, is not judged by how much information, even information about religion and church, that one imbibes. Catechesis aims rather at transmitting the wisdom of a particular religious tradition, which in the context of these discussions is Roman Catholic Christianity. The so-called experiential and anthropological approaches in catechesis try to build and reinforce this heritage by integrating religion with everyday life. It is not a question of whether secular films, profane literature, popular songs, or commercial advertising have a place in the religious studies curriculum; the question is whether they are viewed, read, listened and reacted to from a distinctive point of view. How are the experiences interpreted? Value clarification and the examination of human relationships—friendship, love, sexuality—should be looked at differently in a social science program than in a religion course. It is not enough for catechists to interpret human experience in the context of a vague kind of theistic humanism that too often is passed off as "incarnational faith." Catechesis must rather present the kind of sacramental view of the universe that Langdon Gilkey and others identify as distinctively Catholic: all reality—even sin and failure—is seen as the sign and instrument of salvation.[20] The catechist has no arcane set of special truths not otherwise available, but he or she is the heir to a symbol system that has the power to disclose ultimate meaning and transform the lives of individuals and communities. (The disclosure of ultimate meaning, it should be noted, is not the same as having "all the answers.") In the final analysis, however, it is Jesus Christ, the Master Symbol—the *Ursakrament*—who reveals the mystery of salvation and sheds light on all the lesser symbols.

In the framework of the socialization model, education in the faith has three objectives. They roughly parallel the focal interests of the psychologists, the sociologists, and the anthropologists in their employment of the socialization model. The objectives may be summarized under the headings: (1) growth in personal faith; (2) religious affiliation; and (3) the maintenance and transmission of a religious tradition. In the abstract the three nicely complement one another. In the concrete, however, they are at times the source of tension. Some religious educators build programs to achieve one of the objectives, only to find that there are others in the community who would emphasize another. For purpose of analysis we proceed from the more general to the particular, and, therefore, consider the three objectives in reverse order to their listing here.

Handing On the Symbols of Faith

The Christian community believes it has a message of lasting importance. Like every group that takes itself seriously, Christians believe they have a mission to transmit this message to successive generations. Or in the language of socialization, the Christian community believes it has a responsibility to impress its institutionalized meanings and values powerfully and unforgettably on its members. It knows it cannot engender a basic faith stance, but it leads its members—potentially "all nations"—to adopt its symbols and internalize their meanings.

From Saint Paul to the present every formal effort in religious education in the history of the Church has been in one way or another an exposition of Christian symbols. Although the Christians of the early Church did not have a social science vocabulary, they were in fact consciously "socializing" their members. The catechumenate tested the moral behavior of the proselytes and gradually initiated them into the life of the community. Step by step they were introduced to the sacred texts. Though it referred primarily to the creed, the catechesis in the ancient Church peaked in a special ceremony known as the *traditio symboli*— a ritualized handing on of the symbol of faith. The catechumens who were judged "competent" for full-fledged membership were formally inducted in the baptismal rites and admitted to the eucharistic celebration. While converts from the mystery religions easily understood many of the symbolic rituals, it was necessary to make them familiar with the idiom of the Old Testament. Even the proselytes who came via Judaism had to study the particular interpretation that Christians bring to the Hebrew Scriptures. Cyril of Jerusalem, Ambrose, and Augustine have left us examples of catechetical homilies showing that they continued to explain baptism and the Eucharist even after the neophytes were received into the Church. The meaning of the Christian ritual and creed statements was no more immediately relevant to the Christians of the fourth and fifth centuries than it is to their descendants in the twentieth—perhaps less so. Formal instruction played an important part, but only a part, in the socialization process.

It is obvious that our Christian understandings rest not on our individual experiences alone. Judgments by which we assent to truths of fact and value are seldom, if ever, made independently of the human community in which we find ourselves. Community assumes expression and communication. The world in which one lives is constituted of objects and ideas, patterns of behavior and social structures, verbal and nonverbal language. In the best of times, this objective reality is expressed in a coherent symbol system that yields meaning and purpose. The meaning is not always self-evident, at least to succeeding generations, and therefore needs to be mediated by stories (myths), art, ritual, and theology. In a world constituted of a number of cultures, the symbol system within a religious tradition or the symbol systems of several traditions may conflict and compete with one another. In times of rapid change and cultural upheaval, the resulting chaos and confusion are such that everything seems to lose meaning, nothing appears to have purpose, and all communication is lost.

Catechesis, therefore, has a second task: It is a matter of "world maintenance," the holding together of a shared vision of reality that gives both the community as a whole and the persons who constitute it a sense of identity. (This use of "sense" is adapted from Erikson. The patterns of identity he describes are not able to be objectified by the subject as "knowledge." Rather, he or she comes to a "sense" of who he or she is and tests it in the social and cultural context to see if it is valid.) In biblical terms, "world maintenance" is a matter of adhering to the covenant, with all that it implies for the institutional religion of the people of God as well as the religious individuals who make it up. Education in the faith implies, therefore, an effort to sustain the framework of meaning and value that aids communities and their members to interpret human existence and pattern their behavior.

Religious Belonging

The document *To Teach as Jesus Did*, published by the United States bishops, says that one of the goals of Catholic religious education is "to build community."[21] According to the Canon Law of the Catholic Church (and the same is more or less true for all the mainline churches), every baptized person belongs to the Church (cf. can. 87). Neither juridical membership on the one hand, nor a vague sense of belonging on the other, however, is sufficient basis to establish a community. "To build community" means in this context to socialize the members into an ecclesial community with at least minimal structures and organization.

The model here is Ferdinand Tonnies's *Gemeinschaft*. One is born into the community and accepts it as part of the external order. The archetype is family where people grow up and develop in reliance on one another. The communal bonds are inseparable from their sense of personal identity. The members of the community speak of themselves as "we," and, more or less willingly, accept the social roles that it assigns to them.[22] The primary symbol of this community, at least in the Catholic tradition, is the eucharistic assembly. Inasmuch as the Eucharist brings together the many human differences found within the boundaries of the local community and draws them into the universality of the Church, the Eucharist exemplifies both unity and catholicity. Inasmuch as it is the sacrament of Christ's Passover from death to life, "where natural elements refined by man are changed into his glorified body, providing a meal of brotherly solidarity and a foretaste of the heavenly banquet," it is a sign of holiness (*Gaudium et Spes*, no. 38).

Community in this sense possesses a definite structure and implies a good deal more than a mere "collectivity of people." (It is in this latter sense that Andrew Greeley uses the term when speaking of "communal Catholics." The "Catholic community" is understood in a way roughly equivalent to the "Jewish community" or the "black community.")[23] In this context "religious belonging" becomes the fundamental relationship of a member to his or her group and implies considerably more than looking to one's roots as a source of religious attitudes and cultural outlooks. The conscious identification of a Christian with an organized church "is no longer a fact viewed from the exterior, a fact reported to a census taker, or a religious category; it is a psychological reality."[24] The member sees him/herself in interaction with the group. The group, for its part, welcomes and motivates the member; he/she participates in its activities and is concerned with its well-being and governance.

In the framework of a faith community, catechesis becomes community education. It consists of a fragile network of interlocking and mutually supportive institutions and agencies, professional leaders and private citizens, formal and informal influences, through which a person comes to identify with the Church. It begins with the human community, the family, the neighborhood, perhaps the ethnic tradition of a people like the Irish, the Italians, or the Poles whose history was closely bound with the fortunes of Catholicism. The home nurtures the basic aspirations and attitudes of children and adults alike through the very atmosphere that prevails there. The presence of religious art, a Bible, a crucifix, religious periodicals, and so forth, is an informal way of transmitting the traditional symbols of Catholicism. The very image of the parish church in the eyes of the individuals and the families that constitute it projects an ecclesiology: Is it the image of a building that may be rented for weddings and funerals, a refuge where one may find a moment of peace and quiet away from the pressures of urban life, a place of common prayer and meaningful worship, a center of social action? All or none of the foregoing? The parochial school is an influential instrument of social-ization not only for what it teaches in a formal way but also for what it teaches indirectly and in passing. A very effective social justice curricu-lum may be offset by the unspoken reality that the church school in fact flourishes as an escape from racial integration. Then there is the obser-vance of Sundays and the celebration of the liturgical cycles with the Advent and Lenten rituals culminating in Christmas and Easter. The atti-tudes and priorities manifested in the patterns of belief and behavior in a local Christian community have a more lasting effect than formal in-struction. A parish congregation that self-consciously strives to be truly one, holy, catholic, and apostolic leaves its mark on every other social-izing agent it comes into contact with.

The recent document *A Vision of Youth Ministry*, published by the United States Catholic Conference, outlines a program of community ed-ucation for young people. The many and varied facets of this ministry are brought into focus by a common dedication to two main goals: (1) the "personal and spiritual growth of each young person," and (2) "respon-sible participation in the life, mission and work of the faith communi-ty."[25] It is the latter goal that is of interest at this moment. The document sees catechesis primarily as a form of the ministry of the word, but it recognizes that it is integral to and in practice inseparable from the min-istries of healing, enabling, guidance, worship, and service. The strate-gies whether in schools of one kind or another or in less-structured educational settings are designed "to draw young people into the sup-portive experience of Christian community, and to assist the parish com-munity to welcome the young and share its ministry with them."[26]

"Community," according to *To Teach as Jesus Did*, "is at the heart of Christian education not simply as a concept to be taught but as a re-ality to be lived" (no. 23). The young are socialized through an interac-tion with the adult community that witnesses to faith and provides role models for youth to imitate and emulate. They acquire a religious iden-tity by taking as their own the creedal formulas, rites, activities, and other emblems that symbolize the corporate solidarity of the Catholic community. "For the early adolescent," says John Nelson of Fordham University, "doctrine serves not so much as a formulation of truth as it does a symbol of orthodoxy within a religious group."[27] Even before the meanings of the symbols are internalized, and before they are seen as an organic whole—as a system—the young Christian as it were wears them as badges of belonging.

But not only adolescents are brought to faith through socialization, nor does the process stop in adulthood. The renewed catechumenate, for example, advocated by the recently promulgated *Rite of Christian*

Initiation of Adults, operates from the same premise. Aidan Kavanagh argues that it offers a paradigm for the radical renewal of all Christian life. The new rite, he says, *"re*-unites (italics mine) a complex and long-term process of human formation with ritual-sacramental engagement in a robust ecclesial environment."[28] The modernized catechumenate provides another example of socialization in which the process and ritual of Christian formation create the faith community, sustain and at times modify it, and keep the community a functioning entity. The ultimate success of the socialization process, therefore, must be judged in terms not of how many children or even converts are baptized, but rather by answering how well adults are assimilated into the faith community and how closely they identify with it. It is on this premise that the *General Catechetical Directory* states:

> Catechesis for adults, since it deals with persons who are capable of an adherence that is fully responsible, must be considered the chief form of catechesis. All the other forms, which are indeed always necessary, are in some way oriented to it. (No. 20)

Personal Faith

Even though faith is nurtured in the faith community—in the Church as the Pentecostal assembly—it is, nonetheless, a personal grace. Contemporary theologians speak of it as a personal encounter with God in that faith represents an individual's response to the word of God in Jesus Christ. The encounter is described as personal because it involves one's whole being—entire person—mind, heart, and soul. Faith has a cognitive or intellectual dimension, but it is more than knowing something about God; it is knowing God. Faith implies loving, valuing, caring, and feeling as well.

Catechesis thus seeks to address the whole person. It recognizes the uniqueness of every individual and, therefore, suspects any structures that would indoctrinate and hinder the inner growth of a deep personal relationship with God. Education in faith respects the freedom of the person and, therefore, resists any pressures that try to force a response. Education in faith focuses on individual needs and, therefore, in every case observes the person's natural disposition, ability, age, and circumstances of life.

The *General Catechetical Directory* recognizes that children, adolescents, young adults, and mature grown-ups have different needs and dispositions. It sketches, in broad outline, principles and concerns that should guide catechesis according to age levels. The description is purposefully unsophisticated, but the *GCD* does emphasize that "the life of faith passes through various stages, just as does man's existence while he is attaining maturity and taking on the duties of life" (no. 30; cf. Part V). It admits, moreover, that stage-development allows for various degrees "both in the global acceptance of the total word of God and in the explanation of that word and the application of it to the different duties of human life, according to the maturity of each and differences of individuals" (ibid).

It is now commonplace to hear theologians speak of doctrinal development, and moralists discuss the development of conscience, and psychologists describe cognitive development, but it is a relatively new phenomenon to hear religious educators talking about faith development. Until recently, few recognized the importance of the personal dynamic in the structure of faith. It is not merely that the creedal formula takes on new meanings because of doctrinal development, but the person professing the creed is also subject to change. It is largely due to the work of James W. Fowler III, whose "structuralist-developmental" approach is now well known, that religious educators have become sensitive to this aspect of faith development.

Fowler's research is particularly helpful, moreover, in understanding catechesis as a dimension of the socialization process. He acknowledges his indebtedness to Jean Piaget, Lawrence Kohlberg, and Erik Erikson among others. All three in various ways argue that an individual internalizes patterns of knowing and behavior through his/her interaction with objects and persons. Development comes through a person's efforts to accommodate oneself to one's environment.

Beginning with the premise that faith is a kind of knowing, Fowler has undertaken to adapt the research techniques of Piaget and Kohlberg to the area of "faith-knowing." "Faith," he writes, "is a knowing which includes loving, caring and valuing, as well as awe, dread and fear. Faith-knowing relates a person or community to the limiting boundaries and depths of experience; to the source, center and standard of valuing or responsibility in life."[29] In short, faith presents a set of operations in which cognition and affection are inextricably entwined. Just as Piaget had only a secondary interest in a child's knowledge of physics, mathematics, and logic, and just as Kohlberg's primary interest is not in the outcomes of moral decisions for their own sake, so Fowler does not focus on the content of faith as such. In fact, he has found that "the same or similar content of faith may be appropriated in quite different ways by persons whose faith-knowing is structurally different at different stages." Fowler, however, acknowledges a special difficulty in his research "due to the fact that the dimension of experience we refer to as God or the Transcendent must be symbolically represented and mediated in ways which the parties to moral conflict need not necessarily be."[30]

Taking the six stages of moral development identified by Kohlberg as a starting point, Fowler subsequently modified them in the light of his own research. On the basis of several hundred in-depth interviews conducted with persons of various ages and background, he developed a taxonomy of operations or structures in faith-knowing. Each of the six stages has its own particular wholeness, set of operations, and particular competencies. A brief outline of the stages is given here only to illumine how growth in faith is inextricably bound up with socialization. The reader must go directly to Fowler's own writings for a fuller and properly nuanced description.

Stage I: Intuitive-Projective Faith. The child is powerfully influenced by the examples, moods, actions, and language of the visible faith of significant adults. The phase is characterized by imitation. There is little distinction between fact and fantasy.

Stage II: Mythic-Literal Faith. The person begins to appropriate the stories, beliefs, and rituals that symbolize one's identity with a faith community. Concepts tend to be largely concrete in reference; symbols, one-dimensional and literal. Mythic forms function in lieu of explanation. Appeal to trusted authority (parents rather than peers) serves as the basis for verification.

Stage III: Synthetic-Conventional Faith. Faith is required to help provide a coherent and meaningful synthesis of involvements that grow increasingly complex and diverse and extend beyond the family. The individual, however, does not yet have to make a personal synthesis of meaning. The conventional wisdom suffices.

Stage IV: Individuating-Reflexive Faith. This stage marks the collapse of the kind of synthesis adequate in previous stages. The responsibility for a world synthesis and particular lifestyle shifts more clearly to the individual. Faith is called upon to help reduce the tension between such unavoidable polarities as individuality versus belonging to community, self-fulfillment versus service to others, the relative versus the absolute, and so forth. A person in Stage IV is likely "to see most institutional religion as 'conventional' and to be drawn to the exotic or novel in traditions."[31]

Stage V: Paradoxical-Consolidative Faith. Authority has been fully internalized. "Faith-knowing involves, at this stage, a moral or volitional affirmation of that which is somewhat paradoxical; it affirms the beliefs, symbols and rituals of a community while 'seeing through' them in a double sense. It sees the relativity, partiality, and time-boundness of the tradition—the scandal of its particularity. But it also sees and values it as a way to see through to the Universal it mediates. What Stage V sees in its own faith-knowing and its symbols, rituals and the like, it also acknowledges in the developed traditions of other persons and cultures. Stage V generally involves a reappropriation (and reinterpretation) of one's past, and of the significant persons and groups whose example and teachings influence its growth in faith-knowing."[32]

Stage VI: Universalizing Faith. Few reach this stage. It is characterized "by an integration of life in faith in which immediacy of participation in the Ultimate is the fruit of development, of discipline, and, likely, of genius."[33] The sense of the oneness of all persons becomes a permeative basis for decision and action. Particulars are cherished because they are vessels of the universal. Life is both loved and held loosely.

It is not necessary, however, to discuss all the related issues to establish the usefulness of the stage-theory advanced by Fowler. Catechetics has long needed a paradigm like the stages of faith-knowing to help explain what it means when it says, as the *General Catechetical Directory* and other contemporary works repeatedly do, that the goal of catechesis is "maturity of faith."

Personal faith is caught up in the dynamic of human development. Growth in faith implies ongoing conversion, a gradual transformation of consciousness. Conversion brings individuals (and, though it is not to the point here, communities) to a new awareness of themselves and a fresh orientation to the world around them. It is in this sense that conversion is a principal goal of catechesis. Conversion implies a shift or at least a broadening of one's horizons; and it implies self-transcendence. Bernard Lonergan distinguishes three types of conversion: intellectual, moral, and religious. Since each of the three is connected with the other two, the goal of catechesis comprises them all while being primarily concerned with religious conversion.

Intellectual conversion is a broadening of one's perceptual horizon so that the individual recognizes the world of mediated meaning to be no less real than the world of immediacy. The world of immediacy, the horizon of the child and the empiricist, in Lonergan's categories is the sum of what is seen, heard, touched, tasted, smelled, felt. The world of meaning is "not known by the sense experience of an individual but by the external and internal experience of a cultural community."[34]

Moral conversion changes one's horizons so that one's choice and decisions are made not on the basis of personal gratification but on a basis of values. The person arrives at a point where he/she discovers that choosing affects oneself no less than the objects chosen or rejected. It is a step toward authenticity and becoming "inner directed." In sum, moral conversion, writes Lonergan, "consists in opting for the truly good, even for value against satisfaction when value and satisfaction conflict."[35]

Religious conversion represents a shift in one's ground of being. It is a change from temporal and transitory, particular and personal, interests to a more efficacious ground for the pursuit of intellectual and moral ends. "Religious conversion," states Lonergan, "is being grasped by ultimate concern."[36] Truth and moral goodness imply holiness, but religious conversion adds a distinct quality of its own. It is a total being-in-love; it is other-worldly fulfillment.

Conversion and catechesis are so inextricably linked that they serve to define each other.[37] They work together reinterpreting one's past biography, and checking and rechecking one's judgments and understandings against the judgments and understandings of the community. The transformation of consciousness builds on primary internalizations and, except in those "first conversions" that represent an about-face and radical repudiation of everything that went before, generally avoids abrupt discontinuity with subjective biography of the individual.[38] Conversion and catechesis within the context of the faith community do not necessitate a total resocialization so much as they imply that socialization is a continuing process through life. As long as the process is not fixated at some point in one's development it will result in maturity of faith.

Maturity of faith no longer appears as a static point one may or may not reach in adult years. That faith is a dynamic element in the life of individuals and the community is not an entirely new discovery. The New Testament uses a variety of images to make this point. One must struggle to preserve, cultivate, and bring faith to maturity. Maturity of faith is experienced at each stage when individuals—children, adolescents, adults—harmoniously integrate faith-knowing with other operational structures in the overall patterns of psychological development, cognitional and affective. Each stage is characterized by a delicate equilibrium that has its own comprehensiveness and potential integrity. When this balance is achieved by a child according to his or her years or by an adult in a primitive culture, one can properly speak of maturity of faith. Even though Fowler's descriptions are said to be provisional, they can be most helpful in setting objectives and planning strategies for various groups who are being catechized. They bring the theology of grace and the process of socialization, which too frequently move in different orbits, into dialogue with each other.

III. Implications

The point of departure for this paper and (as I understand it) one of the underlying premises of this dialogue is the need to clarify the purpose, nature, and task of religious education. It is only when an agent, whether an institution or an individual, has a clear grasp of the overall context in which it functions that the significance of particular strategies and tactics can be judged. It is the thesis of this paper that the socialization model provides (1) a heuristic tool for a better understanding of what much of religious education is about, and (2) a clearly defined basis for planning programs.

Insofar as religious education is a socialization process, I refer to it as catechesis. The term, hallowed by tradition (which has caused some to disdain it as "archaic"),[39] embodies the threefold goal of religious education that has concerned the Christian community from New Testament times: (1) the broadening of one's horizons—growth in personal faith, (2) the gradual incorporation of members into a society of believers—religious belonging, and (3) the maintenance and transmission of a particular symbol system that constitutes and expresses Catholic identity—communicating meaning. Although education in faith is related to religious instruction, religious formation, and other dynamics that are part of all religious education, its purpose is at once consciously both personal and communal. Whatever the means used in catechesis, they are seen as tactics in the broader strategy of socialization that ideally leads to maturity of faith.

A number of practical implications flow from viewing religious education as socialization. This is not to say that sacramental preparation, Bible study, human experience, social action, and similar activities are ignored in other models of religious education, but it does suggest that they play a different role and have a different significance in catechesis. Without going into great detail, I mention in closing only a few of the more obvious implications implicit in the socialization model.

1. The socialization model opens the way for a stronger emphasis in religious education on process. This is not to say that methodology assumes the chief role, but rather it is an honest acknowledgment that catechesis in the final analysis is community education. The community of faith with all its formal and informal structures is the chief catechist. Professionals and paraprofessionals engaged in various aspects of the educational ministry are its agents.

2. A corollary of the above is that catechesis not merely with individuals but with the community taken as a whole. The socialization process implies the transformation (though I have not emphasized this aspect in these pages) as well as the transmission of culture. Just as the individual Christian needs to undergo continuous conversion, so too must the Christian community constantly broaden its horizons, reforming and renewing itself. Catechists thus become agents of change.

3. The content of religious education is not "faith" as a kind of abstraction. It is always mediated by a symbol system. The teaching of doctrine becomes a means—albeit one of the most important, only a means—in communicating meaning and giving the community a sense of identity. Religious language—myths, parables, and other narratives—and theology are other means of transmitting the symbols of faith. The success or failure of catechetical programs must ultimately be judged in terms of how effectively the socialization process is proceeding, not in terms of how much information church members have.

4. Unlike theology, which (from a catechetical viewpoint) is a means, ritual and liturgy are part and parcel of community experience. Like all experience they have an educational dimension, but the sacramental liturgy is to be celebrated for its own ends, not merely for its educational purpose.

5. Ultimately, the success of the socialization process is judged in terms of the adult members of the community: how well they understand and carry on the mission of Christ in the world, the mission the Church has assumed as its own.

NOTES

1. M. Sawick and B. L. Marthaler, eds., "Symposium on the Catechesis of Children and Youth" (Papers from the Symposium, Marriottsville, MD, 13–16 March 1977).

2. Cf. I. Ramsey, *Models and Mystery* (Oxford: Oxford University Press, 1964); I.G. Barbour, *Myths, Models, and Paradigms* (New York: Harper and Row, 1974). The world of science identifies several kinds of models that serve different functions. The model attempted here might best be described in Barbour's terms as a "theoretical model." It is "an imagined mechanism or process, postulated by *analogy* with familiar mechanisms or processes and used to construct a *theory* to correlate a set of observations" (p. 30). In this sense modeling is an intermediate stage in Lonergan's modes of consciousness between the realm of common sense and the realm of theory, a necessary step as one moves from the world of immediacy into a world mediated by meaning (Cf. Bernard Lonergan, *Method in Theology* [New York: Herder and Herder, 1972], 81–90).

3. The above introduction to socialization draws heavily on Clausen's essay "A Historical and Comparative View of Socialization Theory and Research," in

Socialization and Society, ed. J. A. Clausen (Boston: Little, Brown and Company, 1964). Cf. also K. Danzinger, *Socialization* (Baltimore, MD: Penguin Books, 1971).

4. H. P. Dreitzel, ed., *Childhood and Socialization*, Recent Sociology 5 (New York: Macmillan, 1973), 6.

5. Clausen, *Socialization and Society*, 31.

6. P. L. Berger and Thomas Luckmann, *The Social Construction of Reality* (New York: Anchor Books, 1967), 78.

7. Ibid., 61. Cf. D. M. Rafky, "Phenomenology and Socialization: Some Comments on the Assumptions Underlying Socialization Theory," in Dreitzel, *Childhood and Socialization*, 44–64.

8. Berger and Luckmann, *The Social Construction of Reality*, 9.

9. G. Baum, "Truth in the Church," in *The Ecumenist*, March–April 1971, 33–48, at 43.

10. Berger and Luckmann, *The Social Construction of Reality*, 131.

11. The quote is from Baum's article in *The Ecumenist* (see no. 9 above), but he says much the same in his foreword to A. Greeley, *The New Agenda* (Garden City, NY: Image Books, 1975), and in his own *Religion and Alienation* (New York: Paulist Press, 1975), 238–265.

12. For an extensive analysis of the nature and task of catechesis, cf. A. Exeler, *Wesen and Aufgabe der Katechese* (Freiburg im Breisgau: Herder, 1966). Exeler offers a lengthy excursus on the history of the term *catechein* (223–232), and a survey of catechesis—its specific function—in the life of the Church (256–276).

13. It should be noted, however, that "Christianity itself starts as a community of believers, united by their faith in the resurrection of Christ and living in shared expectation of that eschatological fulfillment which is described as the 'heavenly Jerusalem.' It is not difficult to assemble New Testament texts that point to the fostering of Christian community as the goal toward which are directed the behavior of Christians, the efforts of the specialized ministry, and the redeeming action of Christ himself in his Spirit" (B. Cooke, *Ministry to Word and Sacraments* [Philadelphia: Fortress Press, 1976], 35).

14. David Tracy, *Blessed Rage for Order* (New York: Seabury Press, 1975), 16, no. 13.

15. John Westerhoff, *Will Our Children Have Faith?* (New York: Seabury Press, 1976), 23.

16. Richard McBrien, "Faith, Theology and Belief," *Commonweal*, 15 November 1974.

17. *Christus Dominus* ("The Bishops' Pastoral Office in the Church"), 14.

18. Peter Hebblethwaite, "Man's Search for Meaning," *Month*, May 1976, 163.

19. *Sacramentum Mundi* 2:311.

20. Langdon Gilkey, *Catholicism Confronts Modernity* (New York: Seabury Press, 1975).

21. See no. 17 above.

22. Cf. Baum, *Religion and Alienation*, no. 45–67. Also J. J. Dewitt, *Making a Community Out of a Parish* (Washington, DC: Liturgical Conference, 1966).

23. Andrew Greeley, *The Communal Catholic* (New York: Seabury Press, 1976), 3, 10–11.

24. H. Carrier, *The Sociology of Religious Belonging* (New York: Herder and Herder), 58.

25. *A Vision of Youth Ministry* (Washington, DC: U.S. Catholic Conference, Dept. of Education, 1976), 4.

26. Ibid.

27. From an unpublished paper delivered at a "Symposium on the Catechesis of Children and Youth"; cf. no. 1 above.

28. Aidan Kavanagh, "Adult Initiation: Process and Ritual," *Liturgy Journal of the Liturgical Conference*, January 1977, 7 (italics mine).

29. James W. Fowler, "Toward a Developmental Perspective on Faith," *Religious Education* 69 (March–April 1974): 211.

30. Ibid., 213.

31. Ibid., 217.

32. Ibid.

33. "Stages of Faith" (a report submitted to a symposium at Fordham University, September 1975), 33.

34. Lonergan, *Method*, 238.

35. Ibid., 240.

36. Ibid.

37. F. Coudreau, *Basic Catechetical Perspectives* (New York: Paulist Press, 1970), 30.

38. Cf. Berger and Luckmann, *The Social Construction of Reality*, 161.

39. E. G. Lee and J. M. Lee, *The Religious Education We Need* (Mishawaka, IN: Religious Education Press, 1977), 4.

READING 7
Introduction

My own special interest in the social and cultural conditions that influence religious persons began in earnest in 1967, when I first read C. Ellis Nelson's groundbreaking book, *Where Faith Begins.* That book has been seminal in my teaching about the possibilities of the local church as the sacrament of the Jesus -secret. Nelson has a pithy way of naming core issues. In the following essay he puts together three clearly stated sentences that offer a profound challenge to the local church and its catechesis: ". . . The interpretation of what it means to have faith in God is culturally conditioned. This creates an interpretive stance that is more complex than that of conventional models of Christian education. We are more a product of, yet blind to, our cultural conditioning than any other element that enters into our interpretation of Christianity."

Nelson reminds us that culture sets out for us its own norms but in an implicit, assumed way. We make judgments based on those norms, without considering the arbitrariness of either the norms or the resulting judgments. Socialization theory can help us pay attention to the culturally shaped presuppositions we bring to our religious faith. It can help us see the discrepancies between the self created by our society and the self summoned by God through Jesus. What is the distance between my self as created by my life in this particular social structure and my self as it is addressed by the Spirit of Jesus? The same question could be asked about our communal religious self.

Nelson adverts to the educationalists' criticism of the socialization approach and suggests that socialization as applied to Christian education or catechesis is actually about the problem of culture. Lifestyle itself harbors its own implicit hermeneutic strategies for interpreting life, sometimes in opposition to religious interpretation. "The problem with the congregation in modern America is [one of] creating and maintaining a community of people who are devoted to seeking first the Reign of God, using the Bible and tradition as their guide." These words of a Presbyterian echo profoundly in me as a Catholic.

C. Ellis Nelson calls for more study of the local church, and offers his own theoretical proposals about congregational change as occurring *(a)* via a core group of leaders; *(b)* by working over a considerable period of time; and *(c)* by being committed to specific kinds of changes. Catechetical leaders at all levels of the church take notice.

Further Reading

Nelson, C. Ellis. *How Faith Matures.* Louisville, KY: Westminster/John Knox Press, 1989.

———. *Helping Teenagers Grow Morally: A Guide for Adults.* Louisville, KY: Westminster/John Knox Press, 1992.

Socialization Revisited

C. ELLIS NELSON

In the fall of 1957, I was invited to join the faculty of Union Theological Seminary. I was acquainted with the educational method used at Union for the introductory required courses because I had been in residence at Union for my Ph.D. degree in the early 1950s. Senior professors in each field usually lectured two hours each week. In addition, the class was divided into small groups and a tutor, usually a Ph.D. candidate in that field, led a weekly discussion on the lectures and assigned readings. This educational method—with classes of about one hundred students—required that the professors present a formal lecture even though students were invited to interrupt with questions. Knowing that I would be expected to have a well-designed set of lectures on Christian education by September 1957 was a frightening challenge. Fortunately, I had seventeen years of experience in many different leadership roles in church education and an acquaintance with Union, Teacher's College and Columbia University professors and their writings, and a year to get ready.

At that time, the introductory course in Christian education was theoretical: that is, the professor presented an interpretation of theology and the social sciences related to the educational work of the church, usually considered to be the Sunday School. My immediate predecessor, Lewis J. Sherrill, published his theory in *The Gift of Power* (1955). His predecessor, Harrison Elliott, published his theory in the book *Can Religious Education Be Christian?* (1940), and his predecessor, George Albert Coe, published his as *A Social Theory of Religious Education* (1917). Today such a course is often described as an approach to Christian education, but the purpose is the same: to present a position that provides a goal, guidance for curriculum and teaching in church-sponsored schools and an educational strategy. In what follows I re-examine the theory I developed while teaching at Union.

Reprinted from *Union Seminary Quarterly Review* 47, nos. 3–4 (1993): 162–176. Copyright © 1993 by the *Union Seminary Quarterly Review.* Used with permission.

The Idea of Socialization

I spent the year before beginning my teaching at Union coordinating theology and data from the social sciences into a coherent theory. During my first year at Union I prepared full outlines of each lecture so the students would have a text to use during their weekly discussion groups. The first five of these lectures on the theological basis of Christian education were written out in full.[1] I used data from this course for the Sprunt Lectures (1965), which were published under the title *Where Faith Begins* (1967).

This approach to Christian education became known as a "socialization" model because it took seriously the way culture influences our lives and colors our beliefs and the way congregations communicate the meaning of faith through the process of socialization. The thesis was stated in these words: ". . . that faith is communicated by a community of believers and that the meaning of faith is developed by its members out of their history, by their interaction with each other, and in relation to the events that take place in their lives."[2]

This socialization idea was not original. I considered it a refurbishing of ancient wisdom about how faith in God is communicated. The Jewish Shemá, for example, described how the meaning of faith is carried along in a society and made practical in family and community settings (Deut. 6:4–9). By combining ancient wisdom about the critical role of the community in the formation of beliefs and character with modern studies of how society influences both the community and the person, this model is open to variations according to the special concerns of the author. My version of the socialization model has been described in various writings since the publication of *Where Faith Begins* and need not be repeated here. John H. Westerhoff[3] has called attention to the educational value of congregational liturgy.[3] William B. Kennedy has given considerable thought to the need for the reform of society in order that education liberate people from the cultural myths that enslave them.[4] It may be useful, however, to identify briefly what difference this socialization approach makes in the practice of Christian education.

First, the goal of Christian education is to help people develop faith in God. Although such a goal seems obvious today, it is different from the goal of the first generation of 20th century educators who expected to build the kingdom of God or the goals approved by the International Council of Religious Education, which emphasize the growth of persons toward seven objectives.[5] The word "God" is a problem in all models of Christian education, for the word stands for a variety of mental images. This is not a new problem; the Bible itself presents different images of God in different social/historical situations. But the goal of faith in God shifted the emphasis from what the educator does to what learners must do for themselves and puts curriculum and educational methods in a subordinate position. This goal considers teachers and group leaders more as guides or coaches than as experts who impart knowledge. Knowledge is an important goal of Christian education, but no more important than developing a Christian style of life. Both elements of Christianity are best expressed by the phrase "faith in God."

Second, the interpretation of what it means to have faith in God is culturally conditioned. This creates an interpretive stance that is more complex than that of conventional models of Christian education. We are more a product of, yet are blind to, our cultural conditioning than any other element that enters into our interpretation of Christianity. At the conscious level, we explain polygamy in the Old Testament, slavery in the New Testament, or the doctrine of "the divine rights of kings" in Western history as characteristic of past eras. This puts us in a position of assuming that our own culture is normative and blinds us to the biblical affirmation that our way of life is under God's judgment as were the ancient ones. The socialization model requires that we make judgments about how culture conditioned people in the past and an understanding of how culture has conditioned us in childhood before we had the mental ability to identify the meaning of faith and the complex culture in which we live.

The insistence that Christianity be interpreted from a cultural perspective makes curriculum and teaching somewhat different from conventional models. Rather than Christian education being a search for what to teach and how to adapt it to people of a certain age, the socialization model requires that we pay attention to the presuppositions we bring to our study of the Bible (interests, concerns or assumptions) and to the historical era out of which the biblical texts emerge. Moreover, this approach does not end with the result of such a study but expects us to ask, "What are we expected to be and do because we have faith in God?" Education is thus more than the acquisition of knowledge and beliefs; it is the development of a Christian style of life in harmony with the future God desires.

Third, the socialization model of Christian education starts with congregations and the education of adults. The Sunday School movement in 19th century United States was at first a para-church movement with an evangelical spirit. Led by laypeople, it flourished as a school for children and youth. Early 20th century Christian educators such as George Albert Coe and Harrison Elliott, and the International Council of Religious Education which they influenced, continued the strategy of a school as the agency of education. These religious educators assumed that if they taught children and youth about the kingdom of God these students would Christianize the social order when they became adults. But the strategy failed because most children grew up to have the values and beliefs of their parents and peers.

The worship and work of a congregation creates a mental image of what the Christian life ought to be and interprets beliefs in the light of events that are taking place. Parents are Christian educators in their home. Church officers, through their role as makers of budgets and policies, translate beliefs into practice. Church schoolteachers are provided a stance from which they interpret the Bible and church history. In addition, church members have an opportunity in their workplace to exhibit what the Gospel means to them. A church school for children and teenagers is an essential part of this strategy, but it is subordinated to the efforts of adults in the congregation to be "the body of Christ."

The Problems of the Socialization Model

The last paragraph, showing how adults in a congregation communicate the meaning of Christianity, is descriptive. The term "socialization" simply describes the process by which a person learns how to be a member of a specific group within society such as the Army, a gang of bank robbers, a congregation or a civic club. The term is neutral; it has no particular moral or religious meaning.

The socialization process as a *strategy* for communicating religious beliefs is clearly illustrated in cults. A religious cult led by a charismatic person who defines the cult's beliefs does not need Sunday schools to train children. The adults of the cult in their role as sub-leaders, parents and teachers, constantly communicate beliefs and enforce a lifestyle in harmony with the leader's wishes. The power of socialization in cults has been demonstrated in two recent tragic events. One was the Jonestown incident on 18 November 1978, when 909 persons on the command of their leader, the Reverend James W. Jones, drank cyanide and died. This cult, made up of members of the People's Temple, had moved from California to Guyana in order to be free to follow the dictates of Jones, believing him to be the Messiah. More recently David Koresh, who claimed to be Jesus Christ, led his group of believers to a compound east of Waco, Texas, to await the end of the world. There, on 19 April 1993, he persuaded 86 members of his cult to die with him rather than to surrender to the Federal Bureau of Alcohol, Tobacco and Firearms.

The same *strategy* (not the same beliefs) is present in religious groups that have endured for long periods of time. Denominations such as the Seventh-Day Adventists, Mormons or Jehovah's Witnesses have been able to maintain distinctive characteristics because their congregations

shape the beliefs and lifestyles of adults who in their role as church officers, teachers and parents communicate the meaning of their faith to
each other and to their children.

From these illustrations one could formulate this rule about the role
of formal education in the communication of religious beliefs and practices: the more deeply a religious community holds its beliefs about God
and practices a lifestyle based on those beliefs, the less it will need
schools to train its children in those beliefs and practices.

The problems of the socialization model are not with the process,
for that goes on in all organizations. These problems deal with: 1. Self
and Society, 2. Instruction, and 3. the Congregation. These parts are interrelated but they will be examined separately.

1. Self and Society

Religious sects and many conservative Protestant congregations know
that society does not support their beliefs and lifestyles. These groups
tend to withdraw from society or to insulate themselves as much as possible from secular influences. Many liberal congregations are aware of
their differences with society. These groups tend to get involved in programs designed to change society. The congregations to which the vast
majority of Protestants belong are seldom aware of any serious discrep-
ancy between their self and society.

Self-transcendence. Unless Protestants learn that society is no
longer their ally in living a Christian life, they will continue under the
spell of "the American way of life." Protestants have no difficulty in understanding how culture has shaped the lives of Africans, Japanese or
other non-Christian people; but middle-class Protestants have great difficulty understanding how our American/democratic/capitalist culture
has formed their beliefs and values. Part of the problem is rooted in our
history. The United States was founded by deeply committed Christians
who were determined to establish the rule of God in a new country.[6] The
documents which established our nation—from the Declaration of In-
dependence (1776) to the Bill of Rights (1791)—were written by leaders
who knew how to translate religious beliefs into a system of government. All through the 19th and into the early part of the 20th century, the
United States was under the influence of an evangelical Protestantism.
Thus, many Protestants are inclined to assume that culture supports
their religion or that culture has a religious slant which the church can
identify and translate into Christian beliefs. Both assumptions are wrong
because today American society is characterized by secular individualism more than by Christian values.[7]

Few Christian educators have been more concerned or have written more persuasively about this matter than William B. Kennedy. He described the role of assumptions and the problem of probing them in these words:

> Assumptions are values unquestioned by those holding them. In most cases they have been introjected into persons through their socialization in a particular community; they have become part of their way of perceiving reality. A society's assumptions form the foundation stories of its ideology, a set of values so basic as not to be questioned, upon which ongoing development of society's institutions and social processes occur. It is therefore difficult to reappraise our assumptions because, like our skin, they are so much a part of us that it hurts to separate them for scrutiny and critique.[8]

Paulo Freire, with whom Kennedy was associated in the education department of the World Council of Churches, described the way in which the ruling class in Brazil exploited the peasant class by myths that appeared to be a true description of social reality. These myths or assumptions were believed by the rulers as well as by the oppressed people. Some of the examples he cites are as follows: 1. *The society is free; people are free to work where they want. If they don't like their job, they can resign.* As a practical matter, people with low-paying jobs—especially peasants—are not free to move. They have few marketable skills and little knowledge about where to go to find work. 2. *The economic order is open; people can start a business and, perhaps, develop it into a large company.* Actually, it is difficult to start a business because money is needed for start-up costs. 3. *Education is available for all children at public expense up to the university level.* In Brazil only a small percentage of the children ever completed secondary education.[9]

With some modifications these assumptions describe American society also. Newspapers frequently report the stories of individuals who get a better job, start a successful new business or achieve distinction through education. But for many people these assumptions do not change their condition for the same reasons the Brazilian peasants are not able to act on these assumptions. These socially induced assumptions become eyeglasses through which all of life is viewed. We must, therefore, bring our culturally conditioned presuppositions to consciousness and evaluate them in the light of God's past revelation. This process of self-transcendence, as Kennedy noted, is extremely difficult to carry out because our socially induced assumptions are as much a part of us as our skin. There are, however, educational processes by which this can be done. Freire uses the term "dialogics" to describe a form of consciousness-raising that has been used in the feminist movement and by other groups feeling oppressed.[10] Kennedy has suggested a variety of ways Americans can identify and deal with socially induced assumptions.[11]

Self-transformation. Although helping people transcend themselves is a necessary first step, it is not sufficient for Christian education. Many people are able through education or critical analysis of their life experiences to change their basic assumptions about the meaning of life. This release from their cultural cage only frees them to make other assumptions. Education, to be Christian, must help adults learn how to have faith in God according to the scriptures and Christian tradition. This is an extremely complex process, but its distinctive features are clearly defined in the New Testament.

In New Testament terms we must be converted to the reign (kingdom) of God. The Greek word *metanoia* literally means a changed mind which will orient us to the things God considers important. The reign of God is a continuation of the Old Testament prophetic tradition which is critical of any society that uses power for itself rather than for the welfare of the people. The reign of God presents us with a difficult problem: what is the will of God for *us?* A partial answer can be given by separating perennial life situations from historically conditioned ones. Perennial life situations include matters related to evil, death, sin and personal ethics, such as honesty and respecting the rights of others. Beliefs about these life situations are rather consistent throughout the Bible and Christian tradition.

Our major problem for interpretation is the historically conditioned events and situations for which we have little biblical guidance. Issues related to abortion, the status of homosexuals in the church, the criteria for fighting a "just war," prolongation of life through medical support systems, genetic engineering, use of contraceptive devices, sharing economic resources, and population control are matters about which there is no Christian consensus. We tend to avoid these issues or we conduct discussions about them only long enough for all opinions to be expressed and then move on to other topics. Although finding the will of God for the events and conditions of our time for which we have little guidance seems impossible, there is hope. The Gospel writer John anticipated the problem and promised that the Holy Spirit would guide Christians into truth about God for new circumstances (John 16:12–15). The apostle Paul demonstrated how the congregation at Corinth could deal with its issues by discussion, prayer and practice of love toward each other (1 Cor. 12–4). These biblical references affirm that a process of honest seeking will produce answers for contemporary issues. I believe this process must be undertaken by adults in a congregation under the leadership of the pastor and this leads us to the critical importance of instruction.

2. Instruction

Because instruction is not the first consideration of the socialization model, this model has been criticized as not being properly concerned with ways a congregation should be educated.[12] This criticism is valid if one considers the socialization model to be only a description of how beliefs and values are transmitted in a community. The problem for Christian education is how to get the congregation to become more like the body of Christ (1 Cor. 12) and less like a place to celebrate secular values.[13] Ernest Paul Hess in a recent analysis of the socialization model found the problem to be ". . . openness to interpret and pass on the Christian tradition faithfully, to receive God's revelation in the present."[14] Hess has correctly identified the theological problem as hermeneutical. The education problem is adult education because adults are the congregational leaders. Beliefs and values are emotionally laden elements within the self that are formed from relationship with parents, relatives and adults who model these elements of the self. We must, therefore, start educational work with adults, for they are the parents, teachers and officers.

Some of the most important aspects of Christianity are learned by adults as they participate in worship, especially through music, celebration of the sacraments, prayers and sermons. Moreover, these elements of worship go counter to cultural values when they extol self-sacrifice for the good of the community, encourage compassion for those less fortunate, or provide a perspective by which current events might be judged. Informal learning in a congregation is continuous as adults participate in committee meetings and work together in various projects.

Formal instruction designed to develop adults' critical intelligence is essential but complicated. One reason is the task itself. We must (1) critique the assumptions we bring to our interpretation of Christianity, (2) understand the meaning of God's revelation in past events and determine what can be brought forward to our situation, and (3) formulate a lifestyle in harmony with the beliefs thus formulated. All of these goals are difficult to achieve; yet we cannot avoid them if we want to have a viable adult Christian education program in a congregation. Another reason for the complexity of adult education is the life situation of adults. Most adults have little motivation to study in order to achieve any of the three goals mentioned above. The assumptions which they bring to biblical interpretation are not easily open to examination. The image of God adults formed in early childhood and perhaps revised in teen years is satisfactory to them. The lifestyle, including religious practices of adults, is in harmony with their background and expectations. As a result, adult education in the typical Protestant congregation does little more than confirm or expand the adult's existing piety.

The socialization approach to Christian education starts with adult education in spite of the difficulties because this approach takes seriously the informal direct instruction that goes on constantly within a congregation. Unless adults within a congregation study to interpret Christianity properly and develop a lifestyle consistent with that interpretation, the informal direct instruction that takes place when adults interact with each other will reflect secular assumptions and values. Informal direct instruction is an unusually powerful form of education because it is event-related. When individuals are involved in an event where they must make a decision, the counsel of other adults who share the same idea about what God desires in that situation is extremely compelling. Thus, adults instruct each other as they manage the work of the church, share life situations and train each other on what to teach in the Sunday School. Informal direct instruction is also a powerful form of education within the family. In addition to the event-related nature of admonitions which adults give their children, there is the dependent nature of the relationship. Young children form a bond with their parents or adult care-givers and depend on them to interpret the world and how to respond to specific life situations. What parents say to children about death, use of money, what to do when a playmate hurts them, what television shows to watch and why, when to stand up for their rights, how to help a person in need, or the necessity for honesty is direct instruction of the most memorable kind. The Shemá states it this way: ". . . and you shall teach them [the words from God] diligently to your children, and shall talk of them when you sit in your house, and when you walk by the way, and when you lie down and when you rise" (Deut. 6:7).

3. Congregation

There is no uncertainty about the origin of congregations in Jewish life or about the centrality of congregations in New Testament times, especially in the writings of Paul. There is agreement that Christians form congregations in order to worship God, to share their lives with each other and to serve the community in which they live.[15] The problem with the congregation in modern America is creating and maintaining a community of people who are devoted to seeking first the reign of God, using the Bible and tradition as their guide (Matt. 7:33).

Why a Godly Community Is Elusive

Except for a few hermits, individuals cannot exist without association with other people. This natural urge to associate with others of similar interests has become more insistent as we face environmental dangers, economic uncertainty and the ever-present threat of street violence. Difficulties appear when we attempt to focus a congregation's attention on the requirements for being a community devoted to seeking first the reign of God. Why is this so?

One reason is the natural human desire of people who manage religious institutions to use them for their own power and prestige. One of many illustrations from the Old Testament is contained in the Song of the Vineyard, a poem already old in Isaiah's time (Isa. 5). A New Testament example is Jesus' frustration with the way religious leaders use religion to enhance their power and prestige (Matt. 23).

In recent times Thomas O'Dea has described how religion, when institutionalized, tends (1) to adjust the original message to fit social expectations, (2) to substitute ritual for experience with the divine, (3) to strengthen the organization at the expense of religion's original purpose, (4) to dilute its message in order to gain and hold followers, and (5) to form alliances with secular groups in order to achieve and maintain status.[16] Mircea Eliade, through his study of world religions, has noted that religion over time undergoes a process "of rationalization, degeneration and infantilization . . . as it comes to be interpreted on lower and lower planes."[17]

Another reason why it is difficult to develop a congregation into a God-centered community is the secular nature of American society. By secular I mean preoccupation with success, entertainment, self-enhancement projects, and, using Thorstein Veblen's term, "conspicuous consumption." This practical form of secularism exists along with a considerable amount of concern for compassion rooted in our Jewish and Christian tradition.[18] But the issue for the church is its ability to organize its activities according to Christian beliefs rather than according to the values of society. The history of this issue is not encouraging. According to Alasdair MacIntyre, American churches during the past two centuries have become the mediators of cultural values. This was due in part to industrialization and the rapid growth in science and technology. It was due in part to the role congregations played in assimilating the large number of immigrants. By serving the needs of immigrants, churches began to form the habit of doing what people wanted and in turn people formed a church-going habit. The results according to MacIntyre: "American religion has survived an industrial society only at the cost of itself becoming secular."[19] This explains why the United States is the only industrialized nation in the world, according to George Gallup, where 92% of the population states a religious preference and 68% say they are members of a church or synagogue. After fifty years of surveying American opinions, Gallup concludes, "While religion is highly popular in America, it is to a large extent superficial; it does not change people's lives to the degree one would expect from their level of professed faith."[20]

The Prospect for a Godly Congregation

Given the natural deterioration of religion when institutionalized and the secular nature of American society, the prospects for developing a congregation into a Godly community are not favorable. There has been an increase in membership in conservative and evangelical congregations in recent years. Sect-type churches continue to grow and some evangelists draw big crowds. But, as Gallup observed, "it does not change people's lives." Moreover, we do not have studies of congregations which will help us understand how congregations can become more oriented to God's desires.

We have only two ethnographic studies of congregations: one is of an Orthodox Jewish congregation located in the northeast and the other is of a 91 member Black Pentecostal church in Pittsburgh.[21]

The studies we have of white Protestant churches are combined with some special concern of the investigator. Nancy Ammerman's study of a fundamentalist congregation opens up the ideology and lifestyle of that form of faith.[22] Jeffrey Hadden has chronicled the events in the life of a congregation formed to foster social action.[23] Mary Hawkes, for her doctoral dissertation in the Union/Teacher's College doctoral program, appraised the adult education program of a New Jersey congregation.[24] Steven Warner has provided a sociological analysis of a church in Mendocino, California, which moved from a liberal to an evangelical theological position.[25] Michael H. Ducey has provided a case study of four mainline white Protestant congregations in Chicago during the social upheaval of the late 1960s and early 1970s.[26] A group of professors reviewed and commented on the yearlong crisis in the life of a Presbyterian church in Ohio.[27] James Hopewell cited short versions of the history and work of several congregations in his analysis of how congregations develop a self-image.[28] Hartford Theological Seminary and the Center for Church and Community Ministries (Chicago) have produced excellent studies of congregations with a special reference to their concern for the community in which they are located.

We do not have studies of congregations where the minister, with the approval and support of lay leaders, attempted to change its ethos, that is, the spirit that animates the congregation.

Needed Research

All of the studies cited above are helpful in describing how the interaction of people in a congregation creates a culture which perpetuates itself by the socialization process. Only three of those studies, however, deal with deliberate efforts to change the culture of a congregation. The Mendocino, California, congregation was changed from a liberal to a conservative theological outlook. The Ohio congregation spent a year discussing the plight of Central American political refugees and then voted to become a sanctuary church. There has been no follow-up study, so we do not know whether there was any lasting change in congregational ethos. Carl Dudley, through the Center for Church and Community Ministries, has accumulated considerable data about how congregations can become aware of their identity and then become more involved in ministry to the community.[29]

What we need is careful research that tests how congregations change their ethos. Research of this kind would require (1) a theory of how a congregation changes, (2) a commitment on the part of the minister and official board to participate in the research for a period of time, (3) agreement on the change that is desired, (4) an appraisal of what the congregational identity is at the start and end of the research, and (5) an evaluation of the original theory and the research method that is used.

Since all of these five items in a research project on congregational change can be interpreted differently, I will describe my proposals as follows.

(1) My theory is that congregations change if the ministers, with the support and help of a small group of leaders, have a vision of what the mission of the church should be and are dedicated to making that vision a reality. This theory comes from political scientists who have observed this process of change.[30] It is also supported by church officials who worked with congregations over a long period of time.

(2) Time is essential for this research. Change in beliefs and practice comes about slowly. Lacking any studies, I would guess that the minimum time for such a study should be three years, but a five-year time span would produce more dependable results. The minister would be required to commit himself or herself for that period of time because the theory of change requires continuity of leadership.

(3) Agreement on desirable changes is complex. Dudley's work is the most useful guide we have because he helped congregations identify themselves as a preparation for enlarging their ministry to include service to the community. Such changes are rooted in beliefs that are shared by Christians of liberal and conservative theologies. Moreover, these changes in service to the community can be observed and documented. Research on changing the ethos of a congregation is more complicated because the leaders of the congregation will need to develop a mission statement or a set of goals acceptable to most of the members. Although there are several ways to produce a set of goals, I propose that at the center of the quest be this question: What are we in this congregation to be and do because we are Christians? This question, adapted from Paul Lehmann, requires a considerable amount of self-analysis as well as a serious consideration of the nature of God from a study of the Bible and tradition.[31] Although this quest for the will of God is elusive and the results are tentative, it is possible to identify a few major goals and to specify events or changes that would indicate whether progress is being made toward the goals.

There are probably several ways congregational leaders can motivate people to move toward the accepted goals. My suggestion is for the minister to form a central study group (CSG). The CSG is to be led by the minister and deal week by week with contemporary issues—personal and social—in relation to the Bible and tradition. There are practical matters related to a CSG (such as selection of members, size of the group, relation to other classes in the congregation and connection to official committees) that I have discussed elsewhere.[32] Moreover, there are probably good ways to deal with these matters other than the ways I have suggested. But the critical matter is to create a group of people at the center of the life of the congregation which has a vision of what is needed and a dedication to make that vision a reality.

(4) It is essential that an appraisal be made of where the congregation is at the beginning and end of the project. There should be no problem with an appraisal of the formal aspects of the congregation. An inventory of the congregation's programs, use of money (budget), statement of mission of the congregation if one has been adopted, attendance, physical facilities and how they are used, and other manifestations of congregational life can be identified and compared at the beginning and the end of the project. Making an appraisal of changes that have been made in the lives of members of the congregation and the ethos of the congregation at the beginning and end of the project is going to be extremely complex. Survey-type questions can be used but they have limited value. Interviews are difficult to interpret in general terms. And

congregational ethos will be almost impossible to quantify; yet people make judgments about this matter, so some assessment can be made. In addition, researchers should attempt to find out what elements in the project were most effective in changing members' understanding of themselves and their vision of what the congregation should be and do.

(5) Finally, such a research project should evaluate the theory of congregational change used in the project, the methods that were used to bring about the change and the way the socialization process functioned to influence new members, children and youth.

Until we design and carry through research of the kind described above, we will be dependent on studies of congregations that explain what they are, rather than what they can be. The key element in this proposed research is a deliberate effort to change a congregation's ethos. Perhaps the statement credited to Kurt Lewin is helpful: "If you want to understand an organization, attempt to change it!" By a deliberate effort to change the ethos of a congregation, we may be better able to understand how congregations become more attuned to God's will for them.

NOTES

1. These five lectures have been published in *Growth in Grace and Knowledge* (Austin, TX: Nortex Press, 1992), 81–149.

2. C. Ellis Nelson, *Where Faith Begins* (Richmond, VA: John Knox Press, 1967), 10.

3. John H. Westerhoff, *Learning Through Liturgy* (New York: Seabury Press, 1978).

4. Alice F. Evans, Robert A. Evans, and William B. Kennedy, *Pedagogies for the Non-Poor* (Maryknoll, NY: Orbis Books, 1987), 232–257.

5. William B. Kennedy's brief history of how Christian education changed during the period from 1935 to 1985 documents this shift in goals. See also David W. Lotz, ed., *Altered Landscapes* (Grand Rapids, MI: William B. Eerdmans, 1989), 280–296.

6. Sacvan Bercovitch, *The Puritan Origins of the American Self* (New Haven, CT: Yale University Press, 1975).

7. C. Ellis Nelson, *How Faith Matures* (Louisville, KY: Westminster/John Knox Press, 1989), 21–42.

8. William B. Kennedy, "Toward Reappraising Some Inherited Assumptions About Religious Education in the U.S.," *Religious Education* 76 (September–October 1981): 467.

9. Paulo Freire, *Pedagogy of the Oppressed* (New York: Herder and Herder, 1970), 135.

10. Freire, 75–119.

11. William B. Kennedy, "Ideology and Education: A Fresh Approach for Religious Education," *Religious Education* 80 (Summer 1985): 331–344.

12. Thomas H. Groome, *Christian Religious Education* (San Francisco: Harper and Row, 1980), 126.

13. The last chapter of *Where Faith Begins* assumes that the congregation is the place where faith in God is fostered and celebrated. It also assumes that congregations can and do corrupt the meaning of faith in God. The chapter ends with the recognition that "apathy, conformity, or downright hostility to change lies beneath the surface of the average congregation." Under these conditions the book ends with the suggestion that it may be necessary to form new congregations "to actualize the ministry of Christ . . ." (211).

14. Ernest Paul Hess, *Christian Identity and Openness: A Theologically Informed Hermeneutical Approach to Christian Education*, PhD diss., Princeton Theological Seminary, 1991 (Ann Arbor, MI: UMI, 1992, no. 9127013), 100.

15. Bruce C. Birch, "Memory in Congregational Life," in *Congregations: Their Power to Form and Transform*, ed. C. Ellis Nelson (Atlanta: John Knox Press, 1988), 20–43.

16. Thomas F. O'Dea, *The Sociology of Religion* (Englewood Cliffs, NJ: Prentice-Hall, 1966), 90–97.

17. Mircea Eliade, *Patterns in Comparative Religion* (New York: Sheed and Ward, 1958), 444–445.

18. Robert Wuthnow, *Acts of Compassion* (Princeton, NJ: Princeton University Press, 1991).

19. Alasdair MacIntyre, *Secularization and Moral Change* (London: Oxford University Press, 1967), 32.

20. George Gallup, *The People's Religion: American Faith in the 90s* (New York: Macmillan, 1989), 16, 21.

21. Samuel C. Heilman, *Synagogue Life* (Chicago: University of Chicago Press, 1973). Melvin D. Williams, *Community in a Black Pentecostal Church* (Prospect Heights, IL: Waveland Press, 1974).

22. Nancy T. Ammerman, *Bible Believers: Fundamentalists in the Modern World* (New Brunswick, NJ: Rutgers University Press, 1987).

23. Jeffrey K. Hadden, *Gideon's Gang: A Case Study of the Church in Social Action* (New York: United Church Press, 1974).

24. Mary N. Hawkes, *The Church as Nurturing Faith Community: A Study in One Congregation*, diss., Columbia University, Teacher's College, 1983.

25. Stephen R. Warner, *New Wine in Old Wineskins* (Berkeley, CA: University of California Press, 1988).

26. Michael H. Ducey, *Sunday Morning* (New York: Free Press, 1977).

27. Nelle G. Slater, *Tensions Between Citizenship and Discipleship* (New York: Pilgrim Press, 1989).

28. James F. Hopewell, *Congregation* (Philadelphia: Fortress, 1987).

29. Carl S. Dudley, *Basic Steps Toward Community Ministry* (Washington, DC: Alban Institute, 1991).

30. Robert A. Dahl, *A Preface to Democratic Theory* (Chicago: University of Chicago Press, 1956), 132.

31. Paul L. Lehmann, *Ethics in a Christian Context* (New York: Harper and Row, 1963) 131, 159.

32. See Nelson, *How Faith Matures*, 204–212.

READING 8
Introduction

David Power wrote the following:

> Perhaps liturgical inculturation never takes place in our times because people are rarely invited to express their reaction to the Gospel, or their faith in Jesus Christ, in their own way. They are given models of doctrinal belief and of prayer to follow, instead of being expected to generate their own expressions of belief and prayer.[1]

Power's essay chosen for this *Sourcebook* exposes the implications of this idea for our day.

As with C. Ellis Nelson's essay above, I have selected David Power's "Households of Faith" mainly because it has become so influential in my own thinking. At first reading, it raised for me issues I had not until then considered in a focused way. These issues stayed with me, and I found myself encouraging many to read this particular piece and, of course, assigning it as required reading in some of my catechetical courses. The issues Power raises are catechetical ones in the sense that they deal with the sacramental power of a local church, a small household of faith. Indeed, Power here radicalizes the issues of inculturation and of local theology.

What initially appears to be a need surfacing among a minority of Christians, Power discerns as a need in the church at large. This is the need for groups of people to struggle face-to-face in the zone of worship with the problem of discipleship in our time. Here, "face-to-face" implies mouth-to-mouth, speaking about ongoing struggles to be faithful to the Jesus tradition. This movement to find new participatory ecclesial structures is not destructive of unity but rather offers a life-giving mix of formal and informal groupings.

Power finds in the Middle Ages evidence that such a movement is part of our tradition. "A grassroots lay movement, a search for new forms of common evangelical life [especially voluntary poverty] attuned to the times, attentiveness to the lot of the poor, and new forms of popular devotion" are some of the characteristics of the renewal movements in the eleventh through fourteenth centuries. For such groups, discipleship meant an active ministry of reflecting and carrying out their inconvenient commitments to the poor. In a time when the cultural colonization of the human spirit by the forces of consumer capitalism has been so efficient, readers will find here integral catechetical impulses that need to be reclaimed.

1. David Power, "Liturgy and Culture," *East Asian Pastoral Review* 21, no. 4 (1984): 348.

Households of Faith in the Coming Church

DAVID N. POWER

While there are those who pursue the model of parish reorganization and revitalization as the way to renew church life and foster Christian community, the emergence of informal groups of believers and of small communities which have little to do with ecclesiastical and even confessional boundaries is of indisputable significance for present and future. Whether some of these will in time replace current official groupings and structures, or whether they will be but a significant phenomenon in a larger church, is not necessary to determine at this stage. Suffice to say that in talking of households of faith in the coming church, it is of such groups that I speak.

The church has always had its plenty of small, informal and often spontaneous groups, associations and communities. One cannot write the history of the church without taking note of them, of their appearance, of their motivations, of their accommodation within the larger church, of their eventual survival or disappearance. They have, however, never been as much studied and analyzed as in today's church, due in great part to the insights provided by sociology and psychology, which greatly assist us in grasping their origins, qualities, motivations and significance. Some of these insights make us acutely aware of how ambiguous a cultural, social and religious phenomenon is this current trend to smaller church or religious groupings. It is not possible to canonize the movement and all its various manifestations without ado.

The challenge to be addressed here is threefold. First, is it possible to isolate and outline the issues at stake? In other words, what are the cultural and social factors that perhaps lie beneath the movement and that are generally verified, no matter how diverse the groups or communities may be? Here, it is necessary to rely largely on the data and insights provided by sociology. Secondly, can a theologian draw on tradition and systematic reflection in offering some Christian or faith

Reprinted from *Worship* 57, no. 3 (May 1983): 237–254. Copyright © 1983 by *Worship*. Used with permission.

assessment of this movement, as well as some suggestions about what it could mean in the future? Thirdly, can a liturgist look to liturgical history to explain some of the emergent prayer-forms and to assess how they may belong in a liturgy which serves the transformation of these groups into ecclesial bodies that testify to Christ's power and presence, and prophetically serve the reign of justice and peace promised in Christ's death and resurrection?

Groups and Their Significance

As already indicated, it needs to be made clear from the outset that in addressing the theme of households of faith I am making the choice of considering groups that belong outside formal structures, such as the parish, and cannot simply therefore be seen as ways of "building community" in a parish, such as the creation of block groups and the occasional holding of Mass in homes throughout the parish. Such innovations have their purpose and may even have affinities with what I am addressing. However, I believe that the cause of serious reflection and healthy critique is better served by taking account of communities wherein disenchantment with the established order and with canonically recognized forms of community organization, ministry and leadership is more obvious. A creative critique of the established ecclesiastical order, supported by a living proposal of alternative models, is needed.

Some groups do indeed seem to be based on fear and the need for mobilization, and respond to highly ambiguous forms of charismatic and autocratic leadership. Others, however, display a strong sense of theocentric freedom, a freedom received as gift of the Spirit. This then becomes a source of energy and of charisms of service, as well as of free decision and choice, dominated by the persuasion of the gift of God's love and mercy. Where communities possess such freedom, structures develop which are more participatory than in the established order. Needless to say, there are communities which betray elements of both these extremes. This is not surprising if both are seen as responses to the same dilemmas of contemporary life and religious belonging. It can also be noted at this point that some groups form around a concentration of interest in the religious well-being of their members, whereas others have a more distinct sense of wanting to expend their energies in transforming society.

The whole movement, comprehensive of its varied forms, has to be related to the social and cultural pressures of our age. A basic question, explaining why the forms of community can be so diverse, seems to be whether it is possible to find reality and an authentic sense of self within contemporary society, or whether one discovers these despite it. Thus, to a crisis of authority in all its forms there is linked a crisis of values. To a crisis of the interpersonal there is linked a crisis of personal autonomy. To a crisis of identity there is linked a crisis of intimacy. To a crisis of religious belonging there is linked a crisis of missions.

Theological Reflection

Intimacy, identity, the interpersonal, authority, mission and the degree of participation in the life of a body are all issues important to the church's nature and its presence in society. We cannot fully recognize the significance of new households and their possible future unless it is seen that they carry within themselves the search for a response to what can only be described as a breakdown in church life, which has in fact over centuries become largely nonparticipatory. This can be ascribed to various factors, such as sacralization, the split between the clergy and the laity or the domination of bourgeois values. A more fundamental description would be that there has been a distortion of Christian symbols, central to the distortion of communications within the church, which has prevented fuller participation of all baptized members in its life, while also impeding the mission of the church in serving society, particularly its lesser members. New groups in one way or another respond to this distortion, in terms which can be described as facing the crisis of the religious imagination. One need only think here of how the symbols of the presence of Jesus Christ have been distorted in meaning, by being used and treated as representative images, to the suffocation of the fuller human and spiritual reality with which this presence is involved. This of course very much affects the question of church leadership, ministry and liturgy. Reductionism obstructs communication, as when bread and wine come to represent only the physical body and blood of Christ, and cease to symbolize the community participating in his life and mystery, as one in him, the new creation in Jesus Christ.

One of the greatest problems in this regard is that the Catholic Church in legitimating its own identity is "organization blind."[1] That is to say, because it adopts certain social structures as essential to its very identity as the church of Christ, it has no real eye for the weaknesses of the organization and little flexibility in allowing for more participatory structures, which, however, is the direction taken by "household churches." As I have quoted elsewhere, "it is not destruction, but growing complexity and diversity, of ecclesiastical organization, a deliberate mixing of formal and informal structural elements, which seems to offer the greatest hopes for the future of the Church as a religious organization."[2]

While attention to this issue of structures cannot be avoided, one has to look to the fundamental reality of community in Christ to assess what is currently coming to pass among us. It is, therefore, to evangelical poverty, to concern for the poor and to a search for the living meaning of poverty in Christ that I would like to make appeal as a key to the future possibilities of households of the faith. By way of insight into this, a parallel is suggested with the twelfth and thirteenth centuries, one made as far back as 1959 by Marie-Dominique Chenu, when he wrote of what was then a very problematic issue, namely, worker-priests and their communities: "Taking a vow of poverty meant, in the thirteenth century, refusing categorically, institutionally, economically, the feudal régime of the Church, the 'benefices,' the collection of tithes, even when sweetened by charitable and apostolic purposes. . . . The mendicant friars rejected feudalism just as today the *Mission de France* has broken its solidarity with capitalism: the same evangelical, not ideological, violence. It is the return to the Gospel which requires the break with the collective superstructures, as well as with personal disorders."[3]

It seems to me that it is true of every renewal movement in the history of the church that, in a way peculiar to its own time and in face of the second temptation, to wit an accommodation with the prevalent temporal power, it has had at its core a renewed awareness of the exigencies of evangelical poverty. This awareness combines the ideal of the Jerusalem community, as described by Luke (Acts 2:42), with the ideal of the community of Jesus with his disciples, both of which ideals are seen as a participation in Christ's mystery in the form of a radical experience and overturning of human poverty. Michel Mollat in his studies on ecclesial poverty ascribes an originality to Francis of Assisi, which is in a way the originality of all renewal movements: "The originality of Francis consists less in an intellectual conception of poverty than in the manner in which he took up the challenges of his time to poverty. It would be too simple to say that he did not expect the poor man to come to apply to him, too simple to affirm that he went toward him. The real innovation is to have placed himself side by side with the poor man and to have sought to rehabilitate him in his own eyes, by bringing him a message against poverty in the name of a victory over poverty. It was to proclaim the dignity of the poor man for himself, not only as an image of Jesus Christ but because Jesus loved him for himself. This explains the episode of the 'kissing of the leper.'"[4]

In all of this, there is not only an affinity with the poverty of Jesus in his self-emptying and a quest for community without barriers, divisions and discriminations, but there is also a response to the deviations of society in its uses of power and wealth, a response based on a certain intimacy with the marginal and debased. Indeed, no response is possible without this intimacy, since it is the poor who provide the diagnosis of a society's ills.

A grassroots lay movement, a search for new forms of common evangelical life, attuned to the times, attentiveness to the lot of the poor, and new forms of popular devotion, these seem to have been the characteristics of the religious renewal movement of the twelfth and thirteenth centuries, of which the principal reminder today is the mendicant orders. A group typical of that age are those known as the *Humiliati*, or Humble Ones, of whom Lester Little notes: "The Humiliati of those early days were mostly laymen, some married who continued to live at home with their families, or else unmarried or formerly married who chose to live a common life in the religious manner. . . . in addition to the personal reformation of their inner lives, the Humiliati sought to reach out into society to oppose actively the enemies of the Christian faith. The Humiliati not only claimed to follow the model of apostolic simplicity in their lives, but with uncommon audacity engaged in the apostolic act of preaching the Christian faith publicly."[5]

By 1201, when they received official recognition from Innocent III,[6] they had "evolved into an officially sanctioned order of the church, with three variant forms of life—canonical, monastic and lay—for both men and women."[7] Important here is to note the continuation of the third order for people who, because of conjugal and familial ties, could not adopt the fuller forms of common life, but kept the basic aspirations: "The particular piety of these laymen," writes Little, "consisted in their fasting two days a week, saying the Lord's Prayer before and after dinner, and reciting the seven canonical hours. They were to wear simple clothing, and should any of their number become ill or face some other kind of hardship, the others were to come to his aid; in case of death, to the aid of the departed person's soul and family."[8]

Those who were not literate did not recite the canonical hours, but recited the Lord's Prayer a certain number of times a day instead. All extended their charity in a particular way to embrace the poor and downtrodden, with special attention to lepers, and sought to live by the work of their own hands.

Mollat, Chenu and Little have all shown how movements of this sort constituted a Christian response to the changing social and economic scene, as Europe moved out of a feudal to a merchant economy, and adopted more communal power structures for the government of society. At the same time, they have pointed out that the scholars associated with the movement, represented particularly by the friars, did not address themselves only to the members of the orders or fraternities, but sought to evolve a moral teaching and a spirituality suited to all Christians, granted that this had its grounding in the vision and way of life of the renewal movement.[9]

One of course cannot talk of this age without recognizing its violence, the social, political, economic and religious violence, as well as the heresies and the exaggerations in forms of piety. That is, however, one of the features that makes it a distant mirror to our times. Society was in upheaval on all fronts, all were struggling to come to terms with it, but in the midst of this struggle there were those who, resisting the deviations, found a new evangelical way of life and new forms of piety. There were indeed the exaggerations leading to heresy, and the valid insights unjustly dismissed as unorthodox, as well as the anti-Semitism, too easily tolerated or even promoted by church leaders. There was popular violence, and there were many forms of institutional violence. It is only by putting together the renewal movements and the deviations that one understands the age. Change is met in many ways, and one looks to the age to see both the failings and the deep evangelical insights.

One may also see how church authority accommodated itself to the scene. The reactions of pontiffs such as Innocent III are often applauded by church historians because they took advantage of the evangelical movement and through it fostered a strong church unity, under the increasing power of the papacy. They are, however, also criticized because they maintained and even strengthened the hierarchical and clerical domination of the church.[10] In particular, there was a failure on the part of liturgists and church authority to allow room in official worship for the new forms of piety and devotion, for a popular expression of faith, so that there remained and increased a gap between liturgy and popular piety, marked by much strong faith on the part of the people but also by extravagances. Some of the worst extravagances, of course, such as the endowment of chantries, multiplication of Masses and absolute ordination, were the result of an accommodation of the clergy to the needs of the rich, and clerical manipulation of popular piety.

Today, the call for the church to be the church of the poor has been sounded, and many forms of evangelical lifestyle are being tried. It is in the lives of those who live a way of life in contrast with some of our more public aspirations, who are in touch with the experience of the suffering and resurrection of Jesus Christ, that many of the world's ills are brought to light. They are remarkably like those of the twelfth and thirteenth centuries: violence, censure of outcasts, a search for a share in the new forms of power, the sophistication of special kinds of knowledge. It is the contrast between certain styles of life and the violence of the times that shows the link between evangelical poverty and emancipatory praxis, since those who capture our attention are those who, while seeking community and simplicity of life for themselves, are also anxious to find ways whereby to release from bondage those who are the victims of the century's greatness. As we know, this interest has been taken up by some of the leading scholars of the day, especially in the theology of Jesus Christ. For them, christology is a praxis, because it is a memory, couched in narrative form, and inclusive of the memory of all suffering and poverty.[11]

Hence one may summarily say of households of faith that respond most fully to the Gospel: (a) the form of life will be that of evangelical poverty; (b) the key to their relation to society will be emancipatory praxis, the desire and the struggle to come to the release of those who suffer bondage in the midst of progress, a resistance to the many forms of violence whereby the poor are oppressed; (c) their liturgies will be forceful commemorations of the suffering and resurrection of Jesus Christ, into which will be gathered a memory of all suffering and of all the forgotten and unnamed of past and present; (d) because their members possess a strong sense of the freedom that comes with the gift of the Spirit, they will develop community structures that are participatory and respectful of a variety and multiplicity of gifts.

Liturgy

Sociological investigations should make us very cautious about ascribing reasons either for decrease in church membership and in worship participation, or for increase in the membership of some churches. One thing, however, that does seem to emerge is that the role of ritual or sacrament in maintaining commitments, or in influencing departures, is not clearly focused. If it is not really at the heart of things, this fact may be more symptom than cause. Yet a theologian or liturgist might make bold to say that without good and convincing celebration, ecclesial life as participation in Christ's mystery does not survive, whatever other functions an ecclesiastical organization or group experiences may serve.

The liturgical expression of households of faith, where the interpersonal is put in evidence, is not a straightforward implementation of the new rites that have received official approval. Indeed, their very appreciation of the ways in which the revisions are based on tradition means that they are put into practice with considerable flexibility and with no little creativity on the part of individual communities. In writing of the right of a community to a priest, which is in effect its right to Eucharist, Edward Schillebeeckx not only highlights the contrast of grassroots communities with more formal structures, and the emancipatory nature of their apostolic sense, but he also points out the contrast of their liturgies, which are more participatory and simple than what one often finds in older traditions. These liturgies are more flexible, allow more room for adaptation, and raise the issue of liturgical ministries in new ways.[12]

The difficulties experienced in the renewal of liturgy and sacrament in mainstream churches might well be described in this quotation from Richard Fenn: "The apparently minor role of ritual in [some recent sociological studies on churches] may reflect the gap between the church's myths and its current reality. The myth of a Christian community is difficult to sustain when the community has scattered, leaving only families and individuals, just as the myth of the people of God is difficult to sustain when the clergy are part executive, part professional, and only partly charismatic at best. The myth of a spiritual body is difficult to sustain when the church has itself become a hierarchical organization with control increasingly centralized in bureaucratic offices. Under these conditions the context of a ritual may provide very poor acoustics for the music of the soul. Conversely, when churches write and impose new liturgies on their members, it may be difficult for the laity to put their heart and soul into the new lines for at least one generation, regardless of the scholastic merits of the new versions, and some would argue that a bureaucratized church can hardly be expected to provide new rites that enable the spirit to soar."[13]

Elsewhere in the review, the same author describes an attitude to worship which may be central to the dislocation of liturgy: "Worship no longer *constitutes* the church, but the church engages in many activities of which some might be called worship. If worship is uneventful, then its time and place must be moved, some suggest, so that the church's celebrations can catch the eventfulness of secular occasions. . . . The key notion . . . is of the congregation as an 'audience'. . . ."[14]

In looking into the mirror of the twelfth and thirteenth centuries once more, one can note the forms of piety and devotion which held the populace and the fraternities, but which were not properly (if at all) integrated into official liturgies. There was the importance given to the recitation of the Lord's Prayer, then completed by the Hail Mary, giving us eventually the Rosary, in recent times highly promoted by Sovereign Pontiffs, but dubbed "devotion" and "nonliturgical." Indeed, through the centuries this form of prayer was allowed to develop almost in opposition to liturgy, quite unintegrated into the liturgical cycle, even though it has profoundly biblical and popular roots. In short, the issue of how such prayer, with its immense popular appeal and simplicity, could be integrated into liturgy never seems to have been faced.

There was also at the time of which we are speaking a great increase in pilgrimages and processions, public and cultural expressions of unity and strength, where the little people of the time could experience their solidarity and express their devotion. The emphasis of these devotions on the humanity of Jesus Christ contrasted with the then current sacramental emphasis on his divinity.

If the people largely played the role of audience and recipient in the Mass and sacramental worship, they did have other ministries and devotions which took the person as subject seriously and which sought to promote and enhance personal conversion and commitment. Preaching, confession and works of penance seem to have gone hand in hand in this regard, since their joint purpose was the conversion and spiritual growth of the human person.

As Little notes in his study, the reform movements showed a deep appreciation of the spiritual worth of the laity generally, and of women in particular.[15] They wanted to break down the perception of society's religious function as the responsibility and domain of the few. Preaching, confession and penance were important instruments in proposing and implementing personal piety and an apostolic way of life among the laity. It was in accordance with their aim that some provision was made for lay preaching and for confession to laypersons. Such practices were not set up in opposition to the role of ordained preachers and confessors, but the extension of these functions to laypersons was justified by an appeal to the importance of the act involved. Current discussion of these matters makes us painfully aware that the alternate argument, stressing the status of the minister, in time prevailed over the possibilities of more active lay involvement. Precisely because of current needs, it seems helpful to note that the question went hand in hand with the development of an evangelical way of life and with a basically New Testament image of Christian fellowship.

Some of the most interesting things liturgically occurred within reform groups that are unfortunately known to history only as heretical, though now it would appear that it was extremes in these groups rather than their mainstream that entered into a collision course with ecclesiastical authority or subscribed to christianly untenable beliefs.[16] The Catharist Church, for example, practiced a ceremony called the *consolamentum*, described as follows: "The formal ceremonies of the Catharist Church . . . were markedly simple, being oriented about a view of what the early church must have been like. . . . In the most important of Catharist ceremonies, the consolamentum, a ceremony of spiritual baptism, the believer gained forgiveness for all his sins, and the perfected ones, those who had been through the same ceremony, administered baptism to the believer by placing their right hands upon him. They did so as 'true Christians, instructed by the primitive church.' In one of the surviving descriptions of this ritual, the reader is urged not to look down upon his earlier baptism in the Roman Church, but to receive his Catharist baptism ('the holy consecration of Christ') as a supplement to that which was insufficient for his salvation. An abbreviated and simplified form of the consolamentum was made available for the sick and dying."[17]

Of similar interest is the *fractio panis* practiced by the Waldensians. This was a simple way of celebrating the Lord's Supper, based on the model of the Last Supper narrative in the New Testament, wherein the simplicity of style and accessibility to the faithful were the major occasions. Again, it is important to note that opposition to church authority or subscription to doctrines at odds with official intentions were not at the base of this development, but that this kind of opposition only came with time, when a harmonious integration of views and practices seemed to become impossible.[18]

From the few examples given, one can see a trend in liturgy toward simplicity of style, lay participation, personal faith, devotion to God's word, devotion to the humanity of Jesus, all gathered together under the umbrella of the desire to return to Gospel models of Christian life and Christian worship. For all the obvious difference between that age and ours, we can sense readily enough similar desires in contemporary households of faith, as well as similar hazards of nonintegration with the established order. How successful can the dialectic be today?

The development of good liturgy, expressive of what the church is, rather than an act which it does, will likewise be rooted in community experience in households of faith for the coming church. Similarly important are the quest for evangelical and apostolic community, the existence of fellowships of the baptized intent on a baptismal rather than on a clerical spirituality, the desire for simplicity in style, the bias against any form of discrimination, the search for contemporary forms of piety, and a christological focus which has been given keen systematic articulation in what are called "christologies from below," highlighting the solidarity of Jesus with the human condition, in particular with those who suffer and are canceled out from the pages of history.

Some of the characteristics and forms of liturgical expression appropriate to households of the faith in the coming church might well appear from what has been said about participatory structures, about Christian freedom in the Spirit, about evangelical poverty, and about the trends of piety in the twelfth and thirteenth centuries that were not well integrated into official worship.

First of all, good worship is based on an aesthetic appreciation of the sacramentality of life and gives it authentic, albeit simple, expression, even while allowing it to be challenged and transformed by the memory of Jesus Christ. It is a worship rooted in the experience of home and family, of communities that are able to transcend family ties by making of a more diverse company "mother, father, brother and sister," keeping the interpersonal and the domestic in their style of living and caring. A first step in good liturgy is the ritualization of core activities and things of community life and community care. The sacrament is not actually the common table itself, or the nursing given to the sick, or the domestic and agrarian uses of water, but it is the ritualization of these acts, the expression of their meaning in some simple but aesthetic form, such as the breaking of a loaf of bread, the pouring of water, the sharing of a common cup, the laying on of hands. Such ritualized forms must allow participants both to see their lives and fundamental acts of shared care and identity reflected in them and at the same time to stand back from life and its activities in order to perceive their meaning and the larger perspective of mystery within which they belong. Discussions about the correct bread recipe, or about what oil to use, or about who may lay hands on whom, are at bottom perverse, since they fail to understand that the intent of basic ritual instruments and gestures is to let the things of life stand forth, in beauty and in mystery. Hence the value of a simple place, of a table, of bread and wine, of oil and water, of lights and shades of darkness, or care-full touch, of the awe apparent in a kiss of peace. In effect, for Christian liturgy this does mean a return to the most primitive and most simple symbols, even though the bread recipes are different from the one used in the upper room.

Such basic symbols and rituals, however, have to be paired with the challenge to barriers and divisions enunciated in the story and remembrance of Jesus Christ. The natural ritual tendency may be to sacramentalize one's own family or kin, one's own ethnic group, one's own social class where one feels at home, one's peers in age and profession, since such are the groups in which one is most secure, and indeed instinctively most aware of the sacred powers that govern life, and most protected against the chaos that could intrude. The challenge of Christian remembrance is to perform the same gestures of sharing and intimacy, to respect and reverence the things of common life, to stand in awe before the sacred and in trust against evil, in settings and groups where divisions and discriminations have no entry. Perhaps this might be stated by saying that Christian worship has to express in ritual, and at the same time parabolic, form an ethic of compassion, where it is the vulnerability of life, the suffering of the other person, the being denied respect and reverence and even name that calls forth the common bond of faith in God's promise. Each one enters into Christian worship conscious of personal vulnerability, naked before Christ and naked with Christ, and alert to this reality in those with whom the gathering is formed, and open to whomsoever approaches seeking compassion and blessedness. This is why, though the ritual act as such is distinct from the meal, it remains bound up with a meal, why "the sharing of food and drink with each other, the celebration of a meal especially among those who are well-to-do and those who have nothing, is essential to the celebration of the Christian eucharistic meal."[19] The beatitudes of the poor and the meek are the qualities of heart that Christians bring to the ritual of the shared table, and to the rituals which invite or restore to that table, or relate mortality and sexuality and power in the community to that table.

Sacred power, sacred place, sacred time, all undergo a transmutation in Christian worship which is a subversion of the carefully established ways in which religious organizations order them, possibly aware of a deep conscious instinct for security in face of the enigmas of power, place and time. Evangelical place and time are qualitative, not quantitative, and hope is accordingly eschatological, not apocalyptic. "Constantly," writes Simon de Vries, "the human mind strives to offset the dread of confronting something entirely unique by reducing it to categories of intellectual understanding, either by way of measurement or by way of comparison. Quantifying measurement enters into use as an abstractive process by which one 'time' is correlated with others purely on the basis of the passage of moving objects (the sun, moon, stars, timepieces, and the like) within a regular orbit or recurring routine. So also the qualifying approach that reduces temporal experience to analogies. Identifying a particular day for its special characteristics, the analytical mind makes intellectual and then linguistic comparisons with other days perceived to be somehow like it. Ultimately, all of life and history may be regularized and brought under control of man."[20]

In contrast with this, DeVries notes, "The essence of the qualitative, non-objectifying apprehension of time is an awareness that God *has* done something 'from the beginning to the end.' One day is not simply related, numerically or categorically, to another day. Rather, each day is seen as transcendentally significant in itself; that is, each is seen as at least potentially revelatory of God's purpose. A day may be different from all other days, not only because it may be the occasion of a decisive event in the history of men and nations, but because it may be the opportunity for a crucial confrontation between God and man."[21]

In ritual, one can find holy days marked off and described as "time out of time," because they are days that provide a sacred pattern for all time, and allow people to reduce their sense of living in time to a reproduction "on other days" of what is represented on the holy day. On the other hand, however, holy days may be seen as significant of the openness of any day to God's promises and decisive action. In practice, though some days are set aside for celebration, any day is open to being a holy day, sanctified not on a calendar but by the gathering of the believing community to remember, make intercession, rejoice and look forward in hope. Early Christians had to look for a space of time on the first day of the week to come together to hear the word and break the bread, and to see to one another's needs. Nowadays, for most people the time is set apart for leisure and it is not work which interferes with gatherings. It may be just as important for households of faith to make space on other days, or indeed to make space on a Sunday, to entertain in their midst those who do not enjoy leisure. It is the Lord's Supper which sanctifies the day, not the day which sanctifies the Lord's Supper.

One could make similar remarks about sacred place and the places where Christians gather. If the place is given some quality of its own, independent of the community, or if it is recognized as the place of a carefully circumscribed divine presence, one can say that the community has missed the point of God's presence in the community itself, in the word spoken and in the table shared. As any time is qualitatively open to a divine event or inbreaking, so also is any place, and the gathering of believers in a place is for them indicative of this openness. The return to a more domestic setting, the celebration of eucharists in homes, the construction of very simple buildings for communities in the shadow of larger basilicas, is simply a quest on the part of evangelical Christians to discover a true sense of place, where worship is given in spirit and in truth.

The locus of God's power is the community itself, for the reality of power is the Spirit of Christ poured forth into our hearts. The symbols of the presence of the Spirit are those which signify interaction between the members in mutual charity and service. Without in the least questioning the place of the sacrament of order in the church, it is necessary to recall that the liturgy is the gathering and action of the baptized, and that it is enlivened by the many services of the Spirit, so that the reality of the apostolic and evangelical community may be shaped. The statement that the one who presides is as the one who serves is not merely rhetoric or an exhortation to leaders to be humble. It is rather the significant declaration that Jesus is present to his community in both actions, or in any action of word, prayer and mutual charity, and in any exercise of the gifts of the Spirit. Indeed, the ultimate reality before which all else fades into the background is the reality of the body of the Lord, and the ultimate ground of the Lord's presence is the community of faith, not any particular gift or ministry. Evangelical communities are conscious of the gifts of the Spirit in their own midst, and trusting of the Lord that they will be provided with the ministries which they need. They are therefore free of stereotypes and ready to discern the gifts of word, of service, of prayer, of presidency, that are most suited to their prophetic and evangelical presence in society.[22]

Because of their historical and eschatological openness, and because they recall the Lord's passion as the act of God's solidarity with
the poor and suffering, evangelical communities give significant proportions to the function of narrative in liturgy, whether as a distinct act or
as part of the prayer of blessing. From relatively early patristic times, the
representation of Christ's mysteries in sacrament and liturgy has often
been sought in signs and actions, or in some declaratory words. It is,
however, much more in keeping with the Jewish roots of Christian liturgy to recognize the importance of haggadah.

The mimesis of the Lord's death and resurrection is not captured in
signs or actions figuratively representative of his cruel death, of his descent into Hades, or of his rising. It is found in a story which redescribes
the events in such a way that they present a ground for hope, and something to imitate in the freedom of new invention and in freedom in front
of all human power structures and expectations. This introduces a creativity into the telling of the story, as well as an actuality, something unfortunately largely lost in liturgy for some centuries. That the narrative
of the passion and resurrection may be told in different ways, for different communities, we already know from the Gospels. These of course
remain the unique canonical source, but they can be returned to for
fresh inspiration in narrative construction, rather than simply repeated.

There is a particularly important christological insight in today's believing communities, which is a new ground for more narrative creativity
in liturgy.[23] This is the emancipatory nature of the Christ story, and the solidarity of that story with the story of the world's forgotten and unnamed.
Jesus is remembered as the one into whose suffering all suffering is taken,
as the one in whose name all those left without a name are named, as the
one in whose remembrance the forgotten of the world are remembered.

Chaos, senselessness and meaninglessness are part and parcel of
actual human experience, but they can be so massive, so terrifying, that
whole societies are built on the capacity to forget. It has been remarked
often enough of our own age that senseless death is so daily, that it is so
massive, so global, so imminent to each of us, so prone to reduce thou-
sands to a kind of nonliving or daily death, that peoples ignore it, sup-
press it in what they choose to remember. The memory of Jesus in
worship can be such as to make room for the expression of fears, of ter-
ror, of emptiness, of blindness, of the offense and the cruelty, present
not only in his death and history, but in all history and in present society,
to wit of all that tends to be suppressed because apparently uncontrollable, or at least dismantling of our favorite ways of being. It is possible
to express all this, because in the pasch there is a vital hope, a hope that
is hope only because it takes all this into account. It is a hope which

alerts the community to the recalling of all those who in suffering, and in opposition to society's collective forgetting, show faith and courage and trust and a belief in life.

In remembering Jesus, therefore, we are allowed to remember "that all human enactments require criticism, revision and reenactment—and that this process is within God."[24] The hopes that this memory evokes are not dull hopes that see people as "better off" in heaven, but hopes that a fuller life is possible, that the past whatever it has been may yet be redeemed, that reconciliation may be effected, that minds and hearts may be opened to compassion, that the material world may be part of God's history, not something to be left behind, and that the poor and the desolate and all who live a shadowy existence will be vindicated.

Such remembrance gives rise to two types of song, namely, to lamentation and to doxology.[25] Communities have to be allowed to grieve, to express their fears and terrors, to lament over the denial of life that is found in alienation, over the refusal of death, over exercises of power that lead to despair. Lamentation is in fact the basis to Christian doxology, because doxology engages us in the promise of newness that comes with the Spirit, who heals, unites and empowers. That which is remembered in grief is redeemed, made whole, renewed. In doxology, in the hope of a new Jerusalem among us, lament turns into rejoicing.

Evangelical communities come to this kind of remembering, grieving and praising out of their own concrete quest for ways of living that are an alternative to the quest for power and happiness that crushes all before it. In living as it does, and in remembering Jesus, Christ and spirit-giver, and asserting its oneness with society rather than accepting to be made marginal to it, a community of faith expresses the reality of God's power active in a concrete historical time and place. The community gathered around such a memory is by its very being and gathering critical of all that is hopeless and alienating in religious and civil society and organization. Because of its belief in God's freedom, it is at the disposal of a God who is not co-opted by human power structures, and so it is free to continue to practice the evangelical way of life, and to speak prophetically to the renewal of society.

An evangelical way of life, a compassion with the poor, a resistance to the institutional and noninstitutional violence of the times, a common life enriched by many ministries, awe toward the sacramentality of life and of matter, a remembering of Jesus Christ which is also a remembering of all the forgotten, of things suppressed, of hopes dismissed, a lamenting before God's face, and praise and thanksgiving for the hopeful newness of the Spirit's creation, these appear to be marks of the households of the faith in the coming church.

NOTES

1. F. X. Kaufmann, "The Church as a Religious Organization," *Concilium* 91 (New York: Seabury Press, 1974), 77.

2. N. Luhmann, "Institutionalized Religion in the Perspective of Functional Sociology," *Concilium* 91 (New York: Seabury Press, 1974), 54.

3. Quoted by N. Fabbretti, "Francis, Evangelism and Popular Communities," *Concilium* 149 (New York: Seabury Press, 1981), 34.

4. M. Mollat, "The Poverty of Francis: A Christian and Social Option," *Concilium* 149 (New York: Seabury Press), 27.

5. Lester K. Little, *Religious Poverty and the Profit Economy in Medieval Europe* (Ithaca, NY: Cornell University Press, 1978), 114.

6. Little, Ibid., 116.

7. Little, Ibid., 113.

8. Little, Ibid., 116–117.

9. M. D. Chenu, "Fraternitas, Evangile et Condition Socio-culturelle," *Revue de l'Histoire de la Spiritualité* 49 (1973): 385–400; Little, 171–217.

10. Lester Little remarks: "The matter of who held power, of who was making the basic decisions for the community or who had the right to define the community, was critical in determining whether initiatives in the direction of change were looked upon as authentic and thus to be accepted or as alien and thus to be rejected. When those in power were not receptive to innovation, the cost of advocating innovation ran perilously high." In "Evangelical Poverty: The New Money Economy and Violence," in *Poverty in the Middle Ages*, ed. David Flood (Werl, Westphalia: Dietrich-Coelde, 1975), 26.

11. One thinks especially of the christologies of Edward Schillebeeckx and J. B. Metz.

12. E. Schillebeeckx, *Ministry: Leadership in the Community of Jesus Christ* (New York: Crossroad, 1981), 79, 136–137.

13. R. K. Fenn, "Recent Studies of Church Decline: The Eclipse of Ritual," *Religious Studies Review* 8 (1982): 128.

14. Fenn, 126.

15. Little, *Religious Poverty*, 16.

16. See *Vaudois Languedociens et Pauvres Catholiques* (Cahier de Fanjeaux 2, Paris: Edouard Privat, 1967), and Little on the Cathars, *Religious Poverty*, 134–135.

17. Little, *Religious Poverty*, 142.

18. Kurt-Victor Selge, "Caractéristiques du Premier Mouvement Vaudois et Crises au Cours de son Expansion," in *Vaudois Languedociens*, 131–132.

19. Elisabeth Schüssler Fiorenza, "Tablesharing and the Celebration of the Eucharist," *Concilium* 152 (New York: Seabury Press, 1982), 10.

20. Simon de Vries, "Time in the Bible," *Concilium* 142 (New York: Seabury Press, 1981), 4–5.

21. De Vries, 8.

22. See Peter Eicher, "The Age of Freedom: A Christian Community for Leisure and the World of Work," *Concilium* 142 (New York: Seabury Press), 50.

23. Schillebeeckx concludes his volume *Christ: The Experience of Jesus as Lord* (New York: Crossroad, 1980) with a homily and a eucharistic prayer.

24. Stephen Happel, "The Structure of Our Utopian Mitsein (Life-together)," *Concilium* 123 (New York: Seabury Press), 101.

25. See Walter Brueggemann, *The Prophetic Imagination* (Philadelphia: Fortress Press, 1980), passim.

READING 9
Introduction

In one way or another, all the essays in this volume focus on the question of Christian formation or the formation of the Spirit of Jesus in would-be disciples, especially considering the challenges posed by the kind of formation given by the wider culture. A question running through all these readings is, How can the church both come to appreciate the value of that wider culture and still be able to reflect on it, evaluate it, and critique it in the light of the Gospel? Another way to pose the same question might be, What method can we use to see what is happening in our world and how various aspects of that world influence our own religious faith?

In responding to this question, I myself have sought a theory of culture that might provide a way of "getting at" culture. I looked for a method of cultural analysis by which the system of signs used by a culture could be scrutinized both for their origins and original purposes and for their shifting social consequences. Herman Lombaerts has also been asking this question, but from an even broader perspective he calls "context." In various ways, all of Lombaerts's essays in this *Sourcebook* volume are about context analysis, though none of them offers a specific formula for such analysis. They are collected here to show how a catechetical thinker probes the various formational forces at work in contemporary society. Those who care to study these essays closely will see social and cultural analyses artfully practiced. They will also see how Lombaerts's art is anchored in some of the best thinking of Vatican Council II.

In treating the formation of catechists, the essay that follows lays out explicitly some of the understandings and competencies implicitly needed by catechists and, in some ways more importantly, those needed by the ones who train the catechists. My reading of diocesan newsletters and information about regional conferences for active catechists suggests that these skills are not well understood or prized in the United States. Those engaged in catechist formation at all levels would do well to study the following features of Lombaerts's approach to formation: (1) his description of Christian identity and the ecclesial nature of forming that identity; (2) the distinctions he makes early in the essay, for example, between catechesis and religious education, and his description of catechetics as a field of study; (3) the functional catechetical competencies needed now and for the future; and (4) his description of a catechetical praxis. In this last section, he sketches the general features of context analysis in four steps, though, as I noted above, the essay as a whole exemplifies this kind of analysis at work. As found in his notes, the broad range of Lombaerts's reading, in both theology and the social sciences, shows the depth of study undergirding his conceptual framework.

Catechetics and the Formation of Catechists

HERMAN LOMBAERTS, FSC
Translated by Michael Warren

This essay deals with catechesis as a field of study. It will give special attention to the educational dimension of the community of faith, especially the community's continuity in a particular time and in a particular sociocultural space. If we are to think carefully about the formation of catechists in the ministry of catechesis, we must focus on the twin axes of Christian living for our time. First, there is the purpose of having present in contemporary society Christians able to express in a significant way the distinctive "thing" we call Christian faith. Secondly, there are those who actually facilitate and coordinate a Christian identity rooted in the authentic tradition from which springs a communal sense of mission. This identity is marked by a kind of inventive freedom that suffuses the believer's persona.

Christian identity itself is anchored at three points: sacred writings, doctrinal understandings, and the community of the church. Each prong of this anchor is so connected to the other two that it ceases, as *Dei Verbum* reminds us, to be functional without them. Working together under the influence of the Spirit of Jesus, scripture, doctrine, and the faithful community contribute to the salvation and liberation of the human (*Dei Verbum*, 10).

The work of catechesis only makes sense in its relation to the two axes mentioned above: contributing to the formation of a Christian identity and to the development of a specific ability to live out the call of Christian faith. The formation of catechists has to be viewed in this perspective. That formation cannot be split off somehow from the responsibility Christians have for the contemporary world, a responsibility marked by solidarity with the human quest and its specific contribution to the name of Christian faith.

Reprinted from *Lumen Vitae* 44, no. 4 (1989): 413–426. Translated by Michael Warren. Translation copyright © 1989 by Michael Warren.

Catechetics

Catechetics is the theory of catechesis. It developed toward the middle of the eighteenth century in an attempt to respond to the challenges of the Enlightenment, including the democratization of teaching and the growing science of pedagogy.[1] Catechetics is the study of the responsibilities and the conditions that mark those who function as catechists.[2] It is the field of specialists who seek to delineate both the definition of catechesis and its tasks, submitting them to the criteria of pastoral theology. Because it serves both the Magisterium and the "sense of the faithful," catechetics has a normative character. Catechetics finds itself situated at the intersection of the essential ecclesial task of teaching and the inevitable creative response of particular communities to specific situations.

Here I wish to distinguish among three dimensions of the discipline of catechetics. The first dimension has to do with the church and its mission of safeguarding its own teaching set forth to guide the faithful. This first dimension, then, involves ecclesial authority as it sets out the boundaries of ecclesial membership and the formation of Christian identity in ever-shifting contexts. This dimension of catechetics is at the service of ecclesial continuity, working as much for the maintenance of stability as for adaptation and innovation. The social perdurance of an institution such as the church calls for unending vigilance lest institutional stability be threatened either from within or from without.

The second dimension of catechetics as a discipline involves laying out the theoretical foundations of its practice in a way that both specifies the criteria of that practice and safeguards authentic practice in new contexts and in the face of new challenges. Such practice calls for a discipline marked by research and interdisciplinary study but also guided by its reference to an ecclesial tradition.

Catechetic's third dimension has to do with the endless probing of the symbolic character of the Judeo-Christian tradition. This symbol system reflects the dynamic and shifting interaction between an unchanging core of divine revelation and the actual social contexts of particular times and places. In this interaction we find endless unavoidable tensions: of space and time, of desire and possession, of obedience and freedom, of presence and absence, of self and other, of silence and word. These tensions represent the indispensable conditions out of which the God of Jesus Christ manifests Godself today.

The first of these dimensions marks the specific, ecclesial character of catechetics, underscoring thereby its difference from the science of religious education, which functions outside of ecclesial authority.

Religious education is marked by the freedom to explore the meaning of educational action on behalf of transcendence or of the various religions, in their interaction with highly varied contexts.[3] Those countries marked by great religious pluralism (English- and German-speaking countries) tend to be more sensitive to these distinctions than the countries more rooted in the Catholic Tradition.[4]

As for the second dimension, the coexistence of these two approaches has led to conflicts about both fundamental catechetical options and actual practice.[5] Faced with voluminous writing about both catechesis and religious education in the larger sense, the Catholic church has in recent decades accused certain efforts at "catechetical renewal" of unacceptable distortions, and in response has called catechists to hold to the transmission of orthodox teaching. A critical reaction to such a call was inevitable, and this reaction pointed out how the boundaries of catechetical action could not be understood in a timeless vacuum. Catechesis has to be related to the changes occurring in the social context or wider environment.

The third dimension of catechetics is the one least often mentioned, though it is without doubt the one posing the most difficulties. It indicates the place where the identity of the believer is constantly being restructured in the very process of personality development but also in the changing sociocultural context of the contemporary world. Religious socialization no longer has the same influence it once had in more stable periods. As alert catechists are acutely aware, religious sensibility is affected by global shifts in culture as these take root in actual societies. These shifts challenge the symbolic meaning system of the Christian tradition itself. Similar to the ongoing tasks facing theologians, the tasks facing catechists go far beyond those of coming up with creative methodologies or innovative use of media.[6]

The Formation of Catechetical Agents

The new Code of Canon Law sets forth clearly the church's teaching function this way: to safeguard the Gospel, to probe its depth, to proclaim and explain it faithfully . . . these constitute a mission received from Christ (Canon 747). Education of the faith involves an organic and systematic teaching of Christian doctrine, an initiation into the fullness of Christian life, and an education to true discipleship (*Catechesi Tradendae [CT]*, no. 19).

Catechetical formation seeks to develop skill and competence in communicating the Gospel's message. Such a competence arises from an adequate formation in theology, in the human sciences, and in methodology. Doctrinal formation is essential if catechists are to discern what is in keeping with the faith, including with its proper ecumenical orientation (see *CT*, nos. 32–33). The human sciences help catechists acquire greater skills in communication. Methodology is a practical ability to use teaching tools in a flexible and appropriate manner (*CT*, no. 31).

Both the *General Catechetical Directory* and *Catechesi Tradendae* highlight the ecclesial character of catechesis and the special responsibility of the bishops for it. In insisting on a doctrinal formation rooted in scripture and guided by the church, these documents disclose the normative character of catechesis: it seeks to develop and maintain a deep identification with the Gospel. Catechesis is an interecclesial and institutional activity; the firmness of the faith of Christians comes about not by happenstance but by design. Such design and planning assures also the strength of the broader ecclesial institution. Through it, the church's organic and doctrinal unity is manifested with greater clarity and power, in the midst of a pluralist culture seeking both truth and liberation (*CT*, nos. 17–18). *Catechesi Tradendae* makes clear that developing a precise formal definition of catechesis, capable of enriching both the concept and its articulation, is a work for specialists (no. 18).

The social significance underlying this institutional understanding of catechesis needs to be decoded with some care. What are its historical roots? Who benefits by its being put into operation?

Catechetical and Pastoral Theology

Pastoral theology (or pastoral practice) focuses on the work of the church situated between its initial mission and its eschatological hope. Seen this way, pastoral theology covers a vast and complex field of practice. The church can appeal to a long tradition of seeking to establish the proper connection between theology and pastoral practice, including catechesis. Edward Farley offers a pastoral theology centered on the vocation of Christians: the action of Christians is located in concrete particular situations.[7] In a "praxis" that frees them to use their own creativity, Christians are meant to interpret particular situations and their outcomes. This capability calls for theological competence, a quality proper to faith itself in its character of reflective wisdom, sustained by the action of the Spirit. Such a perspective is quite different from the understanding of pastoral theology as it existed in a heavily clericalized church of the nineteenth century, entirely oriented to the pastoral formation of priests.

Zulehner[8] distinguishes three areas proper to a fundamental pastoral theology: *criterology*, the setting out of pastoral objectives and of the norms by which to evaluate them; *kairology*, the theory dealing with those situations around which the church organizes action with an eye to having some influence; *praxeology*, the theory dealing both with the improvement of pastoral action toward specified goals and of critical evaluation of concrete situations.

A catechetics tends to structure itself according to a particular pastoral orientation. Positioning catechetics within a particular theological orientation, important as it may be in itself, is insufficient. The task of catechetics is actually broader. Catechetics must name not only its principles but also what particular facets of the Christian vocation its *criteriology*, its *kairology*, and its *praxeology* will prize. Catechetics (as well as the actual doing of catechesis), insofar as it is a work of theological intelligence informed by several disciplines, finds its rationale is a theological one, directed by the Magisterium of the church. Its responsibilities rest on certain assumptions. In submitting its theoretical positions to a methodological work of empirical research, it can decide to move away from certain assumptions and let itself be guided by the logical conclusions indicated by that research. In other words, catechetics cannot position itself in a fixed static place. It evolves and develops in various, indeed, seemingly conflictual, directions, though always seeking to implement the intraecclesial teaching mission.[9]

The "official theology" of the church is not, however, an absolute or static category. That theology will always be marked by the characteristics of a specific historical epoch. Such a theology will respond, and not without justification, to philosophical, methodological, or contextual priorities, of the sort that marked, as we can now see, the patristic period. The direction of the current emphases seem to come from neo-scholasticism.[10]

Therefore, it seems logical to speak of "catechetics" in the plural. It seems unwise to set out by official proclamation a "catechetic" in order to determine a single way to form the agents or doers of catechesis. Such a univocal use might actually overlook aspects of actual practice that both differ and are even incoherent one to the other. It is, then, necessary to lay out precisely which pastoral theology is going to define the field of catechetical practice and which scientific priorities will determine the actual structure of a catechetics.

A Fruitful Tension:
Continuity, Stability, and Contingency

As cited above, the statement of Canon 747, then, poses no problems: it is the task of the Magisterium, in the name of the entire church, to maintain the church's continuity and to direct it toward achieving its total mission. Seen in a wider context, certain of its emphases deserve comment, such as the one offered by J. Passicos, who wrote that the code expresses above all an orthodox system that it intends to protect.[11] Once adopted and ratified, no shifts or changes can be allowed, nor any kind of questioning. Passicos finds that ecclesiology of this sort is not communitarian enough. The witness of faithful assent is to be taken as a constitutive aspect of the teaching mission itself. In contrast, the code suggests that an unhealthy relationship is thereby established between the people and their ministers. Passicos states: "The faith of each person, in its personal expressions, is really the faith of the church. The faith of the church is in the end at the service of the faith of the individuals, and both represent the conditions of authentic union with God."[12]

Passicos warns us against the danger of understanding the various means of speaking and of protecting what is said in a much too narrow way and thereby letting them function too rigidly. In that case ecclesiastical power can function in a meddlesome or too authoritarian manner. It is the function of catechists especially to assure the conditions of proclaiming God's word in various cultures.

Should it ever lose sight of its being part of a much wider teaching authority, the Magisterium would be in danger of positioning itself in a self-enclosed isolation. As an institution and in its own functioning, it comes under the contingency and the influences that mark the production of teaching in the whole of human society. J. Moingt further outlines the dynamic character of the ecclesial teaching authority.

> The exercise of the Magisterium does not obey a simple eternal law, but is functionally determined by strategies clearly circumstantial and, consequently, the theology of the Magisterium is far from being homogenous and finished but is continually and in various ways being constructed . . . in a historically circumscribed situation.[13]

Accepting the evidence for a contextual reading of the function of the Magisterium speaks for itself, but the implications of its concrete operations are less obvious. In effect, the origins of the Magisterium provide the best clue to its proper function. The start of the ecclesial tradition shows circumstances that highlight the revealing power of the person of Christ. Throughout its history, all sorts of circumstances have led the church to turn toward the area of uncertainty as part of the historical character of a mystery focused on the radically "other." This turn to mystery actually accompanied the work of defining, in a disciplined and authoritative manner, both correct teaching and the code of right living.[14]

Awareness of this development is essential if we are to grasp the dynamic and evolutionary interaction between the church and the various peoples. Today the Magisterium must also give attention to public opinion, especially as its value and reality were highlighted by Pius XII.[15] Further, the Magisterium must create conditions for mutual listening and, as a way of encountering the world, allowing itself to go where truth is being forged. After all, the Magisterium was not set up to displace the Absent One, or to set up false power in the space left by the Absent One. As sign of this productive absence, the Magisterium is the symbolic presence of an Absence forever held to be irreplaceable.[16]

One cannot undertake a theoretical study of catechesis without noting the implicit and explicit parameters of such a study. Christian presence in the world depends on a Christian identity continually challenged by what is taking place at the heart of humanity. Once accepted and taken up, this challenge of facing the world will mark our understanding of the work of catechesis and will dramatically influence the way we conceive of catechetical formation.

Formation: A Decisive Act

When it comes to the formation of catechists we do not begin our reflections in a vacuum. Readily available are official church texts specifying what a solid formation of catechists would look like for a catechesis renewed according to Vatican Council II. We also have access to a vast literature, the fruit of thought and based on thorough and wide-ranging research. It is not my intention to offer here an overview of this thought and research. Instead, as a way of thinking about how formation is conceptualized, a focal question deserves our attention: What in fact represents a good formation? In responding to this question, our best guide will be the kind of wide-angle view of catechesis that has already surfaced in this essay.

It is appropriate to re-examine some assumptions that will be crucial for the theoretical and practical grasp of catechesis. In the following pages, I will set forth a reconsideration of functional catechetical competencies, taking into account the praxeological perspective, grouped around four main points.

1. Categories to Be Re-examined

A. The Pedagogical Model

The usual approach to the formation of catechists follows a triangular pedagogical model, marked by a structural connection among: the content, the one who transmits the content, and the one being catechized. Seen this way, it is logical that formation demands a solid preparation in scripture, doctrine, liturgy, ethics, . . . and methodology. Further, in this model the various social and human sciences, especially psychology, can be used to communicate the Christian message in a more efficient way. This way of looking at catechesis has the advantage of intersecting with the most common way of understanding education and teaching. In fact, the basic underlying model is already in place, both in schools and in the church. Such a model has a double advantage of being simple yet having its own indisputable logic. Many official documents and recent publications assume this model.

The model, however, harbors within it certain difficulties. It presents an oversimplified account of what actually happens in the complex process found in any form of education, certainly in religious education. The model lends itself easily to a linear transmission of knowledge, with the students having to submit to the authority of the one who knows. It is also a model easily taken over by institutional ideologies and, more subtly, by the economic and political interests of the wider social system. When misdirected, this model can easily allow minority interests or certain legitimate but troublesome aspirations to be excluded or pushed aside. The model has trouble with the difficult but delicate search for truth and with its call for great respect and patience, because that search is initiated by each student in a unique way.

Catechetics must make use of more nuanced models better able to lay out the various factors affecting catechesis and better able to deal with the complex tasks that will be taken up by catechists. The reality of dealing with the Gospel needs a more open model, since Christian identity cannot allow itself to be under the control of such a linear process.

B. Communication

Since the word *transmit* has connotations that make it unacceptable and even feared today, a different vocabulary is also called for. In spite of this, one finds in a good number of catechetical texts how easily the word *communication* can be replace by *transmission*. Transmission clearly says what it means. Why change this vocabulary?

For the communication sciences, and especially in their examination of models of communication, these words are far from interchangeable. Making them so hides important contemporary issues in communication. The move to the electronic era, now characteristic of postindustrial society, has brought a massive shift in the way information is treated and the way the process of communication is managed at the global level. Automation has created a cultural vacuum that can be countered only by means of interpersonal networks in which communication favors the elaboration of meaning, of values, of interiority, of solidarity, and of deep connections to culture and ritual. All these pose stubborn challenges that cannot be brushed aside. The struggle of faith and of catechesis is found right at the heart of this cultural crisis. Catechesis calls above all for a deep sensibility and an attentive ear, if it is to provide a cultural space where an attentiveness to the "other" might have educative power. A very profound kind of study is called for in order to situate the Gospel proclamation, from which springs faith, within the various forms of communication. Overly facile shifts might short-circuit the entire catechetical effort.

C. Interdisciplinary Character

An analogous comment might be made about the disciplines deemed auxiliary to catechetics. This is the debate of the century. Most attention was focused on theology and pedagogy, the two disciplines thought able to resolve decisively the problems of catechesis and of religious education in a changing world. That judgment was justified, and it will not do to minimize the quality of the work done with the help of theology and pedagogy in recent decades.

It is better to admit that even with a highly diversified pedagogical discipline, the binary schema of theology-pedagogy easily lends itself to a linear way of thinking about the catechetical task: the content (theological) is transmitted by an appropriate method to the catechized. It would seem better for the catechist to identify more clearly the various components involved. The outline would look different if sociology, psychology, anthropology, economics, and philosophy were explicitly put in touch with pedagogy and theology, and connected. Further, all these disciplines understand themselves as plural, characterized by different currents and emphases. When in touch with such a complex mix, catechetical questions become understood and are formulated in new ways.

2. A Catechetical Praxis

The view offered here puts great stress on the interaction between the church understood as an institution and the sociocultural, economic, and political environment, but this latter in two senses. Catechetics will have as its responsibility not only the formation of catechists for three specific tasks: mangagement procedures, the support of scientific frames of thought, and a thorough familiarity with the way the symbolic field works. Catechetics will also prepare catechists to interact vitally with the broad social context in which catechesis is done. Such interaction involves four interpretive skills: discerning the impact of the social context on the church itself, and especially on catechetical situations; listening to what is happening in the midst of ecclesial life itself; foreseeing and fostering the competencies indispensable for Christians ready to fulfill their vocation in the future; and finally, performing the work of summary evaluation in light of these three interpretive analyses.

Catechetics and the Formation of Catechetical Agents

P R A	Sociocultural Environment →	Catechetics		
		Institutional oversight	Scientific discipline	Symbolic field
X E	To discern the influence of the context			
O L	To listen to what Christians are saying			
O G	To foresee the skills that will be needed			
Y	To evaluate			

A. Evaluating the Impact of the Social Context

The church's catechetical documents continually stress the importance of the contemporary world's influence on the church's members. Vatican Council II embraced the insights of the catechetical renewal which has been flourishing for decades, but gave that renewal different agendas: a search for doctrinal coherence; care to find common understanding; and modern adaptations capable of communicating the message more clearly and coherently.

I do not wish to deny either the importance or the ambiguity of these matters, though I do wish to underscore that the catechetical renewal finds itself confronted above all with questions about content. Though a complete, coherent, and systematic synthesis of Christian faith is certainly necessary (and an endless task), it is insufficient in itself for what I have in mind here. We all know of instances where catechists being formed turned their backs on one or another faith summary as not being helpful, whereas their actual questions were about how to relate faith to various sociocultural shifts. Such questions bubble out of struggles to understand and to deal with varied mind-sets. Often such catechists have already tried out various ways of understanding the faith. What they now want is for the previous studies and pastoral work to be evaluated, examined critically, restated, and resituated in a broader, more historical context. What such catechists are seeking is a cooperative effort undertaken among adult Christians.

Perhaps the deepest work of catechetics is to help the agents of catechesis to discern the shifts in cultural sensibility and values, and to discern further the way people today structure their lives either because of economic and social pressures imposed on them or by choices they make to meet real future uncertainties.

There is today a need to mark and note those aspects of our tradition that have been affected by a "spiral of silence" about culture and society,[17] but in the name of what mechanisms and what price of individual isolation? There is a need to attend to the shifts of religious sensibility, to the cultural openness to a religiousness of the past, to the astonishing contributions of contemporary religious art, and to the subtle but important perceptions of Christians or the church as an institution. Does being rooted from birth in a particular religious culture help one resist the uniformity imposed by modern civilization, or does it tend to undergo in our time a cultural shock that is both social and spiritual? Would the coexistence in our time of two logics—secular and religious—mean that people do not want to move from one set of roots to find other roots?[18]

It seems important to accustom catechists to this kind of discernment, especially if they care to maintain and revivify faith. They must be able to apply themselves to such disciplined thought and to contribute thereby to reflection on meaning. The journey of contemporary humanity questions Christian identity right to its very roots.

B. Attentiveness to What Is Being Talked About Among Christians

Christians who are in the church or who meet one another around catechesis also carry within them the presence of their social context. They react and they take positions; they take stances, and they embody various kinds of interests, even contradictory ones. What do they say about this fact?

How does the church see its own sociocultural context? How does it go about analyzing it? What sort of evaluative process will be used to assess a particular pastoral strategy? How will we embrace our concern for the total church, so diversified, in ways able to read and interpret anew its origins and long tradition?

Such attentiveness implies a concern to "become informed," to build a solid knowledge of scripture, of doctrine, and of the living reality of the church. It is essential that catechists be formed to take on the Christian identity of one who seeks to know. Such an identity involves endless study and a lifelong pilgrimage. This attentiveness is the sort that can ponder mistakes, misunderstandings, conflicts, differences, deceit, overstatements, and understatements—but also charisms, the new presence of the Spirit, and the life of faith lived in hidden ways, in simple ways, in profound ways, and in prophetic ways.

This kind of attentive presence brings out endless questions that scientific catechetics and the Magisterium must take up. In the end, the conflict-laden diversity of catechetical study and the demands of the church's teaching authority will contribute to the ever-growing adulthood and maturation of the church. Catechetical agents have a role in fostering that adulthood and so they have a right to be formed in it themselves.

Although strategic planning of future developments is often countered by unforeseen changes, innovation and renewal of the role of Christians in society demand competence, thorough reflection, and preparation. Catechetics will have to explore future possibilities of actualizing the creative strength of Christian identity. Catechists will need to develop the skills to foresee, to anticipate the kind of distinctive, qualitative presence needed to give credible witness to the presence of the Spirit, and to be a sign of universal solidarity with the human community.

C. Expectation

By means of probing and thoughtful attention, catechetics can help catechists identify the appropriate and specific competencies they need to assume their responsibilities among children, teens, and adult Christians. Of course, because the Gospel concerns all humans, wherever they live, catechesis does not stop at an intraecclesial education; the Good News is for all persons. The church's mission takes seriously everything that affects the human project. What kind of presence, or attitude, or language, or rituals, or way of thinking in the church can keep people of today from being touched in their inner life?[19]

The continuity of the church is surely the work of the Spirit—at least such is our profession of faith. But this action manifests itself in and by the efforts of communities of believers. As in a society, such a continuity in the church is an achievement of the kind of intentionality characteristic of the social duration of all human society.[20]

D. Evaluation

This final aspect of the training of catechists implies that catechetics prepares in a way that carefully shapes discernment and attentiveness to the skills needed in the future. It further implies that evaluative norms can be offered catechists by which they can monitor their efforts step-by-step. The process seeks not to "transmit" a static tradition but to give birth to a well-informed consciousness and an attentiveness character-istic of faith. These habits work with the action of the Spirit to recognize the authority and the merciful but dynamic presence of the God of Jesus of Nazareth. Evaluation is not solely a technique applied to work done. Its concern is to integrate all aspects of the task, in collaboration with those others who have special skills and tools of evaluation.

Conclusion

The Magisterium defines the contours of the church's teaching mission, but leaves to those of special skill the task of deepening concepts and ways of articulating them. Catechetics is mandated to develop a solid interdisciplinary study capable of directing actual practice. For this, nuanced models are needed, both for the study and for the formation of catechetical agents. Systematic thought categories must avoid being set out in a static and linear way. Attentive involvement in cultural reality, and a courageous facing of the questions that arise there, can lead to a patient, gradual way of proceeding—a way of artistically fashioning a way forward. Both the catechist and the theologian work with the same aim: speaking a message that is decisive, foundational,[21] faithful to the Creator who has created the living, so that the presence of the living but invisible God might become their strength and their salvation.

NOTES

1. W. Croce, "Katechetik," in *Katechetisches Wörterbuch*, 1961, 369–374.

2. G. Stachel, "Catechetica," in *Dizionario di Catechetica* (Leumann, 1986), 110–111.

3. C. Bizer, "Katechetische Memorabilien—Vorüberlegungen von einer Rezeption der evangelischen Katechetik," *Jarbuch der Religionspädagogik* 4 (1988): 77–89.

4. H. Lombaerts, "Readers of a Century," *The Living Light* 2 (1987): 158–173; U. Hemel, "Quand on dit catéchèse en Allemagne—Les contextes de la catéchèse et de l'enseignement religieux en R.F.A.," *Catéchèse* 116 (1989): 119–132.

5. U. Hemel, *Theorie der Religionspädagogik. Begriff, Gegenstand, Agrenzungen* (Munich, 1984).

6. J. Audinet, "De l'artisanat théologique—Essais de théologie pratique," *Point Théologique* 49 (1988): 95–105.

7. E. Farley, "Interpreting Situations: An Inquiry into the Nature of Practical Theology," in L. S. Mudge and J. L. Poling, eds., *Formation and Reflection: The Promise of Practical Theology* (Philadelphia: Fortress Press, 1987): 1–26.

8. P. M. Zulehner, *Pastoraltheologie. Band 1. Fundamental-Pastoral* (Düsseldorf, 1989), 15.

9. E. Feifel, "Katechese in der katholischen katechetischen Diskussion—Eine Problemskizze," *Jarbuch der Religionspädagogik* 4 (1988): 99–118 at 108ff.

10. C. Duquoc, "Une coexistence conflictuelle: théologie critique et magistère en catholicisme," *Revue de Théologie et de Philosophie* 2 (1989): 165–171.

11. J. Passicos, "La mission d'enseignement de l'Église et le magistère," *Recherches de Sciences religieuses*, 1983, 213.

12. Ibid., 218–219.

13. J. Moingt, "L'avenir du Magistère," *Recherches de Sciences religieuses*, 1983, 300–301.

14. J. M. Aubert, "Modèles politiques et structures d'Église," in *Recherches de Sciences religieuses*, 1983, 177; K. Gabriel, "Die neuzeitliche Gesellschaftsentwicklung der Katholizismus als Sozialform der Christentumsgeschichte," K. Gabriel and F. X. Kaufmann, *Zur Soziologie der Katholizismus* (Mainz, 1980), 201–225.

15. M. Boullet, "Magistère de l'Église et opinion publique," *Christus* 144 (1989): 144–145.

16. Moingt, "L'avenir du Magistère," 305 and 307.

17. E. Noelle-Neumann, "The Spiral of Silence: A Theory of Public Opinion," *Journal of Communication*, 1974, 43–51.

18. H. Lubbe, "Historizismus oder die Erfahrung der Kontingenz religiöser Kultur," in W. Oelmüller, *Wahrheitsansprüche der Religionen Heute* (Paderborn, 1986), 65–83. See also H. Bourgeois, "Au milieu des indifférences et des attraits—Qu'est-ce donc que croire aujourd'hui?" *Catéchèse* 96 (1984): 99–110.

19. F. X. Kaufmann, "Sozialform der Kirche—ein Hindernis für die Weitergabe des Glaubens?" *Katechetische Blätter*, 1987, 138–144.

20. Zulehner, *Pastoraltheologie*, 247–306; E. Farley, *Ecclesial Reflection: An Anatomy of Theological Method* (Philadelphia: Fortress Press, 1982), esp. "Appendix: The General Structure of Social Duration," 345–373.

21. Audinet, "De l'artisanat théologique," 102.

READING 10
Introduction

This essay was originally written as a chapter of a planned book-length portrait of the problem of ecclesial practice. Based on my conviction that the chief form of catechesis is the religious influence of the corporate life of the local assembly, the essay is at least in part an exploration of a catechetical problem. What we often unwittingly inscribe into our corporate behavior shapes, just as unwittingly, the possibilities of discipleship in a particular church body. If the local church is the great sacrament of the presence of the Spirit of Jesus, ways of reflecting on local practice take on special importance. In other words, twin pastoral efforts are called for—greater sensitivity to the teaching represented by the practice combined with a struggle for a renewed practice and better embodying of ecclesial belief in a particular context.

The Local Church and Its Practice of the Gospel: The Materiality of Discipleship in a Catechesis of Liberation

MICHAEL WARREN

In an essay on Christian initiation in the Episcopal Church, William S. Adams explores the place of baptism by examining the use of space and the use of ritual in a sampling of Episcopal parishes.[1] Adams probes whether the symbolic ritual enactments, both in their use of space and in the ritual unfolding itself, back up the Church's stated convictions about the key place of baptism. Officially, the baptismal pool or font, in keeping with its importance in the community's total life, is to have a significant place in the space where the community assembles. Thus there are to be three key areas in the space where the community assembles for worship: the altar, the pulpit from which the word is announced, and the place of baptism. Adams's study sought to determine whether the place of baptism was in fact spatially significant. The study also scrutinized the ritual of baptism as practiced, contrasting the ritual of ordination with that of baptism to see the assumptions embedded in each and whether the practice of these rituals squares with stated teaching that baptism is to have greater significance. In the way the rituals are actually carried out, he found that the "physical observable evidence" shows that ordination has much greater significance, at least when examined as ritual action. Thus, he is examining what the Church does in its ritual and its use of space to see if it is coherent with its teachings. What he is after is *actual practice* rather than stated theoretical positions.

This essay seeks to lay out for educators the significance of the material conditions of Church practice. I begin with attention to Adams's study because of its interesting way of examining whether what we

---

Reprinted from *Worship* 67, no. 5 (1993): 433–460. Copyright © 1993 by Michael Warren.

practice is what we proclaim in our official teachings and its determination to focus on *the teaching represented by the practice*. The teaching embedded in patterns of behavior lived but not reflected on must be an issue for Christian educators or catechists, especially if we accept that what a community lives is at least as formative as what it teaches about itself.

Here I wish to lay a groundwork for considering what might be called "the symbolics of practice" at the level, not of liturgical symbolics, but of that of life structure symbolics. What people say and do in the liturgical assembly, including the arrangement of space in which they speak and act, provides clues to what these people are all about. However—and this is a central point in my argument—what they say and do in the nonliturgical spaces of their individual and corporate lives has a more decisive effect on them than does liturgical speech and action. The material structures of their lives have already formed them—their consciousness, their mentalities, their biases and priorities, their spirits—before they cross the threshold of liturgical space.

Though attention to this matter is growing, I find insufficient attention to it in the literature of religious education under its various subheadings of Christian education or catechesis. Even those who purport to deal with shaping the practice of particular ecclesial groups do not deal with either liturgical symbolics in Adams's sense or life-practice symbolics in my sense. Storytelling as a technique of formation or of reformation of the assembly is not sufficient for coping with the kind of life practice I seek to get at here. One of the few Christian education theorists who has gotten at the issue of the life practice of local Churches is C. Ellis Nelson in his *Where Faith Begins*. Though it was written twenty-five years ago, I know of no other religious/Christian education book that raises the communal practice issue the way his does. Edward Farley's writings consistently raise the issue at an abstract level not yet accessible to many.

Though the matter of practice surfaces consistently in Roman Catholic catechetical documents, and, I presume, in those of all the denominations, the matter has still not been brought forward in a cohesive way that highlights its key place in Christian education/catechesis. Here, in seeking to lay out the importance of the issue and some reasons why it has been so long neglected, I begin with one of the few places where the matter of practice is raised consistently and forcefully: the literature of liberation theology. I hope to suggest some lines of further work to be pursued for the material conditions of practice to receive the emphasis it deserves in Christian education.

Liberation theology begins with the concrete conditions of people's lives, what we call the "material conditions" of life, and engages communities in reflecting on these conditions, in judging them, and, where appropriate, in working to change them. Those material conditions are the earthy clay out of which skilled communal hands guided by a Gospel vision seek to fashion a more useful and beautiful social vessel. While the process of working on the concrete conditions of living is widely known to be crucial to the liberationist approach, this process has yet to be recognized as a key task for the renewal of First and Second World Churches. Is it possible for this task to assume among Christians of privilege the centrality in pastoral reflection and activity it has in the Churches of the oppressed?

Concrete Conditions of Life

In the very first paragraph of his now-classic work *A Theology of Liberation*, Gustavo Gutierrez maintains that built into the way of life of every ecclesial community is a theological understanding in rough outline. The "life, action, and concrete attitude" found in the community provide the soil into which theological reflection "sinks its roots and from which it derives its strength."[2] Though never stressing the negative side of this principle, Gutierrez implies that the material conditions of the community's life can be for good or ill. The title of *A Theology of Liberation*'s first chapter, "Theology: A Critical Reflection," means not so much Gutierrez's critical reflection on theology but rather that theology itself is done as a critical refection on the concrete circumstances of the local Church's life. . . . "*[T]he very life of the Church* [emphasis his] . . . [is] a *locus theologicus*" (p. 8), that is, a zone for doing theological reflection. Throughout this chapter he stresses the importance "of concrete behavior, of deeds, of action, of praxis in the Christian life" (p. 10).

The goal of such reflection on the material conditions of life is to fashion a concrete practice of the Gospel worked out in the face of a probing examination of the specific economic and sociocultural circumstances in which a community finds itself. Far from downplaying "truths" and wisdom, this approach employs them in fashioning a concrete practice of discipleship that itself rescues truth and wisdom from becoming static and sterile. This specific practice is sacrament and verification both of a community's faith in God and of the system of "truths" that elaborates that faith.

Understood in this way, liberation theology seeks the local Church as both an accessible sign of the presence of God's promised Christ and a habitable sign. Neither feature is easily attained. An accessible sign is different from a simply "claimed" or purported sign, because one can see what the accessible sign stands for; the way the sign functions makes its meaning tangible and sense-able. A habitable sign is a sign inviting one to live its meanings in communion, as others do. In the early 1960s when I tried for several years to teach ecclesiology to skeptical teens, I found the unavoidable stumbling block for the young to be, not the claims of the Church, but the lack of coherence between those claims and actual concrete life practice of the local parish. The young found the embodiments of my ecclesial theory to be neither accessible nor habitable. In so finding, they verified Joseph Komonchak's description of ecclesiology as "a theory about a practice";[3] the ecclesiology I was presenting was a theory about a theory, not about a practice. I came to see that the most convincing way of presenting the theory of the Church was to ground it in convincing practice—which at that time was an alternative practice.[4]

Fewer than four years after Gutierrez's book appeared in its first Spanish edition, an important papal statement backed up the basic position. In December 1975, *Evangelii nuntiandi* appeared over the signature of Paul VI, as a papal response to the issues raised at the 1974 Synod of Bishops on the issue of evangelization. Opening with several anguished questions about the possibilities of proclaiming the Gospel in our day, the exhortation returns again and again to the matter of the Church as an accessible and credible sign. The very first step of evangelization involves the Church itself being evangelized and converted to God, becoming a community of believers making real their hope through loving-kindness to others.[5]

Evangelized itself, the Church finds its foundational way of evangelizing others to be by means of witness: the sign of an *ecclesia* embracing the humanizing vision of the Gospel and living not only in communion with its own members but in solidarity with all seeking what is "noble and good." Such witness is basically "wordless," but deeply provocative, that is, raising questions about the vision and intent of those living this way. This witness renders God's presence accessible to others in tangible signs.[6] Though never stating the centrality of the material conditions of the local Church as concretely as does Gutierrez, the document clearly implies their importance in many places, particularly near the end using language of self-confrontation: "Either tacitly or aloud—but always forcefully—we are being asked: Do you really believe what you are proclaiming? Do you live what you believe? Do you really preach what you live? The witness of life has become more than ever an essential condition for real effectiveness in preaching" (no. 76).

Here *Evangelii nuntiandi* echoes the description of belief set forth by a nineteenth-century U.S. philosopher, Charles Sanders Peirce: "Belief consists mainly in being deliberately prepared to adopt the formula believed in as the guide to action; the essence of belief is the establishment of a habit; and different beliefs are distinguished by the different modes of action to which they give rise."[7]

Implied, however, in *Evangelii nuntiandi*'s description of a believable ecclesial community is a process of struggle whereby a group seeks to embrace specific patterns of practice by which a Gospel perspective can be lived out in its concrete circumstances. The conversion of the community sparked by its encounter with the message of Jesus is not a one-time ecstatic event based on euphoric insight into "truth." Translating conversion into patterns of practice that go beyond ritual enactments of the tradition and become embedded in specific ways of living is no euphoric matter. In fact it is the opposite. Ec-stasy means standing outside the self, being lifted out of the self. Establishing Gospel living in a specific set of circumstances involves standing not outside the self but squarely within one's materiality, one's embodiedness within networks of particularities. Ultimately, as we shall see, it involves judgments and decisions about a range of life practices.

Resistance to the Issue of Life Structure

Middle- and upper-class ecclesial communities have for the most part not faced the challenge of specific life practice. One way to support this claim is simply to note the lack of pastoral literature on the matter. In all fields of human endeavor can be found intense interest in standards of practice, with practitioners ready to submit themselves to the best standard so far achieved. This interest in practice and readiness to examine and learn from virtuoso performance can be found in sports, in the arts, in the crafts, even in management theory. Among those who work to hone a particular kind of human skill, any field of practice demands this kind of relatedness among practitioners, involving mutual examination and evaluation—and consequent appreciation or criticism. Basically, "we cannot be initiated into a practice without accepting the authority of the best standards realized so far."[8] This is as true for the playing of the French horn as it is for the practice of virtue.

Quite simply, in pastoral theology the literature showing this interest in practice hardly exists. There is ample literature, called pastoral or practical theology, about the theory of practice but with little to say about the wider patterns of action that make up a specific structure of life for any person or community. There is also a literature of case studies, valuable in themselves, which tend to focus on the pastoral skills of a practitioner but with little critical reflection or even attention to the concrete social conditions of living within which the pastoral skills function. When the problematic of practice surfaces in these studies, it is not the problem of the specific kinds of life patterns embedded in the local community, say, patterns of rampant consumerism—what one could term "operational greed"—being lived out by the majority in the community.

Though patterns of behavior can pass into repetitive, embedded practice without ever going through discourse, they cannot, as Pierre Bourdieu warns us, be contested and changed apart from the intentionality that goes with discourse.[9] In many Churches persons have been empowered to speak knowledgeably about their sacred texts and about those texts' meaning for their inner life. Many, however, do not have a language by which to apply the texts to the patterns of exteriority in their lives, to the way they spend time, money, attention, and energies. These patterns, both among individuals and in the Church's own corporate life, are outside of discourse. When practices, for example those of consumerist greed, are ignored, they tend to generate their own false theory of Christian living, a theory that supposes Gospel fidelity to be unconnected with the use of money. Jacques Ellul reminds us that false practice can generate false theory, but in a particularly subtle and stubborn way:[10] we continue to maintain our stated "theory," when in fact it has been replaced by an unacknowledged operational theory derived from false practice. With the ease of the child in "The Emperor's New Clothes," my secondary school students of yesteryear objected that the actual ecclesiology in force in their parishes was quite different from the stated "theoretical" ecclesiology. Practice of any kind encodes in our lives values and attitudes we may never wish consciously to admit to ourselves. We are unwilling to see or decode what we ourselves have written into our own lives.

If it is true that one is what one does, then patterns of action determine the sort of person one becomes. Some of these patterns are consciously chosen, but many are simply fallen into, adopted through unspoken social permission or initiated in choices made but not examined, choices that bypass discourse. Often initiated without thought or even innocently, these patterns are not maintained without our own complicity. Whatever their origin in choice, all patterns shape the human spirit and a way of being an embodied spirit, that is, a spirituality.[11] At some point in its activity, religiousness must reflect on, not just its system of meanings but the conditions under which these meanings can be realized in concrete behavior. The word *conditions* here is important because it suggests that behavior is not simply individual but also contextual and social. One could ask, "Under what conditions do persons claiming discipleship with Jesus come to overlook the consequences for that discipleship of deeds—if not all deeds, then at least whole categories of deeds?" These conditions for overlooking or attending to deeds are my concern here.

Why has the liberationist concern with concrete patterns of behavior not been taken up by the Churches of privilege? Historical or tradition-laden reasons present themselves, as well as more immediate ones. Paulo Freire suggests to me one of the more immediate ones in a recent brief comment. He notes one of the conclusions of a 1975 UNESCO-sponsored international meeting on adult literacy: that programs of adult literacy "have been efficient in societies in which suffering and change created a special motivation in the people for reading and writing."[12] In other words, social conditions of suffering created among some a need for literacy not felt by those illiterates who were more comfortable. In a similar way, the positions of privilege occupied by those in the Churches of the well-off and very well-off do not spark the need for change. Among the classes of privilege, the conditions of prosperity hinder their probing the religious implications of these same conditions of prosperity.

To be sure, all patterns of practice tend to be taken for granted and invisible until the pattern is somehow disrupted. To return to the previous example, patterns of spending money become sharply visible when for some reason the money dries up; patterns of using transportation, when one's means of transportation breaks down; patterns of eating, when medical imperatives demand change. Built into the very nature of religious meaning is the possibility of calling into question patterns of practice. Religious meanings claim to be ultimate ones, worth suffering for, normative for living. Though this aspect of religiousness is not always called into play or can be muted in various ways, the claim of ultimacy remains embedded in religious traditions and its latent implications for living are always capable of being activated.

The fact remains that religions are not simply ways of thinking; they are also ways of living. Their religious understandings are to become lived realities. Practice remains the test of adherence to the religious system. In another of his writings, Gutierrez explains the prominence of practice for Christianity.

> Practice is the locus of verification of our faith in God, who liberates by establishing justice and right in favor of the poor. It is also the locus of verification of our faith in Christ. . . . Easter life is the life of practice. . . . The only faith-life is the one the Scriptures call "Witness." And witness is borne in works. To believe is to practice. Only from a point of departure at the level of practice, only from deed, can the proclamation by word be understood. In the deed our

faith becomes truth, not only for others, but for ourselves as well. We become Christians by acting as Christians. Proclamation in word only means taking account of this fact and proclaiming it. Without the deed, proclamation of the word is something empty, something without substance . . . [T]he relationship between deed and word is asymmetric. What basically counts is the deed. Of course it will not do to overemphasize this or push it to extremes; its only purpose is the better to express a complex reality. Jesus Christ, the heart of the Gospel message, is the Word made flesh, the Word become deed. Only in this unity of deed and word is there any sense in the distinctions we make in the task of proclaiming liberation in Jesus Christ.[13]

Unfortunately, this relationship of word and deed, of understanding and practice, has not always been maintained in Christianity, and residues of earlier misunderstandings remain in the tradition. How these misunderstandings emerged must now be examined.

Pieris's Analysis of the Displacement of *Agape*

The Jesuit theologian Aloysius Pieris reminds us that any religion must combine both loving action (*agape*) and the search for wisdom (*gnosis*). Along the roadsides of his own country, Sri Lanka, he finds two sets of statues that spell out for him the importance of the unification of loving action or *agape* and wisdom or *gnosis*. Each statue involves a tree, one symbolizing knowledge, the other, love-in-action:

> The tree beneath which Gotama, the Indian mystic, sits in a posture of contemplative calm, and the tree upon which Jesus the Hebrew prophet hangs in a gesture of painful protest— . . . the tree that bears the fruit of wisdom and the tree that bares the cost of love.[14]

For experiencing God and for expressing the fruits of our intimacy with God, each, *agape* and *gnosis*, is important. Together they represent "complementary idioms that need each other to mediate the self-transcending experience called salvation . . . ; any valid spirituality, Buddhist or Christian . . . retains both poles of religious experience, the gnostic and the agapeic."[15] Pieris's analysis of the functioning of the agapeic and the gnostic poles brings to light a historical irony, that the religion using the gnostic symbol of the tree of wisdom, Buddhism, has been able to hold onto the actual practice of love and the one using the agapeic symbol, Christianity, has tended to emphasize a particular gnostic strain. Pieris explains how this occurred.

In its early formative centuries, Christianity found itself in a gnostic milieu tending to assert that knowing the liberating truth is or leads to salvation. From the first, Christianity was able to find a theological formula able to maintain the gnostic pole without compromising the agape-ic. The theologies of John and Paul, according to Pieris, give concrete evidence of this formula. In John, the knowledge of the Father and the Son is given by the Spirit but leads to a discipleship which is a concrete way of loving one's neighbor. Here loving one's neighbor is a way of knowing God. One finds a similar bonding of knowledge and love in Paul's stress on brotherly love.

> Paul admits the possibility of knowing divine things but clearly considers such knowledge worthless without love. Paul puts a greater distance than John between *ginoskein* and *agapan* as between two different modes of human experience. But one can infer that for both [that is, John and Paul] the Sinai covenant of justice has received its final fulfillment in Jesus in whom mutual love among humans is the path to true gnosis—the knowledge of God through the Son in the Spirit.[16]

The wedding of these two elements was maintained in the carefully monitored catechumenal process of the early Church, with its emphasis on helping neophytes restructure their patterns of living. The catechumenate was a method of formation, not just in doctrinal purity, but even more basically in the reimagined self, with a redirected affectivity and restructured life patterns. Willingness to shift primary commitments at odds with Jesus' way is a recurring theme in early Christian writings. Origen writes, "When it becomes evident that the disciples are purified by the word and have begun, as far as possible, to live better, only then are they invited to know our mysteries" (C. Cels. 3, 59), adding in another place, "The profound and secret mysteries must not be given, at first, to disciples, but they must be first instructed in the correction of their lifestyle" (Hom. V,6 in Iud).[17] For Origen (d. ca. 254), restructuring of life had to precede being given the secrets of the Christian way, a matter that for a considerable period meant for some the life-threatening step of resigning from the Roman army. Tertullian (d. ca. 232) also stresses such basic shifts in ways of living: "It [penitence and change of one's ways] presses most urgently . . . upon those recruits who have just begun to give ear to the flow of divine discourse, and who, like puppies newly born, creep about uncertainly, with eyes as yet unopened. . . . We are not baptized so that we may cease committing sin but because we have ceased. . . ."[18]

So important were these re-oriented commitments as prior conditions for admission to full fellowship that the three-year length of the catechumenate was dictated by the usual length of time it took for the redirection of one's life structure.[19]

In the long run, however, the center did not always hold. Though he died three to five decades before either Origen or Tertullian, Irenaeus, bishop of Lyon in Gaul, influenced the shape of theology for centuries. Irenaeus's apologetic treatment of Christianity directed at Greek *thought* had behind it a legitimate academic thrust common to intellectual adherents of all religions.[20] This apologetic thrust, which influenced the Cappadocian and Latin Fathers, eventually became an academic tradition centering on systems of thought, encountering pagan philosophy rather than pagan religious ways. These Fathers looked to non-Christian philosophy for the intellectual means of grasping revelation conceptually. In such a movement, Christianity as a way of living—experiencing concrete symbols and embodying specific practices—though never completely overlooked, tended to be pushed into the background and became, in its radical embodiments, reserved for the monastic tradition, and later for communities practicing the evangelical counsels of poverty, chastity, and obedience. When intellectual elites produced doctrinal statements as norms of the community's authenticity, the text of the community's own life practice as a radical and indispensable means of interpreting the wider world received less focus. The double text meant to be bound together, the text of Scripture and the text of practice, came to drift apart.

In several places in his writings Edward Farley explores the more recent ways the disjunction of doctrine and practice has been carried into our own time. Though the importance of living the Gospel has never been lost—that is, the norms for acclaiming "heroic" holiness have always been centered in life practice—the emphasis on practice for more ordinary individuals and communities diminished. It is possible to conceive of religiousness as unconnected or only marginally connected with patterns of life practice, with the consequence that one's "religion" is a matter of the head, not of the hands and feet. Whole regions of human activity can become exempted from Gospel norms, such as the way one holds property or uses money; one's employment, its kind and outcomes; or one's exercise of social or political power. A tendency to envisage doctrinal instruction as a sufficient means of incorporating the young into the life of the community might be another contemporary instance of this error. Bureaucratic preoccupation with doctrinal exactness while overlooking anti-Gospel patterns of life might be another. To those who ask, "Who envisages doctrinal instruction this way?" I point out that we do not so envisage doctrinal instruction in our theory but rather in our expecting religious commitment to emerge from instruction cut off from the lived patterns of discipleship in communities of worship. My students of the early 1960s nimbly leaped to point out that error.

Pieris's analysis of this history is actually getting at Christianity in its character as a way of life, as *agape*, a way of living out a message of love in concrete practice. "To say 'Jesus is the Word' is not enough; the word must be heard and executed for one to be saved. To say 'Jesus is the path' is not enough; one must walk the path to reach the end. . . . What saves is not the name of Jesus in the hellenistic sense of the term, but the name of Jesus . . . in the Hebrew sense of 'the reality' that was operative in Jesus. . . . In fact, the knowledge of the name or title is not expected by the eschatological Judge, but the knowledge of the path is (Matt 25:37–39 and 44–46)."[21]

Consequently, the kerygma is not a theoretical, logical proposal but a "metalogical proclamation which cannot be demonstrated rationally." Its most convincing proof is witness, the lived-out agapeic behavior of some person or persons. In a passage that challenges all local Churches in the way they embody the Gospel message, Pieris claims: "Saying that Jesus is the medium of salvation requires that the ones who say it display the fruits of liberation. . . . A christology receives its authenticity from a transforming praxis which proves that in the story of Jesus, which continues in his followers, the medium of salvation is operative. . . ."[22]

One can communicate the coherent vision of Christian faith to any person who will stay still long enough to hear it. However, the communication of *the way of being a Christian* and the embracing of that way for oneself are quite another matter. Usually the validation of the Christian way is through action, first the action of those who show it is possible to live it and that indeed it does save, and secondly, the action of the one who embraces it for oneself and finds that, yes, for me it is salvific. Of course Christianity claims more than this. It claims that its way is also socially salvific, as announced by Jesus in the kingdom of God. That part of the Christian reality is verified in the social action of Christians for a just world. Multiple implications for pastoral action emerge from these ideas, as we shall see. An obvious one is that the Church is a zone where all offer thanks to God, ponder God's message, and also struggle with the problematic of practice.

The Material Conditions of Living

So far I have used various expressions to name the kind of life we live: the material conditions of life, life patterns, life structure. Some readers may have found this use of language unhelpful because inexact or vague. I sympathize because I myself have not found a literature laying out the material conditions of life with the specificity I would like. Marx's important work on the material bases of life was groundbreaking, but never worked out with highly specific examples. Possibly the specificity needed can best be attained by particular people struggling to name the patterns they themselves live, first in their own homes and then in their communities of worship and places of work. I have found help in this matter in a few pages of Daniel Levinson's study of sequential stages in the lives of men, *The Seasons of a Man's Life.*

In examining the transition to early adulthood, those five or six years between eighteen and twenty-three or twenty-four, when a person is moving from the world of adolescence into a first taste of adulthood, Levinson finds young men making a series of choices decisive for the life patterns that will determine much of later life. These somewhat tentative initial patterns lay the groundwork on which will be laid a life structure.

Speaking specifically of men, Daniel Levinson describes the life structure this way: "By life structure we mean the underlying pattern or design of a person's life at a given time. . . . A man's life has many components: his occupation, his love relationships, his marriage and family, his relation to himself, his use of solitude, his roles in various social contexts—all the relationships with individuals, groups and institutions that have significance for him. . . . The concept of life structure—the basic pattern or design of a person's life at a given time—gives us a way of looking at the engagement of the individual in society. It requires us to consider both self and world, and the relationships between them."[23]

Seeking a way to analyze a life structure, Levinson becomes more specific, naming the choices a person makes and how the person deals with their consequences. "The important choices in adult life have to do with work, family, friendships, and love relationships of various kinds, where to live, leisure, involvement in religious, political and community life, immediate and long-term goals."[24]

Here Levinson has moved into what I would call "descriptive analysis," which lays out patterns easily overlooked. This is a first analytic step. A second step would be a critical analysis, by which the life structure is not only described but judged from some other, "outside" vantage point. The only such vantage point Levinson uses is "psychological adjustment," that is, whether the person remains tolerably happy in the particular life structure and if not, whether he can make adjustments. My own critical vantage points are different, and have to do with the person's contribution to the human good and with the life structure's coherence with religious commitments.

Unfortunately, Levinson leaves us to work out any more specific descriptive details for ourselves. The task is not a simple one, as I found out in attempting to apply life structure to the brief period of the young adult transition. What many young people do not realize is that in one's late teens one is in a key phase of establishing one's *ways*. At that time one is developing behavioral patterns and life structure that will direct one's life for a long time to come: tastes in food; patterns in the use of time; preferences in and even styles of watching TV; ways of being with older people or of avoiding them; ways of behaving in groups; ways of studying, of reading, even of reading the newspaper—or a way of not reading it. It is not that every one of these ways is being newly formed, for indeed many of them go back to childhood. Still, freed from the countervailing childhood pulls from parents and home, these ways are being cemented into place. Being formed are ways of driving a car, ways of using alcohol, ways of relating to the opposite sex, ways of dealing with the truth, ways of getting one's own will, and far from the least important, ways of thinking about and using money. Behind the nexus of these patterns is a life structure that affects commitments.

Even these suggestions could be fleshed out in ever greater concreteness. Some research into rape by young men shows that a relatively high percentage of such rapists are members of athletic teams. Apparently there are ways of talking about women that become patterned in particular groups, such as fraternities or athletic teams, and these ways of talking can reinforce attitudes toward women that lead to rape.[25] On the other hand, there could also be groups of men who in their way of speaking of women exhibit and reinforce attitudes inimical to rape. What I am getting at here are patterns of interaction and of speech. A life structure is a pattern of choices and ways of living that becomes the accepted and eventually the established way for a person. Once it is established the pattern tends to perdure, in spite of shifts in location, career, or even marriage partner. For every age group after childhood (though children inhabit life structures too, at first chosen *for* them but eventually chosen *by* them), life structure, then, says a lot about what we pay attention to. Evidence of what matters are attended to in a particular life structure is found in specific documents of the sort that could be entered into court records:

> in one's checkbook;
> in a list of the things one has read over the past week or month;
> in what one watches on TV or how one watches TV or whether one
>   watches;
> in the tickets one buys and for what;
> in one's phone bill;
> in the kinds of liquids one consumes and under what circumstances;
> in one's credit card bill;
> in one's ways of spending leisure time;

in the patterns of eating;
in the mileage of one's commute to work or school;
in one's patterns of religious practice or lack of it.

These examples are set out here to provoke application to specific situations and ways of living. One could do a useful descriptive analysis of the material conditions of one's life by examining patterns of ingesting: food, drink, visual and aural information, visual and aural entertainment. What one ingests, where, at what times, with what others, might provide the basis of a fruitful analysis. A similar one could be undertaken about residence, its size, cost, its demand for care; its proximity or distance from work; its proximity or distance from other family or friends, and so forth. For some people the costs and other consequences of buying a home set the overall framework for life structure: the income needed; disposable income available; the transportation needs; the possibilities for leisure; and so forth.

"Sacralizing" Life Structure by Refusing to Judge It

At this point, some readers will have realized this essay is exploratory, in the sense that the writer is seeking to lay out a problem largely ignored in literature of a pastoral nature. Church bureaucracies remain much more troubled by what they consider lapses of orthodoxy than by lapses of orthopraxis. Except for sexuality, entire areas of life are excluded from Gospel norms. In one of his writings, the Renaissance humanist and reformer Erasmus of Rotterdam offers a blistering but comic critique of such blindness to the more important aspects of Christian living in his own time: "It may happen; it often does happen, that the abbot is a fool or a drunkard. He issues an order to the brotherhood in the name of holy obedience. And what will such an order be? An order to be sober? An order to tell no lies? No one of these things. It will be that a brother is not to learn Greek; he is not to seek to instruct himself. He may be a sot. He may go with prostitutes. He may be full of hatred and malice. He may never look inside the Scriptures. No matter. He has not broken any oath. He is an excellent member of the community. While if he disobeys such a command as this from an insolent superior there is stake or dungeon for him instantly."[26]

Again and again in the history of Christianity one finds resurfacing the sort of question Erasmus raises here about lived discipleship. As a social movement affecting European Christians, the Reformation itself is an important instance of such resurfacing.[27]

Once alerted to the dangerous shift in some patristic writings to right understanding as more crucial than right doing, the Churches, we might expect, would have greater sympathy for liberation theology's contemporary re-emphasis on practice. Yet, in the nations of economic privilege and in the Churches of the middle and upper classes this re-emphasis on practice has not taken place. Why not? One could further ask how it might be possible to move this issue more to the forefront of the agenda of local worshiping assemblies. I seek to pursue these two questions before reflecting on some of the problems I myself see in moving toward greater attention to life structure.

Why, then, has not this shift toward practice assumed greater attention in the Churches of privilege? There are many reasons, one of the chief being that in any society some groups are economically privileged by its social institutions. Those in the economically privileged strata find their privileges to be right and just. Their sense of rightness is reinforced by the social order's meaning system—the society's culture. For what a good human life is like, culture presents a set of norms most easily met by the privileged classes. As products of persons of privilege, those meanings maintain the social order supporting their interests.

One should not be surprised if religious understandings are also enlisted to promote such a social order and the privileges it offers some. It could even happen that those trained to mediate religious meaning have themselves sprung from the privileged classes, accustomed from their earliest ages to interpret religion so as not to contradict social class. Unwittingly, perhaps, these religious teachers can sacralize social class. If their sacred texts seem to privilege the poor, they may conclude that the true, deeper poverty is not economic misery, which does not afflict them, but emotional deprivation, which may.[28] It can happen that just as the lives of the privileged classes are dramatically different from those of the poor, so the religion of the privileged can be fundamentally reoriented so as to suit their privileges. Thus, the very places where the privileged assemble to worship provide them with a chorus of other voices affirming their status of privilege, in much the same way as do their network of friends and family, their neighborhoods, schools, places of business, social services, and so forth.

The situation is not hopeless, for the possibilities of conversion away from a "God for me" to Jesus' "God for the dispossessed" are always latent in any Christian group, if only because of the ultimate and normative claims their meanings make on them. Such normative claims make religion a zone of judgment, evaluative of all reality. If some group's sacred texts in fact privilege the poor as a key locus of the manifestation of God and if they as a group ever embrace this feature as normative for their lives, they will soon find they have to live a religion different from the one described above. Such a shift will not happen automatically but only from approaching the interpretation of sacred texts from what I will call a hermeneutics of dislocation. Here the norms of fidelity are not found via self-interest but by crossing over to the needs of those trapped in situations of economic misery and other forms of oppression. Stances of dislocation point to the strangers, to those who first appear nonneighbors but come to be seen as the human face of God. Bonds with such neighbors are forged through actions of solidarity. Such actions dislocate the comfortable from their life structure, allowing it to be scrutinized.

And so, since Christianity does privilege the poor, it bears within itself radical possibilities of contesting the privileges of wealth. Here is the answer to my second question of how it is possible to move the question of practice more to the center of worshiping assemblies. This move will never happen easily but only as part of a struggling, step-by-step recovery of a seminal feature of Christianity's own religious understanding. Once any ecclesial group recognizes and embraces the radical or culture-contesting features of its faith, its search for religious coherence will involve a struggle with life practice.

Reflecting on Life Practice: Further Problems

Working on life practice is not without problems, three of which I describe briefly here: the need to recognize multiple options among valid choices; the temptation to avoid the work of discernment and to substitute moralizing; and the need to accept religion as a zone of judgment.

I have used the term *struggle* here to speak of a local Church's effort to discern its religious faith's consequences for life practice. The word *struggle* implies that the correction of life practice cannot be done by formulaic cut-and-dried patterns that settle the matter forever.[29] The struggle with life practice also suggests there are multiple possibilities for answering the Gospel call for discipleship. Jesus' own way of living and his teaching provide the definitive norms for those who would follow him. But since Jesus' preaching shows wide boundaries of what is acceptable discipleship, even here we have no blueprint done to exact scale. Though the norms provide guidance, their nature is to offer general directions within which persons and communities have leeway, depending on circumstances and insight. The process of discernment is an ongoing, indeed endless, feature of discipleship and of discipleship's discourse about life practice. At the core of the problem of becoming more preoccupied with specific patterns of behavior lies the question of how discernment comes to be located at the heart of a community's life. Superficial communication on superficial issues leads to a superficial Church. Significant discourse on significant issues of discipleship is the antidote. Discernment is not the task of leaders only but of the whole local people seeking to make sense of the Gospel in particular circumstances. What may be acceptable in one situation may be deplorable in another. The history of response to any seminal feature of the Christian way reveals the variety of choices that have in fact led to heroic fidelity.

Moralizing, a process by which one person seeks to prescribe behavior for another but from outside the horizon of that other person, is an inappropriate way of fostering the life practice I am advocating here. Moralizing is a lazy way of dealing with the dilemma of specific response to the call of Jesus. Basically nondialogical, from a position of assumed power, it offers glib oughts and musts, when what is needed is a grappling with the dilemma of multiple acceptable choices in concrete circumstances. In the end the problem with moralizing is that its demands are so cheaply made anyone can walk away from them unaffected. Being invited to enter a community of ethical discourse based on normative sacred texts would seem the proper way of engaging people's religious consciousness. What I advocate here are reflection and analysis, not so much about particular acts as about the entire context of living and how particular acts relate to it. Reflection and analysis engage, in a way moralizing cannot, the problem of behavior from the point of view of particular persons and groups in particular circumstances. When a community engages its members in the problematic of behavior—in exploring Jesus' proposals for human living and their meaning for a particular time and place—those members will have entered a process they can inhabit as their own, not one pushed on them by religious bosses.[30]

Basically, the process I have in mind is one that embraces the role of judgment in religious traditions. By its nature, a religion is a zone of judgment. This same nature involves it in an endless process of interpretation of situations and events toward judgment and decision. Holding its meanings to be ultimate and salvific—normative—a religion uses those meanings as a yardstick for evaluating all of reality. It is not that persons of goodwill may not opt for other norms and arrive at different conclusions deserving respectful dialogue,[31] or that particular areas of life do not have their own norms, such as aesthetic criteria of beauty in the arts. Still, for religious persons ultimate norms are always there in the background able to be activated when claims conflict about what is truly or ultimately good or beautiful or just. As already noted, these norms can be subverted by being reduced, usually unwittingly, to legitimations for society's institutions and culture. In such a case religion undergirds, and in a sense verifies, society's unspoken claim that *its* meanings and institutions are the ones that are truly ultimate. Religion can still sell its heritage for a bowl of pottage.

Searching Out a Method for Reflecting on Practice

I have here claimed an absence in pastoral literature—liberation theology excepted—of the question of living practice of discipleship. The absence is not now total, nor has it ever been, as shown in the long history of the veneration of those who proved themselves virtuosos in embodying Gospel values in their own lives, the saints. There are contemporary authors who deal explicitly with the problem, while others are dealing with questions, such as inculturation, that, if followed through to their logical end, will lead to the matter of life practice.[32] Are there methods for exposing the difficult to discern features of the life practice lived by the local Church or by individual households? Put this way, the question itself must first be examined for its assumptions. Is the practice of discipleship a science or an art? If a science, then, it should be possible to find formulaic methods sure to lead to desired results. Skillful analysis discloses steps designed to produce predicted outcomes. However, the human dilemmas at the heart of finding appropriate responses to the Gospel mandate in particular circumstances do not lend themselves to formulaic solutions. The very elements of such dilemmas: persons already embedded in patterns of action; consciousnesses already affected by culture; normative but open-ended texts calling for response; proposed ways of interpreting these texts; complex situations calling for response; ways of being together in community—such elements indicate what is needed is an art of practice, not a science of using tested procedures for predictable outcomes.

Though both science and art call for vision and skill, art makes greater use of flexible creativity in solving the problems of realizing vision. The visual arts alone show us the infinite ways of depicting some aspect of reality or artistic vision: there is no one correct way. Further, failure in art is not so easily named as in science, where, say, an experiment at its completion is either successful or not. However, artists scorned in their lifetimes can later be hailed as creative geniuses. If there is any method—apart from methods of developing skill—in art, it is best uncovered in an "after the fact" examination of what actually happened rather than in an a priori statement of theoretical outcomes.[33] Here the appropriate descriptive word may be *process* rather than *method*.

In examining an actual process used in art, one may discover valuable methodological clues as to how vision and skill were melded at particular junctures in the actual doing of something.

Conclusion

Some will note that here I have often alluded to specific patterns of life practice but in very few places have I actually named some of these patterns. What are some ways of exposing and naming the practices we actually live or of finding alternative practices? Are there any procedures that might be suggested as a way forward in the task I have sought to examine here? The following are some suggestions for further work on the material conditions of the practice of discipleship.

Case studies of local Churches as they have been able to transform concrete Church practice toward a more radical Gospel life would provide helpful clues about how such a transformation takes place. My hunch is that any such transformation comes from a kind of "cultural dislocation," a shift from the comfortable assumptions driving Church life structure to a series of troubling, problem-filled matters that need attention and a new way of proceeding. These case studies cannot remain with shifts in the Church's inner operations; they must get at how the Church responded to Gospel challenges in its own social context, especially in its responses to the victims of society, those proxies of Christ in our midst. One of the problems I have with the capsule case studies in Patrick Brennan's *Parishes That Excel*[34] survey is that so many of the excellent developments are described at a managerial and programmatic level without sufficient attention to the wider social context in which the Church exists. To describe "excellent youth evangelization" in a church ringed by military bases without at the same time probing the Church's stance toward the programs of death and domination embodied in those bases does not help get at the sort of life structure conditions I have in mind here. Could a youth evangelization program be named excellent at the same time that it has removed from its Good News Jesus' call for nonviolence or a critique of militarization and weapons production? Could there have been parishes that excelled managerially in Nazi Germany?

Concrete procedures are called for, by which local groups might work toward the sort of cultural dislocation that could lead to transformed life practice at the communal level but also in individual homes and lives. Edward Farley offers an outline of such a procedure in his abstruse essay "Interpreting Situations."[35] This outline could be concretized and made accessible to many. A similar sort of procedure is offered in the 1984 statement of the Canadian Roman Catholic Bishops, *Ethical Choices and Political Challenges*.[36] What they call a pastoral methodology for helping the Church make judgments about social conditions is as follows:

A. Being present with and listening to the experiences of the poor, the marginalized, the oppressed in our society;
B. Developing a critical analysis of the economic, political, and social structures that cause human suffering;
C. Making judgments in the light of Gospel principles and the social teachings of the Church concerning social values and priorities;
D. Stimulating creative thought and action regarding alternative visions and models for social and economic development; and
E. Acting in solidarity with popular groups in their struggles to transform economic, political, and social structures that cause social and economic injustices.

In my view this process has built into it clear elements of cultural dislocation.

A third suggestion that might help take forward the project of greater attention to life structure would involve "cognitive mapping." Fredric Jameson suggests such a procedure in his response to the problem of helping people separate out for themselves a moment of truth from the many moments of illusion. He suggests the possibility that the material conditions of our lives, even when we become aware of them, may tend "to demobilize us and to surrender us to passivity and helplessness,"[37] because of their seeming historical inevitability. Indeed, Jameson himself suggests that culture is no longer an area of social life that can be considered separate from economics or politics. In our time he finds "a prodigious expansion of culture throughout the social realm, to the point at which everything in our social life—from economic value and state power to practices and to the very structure of the psyche itself—can be said to have become 'cultural' in some original and as yet untheorized sense."[38] All cultural "space" has been taken over and colonized by the logic of late capitalism.

Jameson believes the new situation can be countered only by means of a new kind of activity he calls "a radical cultural politics." His proposed new form of human agency is grounded in cognitive mapping, an activity analogous to the mapping of urban space. An alienated city is a space where people are unable to map in their own minds either their positions in the city or their relationship to the city as a whole. Such a city is lacking markers like monuments or boundaries like parks or road patterns, to allow people to see where they are. Urban mapping disalienates because it discloses the human construction of urban space hidden to the casual observer. Similarly, cognitive mapping disalienates because it shows persons their relationships to their wider social space: their cultural space.[39]

I find merit in Jameson's suggestion for cognitive mapping—vague as it is. He admits it is an idea that needs to be worked out in concrete strategies. In reading Jameson, I found myself thinking of another kind of space, the space inhabited by those gathered around an altar as a sacred space uniting them to all others as children of God. This space, and the imagery brought to bear there on all of life, offer those gathered a fundamental point of orientation in their perception of reality and in their relation to the world. Because of its claims to ultimacy, here is a "cognitive map" of *potentially* transformative power. Its potential becomes actual when the community embraces the poor, the marginal, the victims, and the despised. My question: will religious persons make use of this power to free themselves from the false imaginations of what human existence is meant to be?

The obvious way to finding new forms of practice in the church is to engage in new, more radical forms of action, since action both will be the heart of a struggle for these forms of practice and will provide a concrete basis for evaluating what the church does.[40] However we look at them, these forms of practice will continue to provide the context for the church's work of catechesis. The teaching taught by the practice is certain to remain more powerful than any kind of teaching that ignores practice.

NOTES

1. William Seth Adams, "De-coding the Obvious: Reflections on Baptismal Ministry in the Episcopal Church," *Worship* 66 (July 1992): 327–338.

2. Gustavo Gutierrez, *A Theology of Liberation*, trans. Caridad Inda and John Eagleson (Maryknoll, NY: Orbis Books, 1973), 3.

3. Joseph Komonchak, "Ecclesiology and Social Theory," *The Thomist* 45 (1981): 283.

4. In this essay I step away from using the word *praxis*, at least in the sense used by Paulo Freire, with its necessary connection to theory. Neither do I delve into the history of the idea of action/praxis so helpfully explicated by Hannah Arendt in *The Human Condition* (Chicago: University of Chicago Press, 1958), 175–247, and *Between Past and Future* (New York: Viking Press, 1961), 91–141.

Sometimes *practice* and *praxis* are used interchangeably, as seems to be the case in Martin Jay's *The Dialectical Imagination* (Boston: Little, Brown, 1973). Here I have selected practice as my category, to call attention thereby to Alisdair MacIntyre's proposals on practice in *After Virtue*, cited in n. 8 below. His positive meaning for practice needs a complementary *pejorative* meaning to describe patterns of behavior that are in place but not reflected on. There seem to be elements of this pejorative sense in Pierre Bourdieu's meaning for practice in *Outline of a Theory of Practice* (London: Cambridge University Press, 1977) and in other writings of his, and in his attempt to recover such patterns for reflection.

Thomas McCarthy's translation of Habermas's two-volume *Theory of Communicative Action* consistently uses the word *action* for what some might prefer to call praxis.

5. Paul VI, Apostolic Exhortation, *Evangelii nuntiandi*, "On Evangelization in the Modern World" (Washington, DC: United States Catholic Conference, 1976), no. 15.

6. Ibid., no. 21.

7. Cited in Thomas McCarthy, *The Critical Theory of Jürgen Habermas* (Cambridge, MA: MIT Press, 1978), 63. The source of the quote is Peirce's essay, "How to Make Our Ideas Clear," in *Writings of Charles Sanders Peirce: A Chronological Edition*, vol. 3 (1872–1878) (Bloomington, IN: Indiana University Press, 1986), 257–275, at 263–264.

8. Here I am following a description of practice and its conditions found in Alisdair MacIntyre, *After Virtue* (Notre Dame, IN: University of Notre Dame Press, 1981), 175–178. The quote is on page 177. For an attempt to apply MacIntyre's ideas to specific practices of the church, see Craig Dykstra, "Reconceiving Practice," in Edward Farley and Barbara Wheeler, eds., *Shifting Boundaries: Contextual Approaches to the Structure of Theological Education* (Richmond, VA: John Knox Press, 1991).

9. Bourdieu, *Outline of a Theory of Practice*, 87–88.

10. Jacques Ellul, *The Subversion of Christianity* (Grand Rapids, MI: William B. Eerdmans, 1986), 4.

11. Here I am following the fine analysis of Roger Haight in "Critical Witness: The Question of Method," in Leo J. O'Donovan and T. Howland Sanks, eds., *Faithful Witness: Foundations of Theology for Today's Church* (New York: Crossroad, 1989), 185–204, esp. 202–204.

12. Brenda Bell et al., eds., *We Make the Road by Walking, Miles Horton and Paulo Freire: Conversations on Education and Social Change* (Philadelphia: Temple University Press, 1990), 77.

13. Gustavo Gutierrez, *The Power of the Poor in History* (New York: Orbis Books, 1983), 17.

14. Aloysius Pieris, "Christianity and Buddhism in Core-to-Core Dialogue," *Cross Currents* 37 (spring 1987): 47–75, at 48.

15. Ibid.

16. Ibid., 52. In another essay Pieris explains the same phenomenon: "In the formative centuries of Christian monasticism, the gnostic spirituality of the non-Christian gradually filtered into the agapeic religiosity of the monks. While this symbiosis was taking place in the silence of the monastic cells, the academic theologians of the church were busy experimenting with the legal language of the Latins and the philosophical thought of the Greeks to make 'precision instruments' that would enable the human mind to fathom the Mystery of Christ, thus producing a vast corpus of theological literature that paved the way for Christological dogmas and, centuries later, *for an overgrowth of scholasticism"* (emphasis added). A. Pieris, "Western Models of Inculturation: How Far Are They Applicable in Non-Semitic Asia?" in *An Asian Theology of Liberation*

(Maryknoll, NY: Orbis Books, 1988), 56. Also in *Vidyajota* (Sri Lanka) (October 1985): 345–445, at 442.

17. Both quotes appear in D. Capelle, "L'Introduction du catéchuménat à Rome," *Recherches de théologie ancienne et médiévale* 5 (1933): 151, notes 38 and 39.

18. Tertullian, "On Penitence," *Treatises on Penance*, trans. W. Le Saint (Westminster: Newman, 1959), 24, 25–26.

19. Regis Duffy, "Liturgical Catechesis: Catechumenal Models," unpublished paper, given as the Mary Charles Bryce Lecture, Catholic University, Washington, DC, April 1983.

20. Here I am following Aloysius Pieris in *Love Meets Wisdom* (Maryknoll, NY: Orbis Books, 1988), 17–42, esp. 18–23.

21. Some particular examples: Edward Farley, "Theology and Practice Outside the Clerical Paradigm," in Don S. Browning, ed., *Practical Theology* (San Francisco: Harper and Row, 1983), 21–41; *Theologia: The Fragmentation and Unity of Theological Education* (Philadelphia: Fortress Press, 1983), esp. chapter 4, "Schleiermacher and the Beginning of the Encyclopedia Movement," 73–94, but also 127–134; "Interpreting Situations: An Inquiry into the Nature of Practical Theology," in Lewis S. Mudge and James N. Poling, eds., *Formation and Reflection: The Promise of Practical Theology* (Philadelphia: Fortress, 1987), 1–35.

For Farley on the materiality of ecclesial life, see *Ecclesial Reflection: An Anatomy of Theological Method* (Philadelphia: Fortress Press, 1982), esp. chapters 9, 10, 11.

22. Pieris, "Core-to-Core Dialogue," 73.

23. Ibid.

24. Daniel Levinson, *The Seasons of a Man's Life* (New York: Alfred A. Knopf, 1978), 41–42.

25. Ibid., 43.

26. Chris O'Sullivan, "Campus Rape Is Usually Fraternity-Related," Letters to the Editor, *New York Times* (5 December 1990), A26. See also Gerald Eskenazi, "The Male Athlete and Sexual Assault," *New York Times* (3 June 1990), L1, L4.

27. I realize the Reformation's complexity is such that it cannot be reduced to this single aspect.

28. See the description of this process in Gregory Baum, *Truth Beyond Relativism: Karl Mannheim's Sociology of Knowledge* (Milwaukee, WI: Marquette University Press, 1977), 60–62.

29. Cut-and-dried formulas also tend to be reductionistic, even trivializing the open-endedness of the Gospel's demands. The lists of sins offered for preparation for the sacrament in Roman Catholic devotional books, even for years after Vatican II, though they do call attention to concrete behavior, reduce the behavior to negative acts easily numbered for the sake of accuracy. This kind of limiting has a long history, as can be seen in the following handbook for determining both sins and the penalties needing to be fulfilled before they could be pardoned: "Haltigar: Prescriptions for Sins," in Charles Jaeckle and William A. Clebsch, eds., *Pastoral Care in Historical Perspective* (New York: Jason Aronson, 1975), 148–164.

30. See the helpful comments on "discourse ethics" in Paul Lakeland, *Theology and Critical Theory* (Nashville, TN: Abingdon, 1990), 174–207.

31. Here I do not emphasize the matter of dialogue, a basic issue in our world. I agree with Johann Baptist Metz that religious people have to enter a "hermeneutical culture" marked by respectful dialogue ("encountering others in their otherness") toward coping with human problems. Johann Baptist Metz, "With the Eyes of a European Theologian," in L. Boff and V. Elizondo, eds., *The Voice of the Victims*, Concilium (London: SCM Press, 1990), 113–119.

32. Among Roman Catholics, Francis Schüssler Fiorenza's *Foundational Theology* (New York: Crossroad, 1984) raises important issues related to practice, as does Edward Schillebeeckx in his more recent *Church: The Human Story of God* (New York: Crossroad, 1990); also, *Faithful Witness*, already cited in note 11. In the writings of the most philosophical of modern Roman Catholic theologians, Karl Rahner, I find practice a seminal concern.

33. My point here is similar to Edith Wyschogrod's argument against moral theory as basically failing to achieve its predetermined goal of transforming moral conduct. Her examination of saints and saintliness chooses instead to examine life histories and recover from them their "exhortative force" and their patterns of practice. See *Saints and Postmodernism: Revisioning Moral Philosophy* (Chicago: University of Chicago Press, 1990), xiii–xxvii.

34. Patrick Brennan, *Parishes That Excel: Models of Excellence in Education, Ministry, and Evangelization* (New York: Crossroad, 1992).

35. See Lewis S. Mudge and James N. Poling, eds., *Formation and Reflection: The Promise of Practical Theology* (Philadelphia: Fortress Press, 1987), 1–35.

36. Canadian Conference of Catholic Bishops, *Ethical Choices and Political Challenges: Ethical Reflections on the Future of Canada's Socioeconomic Order* (Ottawa, 1984), 2.

37. Fredric Jameson, "Postmodernism, or the Cultural Logic of Late Capitalism," *New Left Review* 146 (July–August 1984): 53–92, at 86.

38. Ibid., 88.

39. See ibid., 89–92.

40. Roger Haight writes: "Christian spirituality means living out . . . vision in action. When spirituality is thus conceived as human action, one has the basis for an objective consideration of the adequacy of the method of theology. Christian life and action unfold within the church in its mission to the world and within the world itself." "Critical Witness," 203.

PART D
Evaluating Catechetical Structures and Developments

Introduction

MICHAEL WARREN

The *General Catechetical Directory,* a Vatican Council II document in the sense that it was mandated by the Council, has in its final section (Part VI) seven brief but crucial chapters on pastoral catechetical action at a national level. Such national pastoral action is to be set up under the Conference of Bishops and structured so that pastoral action in the ministry of the word can be carried out in an efficient and coordinated way. These chapters provide wise guidelines for national structures supporting catechesis at all levels.

Since the Directory's publication in 1971, Berard Marthaler has been keeping a keen eye on both these directives and their sometimes erratic implementation in the United States. Residing in Washington, D.C., where the offices of the National Conference of Catholic Bishops (NCCB) and its programmatic arm, the United States Catholic Conference (USCC), are located, Marthaler is conversant with the working of the national catechetical scene. Since, over a period of twenty-five years, he has done perhaps the most sustained of all scholarly research in the archives of the NCCB and the USCC, he writes here with knowledgeable conviction.

Using his skills as a trained historian, Marthaler surveys the story of parish catechetical structures and the way they grew to need more astute diocesan, regional, and then national organizational support structures. He points out that such structures are not frills but indispensable vehicles for the sharing of problems and developments as well as for general communication among catechetical leaders. He sketches the "fragmentation" of catechetical structures at the national and diocesan levels that has taken place since 1975, and hints at the unhappy results.

Those preparing for catechetical leadership—most of those who will consult this *Sourcebook*—do well to give attention and thought to the issues Marthaler raises in his first essay. These matters deserve to be talked out in spirited discussion. Readers may want to do some of their own creative thinking about how local or regional structures for sharing and collaboration might be implemented. Lacking such structures, we find ourselves opting, willy-nilly, to block sharing and collaboration, and, in the end, to diminish ministry itself.

Marthaler's second essay surveys the important role that catechetical conferences and congresses have played in the United States. I presume many readers on reflection will find, as I do, that key formative moments in their pastoral formation are anchored in such gatherings. For me the Liturgical Conference's Congress in Baltimore in the mid-1960s showed me the stirring power of liturgy well planned and carried out. A fledgling educator, I would never be the same. About the same time, my first national meeting of the Religious Education Association, held in Chicago, allowed me to encounter firsthand and for the first time a dimension of learning through involvement in a very large group. At such moments in such groups the chances for new insights and questions seem endless.

Again, with the historian's eye, Marthaler shows us how such events play an important part in the entire modern catechetical movement. Though highlighting the East Coast Conference, he implicitly honors the role of other such regional conferences that followed its lead. We are in the debt of those who work to make such events possible. The work of discerning the need for such events and of setting them up is an open-ended one beckoning to us from the future.

Further Reading

Marthaler, Berard L. "Is It Time for a National Catechetical Office in the National Conference of Catholic Bishops?" *The Jurist* 50 (1990): 2, 553–572.

The Rise and Decline of the CCD

BERARD L. MARTHALER, OFM CONV

Any discussion of the Confraternity of Christian Doctrine would be a great deal easier if someone had thought to make CCD a registered trademark like IBM or Coke. When Pope Pius X revived the Confraternity of Christian Doctrine in 1905, it was clear that he had in mind an association of dedicated, lay catechists banded together for mutual support. As the Confraternity began to take shape in the United States in the years immediately before and after World War I, it was distinguished by its mission and lay character. By the time the National Center of Religious Education—CCD, the brainchild of Bishop Edwin O'Hara—was established in 1935, the Confraternity had developed rather complex structures and methods. In the years after Vatican II, however, CCD came to be used as a label for every kind of religious education program for children, and sometimes for teenagers as well. Andrew Greeley has referred to it rather disparagingly, but perhaps correctly, as a "movement." In the popular mind, the one common feature of CCD programs is that they offer an alternative to parochial schools. Recent editions of the *Official Catholic Directory* name it a "corporation." Were CCD a registered trademark, its proprietors might have been able to preserve a clearer identity and the good name of Confraternity.

This essay surveys the development of the Confraternity in the United States from its modest beginnings as an example of a lay apostolate, through its period of greatest achievement in the years immediately following Vatican II, to its decline in the last decade. The lessons to be learned from this brief history seem to this author to be self-evident, but the readers will have to judge that for themselves.

Reprinted from *Chicago Studies* 29, no. 1 (April 1990): 3–15. Copyright © 1990 by Civitas Dei Foundation. Used with permission.

The Early Years

Pius X brought considerable pastoral experience to the papacy. As a seminarian and young priest, Giuseppe Sarto taught catechism, and as bishop he gave catechesis a high priority in the diocese of Mantua and later in Venice. He repeatedly reminded priests to present Christian doctrine clearly and simply, and to deal thoroughly with the catechesis of adults which, he felt, had been neglected because the instruction of children took precedence. When pope, he set the example: on Sunday he regularly explained the catechism to all who came.

At the turn of the century, country after country in Europe secularized the schools, driving the clergy and religious men and women from the classrooms. As a means of counteracting this deplorable trend, Pius X outlined a series of measures in his encyclical *Acerbo nimis* (1905). It decreed that the Confraternity of Christian Doctrine be established in every parish in the Catholic world, and called for the employment of lay catechists to help in the Church's teaching mission. (On another occasion he said, "It is easier to find a brilliant orator than a catechist who is an excellent teacher.") The 1918 Code of Canon Law incorporated the requirement of *Acerbo nimis* that the Confraternity was to be established in every parish (c. 711.2).

Originally established by Charles Borromeo in the sixteenth century, the Confraternity was a pious association that promised special graces and indulgences to men and women who assisted in the catechetical mission of the Church. And in fact, the Confraternity of Christian Doctrine in the United States predates *Acerbo nimis.* In 1902, a small group of lay people in Our Lady of Good Counsel Church in New York City, concerned about the lack of instruction available to children and adults, organized an inter-parish program for children and youth. The idea caught on. Later that year they published, with the imprimatur of Archbishop Farley, a *Manual of the CCD in the Archdiocese of New York.* The Manual outlined the ideals of the Confraternity, encouraged the recruitment of "generous teachers," described how volunteers could contribute to the task, and stressed the importance of adult catechesis. Given a new impetus by Pius X's encyclical, the movement grew, and in 1909 a diocesan CCD congress was held.

From the beginning, the Confraternity in the United States was a lay movement, a form of Catholic action, that stressed the importance of outreach. Nowhere was this more evident than in the mining towns of Pennsylvania. Mary Downey James tells a moving story of the early days of the Missionary Confraternity of Christian Doctrine (MCDD) in the Pittsburgh diocese, based on newspaper accounts, parish records, personal memoirs, and oral histories. "Lay missionaries," anxious to support their fellow Catholics, went out weekly to teach in towns where there was no church, no priest. They held their classes in tents, private homes, cellars, stables, Miners' Halls, boxcars and a jail. The catechists found many of the Catholics destitute, lacking basic necessities, and members of the MCDD began to solicit funds to help them.

The members of the Confraternity had the full backing of Bishop Canevin, who assigned a priest full-time to assist the volunteers. The city of Pittsburgh was the original hub of the MCDD, and in time, hubs were established in other cities in western Pennsylvania. Workers were recruited locally, organizational meetings were held, officers elected, and the training of catechists was undertaken. By 1919 the MCDD numbered 500 teachers, involved in 153 schools of religion, enrolling more than 13,000 children and young people in the classes. The MCDD laid the foundation and organized many of the communities that would later have resident pastors.

In 1919, *Our Sunday Visitor* carried an article on the Pittsburgh MCDD that caught the eye of Verona Spellmire, a public school teacher and volunteer social worker in Los Angeles. She saw the Confraternity as a way of addressing the needs of the Mexican immigrants who were settling in the city, but not being assimilated into the Catholic parishes. Robert E. Lucy, then director of Catholic Charities in Los Angeles, endorsed the idea, and it received the backing of Archbishop John J. Cantwell. In the early years the members of the CCD worked under the aegis of the welfare agency, often providing clothing and other essentials for poor children attending the schools of religion.

The Los Angeles Confraternity, modeled on the Missionary CCD in Pittsburgh, developed new structures and itself became the model for other CCD programs around the country. The Reverend Leroy Callahan, the first full-time diocesan director in Los Angeles, ably assisted by Spellmire and Alice Vignos, produced catechetical materials and developed instructional stratagems for use outside a formal school setting. "Practical catechetics," wrote Joseph B. Collins of the work in Los Angeles, "was born here in the hard school of necessity." In the summer of 1929, Callahan organized summer vacation schools throughout the diocese: 11,500 children participated in 116 schools under the direction of 500 teachers and helpers.

Through the 1920s and into the 1930s the Confraternity spread from diocese to diocese, especially in the rural areas of the Midwest, Southwest and Far West, but it was chiefly due to the efforts of Edwin O'Hara that the CCD became a national organization. As a young priest in Portland, Oregon, he became consumed with the necessity of catechizing both children and adults. He learned early on, writes Joseph B. Collins, "that catechesis and social welfare go hand in hand." Under his inspiration and direction the National Catholic Rural Life Conference made common cause with the Confraternity of Christian Doctrine to provide comprehensive religious education programs in rural areas. (O'Hara had organized summer vacation schools as early as 1921, and it was O'Hara who had encouraged Father Callahan to develop them in Los Angeles.)

It is reported that on the very afternoon in 1930 that he was consecrated bishop of Great Falls, Montana, O'Hara announced that he was determined to establish the Confraternity in every parish in the diocese. His first pastoral letter laid out specific directives for vacation schools and, ultimately, year-round schools of religion in all parishes and missions. "The Confraternity," he wrote, "is no perfunctory organization, but it is an authorized agency for home mission work within the diocese" (p. 182). The pastoral letter laid the foundation for training courses for lay teachers and a network of study clubs for adults.

A National Organization

As early as 1933, Bishop O'Hara broached the idea of establishing a national office of the Confraternity under the auspices of the Rural Life Office of the National Catholic Welfare Conference. Instead, the American bishops (at O'Hara's instigation) voted to establish an Episcopal Committee of the CCD with Archbishop McNicholas of Cincinnati and Archbishop Murray of St. Paul as members, and Bishop O'Hara as chairman. On the same day that the Committee was appointed (14 November 1934), they met and agreed on opening a national center for the Confraternity in Washington, D.C. It was, O'Hara explained, to be a clearinghouse and a service for diocesan directors and leaders in parish units, not an executive center directing local activities. Within months O'Hara wrote to Dom Augustine Walsh, OSB, who had been appointed director.

> I have been getting certain basic suggestions together which I am submitting to all the bishops prior to their meeting after Easter. I enclose a copy for a suggested constitution of the confraternity for local parish units and also a plan for organization. I am working on a series of leaflets, including those for discussion clubs, vacation schools, parent-educators, etc., so I can submit to my committee of bishops a rounded program for them to approve. (P. 185)

Almost simultaneous with the opening of the National Center, the Congregation of the Council in Rome published the decree *Provido sane;* it was known in the English translation as "Better Care and Promotion of Catechetical Instruction." It stipulated that the Confraternity takes precedence over all other parish associations, and directed that diocesan and national offices be established to promote, support and coordinate the work of the CCD at local levels.

O'Hara's early experience in rural parishes had convinced him of the inadequacy of Sunday schools that were not supported by religious training in the home and the community at large. He found it impossible to educate children and young people unless adult Catholics themselves were interested in learning. His vision was to integrate the Confraternity in the parish, making catechesis a community activity.

The National Center made the parish Confraternity the basic organizational unit. The members included the teachers and the taught, parishioners directly involved in catechetical instruction and others who supported the work in various ways. There were six departments: teachers, fishers, helpers, parent educators, discussion clubs, and the Apostolate to Non-Catholics (later called the Apostolate of Good Will). A lay executive board made up of representatives of each of these departments coordinated the programs in the parish.

In this scheme of things the Confraternity presented a program in total religious education. Instruction was not an end in itself, but a means to foster Catholic identity and inculcate Christian values. Everyone was involved in catechesis in one way or another. The "helpers" were teachers' aides, the "fishers" went after truants, parents were expected to help with homework. A well-organized CCD unit was a beehive of activity that ran year-round. It had vacation schools for young children, sacramental preparation for First Penance and First Communion, social programs for young people, study clubs for adults, and an outreach effort for the unchurched. The National Center published materials for teacher training, sponsored a revision of the Baltimore catechism, and promoted Bible study.

Many factors contributed to the phenomenal growth of the CCD in the years before Vatican II. First of all, it had the enthusiastic support of able and well-placed bishops like O'Hara, Murray and McNicholas. Then, the National Center provided leadership and services, especially in the area of teacher and catechist training, which remained the centerpiece in every program. And third, it was community-based, everyone's responsibility, and it involved adults. The early champions of CCD did not look on the Confraternity programs merely as makeshift or stopgap for children unable to attend Catholic schools, but as a full-fledged institution in its own right.

Schools and the CCD

Parishes too small or too spread out to maintain a parochial school found the Confraternity a suitable vehicle for a community-based catechetical program. Built on the support of adults, parents, lay administrators, and volunteer teachers, the parts supported one another. The Confraternity with its emphasis on social activities as well as on instruction was adapted to work in high school programs. It helped teenagers to identify with the local Church in areas where they lived in several school districts and attended different high schools.

In dioceses and parishes where schools were the focus of Church life, the Confraternity was often a source of friction and dissension. Despite the efforts of bishops and pastors to gloss over the difficulties, smooth hurt feelings and patch up differences as best they could, anecdotes abound that illustrate CCD's role as Cinderella in many parishes. Parochial school teachers resented the use of *their* classrooms for CCD. Distinctions were made between public school children and children who attended parochial schools in the First Communion processions, CCD girls not being allowed to wear white veils! Ultimately, in the years after Vatican II, the question became one of money, teacher salaries versus the cost of hiring a professional DRE and staff for the CCD program.

At the diocesan level the tug-of-war over resources and policy was felt most acutely in medium-sized dioceses. Large archdioceses such as Boston, New York, Chicago and Los Angeles resolved the tension by creating parallel structures to direct and service the schools and CCD programs. Very small dioceses, often with few schools and limited personnel, did not feel the problem because the vicars of education (or whatever the title) dealt with religious education from a single office.

Late in 1963, Mary Perkins Ryan published *Are Catholic [Parochial] Schools the Answer?* The publication coincided with the fanfare that greeted the first session of the Second Vatican Council and seemed to find a good deal of support with the promulgation of the Constitution on the Liturgy. (Mary Ryan had come to religious education via a professional interest in liturgical studies.) First, it must be said in defense of Mary Ryan that her book was not an assault on Catholic *education*. Her thesis was that Catholic *education* is a broader and more complex enterprise than Catholic schools. Her concern was that religious education not stop when one graduates from high school or college. The main purpose of Catholic education is Christian formation that transforms the community––the Church as a whole—as well as individuals.

Although *Are Catholic [Parochial] Schools the Answer?* has little to say about CCD as such, "from that time on," declares Andrew Greeley writing in these pages last November, "CCD claimed that the image of 'movement' in the 'new' Church while Catholic schools were relegated to the status of an institution of the 'old' Church." In the 1960s school offices, faced with dwindling numbers of religious to staff their programs, found themselves in competition with a phenomenon they did not create and often did not understand. The diocesan CCD offices, staffed in large part by laity and former religious, rode the crest of enthusiasm and new interests unleashed by the Second Vatican Council. Diocesan directors of religious education (CCD), in some cases by design, in some cases by default, took the initiative in popularizing the teachings and reforms of Vatican II.

They were in the backfield scoring points and garnering headlines, while the school personnel were doing the grunt work on the line. The diocesan directors, recognizing both the challenge and the opportunity presented by a changing ecclesiology, zealously promoted broad-based catechetical programs and, at the national level, organized as an advocacy group to shape policy and raise consciousness about the need for total religious education.

At the time that Ryan wrote *Are Catholic [Parochial] Schools the Answer?* the Church was investing personnel and resources in a school system to a degree that seemed disproportionate to the numbers served. She quoted statistics to show that the schools reached only about fifty-five percent of the Catholic children on the elementary level, forty-five percent on the high school level, and thirty-seven percent of Catholic young people on the college level. She predicted, correctly it now seems, that without government support these percentages would likely decrease.

Community-Based Catechesis

Ryan presented an overview of history to show that the Church had never relied totally, or even chiefly, on schools to carry on its catechetical mission. She argued that the Church had maintained schools as an "auxiliary service—auxiliary, that is, to its essential mission to build up the Body of Christ, to form hearers and doers of the Word, worshipers of the Father in Spirit and truth" (p. 142). Just as Mary Ryan reacted against an exclusive emphasis on schools, she also pointed out the shortcomings of programs that relied totally on the weekly catechism class as an alternative. The purpose of her book was to shift the focus "from the classroom to the church and to daily life." The primary loci of catechesis and religious formation, according to her thinking, should be the home and the praying community. She envisioned parents taking greater responsibility for the instruction and sacramental preparation of their children. She saw formal religious instruction "as ancillary to the formation and instruction given by Christ Himself, above all in Sunday Mass" (p. 116). At the high school level the emphasis should be on guidance and counseling. Teenagers, she wrote, "do not so much need information about religion as they need personal guidance toward a truly religious view of life in all its aspects, a guidance that can help to remove obstacles to a real and enthusiastic commitment to Christ" (p. 118).

By way of a footnote, it might be added that in the 1989 November *Chicago Studies*, Greeley stated that the effectiveness of Catholic schools comes "not so much through formal religious instruction class, but rather through the closeness to the Catholic community which the experience of attending Catholic schools generates" (p. 251). He acknowledges that not all who attend Catholic schools are "close to the Church," but, he writes, "it is the greater 'closeness' of some of those who got to Catholic schools which 'explains' virtually all of the religious effectiveness of Catholic education" (p. 257).

Ryan may have given the consummate expression to the call for community-based catechetical programs, but she was not alone in arguing that new approaches were necessary in the post-Vatican II Church. Greeley's reflections on Catholic youth in America, reported in *Strangers in the House* (1965), seemed to support many of Ryan's observations. In *The Crucible of Change* (1968), he asks "probing questions about certain kinds of pastoral activity in which we are presently engaged." This latter work presents a vision of the "New Community," and calls for reconsideration of liturgy, youth work and adult religious education. Moreover, Ryan herself relied on the 1964 Rossi-Greeley study for some of her statistics.

On the other hand, Ryan did not propose CCD as the answer. In her framework, the instruction it provides for children and young people is oriented toward the worshiping community where it would find "its proper completion" (p. 120). For the CCD to be successful, the parish must give it priority and make it an integral part of the community's life. The principal causes of failure of CCD programs are two closely related elements: lack of planning and inadequately trained teachers. The task of catechizing children is too important and complex to be entrusted (as it still is in some places) to high school students and volunteers whose chief qualification is good will.

Reorganization and Decline

In January 1975, the United States Catholic Conference was reorganized, and with the reorganization the National Center of Religious Education—CCD—was abolished, the victim of its own success. The Center's staff had grown over the years to include professionals in curriculum development and specialists in youth and adult ministry. It had succeeded in broadening the vision of catechesis from rote memorization of the catechism text to greater emphasis on biblical and liturgical themes. In its thirty-year history the Center produced a steady flow of catechetical materials that took into consideration the developmental stages of the child and adolescent, all the while continuing to stress the importance of catechist training.

Bishop O'Hara had established an organizational structure that gave the Center a good deal of autonomy, while at the same time operating under the direction of an Episcopal Committee. The Center was well staffed and funded by income from publications (including royalties on the Confraternity Edition of the New Testament, the forerunner of the New American Bible). The Center, especially during the Vatican II years when it made common cause with the National Conference of Diocesan Directors, had been a strong advocate for particular policies and practices, a fact that probably contributed to its own undoing. Under the direction of Joseph B. Collins, S.S. and Monsignor Russell Neighbor, the National Center worked assiduously to gain recognition and backing for the CCD. Both Collins and Neighbor were close friends of Mary Perkins Ryan and, like her, did not believe that parochial schools in themselves were the answer to the catechetical mission of the Church.

In the 1975 reorganization of the USCC, the work of the Center was assigned to the Department of Education, whose staff of specialists served as consultants in a liaison capacity with the field. The new structure functioned more as a clearinghouse for information than as a service organization. In 1980, the Department of Education suffered a further reduction in size, leaving in effect a small cadre of professionals who serve as staff to the bishops. A spin-off of the reduction in force and consequent reorganization of the Department of Education was the creation of new organizations such as the National Federation for Catholic Youth Ministry (the NFCYM replaced the old CYO Federation), the National Catholic Young Adult Ministry Association (NCYAMA) and the National Advisory Committee on Adult Religious Education (NACARE). And in 1983, the National Conference of Diocesan Directors—CCD—moved away from the USCC headquarters to its own offices and autonomy.

The breakup of the National Center CCD has been compared with the disintegration of an atom. Once the nucleus disappears the other particles become free-floating and hardly relate to one another. An examination of the NCCB/USCC committees, the national organizations and the diocesan structures listed in the *Official Catholic Directory* reveals a piecemeal approach to Catholic religious education. The Directory lists NCCB committees and staff for Doctrine, Liturgy (which includes among its concerns the RCIA), Pastoral Research and Practices, Marriage and Family Life, Laity, Human Values and Hispanic Affairs, and ad hoc committees for Evangelization, the Implementation of the Pastoral on the United States Economy, and the Pastoral Response to the Challenge of Proselytism. These are in addition to the Department of Education and its related committees. The end result is that major projects like the National Catechetical Directory and now the Universal Catechism are handled by joint committees, while particular concerns like guidelines for doctrinally sound catechetical materials and sex education are handled by task forces. Since the demise of the National Center of Religious Education (CCD), there has been no single agency that keeps abreast of developments in the field, no coordinated effort either in identifying the issues or of plotting a strategy for the catechetical mission of the Church in the United States.

A similar fragmentation occurred at the diocesan level. In the 1980 edition of the *Official Catholic Directory*, many dioceses, among them Boston, Philadelphia, Pittsburgh, Chicago, Milwaukee and San Francisco (to name only a few), list the Confraternity of Christian Doctrine among the diocesan offices and departments. By 1989, mention of the Confraternity and CCD has all but disappeared from the Catholic Directory. One of the few references to the Confraternity of Christian Doctrine in the 1989 edition describes it as "a distinct entity, separately incorporated and directed by a Board of Trustees from the United States Catholic Conference of Bishops." The description continues,

> The purpose of the Corporation is to foster and promote the teachings of Christ as understood and handed down by the Roman Catholic Church. To this end it licenses religious and spiritual literature especially the Lectionary for Mass and the New American Bible. . . . (P. xxi)

The broad vision of catechesis promoted by the Confraternity has shifted to particular concerns. Instead of looking to the National Center to chart directions and serve as an information resource for innovative ideas and programs that "work," diocesan staffs are left to their own devices. The accent on professional leadership and formal training of catechists, once the chief raison d'être of the Confraternity, has been relegated to the field. CCD has come to be a label for generic programs, makeshift substitutes for parochial schools concerned entirely with the instruction of children. Many diocesan offices no longer use the term CCD because of its negative connotations, and individuals have invented new meanings for the acronym, e.g., "Christian Character Development." In many places CCD has given way to the PSR—"parish school of religion."

In their pastoral letter on Catholic education, *To Teach as Jesus Did* (1972), the United States bishops reaffirmed their regard for Catholic schools. No better way has been found to realize the Church's threefold purpose in the educational field: to teach the Gospel message; to build a sense of community and Catholic identity; and to serve the entire human community (nn. 14, 106). But at the same time, the bishops acknowledged that Catholic schools are in crisis (n. 114) and other ways need to be found to realize these objectives. They allowed that the Confraternity of Christian Doctrine and other parish programs of religious education labor under severe handicaps, but they see the limitations as offering challenges and even as being a source of strength (n. 88). They single out the voluntary character of the parish schools of religion as one of the limitations that is also one of its strengths. Local Churches that have continued to pursue the ideal of the old CCD in establishing a strong community-based catechetical program have found that it nurtures Catholic identity and a sense of pride in the local Church. They are chiefly lay movements, involving significant numbers of adults not only as catechists, but as inquirers and learners. Usually administered by a full-time director of religious education, their success depends in large part on the priority that the pastor gives to the program in terms of personal involvement and budgeting.

The lessons of this survey of the past eighty-five years of the Confraternity of Christian Doctrine, as I stated at the outset, seem self-evident. The Church's mission to evangelize and catechize, while remaining ever constant, has been accommodated to changing social-economic circumstances with each succeeding generation. The CCD provided a ready-made support group for the missionary zeal of lay catechists in the mining towns of Pennsylvania and the barrios of Los Angeles in the first part of the century. Bishop Edwin O'Hara created the National Center of Religious Education (CCD) to broaden the understanding of catechesis, to publicize the need for trained teachers, and to produce good catechetical materials, including an English translation of the Bible that twentieth-century American Catholics could understand. That the Confraternity came to be seen as a competitor of the Catholic schools was an unfortunate development that might have been avoided had national and diocesan leadership been able to see the picture whole.

Although the title of this essay seems to be warranted by the facts, it should not be taken as a reason for discouragement. The Confraternity may have gone into a decline, but it has not been a failure. Its vision of the Church's catechetical mission has been incorporated in the National Catechetical Directory, which makes it clear that catechesis is not a piecemeal exercise. For catechesis to succeed, everyone—clergy, religious, laity—must collaborate. Programs for children and teenagers will succeed only when they can draw on committed and well-catechized adults and trained catechists. Catechesis must go hand in hand with the liturgy, Bible study and efforts to implement the Church's social teaching. The whole community has the responsibility for catechesis; it is everyone's responsibility to teach the Gospel message, to build a sense of community and Catholic identity, to nurture a spirit of prayer and to educate Christians for service. Where the ideals and spirit of the CCD prevail, this work still goes on. If diocesan staffs, parish directors and volunteer catechists tend to lose heart, it may be because they have no agency, no arm of the National Episcopal Conference like the old Center of Religious Education (CCD), that publicizes their work, rallies behind them and gives them a sense of direction and self-worth.

The Church Assembled:
Catechetical Congresses and Conferences

BERARD L. MARTHALER, OFM CONV

In an area of rapid change and instability, the existence of any institution that endures and flourishes for twenty years should not be allowed to pass without notice. The significance of the East Coast Conference for Religious Education, however, does not rest solely or even principally on its longevity. In order to appreciate its importance in the life of the Church we must view the East Coast Conference in a broader context. The annual meeting of religious educators and other pastoral ministers, conceived by Tim Ragan and those associated with Time Consultants, is unique in many ways, but it is not an isolated phenomenon.

From apostolic times Church leaders have gathered in councils and synods. It was only with the advent of the railroad and other means of mass transportation, however, that popular movements began to organize congresses, conventions, and conferences to advance causes, raise consciousness, and educate the masses. The first Eucharistic Congress was held in 1881. Some trace the origins of the modern liturgical movement to the Catholic Congress at Malines (Belgium) in 1909 and the paper given there by Dom Lambert Beauduin. Catechetical renewal that had its beginnings with the famous Munich Method became a popular movement at the catechetical congress held in Vienna in 1912.

The Vienna meeting, which came on the heels of the worldwide Eucharistic Congress, had been planned as the first of two meetings to consider scientific pedagogy and educational psychology as these relate to catechesis and to explore ways to implement them at the practical and organizational levels. The second meeting, planned for Munich, had to be postponed because of World War I; when it was held, in 1928, there existed very different circumstances and a quite different agenda.

Reprinted from *Living the Vision: Twentieth Anniversary, East Coast Conference for Religious Education*, ed. by James A. Corr, Carl J. Pfeifer, and Janaan Manernach (Morristown, NJ: Silver Burdett Ginn Religious Division, 1992), 3–10. Copyright © 1992 by Berard L. Marthaler. Used by permission of the publisher.

The Vienna and Munich meetings had the approval of the German and Austrian hierarchies, as did national catechetical congresses held in Italy, France, and Spain. The first national catechetical congress in Italy was held in Piacenza in 1889, and the bishop of Mantua, Giuseppe Sarto, the future Pope Pius X, was among the participants. A second congress, held in Milan in 1910 in connection with the celebration of the third centenary of the canonization of St. Charles Borromeo, was attended by six cardinals, fifty-two bishops, and three thousand official participants representing the 134 Italian dioceses.

During the Holy Year of 1950 the Congregation of the Council, which was responsible for overseeing catechesis (by reason of its mandate to implement the decrees of the Council of Trent, including the promulgation of the Roman Catechism), organized an International Catechetical Congress. More than twenty years later, in 1971, the same dicastery, now known as the Congregation for the Clergy, organized a second International Congress. The 1971 meeting, presided over by Cardinal John Wright, then prefect of the Congregation, was convened to showcase the newly published *General Catechical Directory.*

In the decade between the first International Congress and the convocation of Vatican II, the Congregation of the Council interdicted international catechetical meetings and national congresses that it had not expressly authorized. However, the catechetical movement had picked up too much momentum to be easily intimidated. For example, *Catechesi*, the leading catechetical review in Italy, not wishing to contravene the Congregation's interdiction, organized large but less formal meetings *(riunioni)* of "friends and supporters of catechesis." For the same reason, Johannes Hofinger, SJ, then associated with the East Asian Catechetical Institute in Manila, organized not congresses but "international study weeks."

The prototype for Hofinger's study weeks was a 1956 meeting of catechetical leaders in Antwerp that attracted four hundred participants from thirty-two nations. The theme of the first of the study weeks, held at Nijmegen in 1959, was "Liturgy and the Missions." Although the theme seemed narrowly focused, it was apparent in the discussions that evangelization and catechesis could not be separated from questions of liturgical renewal and the adaptation of language. Nijmegen, in effect, set the agenda for the study week at Eichstatt the following year.

Eichstatt legitimated the goals of the modern catechetical movement. Catechesis could never again be considered simply a matter of catechism texts and teaching methods designed for instructing children. The theme of the study week, "Catechetics and the Missions," invited the participants to view catechesis as a pastoral activity inseparable from the Church's mission and other forms of pastoral ministry. In the wake of Eichstatt, "kerygmatic catechesis" became the slogan of the day. It shifted the focus of catechesis from seemingly disconnected doctrines, commandments, and facts, to the person of Jesus Christ. Catechists could no longer be satisfied with mere teachings; they were called to be witnesses. The were not to retail Church doctrine in the manner of sales clerks, but to share the faith that propels their lives.

One must not overlook the fact that the first two international study weeks, Nijmegen and Eichstatt, were held in Europe. The next three, Bangkok in 1962, Katigondo in 1964, and Manila in 1967, met in the Third World. This change of venue resulted in a different mix of participants and a face-to-face confrontation with non-European cultures. As Eichstatt is linked to kerygmatic catechesis, Bangkok popularized the notion of pre-evangelization and the need for adaptation to the cultural background of the peoples being evangelized and catechized. The emphasis was on the anthropological aspect, the presentation of the Gospel message in human terms. ("The word of God in the words of men," was the slogan in an era less attuned to inclusive language.) The theme of adaptation ran through the study weeks at Katigondo, which was billed as a "Pan-African Seminar," and Manila, as an "Asiatic Seminar." Much more needs to be said about these international gatherings, but for the purpose of this essay it is sufficient to note that the tone and substance of the study weeks, whatever the predetermined theme, were dictated by the Third World ambiance and the cross-cultural dialogue generated by the participants.

As one might expect, it was at the 1968 study week in Medellín (Colombia) that leaders in the catechetical movement entered into serious dialogue with liberation theology. The practices and policies of the Latin American Church are deeply rooted in European Catholicism and culture. Thus the focus of the seminar sessions shifted from cultural adaptation to the social and political factors that impact on the Church's mission and shape approaches to ministry. Medellín went beyond anything that previous study weeks had proposed by calling for a radical change in socioeconomic structures and stressing the need for catechesis to become directed toward the transformation of society. A special commission on international cooperation in catechetics directed two petitions to Cardinal Villot, the prefect of the Council for the Clergy, who had twice addressed the general assembly. The commission asked (1) that the conclusions reached at Medellín be taken into consideration in the development of the *General Catechetical Directory;* and (2) that the *GCD* not be promulgated as a normative document but as guidelines that would allow national hierarchies to adapt them to local needs and circumstances.

Although by that time the contours of the General Directory had already been set, there is reason to believe that the Medellín study week is the principal source of Part I, which was a last-minute addition. It will be recalled that it is in Part I that the *GCD* emphasizes the need for catechesis to confront the challenges of rapid change in contemporary society and to recognize that pluralism and diversity can be positive values. The influence of the earlier study weeks permeates the General Directory and is especially evident in Part II, which echoes the themes of kerygmatic catechesis and the need for adaptation.

In the United States, aspects of religious education and catechetical ministry have been regular agenda items of the annual meetings of the National Catholic Educational Association since its inception in 1904. Although the NCEA has traditionally given priority to parochial schools, it is dedicated to the principle that Catholic education touches every facet of life—individual, domestic, and social. The NCEA conventions are in fact a series of meetings within meetings. They bring together people engaged at every level in the Church's educational ministry, from diocesan superintendents to volunteer catechists. The annual convention provides a forum for professional groups such as the Chief Administrators of Catholic Education (CASE) and, in recent years, the National Association of Parish Coordinators/DREs (NPCD).

The NCEA conventions now attract an average of more than ten thousand people. The sheer size of the crowds, the number of lectures, and the range of activities seem to some to reek of excess. But the convention itself must be seen as a teaching moment. An important part of the annual meeting (and one of the most attractive features) is found in the exhibition halls. A walk through the displays makes one aware that educational programs require more than classrooms, desks, and textbooks. Amid exhibits of school uniforms, playground equipment, computer hardware and software, candy and pizza for fund-raising, and bathroom fixtures, publishers display educational programs. Teachers and DREs can examine in a matter of hours the resources available for grades K through 8, youth ministry, sacramental preparation, and vacation church schools. There are the traditional textbook series with the latest enhancements, audio- and videotapes, as well as teaching aids of all kinds. The size of the convention forces the NCEA to meet in cities with enough hotel rooms to accommodate the participants. Each year the event comes to a different part of the country and thus serves a different clientele, reaching a new audience and making more people aware of the many dimensions of the Church's educational ministry.

The NCEA convention established the pattern, and its success caused other organizations to copy and tailor it to their own specifications. In

1924 the Congregation of the Council encouraged national, provincial, and diocesan catechetical congresses, but it was only in 1935 that the first National Catechetical Congress was held in the United States. The establishment of the National Center of Religious Education—CCD, called for by the decree *Provido sane consilio* of the Congregation, was really the brainchild of Edwin O'Hara, bishop of Great Falls, Montana (1930–1939), and later of Kansas City, Missouri (1939–1956). Even before the establishment of the National Center, the Confraternity of Christian Doctrine had become the ordinary means of catechetical instruction and pastoral ministry in the mining towns around Pittsburgh, the barrios of Los Angeles, and the rural areas of the Mid- and Far West.

The National Center identified a constituency that seemed to be neglected by the NCEA: families for whom parochial schools were not an option. The National Congresses attracted bishops, clergy and religious scholars, diocesan directors, and volunteer catechists. They provided a platform to explain the purpose and the structures of the CCD and to rally popular support. The first congress piggybacked on the thirteenth annual Catholic Rural Life Convention in Rochester, New York, but it was the only time that the two organizations held their annual meetings in the same city. Until interrupted by the outbreak of World War II, the National CCD Congress met annually: New York, 1936; St. Louis, 1937; Hartford, 1938; Cincinnati, 1939; Los Angeles, 1940; and Philadelphia, 1941. After the war the National Congresses resumed, meeting every five years through 1971: Boston, 1946; Chicago, 1951; Buffalo, 1956; Dallas, 1961; Pittsburgh, 1966; and Miami, 1971. It was at the Miami congress that an informal meeting of some participants laid plans for the development of a national catechetical directory.

The National Center of Religious Education was dismantled in 1974 and with its demise the National CCD Congresses came to an end. The catechetical community, including many bishops, looked to the National Conference of Diocesan Directors—CCD for national leadership. The annual conventions of the NCDD, open only to members and invited guests, are working sessions. They identify trends and address common concerns, and most have an in-service component that addresses professional needs and skills. For a time the NCDD was one of the most influential groups in the American Church.

Meanwhile, regional meetings like the New England congress and diocesan meetings like the gigantic Los Angeles congress continued the tradition of the CCD congresses. Regional and local meetings highlighted the importance of the catechetical ministry and at the same time became a means of enrichment for the participants. They focused less on organization, programs, and methods, and became models of religious education for adults. The CCD had from its inception in the United

States been largely a populist movement dependent on laity for its dynamism. Bishops like Regis Canevin in Pittsburgh, John Joseph Cantwell in Los Angeles, and Edwin O'Hara had the vision to provide support and organization. Individual priests and later the NCDD, entirely clerical in its early years, provided leadership and acted as intermediaries, but it was the laity that provided the workers.

The Confraternity of Christian Doctrine, blessed and encouraged by Rome, had official status in most dioceses. It offered a vision of ministry that was open to the laity—men and women—that went well beyond the dictum that defined Catholic action as "the participation of the laity in activity of the hierarchy." The CCD was designed to inform everyone of the responsibility to evangelize and catechize according to one's ability and station in life. Around 1970 a new phenomenon appeared—the parish director of religious education. The DRE provided a model for non-ordained ministry in the post-Vatican II Church—a well-trained, paid professional with a recognized role in the local Church community.

It is against this background that we must look at the East Coast Conference. The conference is the brainchild of Tim Ragan, who in the early 1970s was serving as DRE at Saint John's Church in Severna Park, Maryland. From his own experience he recognized that this emerging class of ministers needed professional support. He brought together a team of friends, individuals with expertise in organization, management, volunteerism, and other skills who made themselves available as consultants to parish programs, and Time Consultants was born. Ragan also recognized that, with the demise of the National CCD congresses, there was a need for a forum where DREs could share their experiences, be kept abreast of developments in pastoral theology, and address their professional concerns. Thus, the East Coast Conference for Religious Education was born. The topic of the first East Coast Conference in 1973, "How to Make Religious Education More Effective," became the underlying theme of all the subsequent meetings. The enduring success of the East Coast Conference is due in large part to the organizational skills of Tim Ragan, who, with his associates in Time Consultants, invested time and risked capital year after year.

The twentieth anniversary of the East Coast Conference is an occasion for reflection. First of all, a word should be said about the site. Meetings and conferences held in Washington, D.C., because it is the nation's capital, project an aura of national importance. Transportation by automobile, train, and plane is relatively convenient for people who live in a radius of five or six hundred miles. Many people have ties to the city either because of their studies at the Catholic University of America or one of the other educational institutions in the area, because of their association with national organizations that have their headquarters here, because their religious communities have houses here, or because of family. Connections like these, as well as the general attractiveness of the city, have prompted participants to attend the East Coast Conference year after year.

Second, the East Coast Conference, in the century-long tradition of catechetical congresses and meetings, convenes people with common interests and concerns. It is not simply that they come together to hear papers and talks by scholars expert in theology, liturgy, and the Bible. The participants themselves are expert to a greater or lesser degree in pastoral ministry. They share experiences with one another and offer mutual support. The schedule permits, even encourages, a great deal of social and professional exchange: academicians with practitioners, practitioners with publishers, and DREs with volunteer catechists.

Third, the East Coast Conference is a forum for non-ordained ministers in the church. It addresses concerns and issues of interest to Roman Catholics, but has no official standing. The right wing find the speakers subversive, and liberals would like to hear voices that champion radical causes, but in fact the Conference is in the mainstream of the American Church. Time Consultants is not a membership organization, and Tim Ragan is a high-class entrepreneur who makes his business acumen serve his Catholic outlook on the world. In this, he is like most of the publishers who display their wares in the exhibit hall. They might want to be on the cutting edge, but because they are market-driven, they find it safer to stay close to the speed limit, just avant-garde enough not to be found irrelevant in a Church that is groping to find its way in a rapidly changing world. Members of the hierarchy and clergy are welcomed as both speakers and participants, but their presence is seen as neither approval of the conference nor as endorsement of the ideas expressed. Nonetheless, the East Coast Conference, run by laity for laity, is very much a part of today's Church.

From another point of view, the East Coast Conference is the latter-day heir of congresses and conventions that date back to the last century. Seen from this angle, some of its success can also be credited to early pioneers like Edwin V. O'Hara and Johannes Hofinger, who had a vision of what the Church can and should be. They saw renewal of religious education and catechesis, allied to the liturgical movement and the renaissance in biblical studies, as a means toward that end. The Second Vatican Council legitimated that vision, and called for new forms of ministry. Now it falls to meetings like the East Coast Conference to keep the vision from becoming institutionalized, so that the Church can continue, as the theme of the 1992 conference expresses it, "Living the Vision in an Age of Change."

PART E
Catechism and Catechesis

Introduction

MICHAEL WARREN

The purpose of these four brief readings is to give readers an angle from which to approach the relation of the catechism to catechesis and to provide some context for the *Catechism of the Catholic Church (CCC)*.

Herman Lombaerts, in a little-known but excellent overview of the "concrete instruments of catechesis," puts the catechism in historical perspective and then looks at the kinds of concrete instruments needed for catechesis today. Lombaerts divides this history into four phases. Phase one is the time of "open formulation." Phase two is the "standardization of the sources." Phase three is the "standardization of the formulation." And phase four, the current phase, is the "electronic era" or breakdown of the standardization and the need for new methods of helping people communicate about faith in face-to-face interaction. Lombaerts sketches a learning process to be "lived with the faith community" in "dynamic interaction" with one another and with the wider world.

In the second article, Joseph Cardinal Ratzinger offers his own chatty reflections on the background of the *CCC*. This is an interesting document both for its overall tone and for the way Ratzinger explains the various steps that led to the actual publication of the *Catechism*. His use of an anecdotal and friendly rhetoric somewhat belies a certain eagerness to explain and defend the various decisions made about the catechism. Ratzinger poses a series of questions, some his own, some from others (such as those of an anonymous French catechist), to which he supplies answers.

In describing its development, he lays out the literary genre of the *CCC* as that of a *catechismus maior,* similar to the *Catechism of the Council of Trent,* and, as such, not something to be used directly in school- and parish-based catechesis, but rather meant as a tool for the bishops. In the course of setting out the process by which the *CCC* was actually produced, Ratzinger is very clear about the human choices and decisions made in skirting the many problems the writers encountered. Even considering the "miracle . . . that out of such a complex editorial process emerged a book of such essential inner harmony and indeed . . . of such beauty . . . speaking . . . in all her fullness as the 'sound of many waters,'" Ratzinger recognizes the process as a this-worldly one, open for critique and interpretation. Ratzinger's harmonious "sound of waters" metaphor ignores the harsh sound the sexist language of the English *Catechism* has for English-speaking people.

The third article, John Paul II's "Apostolic Constitution: *Fidei Depositum*," uses the opening words of the *Catechism*. It also echoes Ratzinger's essay in noting that what we have here is an "authentic reference text," not intended to replace local catechisms approved at various levels in the church but intended to encourage new catechetical writing.

Of all the overviews I have read of the *CCC*, the most useful one for putting the *Catechism* in context is Berard Marthaler's essay, the fourth article in this section. Like Ratzinger's and John Paul II's statements, it lays out what this document tries to do and what it does not intend to do. Set in the context of Vatican Council II and its authoritative conciliar documents, including the *General Catechetical Directory*, Marthaler takes pains both to praise the accomplishments of the *Catechism* and to call attention to its "self-imposed limitations." Only by understanding both dimensions will catechetical leaders make the best creative use of this resource book.

Further Reading

Marthaler, Berard L. "The Cardinal and the Catechism," *The Living Light* 21, no. 1 (October 1984): 32–42.

———. "The Synod and the Catechism." In *Synod 1985: An Evaluation,* Concilium Series, no. 188, edited by Giuseppe Alberigo and James Provost, 91–98. English-language editor Marcus Lefebure. Edinburgh: T. and T. Clark, 1986.

———. "Catechetical Directory or Catechism: Une Question Mal Posée." In *Religious Education and the Future,* edited by Dermot A. Lane, 55–70. Mahwah, NJ: Paulist Press, 1987.

———. "A Book of Common Prayer for Roman Catholics?" *Worship* 61, no. 3 (May 1987): 208–223.

———. "A Catechism Sampler." *Church* (spring 1988): 4854.

———. "The Catechism Genre, Past and Present." In *World Catechism or Inculturation?* Concilium Series, no. 204, by Johann Baptist Metz and Edward Schillebeeckx, 41–49. Edinburgh: T. and T. Clark, 1989.

———. "The Creed and Doctrine in Catechesis for Children." In *Issues in the Christian Initiation of Children: Catechesis and Liturgy,* edited by Kathy Brown and Frank C. Sokol, 65–74. Chicago: Liturgy Training Publications, 1989.

———. "Old Wine, New Wineskins." *Commonweal* (9 March 1990): 143–146.

———. "The Catechism Seen as a Whole." In *The Universal Catechism Reader: Reflections and Responses,* edited by Thomas Reese, 15–30. San Francisco: Harper and Row, 1990.

————. The Catechism Yesterday and Today: The Evolution of a Genre. Col-
legville, MN: Liturgical Press, 1995.

Regan, Jane, et al. *Exploring the Catechism.* Collegeville, MN: Liturgical Press,
1995.

Sloyan, Gerard S. "The Use of the Bible in a New Resource Book." *Biblical Theology Bulletin* 25, no. 1 (spring 1995): 3–13.

Religious Education Today and the Catechism

HERMAN LOMBAERTS, FSC

Introduction

All efforts to find a proper vehicle to express the core of the Christian orthodox faith are to be taken seriously. They represent one further step in the Church's continuous search to be faithful to Christ and to his call to be his disciples. The actual form of a faith profession and the catechetical responsibility of a community are closely related.

When it comes down to the choice of a particular instrument to serve as the vehicle, the discussion starts and many times there seem to be various ways of responding to this responsibility. The process of finding out who is right—or who expresses a correct way of looking at things—might be even more important, and a never-ending concern among Christians.

This process refers largely to the difficulty of setting out criteria according to which the authentic orthodox features of the Christian faith can be identified. A contradictory task. On the one hand, the Scriptures and the Church Tradition profess that God is and remains a mystery; the unknown. On the other hand, the pastoral and catechetical activity is a human and concrete plan in the hands of people and is conditioned by historical circumstances; dimensions we would like to control, from input to output, with every bit in between the two poles. To make absolute the latter effort or aspects of it would put the faithful attention to God's mystery under serious threat.

In this article we will try to reflect upon one of those concrete instruments. Is the "catechism" an essential or an accidental factor in the pastoral activity of the Church? Is the" catechism" to be identified with

Reprinted from *Mount Oliver Review* 1, no. 1 (1984): 3–15. Copyright © 1984 by Herman Lombaerts. Used with permission.

only one way of modeling the Christian beliefs? This reflection focuses attention upon one basic issue: What's happening to Christians today, living in contemporary society? What kind of support seems to be relevant to the process of orienting people in their efforts to believe?

1. The Renewal in Religious Education

Trying to sum up the important historical steps of the catechetical ministry leads inevitably to a caricature. In fact, such a rich and multifaceted history cannot be reduced to a particular pattern. However, for the purpose of our reflection it can be helpful to use a simplified schema to place our concerns in a larger perspective.

The first centuries of the Christian era leave the impression of an astonishing creativity in the development of catechetical activity. The Church fathers left us with famous commentaries on the Scriptures and the mystery of faith. They remain a source of reflection and a frame of reference for the Church in its ongoing development.[1]

In the Middle Ages artists were unique in their creativity in visualizing the profession of faith. Church buildings, statues, carvings, drawings, and paintings offer a solid support for contemplation and reflection. People can easily memorize and remember the core of the Christian tradition, relying upon dramatized presentations, hymns, and prayers. As in the first centuries, many aspects of medieval Christianity represent a living tradition.

In modern times important changes in Western civilization had a very deep effect on religious stability, and forced Church leaders and the Christian population to face the signs of the times. Often, "new ideas," different ways of moving beyond stagnation and sterility, confusion and abuses caused a large variety of reactions, some contradictory, before there were glimpses of a new stability.

If the post-apostolic times provide us with the impressive writings of the Church fathers, if the Middle Ages still leave us with the most wonderful buildings and works of art, expressive of a deep reflective faith, modern times cannot be described without mentioning at length the religious textbooks and the catechism which are the mainstay of religious education.

Technical innovations offered great possibilities for education in schools and there is no doubt that religion benefited from institutional settings and contributed greatly to socialization into modern society. The evolution after World War II, especially in the "Golden Sixties," proved how much scientific and technological developments, the spectacular innovations in the communications media, affected self-image and self-consciousness of the masses.

People who were directly involved in promoting and proclaiming religious belief or the meaning of life (even in other denominations and cultures) and in justifying value systems and moral standards experienced in a vivid way the extent to which the presuppositions of their status and work were called into question. The nature and scope of catechetical instruction during the past fifty years became complex and extensive. Nearly everything has been tried in the effort to re-establish a dialogue about Christian faith in order to motivate people to value a religious commitment, or more simply, just to raise interest in a religious faith.[2]

It became obvious that the problem was not at the level of methods or textbooks, or a revised doctrinal formulation, or even a revised theological reflection—although most of the effort and money was invested in those areas—nor was it solved by the highly praised human and social sciences. A basic question was formulated again and again: Is it meaningful and worthwhile to adhere to a religious tradition at all? Is the Christian faith as such meaningful? Is being Christian to be considered a regressive state of mind, in comparison with the brilliant, autonomous development of the modern "homo sapiens"?

Frightening questions undermined the changing practices and ways of thinking within the Church, and gave rise to fears of ending up with nothing: the empty tomb without anything else![3]

Here again, a simplified analysis of many centuries of interpretation may help us to understand what is at stake in this second half of the twentieth century. The history of the proclamation of the Gospel can be divided into four phases:[4]

1. The biblical tradition rests on an oral proclamation, and an oral proclamation is an *open formulation;* every story, told anew, expresses other nuances. Many versions of the same story develop, but they all move around the same center, around the same dynamic force.

2. The writing down, or the *standardization of the sources*, of the stories that are being passed on constitutes the second phase. The written texts are accessible to the literate, to the educated, and they serve as a reference for the oral proclamation.

At this stage, the hearing, the assimilation by ear of the faith expression, still represents the main catechetical communication. There is the immediate impact of the speaker addressing an audience.

3. The invention of printing brought the possibility of multiplication, and the printed, standardized sources became accessible to the masses. Thus a technological change led to the *standardization of the formulation*, which then became static and mechanically reproducible, as did even the interpretative commentaries on the sources.

As such, this was a most spectacular change which had positive applications. However, a visual perception of the impersonal printed text broke down the personal contact of a living relationship. The learning effort became more individualized, the authority structures less personalized; all conditions to develop a "paper-culture," a bureaucratic, uniform administration of the religious sphere.

4. At the moment we are still exploring all the consequences and possible applications of the *electronic era*. Images and sounds are produced together in such a way and at such a speed and with such a quantity of information stimuli that the whole process moves beyond human control.

New sense-perceptions awaken new self-perceptions and self-images; a new code, a new language is developed; a new intelligence interacts with this fascinating world. The previous balance is destroyed; the standardized formulation—in any field—becomes irrelevant and requires different approaches to reveal specific meanings.

There arises an urgent need to find a new relationship with the sources of a religious tradition in order to relocate the living story and to hear it. In this fourth phase we note the increased interest in talking and listening, in the exchange of perceptions, sensitivities, and interpretations.

Each transition from one phase to the next was caused by a global cultural shift, which in turn caused a crisis in the proclamation of the word of God. A crisis is often met with a panic reaction, namely, with the fear that the "center," the essential, will be lost. There is the fear that one will be alienated from the identity that has been constructed over a very long time, that the equilibrium will be irrevocably upset. The shifts caused by the evolution of society and culture have made all of us all too familiar with efforts to restandardize the formulation, to reappreciate the sources, to guide the story down safe channels again. These are all the expressions of the unavoidable search for a new equilibrium. By now it is also clear that the new equilibrium will be totally different from the previous one. And we are still far from attaining it.

Looking at the catechetical "renewal" from this point of view proves how important it is to work carefully on a sound diagnosis of the actual situation. We are facing important shifts today. How do they affect people? Are there areas where the quest for meaning can be recognized; where Christ's words, "Today you recognize the signs announced by the Prophets . . ." can be heard again?[5]

It is within the context of this more fundamental diagnosis that the discussions about a (new) catechism are to be examined.

2. The "Catechism" as an Instrument for Renewal

Jean Claude Dhotel states in the conclusion of his detailed study of the emergence of the catechism in modern times that this type of book is the historical result of circumstances which vary according to people, place, and time.[6]

In other words, the concept of a "catechism" is a time-bound answer to particular questions and situations. In fact, for fifteen centuries the Church maintained itself and transmitted the Christian faith from generation to generation without a catechism. If catechisms appear in the sixteenth century in their most popular form, it is due to an important number of historical circumstances. It responds to specific aspects of a cultural learning process. Apart from standardized formulations, many other things were learned through memorization.

To ascertain the feasibility of publishing a "new catechism," we need to consider the wider contexts. If we do not do this, the "instrument" could well be completely isolated from the dynamic aspects of the faith experience.

A few historical reminders illustrate these conclusions.

2.1 The Reformation as Renewal

The Catholic Church has had a long tradition of using texts for religious instruction in the parishes. Various texts were used in the fourteenth, fifteenth, and sixteenth centuries, but they only supported the oral instruction and did not separate the hearer from the speaker.[7]

However, the Protestants—especially Calvin—seem to have been responsible for the introduction of the "catechism." A "catechism" is a textbook divided into lessons, in which the text is set out in short questions and answers which can easily be memorized and reproduced. For Calvin, the catechism (*un formulaire*) was intended as a change in the style of presentation of the Christian faith.[8] At the same time it represented a change at the level of content. The synthetic presentation of doctrinal statements expressed a different way of shaping the content of faith.

The presentation needed to justify itself with convincing arguments and, at the same time, be sanctioned by the authority of local churches.

The catechism was meant to be a practical instrument for teaching and learning; it was also a symbolic book.

Its meaning went far beyond the apparent functional purposes and had to do with: freedom in religious thinking; withdrawal from and reaction against aspects of Christian living (cult of saints; papal authority; use of the scripture . . .); the clandestine character of religious propaganda; the diffusion of new interpretations of scripture and tradition or opposition to particular interpretations.[9]

2.2 The Counter-Reformation as Renewal

In its effort to counteract abuses and heresies (propagated by the Reformation) the Council of Trent decided formally to order the production of a catechism as one of the major instruments to achieve that goal (June Session 1563). The Council spent a long time exploring the idea. The task was to produce a catechism that would offer a unified and complete exposition of the doctrine of the faith, as stated officially by the Church, in an era of confusion in the wake of the deep conflicts caused by Luther.[10]

The *Catechismo Romano*, edited in 1566, and written by Carolus Borromeus was re-edited and reprinted many times and had many adaptations until early in the twentieth century. Being a *methodus* or a *compendium* of the Catholic doctrine, it had many purposes: to be the expression of an authoritative argument in matters of doctrine; to be a reference book of the Catholic doctrine for parish priests; to be a criterion for catechetical renewal.

The basic questions provoked long discussions: Was it necessary to write a catechism for the whole Church, or should this task be left to the local bishops? Would it be written by the Roman theologians, or by the theologians of a particular faculty? What type of book should it be? Written for whom, and for what purpose?[11]

Because of the diagnosed abuses and difficulties, the main concern was to guarantee the identification of the canonical books of the Holy Scripture from a doctrinal and disciplinary point of view—to offer a relevant, justified, and safe (orthodox) Catholic sourcebook to be used by the priests for the study of the Bible, the education of children and adults, and the celebration of the sacraments. These aims met the specific problems of the sixteenth century.

These few elements alone show that the Catholic Church assembled in Trent was working on fundamental questions and struggling with basic issues of a changing society. The stability was disrupted. Institutional security was called into question at such a deep level that the presentation of the Christian-Catholic tradition had to be reorganized and rethought. It shows also that the preaching and the teaching of the Catholic faith are a vital locus where the continuity of the faith community expresses its identity, its doctrinal and liturgical unity.

In that sense—and according to the Council of Trent—the catechism was meant to offer a response to the priests and the teachers in their catechetical and liturgical responsibilities. It was a sourcebook, a guide offering a safe background to overcome, in the short run, some of the lacunae and weaknesses revealed by the Reformation.

The catechism, then, was a key instrument in the overall concern to proclaim the Gospel in agreement with the scriptures and the orthodox tradition. It was not meant to be a stereotyped compendium of sentences to be memorized. That was a redaction that occurred in the Lutheran and the Catholic tradition because of the general lack of education in these churches.[12]

Taking into account the historical context, the effects of the Council of Trent and the redaction of catechisms in the sixteenth century cannot be valued enough. They reflect the honest self-questioning efforts of the Church to look at the historical situation and to make a sound diagnosis. They also show the difficulty of standing back and seeing the value of new (and different) approaches. At present, it is easier to see the prophetic role of the Reformation for the whole Church. It took centuries and many other crises, self-critical examinations, and a few more general councils to come to a more balanced response to what happened as modern times evolved.[13]

3. "Catechism" in Today's Catechetical Renewal

Should a new catechism be written? A catechism for the universal Church? Should it be left to the authority of the local bishops? What type of a book should it be? To whom should it be addressed and for what purpose? These sixteenth-century questions sound familiar to priests, catechists, and bishops of the twentieth century. The cultural shifts underlying the four phases in the history of the proclamation of the Gospel must be kept in mind if we want to examine this question. Let's try to summarize a few elements of the recent discussions of this matter.

All these questions have been answered in recent years by many people and in different, sometimes contradictory, conflicting ways. This caused tensions, conflicts, and confusion in local dioceses and church provinces. Instead of promoting a clarifying and deepening growth in faith and Christian living according to Vatican II, the Synod of 1977, and more recent documents, the opposite result seems to occur. In this regard our contemporary situation often illustrates how a one-sided or prejudiced diagnosis leads to a one-sided, sometimes biased answer. And because of the fundamental questions at stake, partial and short-term answers miss the boat and are more harmful than anything else in the long-term perspective.

A global picture of our times is necessary as well as a sound assessment of the influential changes which affect the self-consciousness and the meaning of life. It is proper to our Catholic and Christian tradition to believe that the scriptures and faith in Christ have something to offer in this context. What we have to witness should be a freeing word about the contemporary life-struggle, instead of a self-centered, inward-looking repetition of static utterances, or of expressing uncontrolled and biased forms of anxiety.

The idea of writing a universal catechism for the whole Church was rejected very soon after the publication of the *Directorium Catechisticum Generale* (1971). Cardinal Oddy then wanted to published a *Schema Doctrinae Christianae*, but the International Catechetical Commission, convened by the Congregation for the Clergy, in its meeting of 11 to 17 April 1983, unanimously disagreed with such a syllabus, because it was not an appropriate answer to the real situation.[14] Referring to more recent papal documents and the actual changes, it was even stated that the *Directorium Catechisticum Generale* was outdated and should be substantially revised.

The Commission states that the proper responsibility of the Congregation for the Clergy is to establish certain criteria for the protection of the integrity of the Christian message, rather than to fix the formulation of the message in a stereotyped universal language. Any initiative from the Vatican in matters of the catechetical ministry should consider the necessity of a process of renewal in the context of contemporary society. If the Congregation for the Clergy wants to interfere with doctrinal aspects of the catechetical activity, it should be done in the context of Part Three of the *Directorium Catechisticum Generale*, that is, clarifying norms and criteria. Otherwise, any other text could be duplicated and used as a "catechism." And that would be to run counter to the instructions of the pope himself! A strong recommendation was made to ensure that any presentation of the doctrine would be stated in terms of the "Good News" in an authentic catechetical language, in the spirit of what is stated in *Catechesi Tradendae*, no. 49.

Therefore, it is not enough to multiply catechetical works. In order that these works may correspond with their aim, several things are essential:

a. they must be linked with the real life of the generation to which they are addressed, showing close acquaintance with its anxieties and questionings, struggles and hopes;

b. they must try to speak a language comprehensible to the generation in question;

c. they must make a point of giving the whole message of Christ and his Church, without neglecting or distorting anything, and in expounding it they will follow a line and structure that highlights what is essential;

d. they must really aim to give to those who use them a better knowledge of the mysteries of Christ, aimed at true conversion and a life more in conformity with God's will.

In the last twenty years, various catechetical congresses crystallized a growing awareness among catechists and prepared the basic catechetical orientation to be promoted by Vatican II and post-conciliar movements. The Congresses of Eichstatt (1960), Bangkok (1962), and Katigondo (1964) restored the kerygmatic character of the Christian message.[15] The Congresses of Manila (1967), Medellín (1968), and Rome (1971) emphasized the anthropological dimension of the catechetical ministry. All these congresses systematically drew attention to the rapidly changing situation in the world, which urges respect for and dialogue with other religions; the adoption of important cultural and technical changes and the development of the capacity to deal with pluralistic societies. The many cross-cultural and intercontinental influences are spread around the world through modern communications systems.

In this context, it becomes obvious that a multifaceted and open catechetical effort which allows the Gospel to reveal its unique and prophetic message must be prepared. This urgent appeal for openness is accompanied by a strong protest against any narrow-minded concept of a catechism.

And indeed, the facts do teach us a lesson.

The 1941 edition of the *Baltimore Catechism* (USA) did not differ much from the 1885 volume. It soon proved to be an anachronistic document, in spite of the many efforts to revise the text.

The latest classical German catechism *Katholischer Katechismus der Bistumer Deutschlands* (1955), the *Arbeitsbuch zur Glaubensunterweisung* (1969), and especially the *Katholischer Katechismus* (1975) failed to respond to the many questions both young and older people have about the Christian faith itself. The concerns go far beyond the faith-statements or beliefs—the language used in these books became totally hermetic and didn't reveal anything.[16] What, then, is wrong with an instrument which had such an impact? Obviously, the instrument refers to many other aspects of the institutional Church.

In the nineteenth century, Vatican Council I (1870) debated at length "the compilation and adoption of a single short catechism for the universal Church." The underlying issue, which was in fact discussed under the cover of the catechism, had to do with bishops' rights vis-à-vis the Roman centralization. It had already been stated by Archbishop Félix Dupanloup of Orléans that it was totally impractical and inadequate to impose a single religion text in a multicultural society. Due to historical circumstances the proposal was never promulgated.[17] After Vatican I, centralism and attempts at uniformity contributed to passing on the responsibility for religious education to bureaucracy.

Obviously, for Vatican II and the post-Vatican period, the diagnosis of the catechetical situation was stated clearly enough to make it obvious that to take up again the debate about new catechisms and the compilation of a model text to which all future catechisms should conform would block energies instead of facing the real issues in a creative and sometimes daring fashion.

Instead, the idea of collegiality and subsidiarity made it possible to decide upon the preparation of a general document addressed to bishops only: advisory, rather than legislative, and based mainly on Vatican II documents. In that perspective Vatican II gave birth to new structures capable of maintaining the balance between unity and diversity.

Bishop Lacointe is considered to be the one who formally recommended a directory for a plurality of catecheses for different classes of children and adults.[18] Plurality runs right through one and the same culture, one and the same society, country, or diocese. This phenomenon can only be met by people living the faith, capable of showing the inspirational, prophetic quality of the Gospel in the midst of the crowds of this world.

The Directory itself thus symbolizes the move away from the chimera of a universal catechism. It takes another step away from book-centered catechesis by stating that the role of catechists is more important than texts, methods, and organization.

The immense efforts made by the U.S. dioceses to write the catechetical directory *Sharing the Light of Faith* (1979), on the basis of a very wide consultation, is another example of the shift from catechisms and text-centered uniformity to the development of a sense of catechetical responsibility in the Catholic community, supported by carefully nuanced directives and orientations.[19] Books with theological background information are available; official church documents, the Vatican II constitutions, the synodal recommendations, the papal addresses, all offer plenty of worthwhile material to be used. The "directives," then, indicate in what sense these many aspects should be integrated in a dynamic, dialectic, and hermeneutic interaction with the large variety of situations which Christians are dealing with in this world.

In today's world the search for meaning is more widespread and more explicit than in the past. Education has involved masses of people in this process. At the same time its first preoccupation should be to question the pitfalls of a self-centered society, and to challenge the interest for meaning, as Jesus challenged his world in "the Name of the Father." The call to conversion, to the Gospel, the call to be Christ's disciple, to be committed to his Kingdom, is the first and foremost task of the catechetical ministry.[20]

Finally, let's have a look at a few recent attempts to conceive new models of a catechism which are at least partly intended to meet the more crucial contemporary concerns.

The recent debate in Germany is polarized around two types of catechism.[21] The first one, *Grundriss des Glaubens* (1980), wants to be realistic because many people are confused and lost in the multiplicity of institutional expressions of the Christian tradition. Therefore, this catechism seeks to offer orientations for clarification. The authors suggest meeting contemporary men and women, children and adults, in their real-life situation where they often want to believe, but just cannot go that far. The book offers an approach to the Christian faith in relationship with the life of the Catholic Church and its tradition. It wants to support people in their life decisions and their practical behavior. It is much more a book which invites us to consolidate the evangelical way of looking at things, rather than one which concentrates upon an accomplished and closed product of faith statements.

The second one, *Botschaft des Glaubens* (1979), states that faith is a gift and a source for happiness. The aim of the catechism is to allow people to consider their lives in the light of faith because of the happiness and joy it offers. The Catholic Tradition is a well-developed and clear system which shouldn't cause any problem; on the contrary, in theory at least, it should help us to deal with life's problems. The book offers a systematic presentation of the faith statements; a minicompendium of the doctrine for the school, the family, and the parish. Only in the latter should it be used for discussions of contemporary questions or for argument.

Another example is the famous catechism for *campesinos* (small farmers) presented by the pastoral group of the diocese of Bambamarca (Peru): *Vamos caminando* (1977).[22] The pastoral group addresses itself to the *campesinos* in these terms: "If you want to search for your liberation together with Christ, this book will help you. . . . It is a book to be used in a group, not to be read alone. Your family, your community, those who gather for the preparation of baptism . . . neighbors who want to join for a common job. . . . As we always have to remember: two or more are gathered in the name of the Lord."

Each theme is to be read and reflected upon and offers concrete material about life situations, questions for reflection, further information; texts from the Gospel are quoted, hymns are presented. The daily life and the living conditions of the *campesinos* and the history of God's people are read together. The materials are to be used with the explicit intention of listening to the word of God, of praying, and of living the Christian life.

In 1976 A. Exeler presented a model for a catechism to be used for the theological education of adults.[23] He proposed that this book should offer three types of information for a catechetical learning process:

1. The original apostolic profession of faith should be presented together with comments about the historical context in which it was put together, and the original meaning given to it. Further information should be given about the meaning of this Credo in our contemporary situation.

2. A series of short formulations of Christian faith, as many people or groups are trying to restate their profession of faith in a meaningful way, in response to specific experiences or with an awareness proper to our present life situation.

3. An index of the key words of the Catholic faith tradition and of the Church, with clear explanations and brief historical notes. People are invited to work personally at their faith.

The diversity of materials used historically and geographically should help to deepen the understanding of the Christian tradition and to motivate a more conscious commitment.

In this context, the efforts made over the past fifteen years to work at short formulas of a profession of faith are relevant for a process whereby Christians try to focus on the essential dimension of being believing Christians in contemporary society.[24] Hundreds of these examples were written and used in all kinds of catechetical and liturgical settings. These professions of faith illustrate well that Christians are capable of writing important segments of their own "catechism" and then confronting it with texts of other people and with the official, traditional church documents.

These few examples are sufficient to show the complexity of the catechetical ministry today. It is important, then, to distinguish the essential task from secondary aspects. Some major questions should be given full attention: What is happening to people in the development of our civilization throughout the whole world? In what sense are these changes affecting the Church, Christian (Catholic) thinking, the faith tradition? What seems to be the most striking concern of the ongoing self-educating task of the Christian community, in order to be faithful to the original, orthodox faith in the risen Christ?

Basically, these questions mirror the interaction between a secular society and the Christian faith. Important developments in cultural awareness affect Christians and invite them to clarify what they stand for, to prove that their commitment is real.

The issue is to avoid putting the Christian tradition in competition with the evolution of the world, as if it were a question of winning or losing. Christians are invited to dismantle this dilemma, showing that they are capable of being part of the modern world, but that they respond to another kingdom, because of their faith in Christ, "sitting at the right hand of the Father." It is a totally different way of looking at the reality which is at stake.

The main task of the catechetical ministry, then, is to offer a learning process whereby this "interaction" with the world, specific to Christians, is discovered, interpreted, integrated, and practiced.

This process embodies every aspect of Christian initiation and ongoing commitment: experience and story, study of scripture and of the tradition, faith, including the proper prayer and liturgical celebrations, and the sometimes disconcerting commitment to conflicting life situations.

People have to learn what the reflection proper to faith stands for. They have to learn to reflect upon life in general, according to the Gospel. This is a much larger and more fundamental task than the memorization of standardized (artificial) questions and answers.

The learning process is to be lived with the faith community, calling for dynamic interactions, so much so that the growth of the Catholic faith is the result of the enriching, creative commitment and reflection of many.

"A responsible expression of faith requires a proportional balance between the expressed content of the mystery and the contextual formulation. This balance is reached in a process which has an ecclesiological nature. In this process expressions of faith react critically to and in solidarity with one another" (H. Witte).[25]

The educational level of schooling and the general cultural activity are meant to awaken these capacities in people. They are also meant to deepen the quality of a Christian commitment.

It should not be forgotten, however, that "it is meaningful and necessary to memorize some quotations from the Bible, some liturgical texts, some professions of faith and some prayers, as a living memory of what Christians over the centuries were able to develop in their reflection, because of their faith in Christ; the living memory of God's work among his people."

NOTES

1. G. S. Sloyan, "Religious Education from Early Christianity to Medieval Times," in G. S. Sloyan, ed., *From Shaping the Christian Message* (Macmillan, 1958), 11–45.

2. G. Adler and G. Vogeleisen, *Un siècle de catéchèse en France: 1893–1980; Histoire, Déplacements, Enjeux* (Paris: Beauchesne, 1981); J. Hull *New Directions in Religious Education* (Barcombe: Falmer Press, 1982); P. O'Hare, "Transition and Transformation in Religious Education," *Religious Education*, 1979; D. J. Piveteau and J. T. Dillon, "Resurgence of Religious Instruction," *Conception and Practice in a World of Change* (Notre Dame, IN: Religious Education Press, 1977); M. Warren, *Sourcebook for Modern Catechetics*, volume 1 (Winona, MN: Saint Mary's Press, 1983).

3. A. Knauber, "Over de Grondbetekenis van de Woordgroep Katecheocatchizo," *Verbum* 50 (1983): 234–251.

4. H. Lombaerts, "The Evangelisation of the School Milieu: An Ecological Issue," in *Evangelisation and the Catholic School* (Dublin 6: Secretariat of Secondary Schools, 1982), 29–31; W. Ong, *The Presence of the Word* (London: Yale University Press, 1967).

5. Matt. 11:1–19; Luke 4:16–30.

6. Jean Claude Dhotel, *Les origines du catéchisme moderne d'après les premiers manuels imprimés en France* (Paris: Aubier, 1967), 430.

7. Ibid., 27–38.

8. Ibid., 17.

9. Ibid., 22–27.

10. P. Rodríguez and R. Lanzetti, *El Catecismo Romano: Fuentes e historia del texto y de la redacción* (Pamplona: Universidad de Navarra, 1982), 19.

11. Ibid., 21.

12. Dhotel, *Les origines du catéchisme moderne*, 66–98; E. Germain, *Langages de la foi à travers l'histoire; Approche d'une étude des mentalités* (Tours, France: Fayard-Mame, 1972).

13. Letter of John Paul II to Cardinal Willebrands, *Osservatore Romano* (Rome), 14 November 1983. J. Vercruysse, "Luther vu par les catholiques cinq cent ans après sa naissance," *Pro Mundi Vita*, Dossiers, 1983–1984. Articles in *The Tablet*, 11 December 1983–1 July 1984.

14. W. H. Paradis, "Report on the Fifth Meeting of the International Catechetical Council, Rome, 11–17 April 1983." *The Living Light* 20, no. 2 (1984): 168.

15. Warren, *Sourcebook*, volume 1, 23–109.

16. B. J. Hilberath, "Dogmatische Inhalte Religiösen Lernens: Eine Analyse Katholischer Katechismen aus den Jahren 1955–75," *Katechetische Blätter* 103 (1978): 426–438.

17. M. Donnellan, "Bishops and Uniformity in Religious Education: Vatican I to Vatican II," *The Living Light* 10 (1973): 237–248; Warren, *Sourcebook*, volume 1, 232–243.

18. Ibid., 238ff.

19. Mary Bryce, "Sharing the Light of Faith: Catechetical Threshold for the U.S. Church," *Lumen Vitae* 34 (1979): 393–407; Warren, *Sourcebook*, volume 1, 261–274.

20. Knauber, "Over de Grondbetekenis," 248–251.

21. G. Stachel, "Zum Problem eines Katechismus für den schulischen Religions-Unterricht," *Katechetische Blätter* 104 (1979): 583–588; W. Nastainczyk, "Neuer Katechismus; Einladung und Wegweisung, Religionspädagogischkatechetische Bemerkungen zu 'Grundriss des Glaubens,'" *Katechetische Blätter* 105 (1980): 447–451; K. Rahner, "'Grundriss des Glaubens'—Ein Katechismus unserer Zeit; Überlegungen aus der Sicht eines Dogmatikers," *Katechetische Blätter* (1980): 545–547.

22. Maryknoll, NY: Orbis Books, 1985.

23. Forum Katechismus, *Diakoma* 8 (1977): 254–279.

24. G. Baudler, W. Beinert, and A. Kretzer, *Den Glauben Bekennen— Formel oder Leben?* (Freiburg: Herder, 1975); L. Karrer, *Der Glaube in Kurzformeln* (Mainz: Matthias-Grünewald, 1978).

25. H. Witte, "Plurality in the Expressions of Faith as an Ecclesiological Problem," *Tijdschrift voor Theologie* 23 (1983): 380; Richard P. McBrien, "Does the Faith Change?" *The Furrow*, 1983.

26. Synod of Bishops, *Elenchus Propositionem*, 22 October 1977, no. 19.

The *Catechism of the Catholic Church* and the Optimism of the Redeemed

CARDINAL JOSEPH RATZINGER
Translated by Cyprian Blamires

The catechism confesses the faith as a reality and not merely as the content of the awareness of Christians.

1. The Preparation of the New Catechism

In October 1985, twenty years after the end of the Second Vatican Council, the Holy Father convened an Extraordinary Synod; unlike the normal run of synods, this one was composed of the presidents of all the bishops' Conferences in the Catholic Church. It was to be something more than simply a solemn commemoration of the great event of twenty years before, an event in which only a handful of the bishops present at the 1985 synod had been involved. The idea was not just to look back, but also to look forward: to take stock of the situation of the Church, to take another look at the basic intentions of the Council, and to reflect on how its directives might best be followed out today so that they can bear fruit in the years to come.

Out of this came the idea of producing a Catechism of the Universal Church that would be comparable to the Roman Catechism of 1566, which had contributed so decisively to the renewal of catechesis and preaching in the spirit of the Council of Trent.

The proposal for a Vatican II Catechism was nothing new. In the closing stages of the Council, for example, Cardinal Jäger from Germany had suggested that such a book be commissioned as an embodiment of the process of *aggiornamento* in the area of doctrine. With the same sort of intention, no doubt, the Dutch Bishops' Conference had already

Reprinted from *Communio* 20 (fall 1993): 469–484. Copyright © 1993 by *Communio: International Catholic Review*. Used with permission.

published its own catechism in 1966. This catechism had aroused widespread global interest as a new approach to catechesis, but it soon also provoked serious anxieties. The pope therefore appointed a commission of six cardinals to study the matter: reporting in October 1968, the commission declared that while they did not wish to criticize the catechism's strongly individual tone—which they thought highly praiseworthy—the text nonetheless had to be clarified and indeed corrected on certain essential points.

This being the case, it was natural to ask whether the best way of handling the matters at issue was not to produce a catechism for the whole Church. At the time I said that the moment had not yet come for such a project, and I am still convinced that my assessment of the situation was correct. Apparently Jean Guitton has said that our catechism is twenty-five years late, and in a sense he is right, but equally it has to be admitted that in 1966 it was still very difficult to size up the situation. We were just entering a period of ferment that would be very slow to subside in order to make possible the clarity of vision requisite for a new expression of our common belief.

In the course of their discussions at the 1985 Synod, the bishops came to the conviction that the time was finally ripe for work to begin on the new catechism. The phase of feverish post-Conciliar endeavor that had seen the birth of so many new catechisms too hurriedly composed to reflect any maturity of deliberation had given way to a tendency to move away from the idea of the catechism as such. The new books with their rather frenzied modernization had begun to look dated as soon as they were published; anyone who is too quick to embrace today's ideas will inevitably look out of date by tomorrow. For a while the phenomenon of perpetual change in life and thought seemed to mean that long-term affirmations were simply no longer possible, and that any catechism would need to be repeatedly rewritten. It is certainly true that catechesis must always present the Christian message afresh to particular persons living at a particular historical moment. But this translation of doctrine for each new "today" presupposes something that transcends those "todays," transmitting from era to era a content that always remains valid; otherwise catechesis would have nothing to transmit.

The truth is that when, in the seventies, the catechism ceased to be viewed as the basis for mediating the faith, catechesis lost its content, and humanly speaking it became not merely a much more difficult enterprise but pedagogically and didactically a very ineffective one.

In this connection I am reminded of a letter that a catechist wrote to me after I had lectured on catechesis in Lyons and Paris. The letter was clearly written by a woman who loved children and knew how to work with them, a woman who loved her faith and who was not only remarkably intelligent but fully involved in using the catechetical instruments available to her from the appropriate sources. She observed in her letter that for some time she had been noticing that at the end of their catechetical preparation the children seemed to be left with nothing solid, with no firm basis of doctrine, because of the lack of any real substance in what they had learned. She said she had originally embarked on her task with pleasure, but was finding it increasingly unsatisfying, and had noticed that the children seemed to find it unsatisfying despite all her efforts. She had turned over and over in her mind what might be the reason for this.

This woman was too intelligent to attribute the ineffectiveness of catechesis simply to the evils of the times or to some inability to believe on the part of the present generation; she saw that there must be some other reason. Eventually she decided to conduct a thorough analysis of the catechetical material, asking the question: what were the didactic media employed actually being used to communicate? This analysis gave her both an answer to her question and the motivation to search for a new place to start. The conclusion of her analysis was that, for all its refined modern didactic methods, catechesis had lost almost all of its substantive content and was focusing exclusively on itself. This kind of teaching, going round and round in circles and communicating virtually nothing, could not hope to hold anyone's attention. Priority needed to be given back to content.

We would not be safe to generalize from what is a rather extreme example. But it does illustrate the problems of the seventies and early eighties, when even such content as survived in the practice of Catholic instruction was most unattractive, and anthropocentrism was the order of the day. Even the best catechists were feeling discouraged, and naturally the children themselves, to whom the catechesis was addressed, felt just as discouraged. A widespread conviction developed that the content of the message in all its splendor needed to be put back at the center of things.

In saying that the time was ripe for a Vatican II Catechism, the bishops who took part in the 1985 Synod were giving voice to just such a conviction. It was easier to set out the task than to implement it, but on 10 July 1986 the Holy Father appointed a special commission of twelve bishops and cardinals as a first step. The commission included representatives of the most important curial offices and all the major cultural areas of Catholic activity.

The challenge facing the commission when it met for the first time in November 1986 was an arduous one. The first priority was for it to try to define exactly what it had to do. The nature of the task entrusted to it by the synodal fathers, a task the pope had made his own, was still rather vague. The commission was to draw up "a draft catechism for the universal Church or a compendium of Catholic doctrine (in the areas of faith and morals) that could serve as a point of reference for the catechisms that had been composed or were being composed for individual regions." The Fathers had also said that doctrine was to be expounded "biblically and liturgically." It was to be "sound doctrine suited to modern Christian life."

2. Literary Genre, Readership, and Methods

The first dilemma was—catechism or compendium? Are they the same or different? This raised the question of what a catechism is and what a compendium is. It is widely considered (even among specialists in catechetics) that a catechism necessarily involves a set of questions and answers; but there was a great deal of resistance to presenting doctrine in this way. In fact, however, neither the Catechism of Trent nor Luther's Great Catechism followed this pattern, which is not historically essential to the catechism as a literary genre.

The first thing to be done, therefore, was to clarify the exact meaning of these two terms, "catechism" and "compendium." Historically the concepts had developed very slowly—during the Council of Trent and immediately afterwards—and only after a long process of study and reflection. In the First Session of the Council of Trent, there had been talk of the need both for a brief introduction or *metodus* (means of access) to the Holy Scriptures for students, and for a further "catechism" for the uneducated. In the Second Session (1547–1548), it was the "catechism" idea that dominated, but at the same time the conception of the two types of book (in time distinguished as *catechismus maior* and *catechismus minor*) persisted. When he closed the session Cardinal Del Monte remarked, "Let the book be written first, and then we can worry about the title," and apparently when the Tridentine Catechism was sent to the printers it still lacked a title. There certainly is no title in the manuscripts, which means that it was not finally settled until the book was at the press.

The distinction between a "greater" and a "lesser" catechism proved essential in the discussions within our commission of twelve. The word "compendium" would have suggested a whole collection of volumes intended for the shelves of the learned and not for the ordinary reader. The title "catechism" excluded the book from the category of the scholarly work—and indeed it is not a work of learned science, but a proclamation.

Here we come to the real question behind the debate over a title: Who was the book to be written for? And there were other related questions—what method should be used? What sort of language was to be adopted? It was clear from the start that this could not be a *catechismus minor*, a manual to be used directly in parish- or school-based catechesis. Differences between cultures are too great for there to be any possibility of writing a single book of the teaching of the Universal Church; teaching methods need to differ in response to differing circumstances.

So it had to be a *catechismus maior*. But who was it really going to be for? The Council of Trent had specified that its catechism was to be *ad parochos*, for parish priests. In those days they were practically the only catechists, or at least they had the main responsibility for catechesis. But through the centuries this responsibility has been transferred to a much wider class of persons, while at the same time the Catholic world for which the book was intended has grown a great deal. We therefore agreed that the book should be aimed above all at the persons who have responsibility for holding together the whole overall catechetical structure—the bishops. It was to be first and foremost a tool for them and for their helpers, a means of assisting them in the task of consolidating the work of catechesis in the various local churches.

Through the bishops and their collaborators, the catechism was to be the Church's book of inner unity in faith and proclamation, while at the same time providing a benchmark to test the doctrine being preached at the local level. This did not mean that the catechism was to be the preserve of a handful of the elect. This would have been out of kilter with the renewed way of understanding the Church and with our common responsibility in it as taught to us at Vatican II. The laity have a share in responsibility for the faith of the Church; they are not mere passive recipients of a doctrine, but pass it on and develop it according to their own sense of the faith. They are committed both to its continuity and to its vitality. At the time of the post-Conciliar crisis, the laity's sense of the faith was of crucial importance in the discernment of spirits. For this reason, the book had to be able to be read by the laity and needed to be an instrument for making them mature and able to be responsible for the faith.

The situation today seems to bear out this conclusion. Many believers are wanting to become better acquainted with the Church's teachings. In the midst of the confusion generated by a succession of novel theological hypotheses and their diffusion (unfortunate in many cases) through the media, the faithful want to know what the Church teaches or does not teach. I personally consider that the way this book has been welcomed represents a kind of vote by the people of God against those forces that see catechisms as enemies of progress, products of the centralizing tendencies in Rome, or something similar. Such opponents of catechisms often represent particular groups that want to defend their own monopoly over the formation of theological opinion in the Church and the world and that do not want to be troubled by the voice of a theologically competent laity.

Of course the catechism must also serve the fundamental goal of catechesis, namely, evangelization. It offers a resource to agnostics too, and to those who are questioning and searching, it tells them what the Catholic Church believes and tries to live.

It has to be admitted that within the commission questions were constantly asked as to whether the composition of a common catechism for the whole Church is not an impossible task. Will it not inevitably lead to an unacceptable uniformity? We were constantly and sometimes reproachfully asked whether we were not simply going to create a new tool for the censorship of theological research. But when humanity and Christendom alike are relentlessly disintegrating in spite of their technical uniformity, elements of unity surely do not need to be defended. On the contrary, we have urgent need of them. When we see how in many countries the ability to live together and to maintain moral and civil consensus is collapsing, we have to ask ourselves why. How can we learn to live together again? Only by rediscovering spiritual principles that heal divisions and reawaken our capacity for mutual acceptance. Even within the Church there are distinct parties and groups that hardly recognize one another anymore as members of the same community. The decay of ecclesial unity goes hand in hand with the decay of civil unity. And yet it is not true that today what we have in common can no longer be expressed. The catechism is not intended to reflect the opinions of one particular group, but the faith of the Church—something that has not been invented by us. Only where there is real unity on basic fundamentals can there also be a vital pluriformity.

The discussion so far has focused on important choices concerning the method employed in the catechism and concerning its validity within the Church. The important factor for the commission was that the catechism must not express the personal opinion of its authors, and this meant that the greatest care had to be taken over the accuracy and fidelity of the expression of the faith of the Church. For the Church, the word "catechism" implies that her doctrine is being mediated and her faith is being expressed in such a way that it becomes accessible to us as something present, as a word for *our* today.

The methodology of the catechism was a tricky problem, one that took a long time to resolve. Should we follow a more "inductive" method, starting from man in the modern world and finishing with God, Christ, and the Church, which would involve structuring the text in a more "argumentative" manner allowing for a constant unspoken dialogue with today's issues—or should we start from the faith itself and argue from within its own logic, that is, testifying rather than reasoning?

The question immediately became a very practical one when we asked ourselves how to begin the book—what to take as a starting point. Would it not perhaps be appropriate to set out with a description of the context of the modern world, only then going on to open the doors of access to God? Would it not otherwise look as though we were operating in some realm of abstraction, far removed from concrete reality? The two possible starting points were frequently discussed and minds often changed.

In the end, we agreed that analyses of our time always involve an element of arbitrariness and depend too much on the point of view adopted in advance, for in fact there is no such thing as a uniform world situation. The situation for someone living in Mozambique or Bangladesh (to take two purely arbitrary examples) is completely different from that of someone living in Switzerland or the United States. Moreover, we have seen how quickly social circumstances and social awareness change. It is of course vital to maintain dialogue with each different mentality, but that is a task for local churches; it is they who have to respond to the particular challenges of individual situations in our world.

Nonetheless, the catechism does not actually proceed in a purely deductive manner, since the story of faith is a reality of this world and has created its own experience. Here is found the starting point for the catechism, attentive as it is to the Lord and his Church, mediating in its intrinsic logic and inner force the word it hears in this way. At the same time the message is not simply "supratemporal" and is not intended to be so: it is just that the catechism avoids tying itself too much to the circumstances of the moment, since it aims to offer the service of unity not merely synchronically—for our particular era—but also diachronically—for the generations to come, as did the great catechisms of the past, and most notably the sixteenth-century one.

3. The Author of the Catechism and Its Authority

At this point we were faced with the question of finding an appropriate structure for the text. First, however, we still had to reflect on two other questions—how binding was the work to be and who was actually to write it? Let us begin with this second question. Among all the tricky problems we faced this was probably the most delicate. One thing was clear: it had to be a "catholic" book in the truest sense of the term—and that included the mode of its composition—but at the same time it had to be both readable and, at least to some extent, unitary in style. The fundamental decision was made in a rush: the catechism should not be the work of specialists but of pastors, based on their experience of the Church and the world. It was to be a work of proclamation. The three sections that had been planned from the beginning were assigned to three pairs of bishops: the part relative to the confession of faith was entrusted to Estepa (Spain) and Maggiolini (Italy); the section on the sacraments to Medina (Chile) and Karlic (Argentina); the section on morals to Honoré (France) and Konstant (England). As soon as it was recognized that a separate fourth part on prayer needed to be added, we looked for someone representative of Eastern theology. Unable to find a bishop to do the job, we approached J. Corbon, who wrote the marvelous text on prayer at the end of the catechism while under siege in Beirut and at grave risk from bombardment. Archbishop Levada from the United States was called on to produce a glossary. To be frank, I did initially feel it was rather rash to suppose that a group of authors like this spread all over the world—authors who as bishops were in any case already carrying heavy workloads—could manage to complete a book together. Apart from anything else it was far from clear what language the text should be in. The first draft, sent to forty consultants in different parts of the globe in 1987, had kept to Latin. But we came to realize that Latin translated (often very badly) into a modern language would be a source of misunderstandings and would sometimes result in distortions rather than a clear expression of the intentions of the writers. Having discussed the matter together, we decided that French should be our working language, since all the writers had at least some ability to express themselves in it. The decision was reached that the catechism should be drawn up in French and that only the definitive official text was then to be written in Latin—so as to make it quite independent of all the current national languages. Moreover, this definitive text would be published only after the editions in the chief national languages and would take account of observations made in the first phase of the reception of the catechism, without of course altering the overall thrust of the text. The individual texts in the national languages would then be revised on the basis of this definitive text, on which work was begun in the meantime.

To return to the question of the actual composition of the catechism, it was evident that work could begin only when some fundamental decisions had been made by the pope's chosen commission of twelve. As it was composed, the text was regularly presented for approval to the commission, which pronounced (after discussion) on all the more important

problems raised in the course of the redaction. This collaboration between the commission and the editorial committee proved extremely
fertile, but also demonstrated the lack of an intermediate element: the
individual sections were stylistically and conceptually too diverse, and
there was need for an editorial hand to weave together all the separate
parts of the tapestry. So we looked for an editorial assistant to keep an
eye on the way the texts were composed and then to give them unity of
style without altering their substance. The person we chose for this task
is the present auxiliary Bishop of Vienna, Christoph Schönborn, who accomplished magnificently the often ungrateful task of giving unity to
some very diverse modes of thought and stylistic forms. It still appears
as something of a miracle to me that out of such a complex editorial
process emerged a book of such essential inner harmony and indeed (to
my eyes) of such beauty. The fact that minds of such differing stamp on
the editorial committee and on the commission could so consistently
find ground for agreement in their aims was for me and for all the participants an extraordinary experience, an experience which we were
very often inclined to interpret as a sign of guidance from above. The
commission of twelve unanimously approved the text on 14 February
1992, the Feast of Saints Cyril and Methodius. If it is borne in mind that
more than a thousand bishops made their opinions known on the revised draft sent out in November 1989 and that upwards of twenty-four
thousand of their observations were taken into account in the text, we
can see this book as truly representing an exercise in episcopal "collegiality," and we can hear in it the voice of the universal Church speaking
to us in all her fullness as the "sound of many waters."

At this point let us return to the question raised earlier about the authority of the catechism. To resolve this question, we need first of all to
analyze the juridical structure of the book more closely. Like the new
code of canon law, the new catechism is in fact a collegial work, but
from a strictly juridical point of view it is a papal work, that is, it has
been transmitted by the Holy Father to Christendom by virtue of his specific magisterial power. In this sense, it seems to me that from the point
of view of its juridical structure the new catechism offers an excellent
example of the reciprocal interaction between papal sovereignty and
collegiality, corresponding to the spirit and letter of the Council. The
pope is not talking over the heads of the bishops, but invites his brothers in the episcopate to sound out the symphony of the faith together. He
stamps the result with his authority, which then guarantees the juridical
value of the book. This authority is not something imposed from outside,
but brings the common witness to the forefront. That does not mean
that the catechesis is a kind of new "Superdogma," as its detractors are
prone to insinuate, wanting to imply that it endangers the freedom of

theology. The significance of the catechism for the common teaching of the Church can be gathered from the Apostolic Constitution *Fidei Depositum* with which the pope launched it on 11 October 1992, exactly thirty years after the opening of the Second Vatican Council: "I acknowledge it [the catechism] to be a valid and legitimate instrument available to the Ecclesial Communion and a reliable norm for the teaching of the Faith" (no. 4). The individual doctrines that the catechism affirms have no other authority than that which they already possess. What is important is the catechism in its totality: it reflects the Church's teaching; anyone who rejects it overall separates himself unequivocally from the faith and teaching of the Church.

4. Structure and Content

a. The Structure of the Whole

Once the commission had chosen its working methods and decided to whom the work was to be addressed, it had to settle the way in which the work was to be structured. There were a variety of ideas about this. Some thought the catechism should be patterned on a christocentric conception, others felt that Christocentrism needed to give way to Theocentrism. In the end we felt it right to take the concept of the Kingdom of God as our unifying principle. After some vigorous debate, we became convinced that the catechism should not represent the faith as a system or as something to be derived from a single central concept. The best way to organize the content of catechesis would emerge out of particular concrete circumstances and could not be imposed on the whole Church through the common catechism. We had to do something simpler: we had to set out the essential elements that were to be considered as conditions for admission to baptism and the communal life of Christians. Every Muslim knows the basic principles of his religion: faith in one God, in his prophet, in the Koran; the commandment to fast and make pilgrimages to Mecca. But what makes a person a Christian? The catechumenate in the early Church assembled the fundamental elements on the basis of Scripture—faith, the sacraments, the commandments, the "Our Father." Then there was the *redditio symboli*—the handing over of the confession of faith and its "redditio," the committing of it to memory by the one being baptized; the learning of the "Our Father," of the moral teaching, and of the mystagogical catechesis—that is, the introduction to the sacramental life. Perhaps all this looks rather superficial, but in reality it leads into the heart of what is essential: to be Christians, we must believe, we must learn how to live as Christians, we must as it were learn the Christian style of life; we must be ready to pray as Christians and accede to the Church's mysteries and her liturgy. All these four elements are closely interlinked; the introduction to the faith is not the transmission of a theory, as if faith were a kind of philosophy—"Platonism for the people," as someone once rather contemptuously defined it. The confession of faith is only the elaboration of the baptismal formula. The introduction to the faith is itself mystagogy, our introduction to baptism, to the process of conversion, in which we do not act purely on our own, but allow God to act in us. Therefore the exposition of the confession of faith is closely connected with liturgical catechesis; it is in fact a guide to the celebration of the mysteries. Being introduced to the liturgy also implies learning to pray, and knowing how to pray means learning how to live, so it involves the problem of morals too.

Thus in the course of our debates it became clear that the quadripartite structure of the Tridentine catechism—confession of faith, sacraments, commandments, and prayer—was the most appropriate way for a *catechismus maior*. This division, moreover, allows anyone who uses the book to find a way around it in the quickest and easiest way and to look up the particular questions that are of interest. We were not a little surprised, however, to find that in what was for all intents and purposes a mere juxtaposition of elements, something not unlike a "system" could be directly discerned. The things that the Church believes, celebrates, lives, and prays are presented one after another. Someone suggested that we link the individual parts through these titles so as to make clear the inner unity of the book. This idea was, however, ultimately rejected, and for two reasons. The method would have given rise to a kind of ecclesiocentrism from which the catechism is very remote. Such an ecclesiocentrism—and this was the second reason—then would easily lead to a kind of relativism and subjectivism in the faith: only the Church's awareness is presented, while the question of whether this awareness corresponds to the reality is left open. Many books on religion no longer dare to say "Christ is *risen*," affirming only that the community experienced Christ as risen. The question of the truth of this experience remains an open one. Such a vague ecclesiocentrism eventually leads to the approach of German idealism, according to which everything takes place purely within our consciousness—in this case the consciousness of the Church (the Church believes, celebrates, etc.). The catechism intended and intends to speak frankly and clearly on the question: Christ is *risen*. The catechism confesses the faith as a reality and not merely as the content of the awareness of Christians.

b. The Structure of the First Part

After having outlined the general structure of the catechism, there still remained a whole series of questions about its concrete form, and especially about its first and third sections. For purposes of brevity I will restrict myself to the chief decisions relative to these two parts. The first concerns the profession of faith: what kind of profession? From the earliest times the Western catechetical tradition had adopted the baptismal confession of the Church of Rome, which, as "the apostolic confession of faith," became one of the chief prayers of Western Christendom. But on this point an objection was made: the *Apostolicum* is a Latin creed, whereas the catechism belongs to the whole Catholic church, Western and Eastern. This led to the idea of following the so-called Niceno-Constantinopolitan Creed—as does the catechism for German adults, for example. But an observation that was made about the particularity of individual creeds encouraged us to move away from the idea. For in the case of the Nicene Creed, the confession was that of a council and it was therefore a bishops' creed, which then afterward also became the creed of the community gathered to celebrate the Eucharist. Catechesis is presupposed here, but catechesis as such has always kept to the baptismal creed because in essence the latter is an introduction to baptism or a renewal of the life of the baptized. Unlike some of the great conciliar confessions of faith, baptismal creeds all show local differences: it was necessary to adopt the creed of a local church. But these creeds are actually all so similar in their basic structures that the decision to opt for the Roman creed—the Apostles'—did not imply a unilateral preference for the Western tradition but opened a way into the common tradition of faith of the universal Church.

This universal character of the creed is evident if we hold to its essential structure, as demonstrated with particular force by Henri de Lubac. The division into twelve articles corresponding to the twelve apostles is certainly very ancient but is subordinate to the original ternary structure that follows the trinitarian formula of baptism: "I baptize you in the name of the Father, and of the Son, and of the Holy Spirit." In essence the baptismal creed is a confession of the living God, the one God in three persons, and this is the supreme structure which shows the basic essence of the faith that is always and everywhere the same; we believe in the living God, who as Father, Son, and Holy Spirit is one God. He gave himself to us in the Incarnation of the Son and always remains close to us by the sending of the Holy Spirit. Being Christians means that we believe in this living God of revelation. All the rest is a development of this nucleus. So even by its structure the catechism shows the hierarchy of truth of which the Second Vatican Council spoke.

c. Chief Questions About the Third Part

Finally a few points on the third part, on morals, the most-discussed section and for many reasons the most difficult task in the composition of the catechism. On the basis of the tradition it seemed appropriate to choose the schema of the Ten Commandments, which is also the foundation of the Sermon on the Mount and which is used by Saint Paul (for example in Romans 13:8–10) as a fundamental model for moral teaching. The view that this is a purely Old Testament matter and that the commandments have been superseded for the Christian is not, therefore, in any way correct. The Ten Commandments are often erroneously identified with the "Law" from which we have been liberated—as Paul teaches—thanks to Christ. But the Law Paul is talking about is the Torah in its entirety, which Christ took onto the Cross and which was fulfilled and transformed on the Cross; the moral teaching of the "ten words" retains its full validity, though now of course in the new vital context of grace. With the New Testament, the Ten Commandments emerge as a living word, growing in the history of the people of God and being continuously disclosed in its true depth there, finally attaining its full significance in the work and the person of Jesus Christ. But as we understand the mystery of Christ in a new way and find new things in it in each historical period, so the exposition and comprehension of the commandments never come to an end. On the basis of this kind of interpretation of the commandments in the context of the history of salvation with its christological center, we could link up again with the catechetical tradition that has always found in the commandments fundamental guidelines for the Christian conscience.

In order to expound this concrete and dynamic interpretation of the commandments, we had to place them clearly in a Christian context, as they are read by the New Testament and the great tradition; the Sermon on the Mount, the gifts of the Holy Spirit, the doctrine of the virtues provide the context for the right reading of the commandments. On the question of where to place the doctrine of sin and the doctrine of justification by law and Gospel, after lengthy discussion we decided that the right place was in the third part of the catechism. In this way it becomes crystal clear that Christian moral teaching comes within the sphere of grace which goes before us, touches us, and in the moment of pardon renews us. This close connection must be kept constantly in mind while individual parts of the section on morals are being read, otherwise the section will be open to serious misunderstanding.

At the present time there is a huge debate within moral theology regarding its specific foundations, and the question of the revelation-reason and reason-being (nature) relationships is being bitterly contested. But it was not the job of the catechism to become involved in theological debate. It had to presuppose the great fundamental decisions of the faith. We come into conformity with Being when we come into conformity with Christ, and we come into conformity with Christ when we become persons who love with him. Discipleship of Christ and an understanding of all individual duties on the basis of the commandment of love are connected; neither may be separated from our response to the word of Creation, hidden yet perceptible. Just as Creation and Redemption, proclamation of Being and proclamation of Revelation are inseparable, so too are faith and reason, being and reason. To the extent that the catechism makes use of this category of nature, we must interpret the term in this way. The catechism does not accept the sort of naturalism defined by Ulpian (d. 228 A.D.), when he said that what is natural is what nature teaches all living beings. For the catechism, reason belongs to human nature; what is "natural" for man is what is in conformity with his reason, and what is in conformity with his reason is what opens him to God. In other words, physiology alone cannot define "nature" nor can it be a norm for morals; when we speak of human nature we must always bear in mind the indissoluble unity of body and soul, the spiritual and corporeal dimensions of the unique being that is man. On the other hand, neither can the catechism accommodate any "autonomous" or auto-sufficient reason, a reason for which the barrier between reason and being, reason and Divine Logos is impenetrable, leaving man in a position where he not only may but must base his moral judgments entirely on his own standard of assessment. The catechism follows tradition in viewing reason as being weakened by sin yet retaining uncompromised its capacity to perceive Creator and creation. This capacity is renewed by the encounter with Christ who as Divine Logos does not exclude reason, but brings it back to himself. In this sense, it is above all in its section on morals that the catechism is imbued with the optimism of the redeemed.

I would like to end with a little anecdote. One of the last redactions of the catechism to be drawn up before publication was sent to an old bishop much venerated for his erudition, with a request for his opinion on it. He sent back the manuscript quite delighted. "Yes," he said, "this is the faith of my mother." He was thrilled by the fact that the faith he had learned as a child, the faith that had guided him throughout his life, had been reformulated in all its richness, in all its beauty, but also in all its simplicity and indestructible uniqueness. "It is the faith of my mother"—the faith of our mother, the Church. This is the faith to which the catechism invites us.

Apostolic Constitution: *Fidei Depositum* On the Publication of the *Catechism of the Catholic Church*

Prepared Following the Second Vatican Ecumenical Council

JOHN PAUL, BISHOP (POPE JOHN PAUL II)
Servant of the Servants of God for Everlasting Memory

To my Venerable Brothers the Cardinals, Patriarchs, Archbishops, Bishops, Priests, Deacons, and to all the People of God.

Guarding the deposit of faith is the mission which the Lord entrusted to his church, and which she fulfills in every age. The Second Vatican Ecumenical Council, which was opened thirty years ago by my predecessor Pope John XXIII, of happy memory, had as its intention and purpose to highlight the Church's apostolic and pastoral mission and by making the truth of the Gospel shine forth to lead all people to seek and receive Christ's love which surpasses all knowledge (cf. Eph. 3:19).

The principal task entrusted to the Council by Pope John XXIII was to guard and present better the precious deposit of Christian doctrine in order to make it more accessible to the Christian faithful and to all people of goodwill. For this reason the Council was not first of all to condemn the errors of the time, but above all to strive calmly to show the strength and beauty of the doctrine of the faith. "Illumined by the light of this Council," the Pope said, "the Church . . . will become greater in spiritual riches and gaining the strength of new energies therefrom, she will look to the future without fear. . . . Our duty is to dedicate ourselves with an earnest will and without fear to that work which our era

Reprinted from "Apostolic Constitution: *Fidei Depositum*," on the Publication of the *Catechism of the Catholic Church*, 1–6. 1993.

demands of us, thus pursuing the path which the Church has followed for twenty centuries."[1]

With the help of God, the Council Fathers in four years of work were able to produce a considerable number of doctrinal statements and pastoral norms which were presented to the whole Church. There the Pastors and Christian faithful find directives for that "renewal of thought, action, practices, and moral virtue, of joy and hope, which was the very purpose of the Council."[2]

After its conclusion, the Council did not cease to inspire the Church's life. In 1985 I was able to assert, "For me, then—who had the special grace of participating in it and actively collaborating in its development—Vatican II has always been, and especially during these years of my Pontificate, the constant reference point of my every pastoral action, in the conscious commitment to implement its directives concretely and faithfully at the level of each Church and the whole Church."[3]

In this spirit, on 25 January 1985, I convoked an extraordinary assembly of the Synod of Bishops for the twentieth anniversary of the close of the Council. The purpose of this assembly was to celebrate the graces and spiritual fruits of Vatican II, to study its teaching in greater depth in order that all the Christian faithful might better adhere to it, and to promote knowledge and application of it.

On that occasion the Synod Fathers stated: "Very many have expressed the desire that a catechism or compendium of all Catholic doctrine regarding both faith and morals be composed, that it might be, as it were, a point of reference for the catechisms or compendiums that are prepared in the various regions. The presentation of doctrine must be biblical and liturgical. It must be sound doctrine suited to the present life of Christians."[4] After the Synod ended, I made this desire my own, considering it as "fully responding to a real need of the universal Church and of the particular Churches."[5]

For this reason we thank the Lord wholeheartedly on this day when we can offer the entire Church this "reference text" entitled the *Catechism of the Catholic Church* for a catechesis renewed at the living sources of the faith!

Following the renewal of the Liturgy and the new codification of the canon law of the Latin Church and that of the Oriental Catholic Churches, this catechism will make a very important contribution to that work of renewing the whole life of the Church, as desired and begun by the Second Vatican Council.

The Process and Spirit of Drafting the Text

The *Catechism of the Catholic Church* is the result of very extensive collaboration; it was prepared over six years of intense work done in a spirit of complete openness and fervent zeal.

In 1986, I entrusted a commission of twelve Cardinals and Bishops, chaired by Cardinal Joseph Ratzinger, with the task of preparing a draft of the catechism requested by the Synod Fathers. An editorial committee of seven diocesan Bishops, experts in theology and catechesis, assisted the commission in its work.

The commission, charged with giving directives and with overseeing the course of the work, attentively followed all the stages in editing the nine subsequent drafts. The editorial committee, for its part, assumed responsibility for writing the text, making the emendations requested by the commission and examining the observations of numerous theologians, exegetes, and catechists, and, above all, of the Bishops of the whole world, in order to produce a better text. In the committee various opinions were compared with great profit, and thus a richer text has resulted whose unity and coherence are assured.

The project was the object of extensive consultation among all Catholic Bishops, their Episcopal Conferences or Synods, and of theological and catechetical institutes. As a whole, it received a broadly favorable acceptance on the part of the Episcopate. It can be said that this *Catechism* is the result of the collaboration of the whole Episcopate of the Catholic Church, who generously accepted my invitation to share responsibility for an enterprise which directly concerns the life of the Church. This response elicits in me a deep feeling of joy, because the harmony of so many voices truly expresses what could be called the "symphony" of the faith. The achievement of this *Catechism* thus reflects the collegial nature of the Episcopate; it testifies to the Church's catholicity.

Arrangement of the Material

A catechism should faithfully and systematically present the teaching of Sacred Scripture, the living Tradition in the Church, and the authentic Magisterium, as well as the spiritual heritage of the Fathers, Doctors, and saints of the Church, to allow for a better knowledge of the Christian mystery and for enlivening the faith of the People of God. It should take into account the doctrinal statements which down the centuries the Holy Spirit has intimated to his Church. It should also help to illumine with the light of faith the new situations and problems which had not yet emerged in the past.

This catechism will thus contain both the new and the old (cf. Matt. 13:52), because the faith is always the same yet the source of ever new light.

To respond to this twofold demand, the *Catechism of the Catholic Church* on the one hand repeats the "old," traditional order already followed by the Catechism of Saint Pius V, arranging the material in four parts: the *Creed*, the *Sacred Liturgy*, with pride of place given to the sacraments, the *Christian way of life*, explained beginning with the Ten Commandments, and finally, *Christian prayer.* At the same time, however, the contents are often presented in a "new" way in order to respond to the questions of our age.

The four parts are related one to another: the Christian mystery is the object of faith (first part); it is celebrated and communicated in liturgical actions (second part); it is present to enlighten and sustain the children of God in their actions (third part); it is the basis for our prayer, the privileged expression of which is the *Our Father*, and it represents the object of our supplication, our praise, and our intercession (fourth part).

The Liturgy itself is prayer; the confession of faith finds its proper place in the celebration of worship. Grace, the fruit of the sacraments, is the irreplaceable condition for Christian living, just as participation in the Church's Liturgy requires faith. If faith is not expressed in works, it is dead (cf. James 2:14–16) and cannot bear fruit unto eternal life.

In reading the *Catechism of the Catholic Church* we can perceive the wonderful unity of the mystery of God, his saving will, as well as the central place of Jesus Christ, the only begotten Son of God, sent by the Father, made man in the womb of the Blessed Virgin Mary by the power of the Holy Spirit, to be our Savior. Having died and risen, Christ is always present in his Church, especially in the sacraments; he is the source of our faith, the model of Christian conduct, and the Teacher of our prayer.

The Doctrinal Value of the Text

The *Catechism of the Catholic Church*, which I approved 25 June last and the publication of which I today order by virtue of my Apostolic Authority, is a statement of the Church's faith and of Catholic doctrine, attested to or illumined by Sacred Scripture, the Apostolic Tradition, and the Church's Magisterium. I declare it to be a sure norm for teaching the faith and thus a valid and legitimate instrument for ecclesial communion. May it serve the renewal to which the Holy Spirit ceaselessly calls the Church of God, the Body of Christ, on her pilgrimage to the undiminished light of the Kingdom!

The approval and publication of the *Catechism of the Catholic Church* represent a service which the Successor of Peter wishes to offer to the Holy Catholic Church, to all the particular Churches in peace and communion with the Apostolic See: the service, that is, of supporting and confirming the faith of all the Lord Jesus' disciples (cf. Luke 22:32), as well as of strengthening the bonds of unity in the same apostolic faith.

Therefore, I ask all the Church's Pastors and the Christian faithful to receive this catechism in a spirit of communion and to use it assiduously in fulfilling their mission of proclaiming the faith and calling people to the Gospel life. This catechism is given to them that it may be a sure and authentic reference text for teaching Catholic doctrine and particularly for preparing local catechisms. It is also offered to all the faithful who wish to deepen their knowledge of the unfathomable riches of salvation (cf. Eph. 3:8). It is meant to support ecumenical efforts that are moved by the holy desire for the unity of all Christians, showing carefully the content and wondrous harmony of the Catholic faith. The *Catechism of the Catholic Church*, lastly, is offered to every individual who asks us to give an account of the hope that is in us (cf. 1 Pet. 3:15) and who wants to know what the Catholic Church believes.

This catechism is not intended to replace the local catechisms duly approved by the ecclesiastical authorities, the diocesan Bishops and the Episcopal Conferences, especially if they have been approved by the Apostolic See. It is meant to encourage and assist in the writing of new local catechisms, which take into account various situations and cultures, while carefully preserving the unity of faith and fidelity to Catholic doctrine.

At the conclusion of this document presenting the *Catechism of the Catholic Church*, I beseech the Blessed Virgin Mary, Mother of the Incarnate Word and Mother of the Church, to support with her powerful intercession the catechetical work of the entire Church on every level, at this time when she is called to a new effort of evangelization. May the light of the true faith free humanity from the ignorance and slavery of sin in order to lead it to the only freedom worthy of the name (cf. John 8:32): that of life in Jesus Christ under the guidance of the Holy Spirit, here below and in the Kingdom of heaven, in the fullness of the blessed vision of God face-to-face (cf. 1 Cor. 13:12; 2 Cor. 5:6–8)!

Given 11 October 1992, the thirtieth anniversary of the opening of the Second Vatican Ecumenical Council, in the fourteenth year of my Pontificate.

NOTES

1. John XXIII, Discourse at the Opening of the Second Vatican Ecumenical Council, 11 October 1962: AAS 54 (1962): 788–791.

2. Paul VI, Discourse at the Closing of the Second Vatican Ecumenical Council, 7 December 1965: AAS 58 (1966): 7–8.

3. John Paul II, Discourse of January 25,1985: *L'Osservatore Romano*, 27 January 1985.

4. *Final Report* of the Extraordinary Synod of Bishops, 7 December 1985, *Enchiridion Vaticanum*, vol. 9, II, B, a, n. 4: p. 1758, n. 1797.

5. John Paul II, Discourse at the Closing of the Extraordinary Synod of Bishops, 7 December 1985, n. 6: AAS 78 (1986): 435.

The *Catechism of the Catholic Church* in U.S. Context

BERARD L. MARTHALER, OFM CONV

Even though the *text* of the *Catechism of the Catholic Church* is not generally available in the United States, we are in a position to examine the *context* of the catechism. So that our examination does not become too ethereal, a mere literary exercise in exegesis or eisegesis, we would do well to recall that the Latin root of *text* is *textere*, "to weave," and *context*, in the sense that it is "woven with," is an integral part of the fabric. A document's context is twofold: the circumstances in which it is written and the circumstances in which it is read. Both are important.

The Catechism Genre

Words and phrases are the threads of a literary text. The cultural setting and historical conditions in which a manuscript or book comes to be are the context. Everything exists in some context or other, and words do not have meaning apart from a context. The term "catechism" is a case in point. The Baltimore Catechism, the standard catechetical tool in the United States for eighty years or so, is part of the context in which the *Catechism of the Catholic Church* (*CCC*) will be received in this country. Baltimore shaped Catholicism in the United States through the first six decades of this century and became the paradigm for all catechisms and the syllabus for textbooks. During the consultation process that produced the *CCC*, many in this country criticized the provisional text as being too long and detailed. They were using the Baltimore Catechism as the yardstick.

To appreciate the nature and purpose of the *Catechism of the Catholic Church*, it is necessary to see it in a broader context. The *CCC* is the

Reprinted from *The Living Light* 30, no. 1 (fall 1993): 65–71. Copyright © 1993 by the United States Catholic Conference, Washington, D.C. Used with permission.

latest exemplar of a genre whose roots are deep in the Middle Ages. In the Middle Ages, *catechismus* referred to oral teaching, both the act of instruction and the doctrine taught. The fabric of the medieval catechism was sewn together from the Apostles' Creed, the commandments, the Lord's Prayer and, later, the sacraments. The term was first applied to a book in 1357, when *The Lay Folks Catechism* was issued by Archbishop Thoresby of York. Even then it was ambiguous, because *The Lay Folks Catechism* seemed to refer to the content rather than the form, and despite the title it was really intended for the clergy who were to use it to instruct the laity.

The printing press changed the context of the catechism. It was now mass-produced, even illustrated with woodcuts. Martin Luther made masterful use of the catechism as a vehicle in his program for reform and for instructing clergy and laity alike in the rudiments of the faith. Luther set the pattern that would be followed by Saint Peter Canisius, Claude Fleury, and others in producing two versions of the catechism: the *catechismus maior*, a systematic presentation of doctrine for use by clergy and the educated; and the *catechismus minor*, a short catechism in the form of questions and answers to be used as a didactic tool. The *Catechism of the Catholic Church* belongs to the genre of the former.

In the midst of the Protestant Reformation, the catechism took on still another function. With the publication by Reformed theologians of the Heidelberg Catechism in 1564, the catechism began to serve as a criterion for orthodoxy. Thus the *Catechism of the Council of Trent*, published three years later, served both as a resource for the pastoral ministers and as a witness to authentic Catholic teaching. It was a bridge between the past and the future. The Roman Catechism, as the Tridentine work was popularly known, emphasized the four pillars of medieval catechesis on the one hand and, on the other, nurtured Catholic identity by stressing points of difference with Protestants without ever mentioning them.

The ordinary American Catholic did not have access to the *Catechism of the Council of Trent*. An English translation, dating from 1829, more than 250 years after the Roman Catechism first appeared, was only published in the United States in 1905. Up to the time of the Third Plenary Council of Baltimore in 1884, dozens of catechisms were in circulation. Some were imported, but many bishops produced catechisms for the special needs of the frontier and the indigenous peoples. (One thinks of John Ireland in Charleston, South Carolina, and Fredric Baraga in Marquette, Michigan. The latter wrote a catechism in the language of the Ottawa Indians and later translated it into Ojibway for the Chippewas.)[1] The Baltimore Catechism, much criticized even by bishops at the time of its publication, displaced the earlier catechisms in the name of uniformity. As time passed, it took on the aura of the McGuffy reader, and like that old standby from another era, was credited with an importance it never had or deserved. Seen through the rose-colored lens of nostalgia, it was associated with all that was good, holy, and unchanging in the Church. Less than one-quarter the size of the Tridentine Catechism and intended for beginners—children and the uneducated—the Baltimore Catechism became for clergy and laity alike the paradigm of catechisms and the criterion of orthodoxy. (Language that did not resonate with Baltimore sounded Protestant.)

Americans familiar with only the Baltimore Catechism have a limited context in which to assimilate the *Catechism of the Catholic Church*. The size, depth and, in places, the complexity of the *CCC* has been a source of surprise and, for some, puzzlement. It does not fit the popular image of a catechism: it has no questions and answers, and it defies memorization. Like the *Catechism of the Council of Trent*, the *Catechism of the Catholic Church* is a resource for pastoral ministers and teachers, not a textbook to be brought into the classroom.

Influence of Vatican II

The Second Vatican Council changed the face of Catholicism and created still another context for catechisms. Pope John Paul II wrote in *Catechesi Tradendae* that "the ministry of catechesis draws ever fresh energy from the councils," and he expressed the desire that the Second Vatican Council stir up enthusiasm and activity in our time similar to that which followed in the wake of the Council of Trent (n. 13). That indeed happened. The emphasis placed on adult catechesis by the *General Catechetical Directory* (*GCD*), mandated by Vatican II, and the Order of Christian Initiation of Adults sharpened the focus of the catechetical ministry. The *GCD*, together with the Apostolic Exhortation *Catechesi Tradendae* of Pope John Paul II, have provided the most comprehensive statement on the nature and purpose, means and methods of catechesis in the annals of the Church. They make it clear that the Church's catechetical ministry, closely linked to its evangelical mission, is shared by all Christians.

The vision engendered by the council stirred new enthusiasm and activity. It opened new opportunities for the laity—women and men—who committed themselves full-time to the catechetical ministry. Graduate programs were introduced in universities and colleges. Adult religious education and catechist training programs flourished at the local level.

Publishing houses, large and small, brought their considerable resources and know-how into the field of religious education. These have produced a variety of catechetical materials distinguished by the richness of their doctrinal content and up-to-date pedagogical methods that have made the American Church the envy of the Catholic world. Regional congresses, diocesan conventions, and parish workshops provided continuing education for volunteer catechists, inspiring them to persevere in their work.

Vatican II did not mandate a catechism for the universal Church, but it did envision national and regional catcchisms. It was in this context that *A New Catechism* was commissioned by the hierarchy of the Netherlands—the notorious Dutch Catechism that appeared in 1966. It was followed by a German Catechism (1985), a Belgian Catechism (1987), and a French Catechism (1991), all sanctioned by the national hierarchies of those countries and approved by Rome. Despite the imbroglio that surrounded its publication, the trajectory from the Dutch Catechism to the *Catechism of the Catholic Church* is direct. All the national catechisms just cited, inspired by the council, are addressed to adults; they are intended as "reference texts" for church teachings; they bring the Gospel message into dialogue with the contemporary world; they emphasize the need for unity among Christians; and they are sensitive to ecumenical issues. All seek to present doctrine in ways that will foster maturity of faith and a deeper understanding of the Christian mysteries.

A Catechism for the Universal Church

The *Catechism of the Catholic Church*, as it has come to be, owes its origins to the proposal made by Cardinal Bernard Law at the Extraordinary Assembly of the Synod of Bishops in 1985. Cardinal Law observed that modern means of transportation and communication have made today's world a "global village." On the other hand, even though the world is growing smaller, there is little agreement on ideals and values. Pluralism is accepted as a virtue, diverse cultural expression is considered a right, and change is the only absolute. The social sciences have displaced philosophy as the arbiter of the true and the good. New nations have emerged and colonialism is a bad memory. Hierarchy is challenged along with patriarchy.

It is a mistake to attribute these developments to the Second Vatican Council. The Church, incarnate in the world, has not—cannot—escape the cultural, social, and intellectual forces that have divided the contemporary world. And to think that better education alone, even in the form of an updated catechism, will dispel the confusion is to repeat the mistake of the Enlightenment. Just as it is a political cop-out to indict schools for all the difficulties that beset society, it is irresponsible to censure religious education programs for everything that ails the Church, from the shortage of priests to the neglect of the sacrament of penance.

The Church, worldwide, is struggling to divest itself of its "Eurocentric" image. It pursues internal unity without insisting on the need for external uniformity. At every level, the faithful are seeking ways to reconcile the tension between the particular needs of the local church and their loyalty to the Church Catholic, represented by the bishop of Rome, to which are all committed. In acknowledging that a divided Church is a scandal, ecumenical efforts stress what Christians hold in common and search for ways to transcend age-old frictions. It is a sound Catholic principle that there is one faith, but many theologies and theological methods.

Vatican II and the *General Catechetical Directory* recognized cultural diversity as a legitimate expression of peoples. When John Paul endorsed the 1985 Synod's proposal for "a catechism or compendium of all Catholic doctrine," he already saw it as "a point of reference for the catechisms or compendiums that are prepared in the various regions." No one catechism can address the disparate needs of the First and Third Worlds, agricultural societies and industrialized nations, suburbia and inner cities, not to mention people of different age groups and educational backgrounds.

In the Apostolic Constitution *Fidei Depositum* that prefaces the *Catechism of the Catholic Church*, Pope John Paul II writes:

> This catechism is not intended to replace the local catechisms duly approved by the ecclesiastical authorities, the diocesan Bishops and the Episcopal Conferences, especially if they have been approved by the Apostolic See. It is meant to encourage and assist in the writing of new local catechisms, which take into account various situations and cultures, while carefully preserving the unity of faith and fidelity to Catholic doctrine. (No. 4)

Sharing the Light of Faith: National Catechetical Directory for Catholics of the United States (*NCD*), like the *General Catechetical Directory* before it, insisted on the point that while certain norms and criteria guide all sound catechesis, "it is neither possible nor desirable to establish a rigid order or to dictate a uniform method for the exposition of content" (*NCD*, 47; *GCD*, 46).

The Purpose of the Catechism

The chief purpose of the *Catechism of the Catholic Church* is to stress "the presentation of doctrine" and "to deepen and increase a mature understanding of faith, firmly taking root in personal life and evident in conduct." It recognizes that adaptation of the doctrinal presentation and catechetical methods "required by the differences of culture, age, spiritual life, and social and ecclesial conditions" are "indispensable," but it leaves this adaptation to local catechisms and "those who teach the faith" (nos. 23, 24).

In an address to the International Catechetical Council in 1992, Cardinal Ratzinger reaffirmed the importance of catechetical materials produced at the local level.[2] The *Catechism of the Catholic Church* does not lessen but enhances the relevance of national and diocesan catechisms. It is only in conjunction with other catechetical materials and local catechists' efforts that the *Catechism of the Catholic Church* can achieve its goals. Addressed to the universal Church, the catechism relies on the local churches to inculturate the faith. Cardinal Ratzinger also cited contributions to the final draft submitted from diverse parts of the world by countless individuals competent in the theological disciplines—moral theologians, exegetes, systematicians, pastoral theologians, liturgists, and catechists—as evidence that the authors were attentive to the global context of today's Church.

Thus, the *Catechism of the Catholic Church* has already mediated the kind of symbiosis between the universal Church and particular churches that strengthens unity. In the future, the Cardinal anticipates it will be a bond that reinforces communion of local churches among themselves and of pastors and the faithful within local churches.

For all its attributes, the *Catechism of the Catholic Church* has certain self-imposed limitations. It is attentive to the human condition in today's world and the kind of fundamental questions it raises for the Church. It does not, however, attempt to describe the varied types of anthropology that, in different meaning systems, characterize the modern world in diverse geographical spheres and in complex sociocultural contexts.

The new catechism should not be an excuse for overlooking catechesis aspects that call for adaptation and variations according to time, place, and sociocultural context. In Cardinal Ratzinger's framework, the catechism presents the "what," and leaves the who, with whom, for whom, where, when, and how to catechetical works produced at the local level. It is not because these other dimensions of catechesis are unimportant, or less important, but they can best be dealt with by people who are familiar with particular needs of the local church.

The American Contexts

The catechetical establishment in the United States prides itself on being informed about the American cultural context and particular needs of the Church in the areas in which we work. We are aware that our dominant culture has its roots in Europe but, also, that it has been shaped by the peculiarities of geography, immigration, economy, transportation, and communications of North America. We are aware that Native Americans, African Americans, Hispanic Americans, and, most recently, Asian Americans, retain their own cultures, more or less tainted by the dominant culture. We are aware that socioeconomic forces are also important in shaping the context in which we work, areas such as rural America and urban America, the latter being subdivided into suburbia and the inner city. Then there are regional differences—North and South, East, Midwest, and Far West—that fashion our attitudes toward government and religion, toward church and ecumenism.

These factors that challenge the catechetical ministry in the United States are well known to you, but there are also other forces integral to the context in which the *Catechism of the Catholic Church* will be received. There are many differences within the American Church regarding policies and priorities. The catechetical community will study the pages of the catechism to see the light that it will throw on a whole series of questions that affect programs and methods. By way of illustration, I cite a few examples.

I mention first the age of confirmation because it is an issue on which even bishops are at odds. It has a theological dimension that touches on the very nature and number of the sacraments. It is a pastoral issue that has ramifications for all of catechesis. Joining confirmation with baptism as we do in the Order of the Christian Initiation of Adults restores an ancient practice, but should it be normative always and everywhere? The age of confirmation makes a great difference to the structure of catechetical programs: confirmation joined to the baptism of infants, confirmation at the time one reaches the age of reason, confirmation as a requisite for First Communion, confirmation at adolescence—each creates its own dynamic.

The *Catechism of the Catholic Church* appears at a time when there is a move toward lectionary-based catechesis. Advocates of this propose it as an alternative to and an improvement upon the accepted catechetical curriculum that has, even in recent textbook series, been based on the "four pillars"—creed, sacraments, commandments, and prayer. Does the *CCC* offer a way to reconcile the two approaches?

The catechism's publication coincides with a review of the national directory, *Sharing the Light of Faith*. Should it be revised in light of the

Catechism of the Catholic Church? I raise the question because in a recent article, Cardinal José Sánchez, prefect of the Congregation for the Clergy, the curial agency charged with establishing guidelines to oversee the "mediation and inculturation" of the catechism by means of local catechisms, states that the Congregation "is not starting from scratch." Cardinal Sánchez explains that "the *Catechism of the Catholic Church* and its mediation must be placed in the context and wake of the *General Catechetical Directory* and *Catechesi Tradendae.*"[3] His remarks clearly imply that the new Catechism does not pre-empt the role of catechetical directories, but what is their function vis-à-vis the *Catechism of the Catholic Church?*

The catechism seems to leave questions of this kind—questions of special interest to the catechetical community in the United States—to the local church to resolve.

The Challenge of the *Catechism*

In concluding, I mention two other issues—less obvious and more intangible—that are part of the cultural context that will have an impact on the way that the *Catechism of the Catholic Church* will be received in the United States. Whether we like to admit it or not, Americans have a tendency toward fundamentalism. We read texts, not contexts. We do not have a sense of history, and we sometimes forget that our Church spans centuries as well as continents. Issues that are of importance in this country seem less important to other peoples and vice versa. In places, the catechism helps us to sort out the more important from the less important by the use of large and small type, but we should still recognize that the teachings in the catechism are part of a living tradition that must be interpreted accordingly.

Another peculiar trait of American culture is the enthusiasm with which we greet the new. At times it seems like sheer faddism that causes us to latch onto the latest book, buzzword, or technique as if it were a panacea, only to discard it when something newer comes along. There is a danger that even the *Catechism of the Catholic Church*, which was a best-seller at Christmas, will be collecting dust on the shelves by Easter. And our task is made even more difficult by the delay in making the catechism available in English. With the publication of the French text last year, enthusiasm for the catechism began to build in eager anticipation. But as the publication date of the English translation is pushed further and further back, the excitement wanes and interest begins to wilt.

In these remarks, I have described the context in which the catechism was conceived and sketched in broad strokes some of the factors that impact on its reception in the United States. Whether or not the *Catechism of the Catholic Church* has a long shelf life and achieves its intended purpose depends on how it is welcomed. My guess is that the catechetical community in the United States is ready to accept it with an open mind. We recognize that the catechism witnesses to the saving truth of the Gospel as it affects our lives and the lives of men and women in our time. It is not a syllabus of errors, but a positive presentation of Catholic doctrine that draws, as Pope John Paul II directed, from biblical and liturgical sources. It states the "what," and leaves it to us at the local level—beginning with the bishops who are the "chief catechists"—to explore the how, the when, and the means whereby its contents will be disseminated. The *Catechism of the Catholic Church* renews the challenge that we face in presenting the Gospel message in a way that speaks to the contemporary world.

NOTES

1. See Mary Charles Bryce, *Pride of Place: The Role of the Bishops in the Development of Catechesis in the United States* (Washington, DC: The Catholic University of America Press, 1984), 34–36, 50–54, and passim.

2. See Cardinal Joseph Ratzinger, "Catechismo e inculturazione," *Il regno-documenti* 19 (1992): 585–589.

3. *L'Osservatore Romano*, Weekly Edition, 14 April 1993.

PART F
Church (Catholic) Schools

Introduction

MICHAEL WARREN

Leslie Francis, an Anglican priest, is a professor of pastoral theology at both Saint David's University College and Trinity College in Wales. Over a twenty-year period, in various English-speaking countries, he has done extensive sociological study of the attitudes both of children attending church schools and those of their parents. His studies use sophisticated statistical methods to get at the various kinds of expectations attached to the specifically religious aspects of church schools. In differing ways, the studies are all significant.

Here he collaborates with Josephine Egan to study Catholic secondary schools in the United States, especially through the lens of the "faith community" ethos proposed by the United States bishops in their 1973 pastoral on Catholic education, *To Teach as Jesus Did.* Francis and Egan note the presence of three groups of students in most Catholic schools: those from practicing Catholic families; those from nonpracticing families; and those who are not Catholic.

Readers will want to note how the authors relate the United States study to studies of Catholic school students in other countries and the caveats those latter studies raise about the claims made for the religious influence of Catholic schools in the United States. Francis and Egan find the results of their United States study very similar to those done in England and Wales: that as an influence the Catholic high school does not function in isolation from the attitudes of parents or from the actual religious practice of the young people themselves. Where students voluntarily attend Mass, they tend to have positive attitudes toward both the school and their religious instruction. However, parental Mass attendance remains the most significant factor affecting the worship practice of young people.

That Francis and Egan's results support long-standing catechetical theory will be evident to most readers of this *Sourcebook* volume. Catechesis involves rhythms and contexts different from those of religious instruction. Their study does not fault the Catholic school, though it does find that identifying the school as a faith community may not be appropriate to what is actually done by the school. If the school took the faith community model as normative, it would have to adopt a different, more selective, and restrictive set of operating policies. Many would find these adjusted policies undesirable, because they would seek to make the school the church instead of a sign of the church.

Further Reading

Francis, Leslie J. "Roman Catholic Schools and Pupil Attitudes in England." *Lumen Vitae* 39 (1984): 99–108.
———. "Roman Catholic Secondary Schools: Falling Rolls and Pupil Attitudes." *Educational Studies* 12 (1986): 119–127.
———. "Drift from the Churches: Secondary School Pupils' Attitudes Toward Christianity." *British Journal of Religious Education* 11:2 (1989): 76–86.
Francis, Leslie J., and Josephine Egan. "School Ethos in Wales." *Lumen Vitae* 41 (1986): 159–173.
———. "Catholic Schools and the Communication of Faith: An Empirical Inquiry." *Catholic School Studies* (Australia) 60, no. 2 (1987): 27–34.
———. "The Catholic School as Faith Community: An Empirical Inquiry." *Religious Education* 85, no. 4 (fall 1990): 588–603.
Francis, Leslie J., Harry M. Gibson, and Peter Full James. "Attitudes Toward Christianity, Creationism, Scientism, and Interest in Science Among 11–15 Year Olds." *British Journal of Religious Education* 13:1 (1990): 4–17.
Francis, Leslie J., and John E. Greer. "Catholic Schools and Adolescent Religiosity in Northern Ireland: Shaping Moral Values." *Irish Journal of Education* 24, no. 2 (1990): 40–47.
Rhymer, Joseph, and Leslie J. Francis. "Roman Catholic Secondary Schools in Scotland and Pupil Attitudes toward Religion." *Lumen Vitae* 40 (1985): 102–110.

See also the series of three readers on Christian education edited by Dr. Francis and Dr. Jeff Astley: vol. 1: *Critical Perspectives on Christian Education* (United Kingdom: Fowler Wright Books, 1994); vol. 2: *Theological Perspectives on Christian Education;* and vol. 3: *Psychological Perspectives on Christian Education.* The last two volumes are yet to be published.

In the second essay, Herman Lombaerts gives another example of the context analysis he used in part C, reading 9, "Catechetics and the Formation of Catechists." His method deserves study. Using his research in the literature of several different languages, he examines the place of religion in schools in the context of multifaceted social and cultural shifts that also affect religious institutions. Readers should give special attention to sections where Lombaerts is clearly dealing with religion in denominational schools controlled by a church with an evangelizing agenda or dealing with state schools where religion is taught as a subject without catechetical intent. In Europe it is common for religion to be part of the curriculum in state schools. In most of his essay, Lombaerts is dealing with the second kind of school, but he often applies his critique to the way church officials think of the study of religion, thereby connecting the two situations. In either context of study, young people have been shaped by the same influences.

Lombaerts's framework for context analysis here is not the situation of any one country but that of Europe as a whole. Even then, he refers often to shifts that are not European but global. Perhaps readers could think of this writer as a catechist who has absorbed the kind of formation he described in his essay in part C and now applies these skills to a very challenging topic. He begins with an analysis of the place of religion in European society, and examines its social status, unhelpful forms of religious socialization, and the relationship between religion in society and in the churches. The underlying message is that religion's place is undergoing momentous change that affects the way it is dealt with both within the churches and outside them.

The next main section deals with the teaching of religion in schools. In several places Lombaerts's position complements the research done by Francis and Egan. Lombaerts is always implicitly asking: What influences are shaping the spirit of the young before they ever gather in a classroom to consider the matter of religion? He also studies shifts in the way schooling itself is being done. Much of what he says about the situation in Europe is true of schooling in North America, and needs to be pondered.

In his third section, "Perspectives for the Future," Lombaerts offers tentative proposals about how society and the churches might proceed in helping young people reconsider the place of religion in life and embrace interreligious appreciation and tolerance. Not seeking to offer a blueprint for action, Lombaerts instead opens up avenues for further reflection. Those needing blueprints will be disappointed; those prizing insightful analysis that opens the way to insightful action will want to study this section carefully.

The Catholic School as "Faith Community"— An Empirical Inquiry

LESLIE J. FRANCIS AND JOSEPHINE EGAN

Introduction

Our earlier studies have examined the relationship between Catholic secondary schools and pupil attitudes in England,[1] Scotland,[2] Wales,[3] and Australia.[4] Because these studies have deliberately adopted a common methodology and focus, it has been possible to compare and integrate their findings. When the same pattern of relationships begins to emerge between Catholic schools and pupil attitudes in more than one country, there is greater reason to take seriously the practical implications of the empirical findings. A significant conclusion that has developed through the English, Welsh, and Australian studies concerns the disparity between the theoretical view of the Catholic school as a faith community and the empirical reality in terms of the pupils' backgrounds, expectations, and attitudes. The aim of the present study is to extend this research perspective to the United States. First, a review is made of the weight given by American Catholic educationalists to the theory of the Catholic school as a faith community. Then this theory is tested against the perceptions of 1,204 16-year-old students.

Quantitatively Catholic schools in the United States reached their all-time high in 1965–1966 when they provided places for 5.6 million elementary and secondary pupils, constituting 87 percent of nonpublic school enrollment. By this time, however, the Catholic school system was coming under a number of pressures from within the church itself,[5] while the research reports by Greeley and Rossi[6] and Neuwein[7] seemed to suggest that Catholic schools were not central to the church's survival.

Reprinted from *Religious Education* 85, no. 4 (fall 1990): 588–603. Copyright © 1990 by University of Judaism, Los Angeles, CA. Used with permission.

Dr. Leslie J. Francis is an Anglican priest concerned with church-related research in the social sciences. Dr. Josephine Egan is a member of the Community of the Daughters of the Holy Spirit.

By 1981–1982 the Catholic school population had declined to 3.1 million, accounting for 64 percent of nonpublic school enrollment.[8]

Alongside this period of quantitative decline, there developed a process of qualitative reassessment. The bishops' pronouncement in 1967, entitled "Catholic Schools Are Indispensable," led to the restatement of the role of Catholic schools during 1972 in the pastoral letter *To Teach as Jesus Did*.[9] The bishops argued that only in the "unique setting" of a Catholic school could children and young people "experience learning and living fully integrated in the life of faith." This report set in motion a new quest after the distinctiveness of Catholic schools. At the same time, Greeley's more recent research had concluded that "far from declining in effectiveness in the past decade, Catholic schools seem to have increased their impact. . . . In terms of the future of the organization, Catholic schools seem more important for a church in time of traumatic transition than for one in a time of peaceful stability."[10]

O'Neill[11] argues that recent emphasis on Catholic schools becoming "more of an alternative, more unique" was being accomplished by a strong emphasis on the schools developing as a "faith community" of students, teachers, and parents. According to O'Neill,[12] a faith community is characterized by a common intentionality:

> when people in a school share a certain intentionality, a certain pattern or complex of values, understandings, sentiments, hopes, and dreams that deeply condition everything else that goes on, including the maths class, the athletic activities . . . everything.

A number of other recent documents on the development of the Catholic school system in the United States through the 1980s and into the 1990s also talk in terms of developing aspects of the distinctive faith community. For example, Sullivan[13] argues that Catholic schools offer parents an atmosphere in which "home and school share a common and explicitly religious understanding of the meaning of life"; McBride[14] identifies the "most basic" challenge facing Catholic schools in the 1980s as keeping "Catholic schools Catholic, institutionally, morally and spiritually"; the *National Catechetical Directory*, issued by the National Conference of Catholic Bishops,[15] speaks in terms of the acceptance and living "of the Christian message" and the striving "to instill a Christian spirit" in the students.

The faith community view of the Catholic school, especially in the strong form expressed above by Sullivan,[16] seems to imply support for a very separatist notion of the Catholic school providing an alternative educational environment primarily for the practicing Catholic children of practicing Catholic parents. In practice, however, there are usually three different groups of pupils attending Catholic schools: Catholic pupils from practicing backgrounds, Catholic pupils from nonpracticing backgrounds, and non-Catholic pupils. According to O'Neill,[17] the Catholic school as faith community is not impaired by students who do not share the same beliefs; rather he believes that their presence "in many cases" will stimulate the other persons in the school to deepen and broaden their own perspective. This view has helped Catholic schools to respond to issues of racial integration through the admission of minority students who are not themselves Catholic.[18] However, there remains a significant lack of empirical information about the impact of non-Catholic pupils and, indeed, nonpracticing Catholic pupils on the character of American Catholic schools as faith communities.

In a study from 1986 conducted in England, Francis[19] demonstrates that non-Catholic pupils attending Catholic schools record a less sympathetic attitude toward Christianity than Catholic pupils. About 17 percent of the pupils admitted to these schools were not baptized Catholics. He concludes that if one of the aims of the Catholic church in maintaining Catholic schools in England is to provide a faith community in which Catholic pupils are supported by positive attitudes toward Christianity among their peers, these findings place a caveat against the policy of recruiting a significant proportion of non-Catholic pupils, even from churchgoing backgrounds. He suggests that the lower attitudes toward Christianity among the churchgoing non-Catholic pupils might well be a function of the incompatibility between their own religious background and the doctrinal, liturgical, and cathechetical assumptions of the school.

In a recent study in Wales, Egan and Francis[20] demonstrate that the most serious disaffection with the Catholic school is attributable not so much to the non-Catholic pupils as to the nonpracticing Catholic pupils. This is a much larger problem for the Catholic church in Wales. While less than 9 percent of the Welsh sample was non-Catholic, less than half of the girls and only slightly more than two-fifths of the boys were weekly mass attenders, while only two-fifths of both sexes were supported by weekly mass-attending mothers and only one-quarter by weekly mass-attending fathers. They suggest that if Catholic schools are to exercise an effective ministry among Catholic pupils from nonpracticing backgrounds, these schools need to consciously abandon the assumption that all pupils can be treated as if they are part of the faith community characterized by practicing Catholics.

The present study sets out to examine the religious background and practice of pupils attending some Catholic schools in the United States, to explore the relationship between religious background and practice and the pupils' attitude toward Catholic schools, and to assess the implications of the findings for an understanding of the Catholic school as a faith community.

Method

Four Catholic schools from New Jersey, Connecticut, and New York participated in the study by administering a questionnaire to all their 16-year-old pupils. The questionnaire included three main indices. First, frequency of pupils' mass attendance, fathers' mass attendance, and mothers' mass attendance was recorded on a four-point scale: every week; once or twice a month; a few times a year; never. Second, an indication of pupils' religion, mothers' religion, and fathers' religion was recorded on a two-point scale: Catholic and non-Catholic. Third, a detailed 66-item Likert-type[21] attitude inventory,[22] containing items concerned with the pupils' views of the purpose and practice of Catholic schools, was responded to on a five-point scale: agree strongly; agree; not certain; disagree; disagree strongly.

All the questionnaires were administered by teachers within the schools, following a standardized procedure. Completed questionnaires were returned from 535 boys and 669 girls. The data were analyzed by means of linear multiple regression and path analysis, with listwise deletion of missing cases, using the SPSS package.[23]

Results

The replies to the questionnaire indicate that 13 percent of the boys and 13 percent of the girls attending the Catholic schools in the sample were not themselves baptized Catholics. This compares with 7 percent of the same age group in the English study and 9 percent in the Welsh study. Over three-quarters of the pupils in the present sample have been recruited from homes in which both parents are Catholic. As far as the boys were concerned, 86 percent reported that their mothers were baptized Catholics, 81 percent that their fathers were baptized Catholics, and 77 percent that both their parents were baptized Catholics. As far as the girls were concerned, 83 percent reported that their mothers were baptized Catholics, 80 percent that their fathers were baptized Catholics, and 76 percent that both their parents were baptized Catholics. Both the English and Welsh studies show much greater evidence of pupils coming from religiously mixed homes.[24] In the English study, 62 percent and, in the Welsh study, 43 percent of the pupils report that both their parents are baptized Catholics.

While the majority of the pupils (87 percent) attending Catholic schools in the present sample are baptized Catholics, just half of the girls (50 percent) and considerably less than half the boys (43 percent) claim to be fully practicing Catholics in the sense of attending mass most weeks. As is consistent with much previous research, the girls demonstrate more religious practice than the boys.[25]

Totally consistent with the Welsh and English data is the fact that both the boys and the girls receive more religious support, in terms of mass attendance, from their mothers than from their fathers. Half the mothers (51 percent) and two-fifths of the fathers (40 percent) are weekly mass attenders. The comparison with the English data deserves closer scrutiny. While in England more pupils are likely to come from religiously divided homes, those parents who are baptized Catholics are more likely to be mass attenders. In other words, while the American pupils are more likely to come from homes in which both parents are baptized Catholics, it is also more likely that the faith is not being practiced in these homes.

Two key subscales of the 66-item Likert attitude inventory used in this study are particularly appropriate to testing the pupils' own attitudes toward the Catholic school as a faith community and to exploring the differences in the perceptions of pupils from practicing Catholic, nonpracticing Catholic, and non-Catholic backgrounds. These two scales can be described as measuring attitude toward attending the Catholic school and attitude toward religious education in the Catholic school. The items composing these scales, together with their statistical properties, are presented in appendix 1.

The scale of attitude toward attending the Catholic school demonstrates that the pupils who are happiest in Catholic schools believe that their parents made the correct decision by sending them to a Catholic school. Given the choice all over again, they would still opt to attend a Catholic school. They believe that there is a friendly relationship between the Catholic teachers and pupils in their school, and they attribute this friendly and happy atmosphere to a shared community of faith in which "teachers and pupils work together to live the Christian way of life." They claim that attendance at Catholic schools has helped them to understand the real meaning of life. The six items of this scale produce an alpha coefficient of .81707.[26] Since individual scores can range between 6 and 30 on a six-item Likert scale, the fact that the overall sample produces a mean of 22.22 (SD=4.58) indicates that the majority of the students lean toward the positive end of this attitudinal continuum.

The scale of attitude toward religious education in the Catholic school demonstrates that pupils who are most supportive of religious education in their schools claim that religious education lessons have helped them both to know Christ more deeply and to deal with the important problems of life. This is the kind of integration of faith and life envisaged within the faith community. The four items of this scale produce an alpha coefficient of .72868. Since individual scores can range between 4 and 20 on a four-item Likert scale, the fact that the overall sample produces a mean of 12.04 (SD=3.07) indicates that the majority of the students tend to hold a position toward the middle of this attitudinal continuum.

The path diagram[27] in Figure 1 sets out to explore the extent to which the variation in the pupils' attitudes toward attending the Catholic school and toward religious education in the Catholic school can be accounted for in terms of their sex, their personal baptismal status, their parents' baptismal status, their personal mass attendance, and their parents' mass attendance. The correlation matrix from which this path model is developed and the accompanying multiple regression significance tests are presented in appendix 2. Four main conclusions emerge from this path model.

First, it is the pupils' personal contact with the church, expressed in terms of mass attendance, which is the key predictor of the pupils' attitude toward attending the Catholic school and toward religious education in the Catholic school. Pupils who attend mass more regularly also tend to feel more positively about attending the Catholic school and

Figure 1: Path Diagram

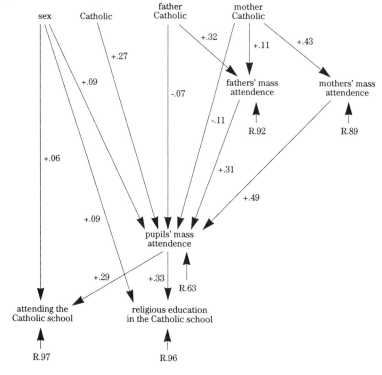

about the kind of religious education they receive in school. According to the beta weights, after the pupils' personal mass attendance has been taken into account, information about their personal baptismal status, their parents' baptismal status, and their parents' mass attendance contributes no additional predictive power to explaining variance in attitude scores.

Second, given the centrality of the pupils' personal pattern of mass attendance in predicting their attitudes, it is important next to examine the factors that help to predict the pupils' pattern of mass attendance. Here parental example and practice hold the key. If their parents attend mass regularly, the pupils are also much more likely to attend mass regularly. The path model also attributes greater significance to maternal influence than to paternal influence. This is consistent with Michael Hornsby-Smith's findings.[28] What is extremely interesting at this point in the model is the direction of the influence from parental baptismal status. According to the correlation matrix, both fathers' and mothers' baptismal status is positively related to the pupils' mass attendance. According to the beta weights, when parental mass attendance has also been entered into the equation, both fathers' and mothers' baptismal status produces a negative relationship with the pupils' mass attendance. This means, for example, that the pupils from a Catholic home where one or both parents have ceased to attend mass are less likely to attend mass themselves than the pupils from a religiously mixed home where one parent is a mass-attending Catholic and the other parent is not a Catholic. In other words, parental disaffection has a stronger negative influence on the pupils than a partially non-Catholic background. This is consistent with Egan and Francis's findings in Wales.[29]

Third, given the centrality of parental mass attendance in predicting the pupils' pattern of mass attendance, it is important next to examine the factors that help to predict parental mass attendance. Here parental baptismal status holds the key. This, of course, is not surprising, since it is presumably the Catholic parents who go to mass. The path model does, however, enable us to go one step beyond this simple conclusion. Fathers' mass attendance is related not only to fathers' baptismal status but also to mothers'. This means that Catholic fathers tend to be more regular mass attenders when they are married to a Catholic wife. Mothers' mass attendance is not, however, related to the baptismal status of their husband. Catholic mothers are just as likely to be regular mass attenders whether or not their husbands are also Catholics.

Fourth, the pupils' sex is a significant predictor of their attitude toward attending the Catholic school and toward religious education in the Catholic school. This influence works in two ways: indirectly through the frequency of mass attendance and directly in addition to the influence mediated through mass attendance. This means, for example, that girls are more likely to attend mass regularly than boys and that regular mass-attending girls tend to hold more favorable attitudes toward attending the Catholic school and toward religious education in the Catholic school than regular mass-attending boys. This is consistent with a range of research that reports higher levels of religiosity[30] and more favorable attitudes[31] toward religion among girls and women than among boys and men.

This path model would lead to the predictions that the pupils with the most positive attitudes toward attending the Catholic school and toward religious education in the Catholic school are the practicing Catholics from homes where both parents are practicing Catholics, and that the pupils with the least positive attitudes are the nonpracticing Catholics from homes where both parents are nonpracticing Catholics, while non-Catholic pupils from non-Catholic homes occupy a midway position between these two extreme groups. Table 1 compares the responses of these three groups to the individual items of the attitude scales, confirming the predictions made from the path model and providing further detail about the variation in attitudes between the three groups. For example, just 62 percent of the nonpracticing Catholics from nonpracticing Catholic homes agree that their parents made the correct decision by sending them to a Catholic school, compared with 75 percent of the non-Catholic pupils from non-Catholic homes and 88 percent of the practicing Catholic pupils from practicing Catholic homes.

Conclusion

The above data analysis has set out to explore the sense in which Catholic schools in the United States can be regarded as a faith community. Three key conclusions emerge from this analysis.

First, an examination of the baptismal status of the pupils attending these schools, together with the baptismal status of their parents, demonstrates that only 13 percent of the pupils are not themselves baptized Catholics, while 77 percent of the pupils come from homes where both parents are baptized Catholics. In the sense, therefore, of shared baptismal status and shared religious background, Catholic schools in the United States show much evidence of potential for being a community of faith.

Second, an examination of the pattern of mass attendance of these pupils, together with the mass attendance of their parents, demonstrates that only half the girls and considerably less than half the boys are weekly mass attenders. At the same time, only half their mothers and two-

Table 1: Comparison between practicing Catholic, nonpracticing Catholic, non-Catholic pupils

	Practicing Catholic %	Nonpracticing Catholic %	Non-Catholic %
Attitude toward attending the Catholic school:			
My parents made the correct decision by sending me to a Catholic school.	88	62	75
There is a friendly relationship between the Catholic teachers and pupils in my school.	77	52	71
There is a happy atmosphere in my school because teachers and pupils work together to live the Christian way of life.	62	48	51
Attendance at Catholic school has helped me to understand the real meaning of life.	53	16	44
If I had the choice all over again, I should still wish to attend a Catholic school.	77	56	58
I am happy to be a pupil in my school.	81	60	74
Attitude toward religious education in the Catholic school:			
Religious education is more important to me than any other subject I study in my school.	10	0	12
Religious education lessons have helped me to know Christ more deeply.	69	40	64
Religious education lessons provide me with the principles with which to deal with the important problems of life.	65	44	60
If attendance at religious education lessons were voluntary, I would still want to attend them.	46	20	41

Note: "Practicing Catholics" means weekly mass-attending pupils from homes where both parents are weekly mass attenders.

"Nonpracticing Catholics" means baptized Catholic non-mass-attending pupils from homes where both parents are baptized Catholics but non-mass attenders.

"Non-Catholics" means pupils who are not baptized Catholics from homes where neither parent is baptized Catholic.

fifths of their fathers are weekly mass attenders. In the sense, therefore, of T. F. Sullivan's[32] notion of home and school sharing "a common and explicitly religious understanding of the meaning of life," there is considerably less evidence of Catholic schools being able to realize the potential for being a community of faith.

Third, an examination of the pupils' attitudes toward attending a Catholic school and toward religious education in a Catholic school demonstrates that a positive attitude among pupils toward the Catholic school as a faith community is clearly related to their own pattern of mass attendance. At the same time, the pupils' pattern of mass attendance is closely related to their parents' mass attendance. In short, Catholic pupils from nonpracticing homes are less likely to be regular mass attenders, while pupils who are not regular mass attenders are less likely to feel positively about either attending a Catholic school or the religious education they receive in the Catholic school. Similarly, non-Catholic pupils are also less likely to feel positively about the Catholic school than practicing Catholic pupils. In the sense, therefore, of M. O'Neill's[33] notion of a common intentionality "when people in a school share . . . a certain pattern or complex of values, understandings, sentiments, hopes and dreams," the evidence seems to suggest that by catering to pupils with three different backgrounds—practicing Catholic, nonpracticing Catholic, and non-Catholic—the Catholic school vitiates the claim to be a faith community. As currently expressed, Catholic schools are most appreciated by practicing Catholic pupils. The presence of non-Catholic and nonpracticing Catholic pupils in these schools increases the pool of those who are not supportive of the common intentionality of the school, who are not positively disposed toward attending a Catholic school, and who do not value the religious education provided within the school as an integrative factor.

While the student body embraces some pupils who are hostile toward the Catholic school system itself alongside many who are supportive of the system, it is difficult to maintain that these schools represent a true community of faith. Given the hard reality of adolescent attitudes toward religion and the church,[34] together with the many positive contributions the Catholic school system is able to make to the education of non-Catholic pupils,[35] it is considerably more realistic to modify the theory underpinning the Catholic school system to take into account the presence of non-Catholic pupils, pupils from nonpracticing Catholic backgrounds, and nonpracticing Catholic pupils, than to attempt to redefine enrollment policies to ensure that Catholic schools more truly represent a community of faith.

Appendix 1:

Scale of attitude toward attending the Catholic school

	corrected item-total correlation
My parents made the correct decision by sending me to a Catholic school.	.62180
There is a friendly relationship between the Catholic teachers and pupils in my school.	.45428
There is a happy atmosphere in my school because teachers and pupils work together to live the Christian way of life.	.53536
Attendance at Catholic school has helped me to understand the real meaning of life.	.52333
If I had the choice all over again, I should still wish to attend a Catholic school.	.64986
I am happy to be a pupil in my school.	.70612

Note: alpha = .81707

Scale of attitude toward religious education in the Catholic school

	corrected item-total correlation
Religious education is more important to me than any other subject I study in my school.	.44470
Religious education lessons have helped me to know Christ more deeply.	.56229
Religious education lessons provide me with the principles with which to deal with the important problems of life.	.47529
If attendance at religious education lessons were voluntary, I would still want to attend them.	.59941

Note: alpha = .72868

Appendix 2: Correlation matrix

	attending Catholic school	religious education	fathers' mass attendance	mothers' mass attendance	pupils' mass attendance	father Catholic	mother Catholic	pupil Catholic
sex	+.0857 .001	+.0857 .001	-.0438 NS	-.0125 NS	+.0730 .01	-.0113 NS	-.0386 NS	-.0010 NS
pupil Catholic	+.0821 .01	+.0756 .01	+.3127 .001	+.3834 .001	+.4209 +.001	+.6779 +.001	+.7696 +.001	
mother Catholic	+.0331 NS	+.0138 NS	+.2932 .001	+.4443 .001	+.3650 .001	+.5963 .000		
father Catholic	+.0229 NS	+.0134 NS	+.3861 .001	+.2982 .001	+.3124 .001			
pupils' mass attendance	+.2287 .001	+.2450 .001	+.6354 .001	+.7158 .001				
mothers' mass attendance	+.1160 .001	+.1137 .001	+.6091 .001					
fathers' mass attendance	+.1134 .001	+.1057 .001						
religious education in the Catholic school	+.5446 .001							

Appendix 2: Multiple regression significance tests

Criterion variables	Predictor variables	R²	Increase in R²	B	Beta	St error B	F ratio	d.f.	P<
fathers' mass attendance	father Catholic	.14707	.14707	+1.06012	+.32116	0.11039	92.22	1,1165	.001
	mother Catholic	.15426	.00719	+0.38298	+.10522	0.12173	9.90	1,1165	.01
mothers' mass attendance	mother Catholic	.20554	.20554	+1.41653	+.42726	0.10738	174.03	1,1165	.001
	father Catholic	.20680	.00126	+0.13251	+.04407	0.09738	1.85	1,1165	NS
pupils' mass attendance	sex	.00624	.00624	+0.19309	+.08859	0.04023	23.03	1,1161	.001
	pupil Catholic	.18900	.18275	+0.89137	+.27212	0.10379	73.76	1,1161	.001
	mother Catholic	.19340	.00440	-0.34347	-.11262	0.09278	13.70	1,1161	.001
	father Catholic	.19406	.00066	-0.18643	-.06740	0.07227	6.66	1,1161	.01
	mothers' mass attendance	.55128	.35722	+0.45228	+.49166	0.02302	385.86	1,1161	.001
	fathers' mass attendance	.60692	.05563	+0.26023	+.31057	0.02030	164.32	1,1161	.001
pupils' attitude toward attending the Catholic school	sex	.00809	.00809	+0.59009	+.06408	0.26481	4.97	1,1160	.05
	pupil Catholic	.01501	.00692	+1.03191	+.07455	0.69763	2.19	1,1160	NS
	father Catholic	.01744	.00243	-0.78221	-.06693	0.47237	2.74	1,1160	NS
	mother Catholic	.01850	.00106	-0.65401	-.05075	0.60828	1.16	1,1160	NS
	fathers' mass attendance	.03083	.01244	-0.01243	-.00351	0.14137	0.01	1,1160	NS
	mothers' mass attendance	.03329	.00236	-0.29053	-.07474	0.17322	2.81	1,1160	NS
	pupils' mass attendance	.06553	.03244	+1.21013	+.28639	0.19129	40.02	1,1160	.001
pupils' attitude toward religious education in the Catholic school	sex	.01362	.01362	+0.52886	+.08579	0.17582	9.05	1,1160	.01
	pupil Catholic	.01862	.00500	+0.64632	+.06975	0.46320	1.95	1,1160	NS
	mother Catholic	.02173	.00311	-0.65115	-.07548	0.40387	2.60	1,1160	NS
	father Catholic	.02366	.00193	-0.48230	-.06164	0.31363	2.37	1,1160	NS
	mothers' mass attendance	.03583	.01217	-0.20568	-.07904	0.11501	3.20	1,1160	NS
	fathers' mass attendance	.03894	.00311	-0.06625	-.02795	0.09386	0.50	1,1160	NS
	pupils' mass attendance	.08080	.04186	+0.92312	+.32634	0.12701	52.83	1,1160	.001
constants	attending the Catholic school			19.28432					
	religious education in the Catholic school			10.09518					

NOTES

1. L. J. Francis, "Are Catholic Schools Good for Non-Catholics?" *The Tablet* 240 (1986): 170–172; L. J. Francis, "Roman Catholic Secondary Schools: Falling Rolls and Pupil Attitudes," *Educational Studies* 12 (1986): 119–127.

2. J. Rhymer and L. J. Francis, "Roman Catholic Secondary Schools in Scotland and Pupil Attitude Toward Religion," *Lumen Vitae* 40 (1985): 103–110.

3. J. Egan and L. J. Francis, "School Ethos in Wales: The Impact of Non-practicing Catholic and Non-Catholic Pupils on Catholic Secondary Schools," *Lumen Vitae* 41 (1986): 159–173.

4. L. J. Francis and J. Egan, "Catholic Schools and the Communication of Faith—An Empirical Inquiry," *Catholic School Studies* 60, no. 2 (1987): 27–34.

5. M. P. Ryan, *Are Parochial Schools the Answer?* (New York: Guild Press, 1964); J. L. Reedy and J. F. Andrews, *The Perplexed Catholic* (Notre Dame, IN: Ave Maria Press, 1966).

6. A. M. Greeley and P. H. Rossi, *The Education of Catholic Americans* (Chicago: Aldine Publishing Company, 1966).

7. R. A. Neuwien, ed., *Catholic Schools in Action* (Notre Dame, IN: University of Notre Dame Press, 1966).

8. T. C. Hunt and N. M. Kunkel, "Catholic Schools: The Nation's Largest Alternative School System," in J. C. Carper and T. C. Hunt, eds., *Religious Schooling in America* (Birmingham, AL: Religious Education Press, 1984).

9. National Conference of Catholic Bishops, *To Teach as Jesus Did* (Washington, DC: United States Catholic Conference, 1973).

10. A. M. Greeley, W. C. McCready, and K. McCourt, *Catholic Schools in a Declining Church* (Kansas City, MO: Sheed and Ward, 1976).

11. M. O'Neill, "Catholic Education: The Largest Alternative System," *Thrust* 7 (May 1978): 25–26.

12. M. O'Neill, "Toward a Modern Concept of Permeation," *Momentum* 10 (May 1979): 48–49.

13. T. F. Sullivan, "Catholic Schools in a Changing Church," in T. C. Hunt and M. M. Maxson, eds., *Religion and Morality in American Schooling* (Washington, DC: University Press of America, 1981).

14. A. McBride, "Major Challenges Facing Catholic Education in the 1980s," *Momentum* 13 (December 1982): 10–11.

15. National Conference of Catholic Bishops, *Sharing the Light of Faith: National Catechetical Directory for Catholics in the United States* (Washington, DC: United States Catholic Conference, 1979).

16. See note 13 above.

17. See note 12 above.

18. A. M. Greeley, *Catholic High Schools and Minority Students* (New Brunswick, NJ: Transaction Books, 1982).

19. See note 1 above.

20. See note 3 above.

21. R. A. Likert, "A Technique for Measurement of Attitudes," *Archives of Psychology* 140 (1932).

22. J. Egan, "An Evaluation of the Implementation of the Principles of Catholic Education in the Catholic Comprehensive Schools in Wales" (PhD diss., University of Wales, Cardiff, 1985).

23. SPSS Inc., *SPSSX User's Guide*, 2d ed. (New York: McGraw-Hill, 1986).

24. These differences in pupil background between the English, Welsh, and USA studies are reported here to help the reader compare the path models constructed on the basis of the different studies, not to imply that inferences about national differences can be drawn from the present sample of schools.

25. See, for example, J. J. Boyle and L. J. Francis, "The Influence of Differing Church Aided School Systems on Pupil Attitude Toward Religion," *Research in Education* 35 (1986): 7–12.

26. L. J. Cronbach, "Coefficient-Alpha and the Internal Structure of Tests, *Psychometrika* 16 (1951): 297–334.

27. See K. I. Macdonald, "Path Analysis," in Colm A. O'Muircheartaigh and Clive Payne, eds., *The Analysis of Survey Data*, vol. 2, chap. 3 (New York: John Wiley and Sons, 1977).

28. M. P. Hornsby-Smith, *Catholic Education: The Unobtrusive Partner* (London: Sheed and Ward, 1978).

29. See note 3 above.

30. M. Argyle and B. Beit-Hallahmi, *The Social Psychology of Religion* (London: Routledge and Kegan Paul, 1975).

31. L. J. Francis, "The Child's Attitude Toward Religion and Religious Education: A Review of Research," *Educational Research* 21 (1979): 103–108.

32. See note 13 above.

33. See note 12 above.

34. L. J. Francis, *Teenagers and the Church* (London: Collins Liturgical Publications, 1984).

35. See note 18 above.

Religion, Society, and the Teaching of Religion in Schools

HERMAN LOMBAERTS, FSC
Translated by Michael Warren

Europe finds itself at a historical crossroads. The year 1992—a symbolic date—indicates a new stage in the history of the continent. Europe sees the chance of regaining its control and valuing its historical resources at the service of a greater political and economic autonomy. In 1992, Europe has also departed from the disastrous consequences of the two world wars. Reasons to celebrate, although modestly. For, given its history, the passage from "the Europe of the whole world to modern nationalisms,"[1] to the United States of Europe, is not without ambiguity. The dismantling of the Eastern Communist bloc, after more than forty years of dictatorship, arouses certainly the hope to integrate the different cultures. But this ideal is challenged by the several transformations to be gone through in order to honor a very ancient myth of oneness. The recent political events illustrate also that the change in relationship, on the one hand, between the capitalistic and the Communist worlds affects the relationships between the Northern and Southern Hemispheres, and on the other hand, between the Western world of Christian origin and the Arab world closer to Islam.

Having been the reference point for the whole world for centuries, the old Christian continent finds itself today in a historical phase where the certainties of the past encounter once again the challenges of the present times. But, about what kind of certainties are we speaking?[2] Where will this new Europe find its inspiration to orchestrate the qualitative leap? How will it be able to overcome a critical regression due to its economic and political options? All these transformations have been

Reprinted from *L'Enseignement de la Religion Catholique*, ed. J. Bulkens and H. Lombaerts (Louvain: University Press, 1993), 3–30. Copyright © 1993 Bibliotheca Ephemeridum Theologicarum Lovaniensium. Article translated by Michael Warren. Translation copyright © 1997 by Michael Warren.

in the making for decades. The institutional and relational shocks have brought to light the necessity for the remodeling of society. More particularly, the democratization of schooling created impasses connected to a global restructuring of society. The school, with the mythical aspirations of the First World, is driven to assume the extreme exigencies of assuring the future of the new generations.[3] When a child is in nursery school, his or her school career is already planned. The choices thus made are directly linked to the political and economic interests of society.[4]

It is in this context that the question of teaching of religion in schools finds its beginning. The recent debates about this question in the different European countries prove that society has changed its position, not only in relation to the teaching of religion, but especially in relation to religion in general. The revision of the concordats,[5] the controversies around the schedules and programs,[6] the growing indifference of students, and the demotivation of a good number of teachers, do not merely show the lack of adaptation to the modern world. To understand what is happening requires a fundamental rethinking of the issue of teaching of religion as such in schools, which is linked to a sociocultural shift.

In his proclamation of a "second evangelization" as necessary for the whole work of the church, Pope John Paul II stressed the importance of Christian roots for the unification of a European continent.[7] Yet, at the same time, cultural and social developments, such as a European population of wide religious diversity, indicate that the teaching of religion in schools will progressively be done outside of such evangelizing intentions.

This paper seeks to set out a global perspective, a procedure, and an interpretative frame in order to appreciate better the challenge that comes to us from the future of Europe. To achieve this purpose I will lay out three moments of reflection: (1) to detect the link between the present socioreligious situation of the continent and the changes of the global society; (2) to revalue the role of the school in this society; (3) to reflect upon the specific contribution of the teaching of religion in the context of a democratized schooling system.

I. Society and Religion

The status and importance of religion in each European country are the result of a long historical process. The specifics of these developments in each country render continent-wide generalizations problematic. At the same time, however, we can see in Europe a generalizing model of civilization and culture working its way into the political and socioeconomic realms. If adopted continent-wide, this model will produce conditions affecting both values and the search for meaning among many people. Here I will point out some characteristics of these developments and show their influence on religion.

1.1 The Social Status of Religion

Numerous studies have evaluated the evolution of the relation of the European population to a particular religious tradition, to religious practice, and to the impact of religion on daily life. The most conspicuous of these studies is the one conducted by the European Value Systems Study Group, relevant to most of the European countries between 1981 and 1983. These studies were done again in 1991.[8] Although important differences exist between countries, and inside each country the profile of the believer is far from being homogeneous, the great majority of the European population still continues to name itself Christian. The findings reveal that Catholics and Protestants adopt a more reserved attitude in relation to their ecclesiastical institution and tend to select their beliefs against the doctrine proposed by their churches. The graph of religious practice continues to go down. And although the church is having a real influence on society, institutional affiliation is characterized as problematic. It is as if Christians vacillate between different value systems and lines of thinking. The analysis of church affiliation has led P. M. Zulehner to formulate the hypothesis of an ecclesial atheism.[9]

A detailed analysis of the results of different surveys in France shows that strong positions against religion or radical identification with a particular tradition are getting blurred. Besides, an important group with no clear profile—religiously hesitant persons—seem to take progressive distance from their institutions. Susceptible to multiple influences, this population evolves toward an unbelief that is more and more explicit.[10]

In this context, it is not possible to overestimate the importance of the collapse of the Communist bloc in Eastern Europe. The atheistic pole of Europe has now abandoned its paranoid position, no longer obliging the churches to situate themselves against an enemy. One could speak of a historical victory. The way is open now to establish an ecclesiastical presence throughout the continent, in continuity with the first missionaries and encouraged by new canonizations. But the fear of the foe continues to be cultivated, though now in relation to an eastern reconquest: from Communism toward freemasonry. The impact of multiple influences seems to remove the possibility of linear action in favor of either one religious tradition or a particular ideological tradition. In such a situation, would the Eastern churches have the time, space, and support needed to grasp what has happened outside their countries over a period of forty years? Will they have the resources needed for objectivity and for the sort of study needed if they are to analyze their history and link it with the evolution in the rest of the world? Will they have the time to anticipate the implications of the probable evolution of the Eastern countries toward capitalism? It is also important for Christians of the West to be conscious of the models according to which the Eastern churches have acted in the context of Communist domination.[11] The position of the churches toward society cannot ignore the threat, not from freemasonry, but rather from the capitalist world and modernity.

At the same time one cannot underestimate the necessity of readjustments between the different Christian traditions. Some countries are strongly marked by the Reformation; others have practically not known its existence. The ecumenical movement poses the problem of the credibility of Christianity in relation to society's emerging priorities. This movement insists on re-establishing a prophetic solidarity at the service of coexistence on earth, in response to the call of the God of life, rather than overemphasizing the importance of the separation between churches.

The third problematic aspect is anxiety about a united Europe. Almost the way modernism was blamed at the end of the nineteenth century, "postmodernity" and the influence of sects and cults are considered responsible for the present confusion and de-Christianization. Given the persistence of the evolution of the modern world and subsequent awareness about opportunities for life's chances that society and modern culture are offering for all, certain trends in the church continue to interpret "the crisis" in terms of a suspicion of the world. The logical answer would seem, then, to reinforce the attachment to the body of doctrine and to institutional discipline in order to "conquer" the world. At least such is the purpose Abbruzzese perceives in the Italian movement *Comunione e Liberazione.*[12] His analysis is one of the many studies about the reciprocal influences between modernity and Christianity in Europe.[13] The interest in sects or "the new religious movements" must be directly linked to the impact of the crisis of modernity.[14] These phenomena require a clear and detailed study and a nuanced interpretation in order to evaluate their significance.[15] Only thus will adults be invited to overcome futile polarization, to set up a climate of dialogue, and to clarify the presuppositions from which individuals and groups situate themselves in relation to faith. This sort of response calls adult Christians to develop new skills, which allow them to distance themselves from a passive dependence on the authority of a religious tradition.

The debate about the teaching of religion in schools is only one symptom, but a major one, of the present shift going on in European society and culture. In order to understand the real roots of the problem, it is important to formulate certain observations and to raise some questions.

1.2 Dysfunctional Religious Socialization

The religious socialization of children and teens is affected by the same contextual factors we have just examined. All the psychosociological studies on religious education show the indisputable importance of the family in religious socialization (primary socialization).[16] The school continues the work of integrating ritual traditions, doctrine, and codes of social behavior, in order to assure the development of a social and cultural identity (secondary socialization). The school has, then, a fundamental influence on religious socialization, but under certain conditions only: we have to underline the importance of the development of cognitive faculties and of the capacity to reflect on human knowledge itself.[17] For adults, integration in a professional and social milieu represents a third network of socialization, which is a guarantee of continuity and stability.

Today this continuity is at risk. Sociological studies of religion show complex and nuanced findings that signal certain important structural modifications. In Europe it is obvious that the Christianization of new generations has been assured essentially by families and by schools. Until a short time ago, various churches could rely upon these two educational agents to maintain the continuity of their religious adherence.

As for primary socialization, a great number of families do not transmit religious tradition to their children. They prefer to hand over this responsibility to teachers who have been trained to do it. Many young parents are not opposed to having their children initiated into a particular religion. After all, they think, it is the concern of their children, who will make their choice when they reach the age of maturity. Such parents do not concern themselves directly with religious initiation.[18] In more abstract terms, sociologists speak about a separation between the church and the family. After the separations between church and state, religion and science, state and science, the structural differentiation of society continues in a more and more global manner. This evolution coincides with a whole set of changes in religious behavior identified for decades in various disciplines. The progressive decline in the number of baptisms at birth, a greater number of ruptures with ecclesiastical institutions, the decline of religious practice, and a clear reservation with respect to ecclesial membership all seem to create a religious void,[19] which in turn results in an excess of responsibilities for the school and for the teacher of religion in particular. These pressures on schools explain partly the crisis in the teaching of religion in schools.[20] The religious ignorance of students is often invoked as an important obstacle that causes frustration for teachers of religion.

Church authorities continually point to the dramatic character of religious ignorance, of the lack of church identity, of a deep religious illiteracy and inability to even speak about religion, of a contagious indifference to the significance of religion and Christianity for daily life, and of the growing individualism found in a culture of consumption. The list goes on to name the culprits as atheism, hedonism, secularism, materialism, and modernism.[21] In the face of such a negative diagnosis, parents, teachers, and catechists find themselves accused of having failed in their mission.[22]

Should this crisis be laid at the feet of the "agents" of religious socialization and stop there? Equally at issue here are institutional structures interacting with a changing environment. These structures for their part are directly connected to the way the profession of faith and the tradition itself have historically been conceived.[23] Instead of focusing on a problem within the churches, there is room for a closer look at the mutual interaction between the churches and their social and cultural context. Systems theory invites institutions themselves to lay out a more complex picture of the structural interactions connecting the ecclesial or religious organization's members with one another and with their environment.[24]

1.3 The Reciprocity of Influences

As F. X. Kaufmann has remarked: just as the Catholic church weighs the influence it has had on the European continent and on Western culture, so too it must recognize that global society, with its sociocultural, economic, and political evolutions, has also influenced the church in a decisive and fundamental way.[25] The relationship between societal change and religion's shifting social position discloses their reciprocal influence on each other. The functional-structural differentiation of modern societies produces a different position for Christianity in those societies. In facing these new circumstances, Christianity is first identified with an ecclesial organization. This shift in turn frees Christians to search more openly for a personal sense of life and of values. In a move generally identified as a movement of secularization,[26] they distance themselves from the influence of the church. Ironically and mistakenly, the churches react by appropriating to themselves almost exclusively the official representation of Christianity and by seeking to dominate religious

communication in society. Faced with both the decline of religious practice and the formal trappings of a particular church, a seemingly logical
response is to hold fast to "priestly ministry" as the essential core of ecclesial identity. A stronger bureaucratization is put in place in order to
save the continuity of tradition and to reinforce institutional power and
discipline.

The crisis of transmitting an ecclesial tradition must be situated in
this context. The successive attitude adopted by the churches in relation
to changes in society and culture has contributed to this situation. This
thesis differs from the one claiming that environmental influences are
primarily responsible for both massive religious confusion and the loss
of effective members and that these influences represent a danger for
the continuity of the churches at the moment.

1.4 An Urgent Issue

It is then possible to ask oneself about the strategy adopted today by the
churches, namely, the one that consists of reinforcing the boundaries of
the institution and of controlling influences that effectively come from
the environment. This reaction seeks to promote a return to certitudes
and to securities. Is this a felicitous strategy, able to answer the challenge of the credibility test to which the churches are confronted at this
moment? One may also question the usefulness of reactions, apparently
logical, of pastors and certain ecclesiastical authorities who want to take
over control of the teaching of religion in schools in order to stop all the
modernist and secularist influences coming from the environment. In order to evangelize Europe, the teaching of religion should give priority to
the "spiritual."

When certain adults and teens criticize the church's organizational
aspect in order to justify the distance they themselves have taken, they
bring into focus a real weakness. In every institution, the organizational
aspect represents a continuous source of tension. The members experience the distance between the ideal, the dream, or personal interests on
the one hand, and the demands of a fragile collective project on the other hand. The church could take a more flexible approach to the varied
search for meaning or for truth so common today but also so little connected to or interested in church discipline. The church has a double
duty: first, to situate itself clearly as mediator of the divine presence of
Jesus Christ and as guardian of the boundaries of its specific identity;
second, to value and ponder respectfully the initiatives and spiritual
journeys of varied people and to discern the unexpected presence of the
God of life.

Where the second of these duties is resisted, K. Gabriel finds what he calls a "spiral of silence." Many efforts, experiences sometimes of great quality, and multiple spiritual journeys remain unnoticed, or are treated with distrust. More attention is given to less threatening attitudes and types of reflection. Gabriel thinks this spiral needs to be broken in favor of openly recognizing situations in which the presence of Christ may be manifesting itself.[27] The historical studies brought together by Delumeau on the role of women in the transmission of faith offer provocative material on how church discipline sought to control Christian women's use of scripture and their intuitive foreseeing of coming developments.[28]

There are many reactions to the threatening void. Among them are the temptations to avoid all puzzlement, to move toward secure, select interpretations, or to reread history in the light of solutions deemed necessary to solve some current problem. In the view of Danièle Hervieu-Léger, such reactions are not lacking their own persuasiveness:

If religious language does not stand by itself, it is because in modernity it is no longer possible to distinguish between the objective order of the world, the collective universe of signification, and the subjectively lived experience of meaning. Or better, this coherence can no longer be presented only as a human objective, a horizon to be continually broadened by collective work. Coherence is not of the order of revelation given once and for all. In a modernity uncertain about its own origins, what is so fascinating about the lost meaning systems of religious traditions is this: in their obsolete way of thinking, these traditions shed light on the imperative character of the individual and collective need of coherence. But at the same time, they reveal clearly how impossible it is to offer coherence in a religious mode when that mode is culturally unacceptable. In valuing the experienced presence of the divine—against every type of nuanced theological reflection—contemporary emotional [religious] trends seem to avoid the structural conflict experienced by a religious faith in the context of modernity, because the "intellectual reflection on experience," necessary for its articulation in a nuanced religious language, is quietly sidestepped. One can wonder, though, whether avoiding such a conflict is not in the end a refusal of a coherence inherent (and perhaps overdone) in traditional religious language.[29]

What is called for in this situation is for religious groups to face a new cultural situation in modernity: taking emotion up again as a way of dealing with the "desymbolization" of the modern world that at a cultural level accompanies the social dismissal of religion.[30] One could put forth the theory that many persons and groups respond to a reuse of emotionally based experience. However pursued, this will not be a process done in a linear, uniform way but according to what we might call "a flourishing diversity." And "in this overflowing of the affective expression of religious experience, people could read something of a protest against the bureaucratic framing of a personal believing experience."[31]

Multiple dilemmas now emerge at the end of the twentieth century. There is the destabilization of both institutional religion and ideological systems. In addition, troubling armed conflicts erupt throughout the world, in spite of the horrible evidence of their destructiveness in this century. There is, further, the ecological menace, as well as disturbing evidence of the growing desire to control both the start and the end of life. There is also the fatal danger of AIDS, the production and sale of arms, and the murderous dependence of the Southern Hemisphere nations on the Western world.

Each topic is a matter of urgency. People may understand the perplexity of the religious authorities confronted with these situations. The analysis of the moral question may help us to clarify our attitude in the context of these changes in the religious field.

> Instead of lamenting an unfavorable context, it will be better to recognize that we confront one of the inescapable conditions of moral judgment today. Rather than dreaming of an immovable or static moral judgment, it would be better to learn to decide and to discover the ways through which risky judgments may and have to be taken in these urgent contexts.[32]

Writing of "postmoral societies," G. Lipovetsky stresses the need for a sharp vigilance to spot real tendencies "to dissolve the religious form of ethics—duty itself." At issue here is a new kind of logic, different from the thinking that argued in favor of a moral autonomy separated from religion.[33]

The churches are finding their credibility questioned when they speak out on important questions facing people today. In urgent situations, it is important to focus on essential matters. What is essential is shaped by a shifting and changing context. Criteria can be invoked, unwisely, as a way of ensuring institutional credibility. Religious and priestly vocations, the number of participants at religious events, the intensity of affiliation, the public acknowledgment of official authority—when these indications are offered as criteria, they suggest an interiorization of a religious institution. At its extreme, the uncritical identification with a religious institution is unwilling to face any questioning of that institution as not worth the risk.

In spite of the institutional precautions, the influences sketched here affect the members and modify the interactions between an organization and its environment. Figures show that these influences cannot be ignored.[34] We are in an emergency situation that obliges us to take appropriate action. These are the signs peculiar to an ethical situation. The overpowering impact of the challenges is obvious. Some hesitate when obvious action must be taken. The very diversity of views shows many people's inability to think their attitudes through. "Action organizes itself around intuitions of an evil to be avoided, of an insupportable situation to be denounced, or of a challenge to be answered under the penalty of uncontrollable consequences."[35]

F. X. Kaufmann insists on three important orientations in order to assure a greater credibility for the churches.[36] We could add to them, for they are three orientations that can promote the creation of a space free of organizational domination, where the religious question can be raised in all truth. First, to distance oneself from a bureaucratic organizational model of the state, in order to be more available to the necessary slow progress toward faith and ecclesial belonging, that is, to respect the freedom and personal path of each one and to show more interest in the adult search for religious life, rather than to stay with the decisions of total and definitive identification. Second, to promote a theology and a structure of ministry closer to the concrete reality of the communities, in order to avoid immobilism and to stimulate communitarian dynamism. Third, to favor subsidiarity: what can be decided and realized in a lower level, closer to the concerned persons, must be assumed by this level. The resulting decentralization enables more personal and autonomous responsibility at the level of persons and groups. To accept the contingency and fragility of the human condition, the flexibility necessary for the diversity of people and their mind-sets, and the fact that "the good" starts with imperfect and sometimes temporary solutions—all this demands at the same time that we abstain from an objectivist morality.[37]

II. The Issue of Teaching of Religion in Schools

The teaching of religion is, then, directly affected by the consequences of the reciprocal interaction, generally taken for granted, between the church and society. Within this interaction, the teaching of religion can find a place and status that would re-establish its credibility. A society harmoniously integrated into a religious tradition looks for ways of guaranteeing that religion's monopoly, for example, by the restructuring of history itself. In several European countries, school networks were variously the expression of the mission of the church or of other philosophical systems, antireligious or atheistic. The history of teaching in schools is complex because of the overlapping of such a number of economical, political, religious, and sociocultural interests. Thanks to the considerable contribution of the churches, notably the religious congregations, the impact of Christianity on Western society has been able to maintain itself in spite of a militant, antireligious, antichurch movement.

2.1 School and Society

The historical conflict has not been resolved in favor of one or the other of these partners. In certain countries the confessional network maintains its privileged position and continues its "mission." But today, the school becomes more and more an economic, political, and sociocultural instrument of society. The type of society emerging at the end of the twentieth century and the beginning of the twenty-first affects progressively every discussion, including the education system. New criteria of a generalized school socialization affect all schools, no matter what their possible confessional orientation. Resistances to these social forces are only temporary. The political and economic agendas pushing modernization are prior to the ideological justification of a hierarchy of values or of ethical and confessional priorities. The school thus moves progressively, with different rhythms, beyond polarization.

A democratic society takes as one of its main concerns the teaching done in schools. All citizens have an equal right to be educated. The school is asked to be at the service of the interests and desires proper to a pluralist population of modern society. Today, students and teachers negotiate their status and their style of collaboration. The place of cultural and ethical systems, including religion, is situated within this perspective. These systems do not identify themselves anymore with the ideological or spiritual inspiration of the past. The majority of teachers—mostly laypeople—motivate their teaching from a professional deontology, which is not opposed to serious and generous commitment. But the professional space is consciously limited. A professional ethics contrasts with the ethics of sacrifice and total, free, and genuine availability for education and health care as it used to be in previous centuries.

The life project today's society is promoting is no longer stated in terms of religious belonging. The myth of excellence is the code of successful careers in a postindustrial and international society. As a result a syndrome of competencies to be acquired is emerging through highly specialized teaching careers: the study of languages—both modern and ancient—mathematics, sciences, technology, computer, and art, all aiming at high qualifications. The church is not propagating these dreams. High qualification standards are promoted in schools, cinemas, television, by advertisements, and by the big multinational companies that created this attractive model. Through this model, the youngsters are confronted with the urge to acquire: such a style of charm, smile, intelligence, know-how, happiness due to unexpected coincidences, intimacy, feminine or masculine identity, a type of maternity, a combination of personal convictions, a public recognition, an exotic universe accessible only to a few, a taste for clothes, a projection of an original identity, and so forth. The massive orchestration of consumption introduces a new kind of social differentiation. The school plays an important role also in introducing violent differences: the school campus and the classroom as such often become a place for imposing a specific style of fashion, managed by the advertising strategy of big corporations.[38]

Given this situation, and this is the case in all the European countries, the status of religion in schools is put to a historical, ideological, and juridical test. From this angle, the school of tomorrow will be of a different nature. That is why we are invited to reinterpret and to revalue the relevance of religion for the school curriculum. This question is linked with the evolution of the social status of religion within society itself. This evolution obliges every school to resituate itself socially and culturally, and to clarify its ideological identity. That is why the debate about the link between school and religion is a complex one.[39] That is also why it is such a delicate matter to formulate a diagnosis.

In spite of being tolerated, it is obvious that religion does not fit the present evolutions. The very presence of religion is seen as a source of embarrassment. From several angles and with different strategies according to specific countries or local circumstances, one finds efforts to minimize its influence and its importance.

How do we handle religion in schools? The options are multiple: either isolate religion from schools; or give religion a proper space and time, strictly regulated by law; or diversify religious or ethical teaching with respect to the pluralism of the school population; or question the religious content (Christian) of a ritualized orientation of the school life; or question the direct link between the teaching of religion and the church (Catholic or Protestant); or adopt a critical view about the presentations of religions in the school manuals. On this issue of religion in schools, Europe represents a mosaic of views.[40] Considering the institutional and personal confusion, there are good reasons to argue in favor of both the prophetic mission of religions and the priority of the spiritual, in response to the emptiness experienced by contemporary people and particularly by the young.[41]

2.2 A New Culture of Schooling

During the second part of the twentieth century, we have been witness-ing a cultural crisis. Though simmering for a long time, its public mani-festation has now accelerated a general awareness of cultural problems. The process includes two simultaneous movements: grief over the loss of certain long-accepted ways of thinking and the loss of well-established points of reference. But the crisis also offers an opportunity: to find in-spiration in a new freedom of spirit, allowing us to establish unusual links between factors little or not known. Yet, the crisis is full of risks, because it is impossible to master its results in advance.

This crisis marks the emerging reality of the school world today. In solidarity with the decisive change of so-called secularized European society, the school becomes part of a movement of exploration of an open and pluralistic culture, of simultaneous and creative integration in multiple networks. Like the young, children are also invited to make choices in the face of an overwhelming abundance of information. They discover new questions; they learn how to work out original and effi-cient solutions. Teachers find themselves face-to-face with the young "informed" on a certain number of themes and experimenting in certain domains. Teaching is no longer practiced according to a one-way com-munication. In turn, the school is confronted with the dilemma of aban-doning, on the one hand, speculative pedagogy, centered on a hierarchy of traditional values, and, on the other hand, the adoption of a teaching approach inspired by the priorities of contemporary society. The proj-ects for making school more efficient, so common in all the European countries, actually officialize the decisive change. We are witnessing a mutation of the school; the teaching profession is being shaped by other criteria of professionalism. As young people begin a school career, par-ents are preparing to participate in the management of the schools.

Who, then, has the power over the school? From now on, there will be several centers of power: the formal structure of school management, of course, but also the agents of commercial and advertising interests. The boundaries between the school and its environment are now blurred by these multiple interests; students and teachers find themselves more at the periphery of the school than at the center. This evolution that is characteristic of the school institution requires a presence of dif-ferent kind, a different attention, a collaboration among partners, each one making use of seemingly amazing resources to stimulate learning. Who does not realize that this reality creates dangerous situations as much for the persons who are involved as for the school institution it-self?

What is the core of the debate about teaching of religion in schools? It is possible to misread this issue. The question is real, and its "technical" aspects deserve full consideration. At the same time, the debate represents a vast problem, it is also a symptom. The underlying question is, What will be the constructive contribution by the school in contemporary society? Then, according to the logic of this response, one should specify the proper contribution of teaching of religion in this context. "The real answer does not lie in focusing on a discipline, 'the teaching of religion,' but in the evolution of the school culture and in the internal rebalancing of disciplines."[42] The teaching of religion (religions) needs a new foundation of credibility. This credibility is directly linked to the way the school, as sociocultural, economic, and political institution, redefines its status and its specific contribution in society. Insofar as the school can embrace an educational model, capable of giving youth the space where they can integrate constructively whatever affects them in an overinformed context, it creates a space for an interesting dialogue with religions.

The temptation to isolate the "religion class" as a proper discipline may destroy its very goal. It is encouraging to listen to the arguments of atheists in favor of a course on religions. Although this way of looking at the issues is not sufficient, the arguments deserve further analysis.

The European Council of Cultural Cooperation insists on the importance of European people taking responsibility for their common patrimony. What is often consciously or unconsciously forgotten is that this patrimony has a religious (and moral) core which, whatever its confessional status, goes beyond rationality. This council insists upon the importance of intercommunity understanding of the religious dimension of this European identity. From this point forward, religion at school should be understood as a plural noun. The school is a key place for an intercultural and multiconfessional education.

Next comes the issue of addressing "religious illiteracy," a big cultural gap in religious knowledge characteristic of general education. A nonconfessional rationality admits today a nonconfessional teaching of religions. The aspiration is that all students should develop a "religious culture" emerging from a new sensibility of the common consciousness of Western society. The authority—the collective imagination—is no longer situated within a religious tradition or with the functionaries of a particular ecclesial tradition. Contemporary human persons base themselves on the authority of their competencies in managing their individual and collective life. The integration of a "religion class" is invoked for human, cultural, and functional reasons.[43]

The blind alley in which religious education finds itself in schools is linked with a certain number of preconceived ideas concerning religion, says Danièle Hervieu-Léger. (1) The believer is supposed not to be able to speak from within his or her belief; the nonbeliever is supposed to fight against that which he or she does not share. This situation is an obstacle for a climate of serenity. (2) Religion is par excellence a question that divides, that puts the individual one against the other. This makes religious pluralism inaccessible within the religion class at school. (3) The demand of a religious culture is in fact a demand of a "Catholic culture," which the church addresses in an inadequate manner. This leads to a loss of cumulative religious culture, from generation to generation.

The debate is about the status itself of religion in a modern society. The debate on the religion class is about the value of school teaching as a quest for truth in a heterogeneous sociocultural context. Rather than argue in favor of the school as an instrument for providing necessary religious information—historically and even theologically confined to the suspected isolation of a "one-hour religion class"—the remedies consist in fostering qualitative change of the teaching profession.[44]

> The plurality of perception of religious reality allows religions to contribute to the development of the culture itself, and each one can become conscious of the role of religion in human culture, so much so that religions can be understood in truth.[45]

What the discovery of religion means or stands for depends on the establishment of a new "school culture" and a new policy of education. And G. Coq concludes: "It is still true that a school culture renewed by an active nonconfessional rationality would not be able to assume all the issues linked with the notion of the lack of religious culture."

In fact, on the side of the believing institutions, it is convenient that the church asks clearly the question of its inscription in a "lay society." Has it truly assumed its responsibility in the matter of religious culture? A lot has been done in catechesis, but when people asked for a better grasp of the Christian message, Christian communities did not really prepare themselves to create open spaces, to offer this "service to the collective memory." In the Catholic church notably, a stubborn anti-intellectualism and a ridiculous attachment to confessional teaching witness to a kind of self-doubt.

We must go further:

> Instead of being attached to the survival of Christianity, there is an urgency to help construct a real lay-centered society. This task should have found in Christianity faithful disciples, because Christianity will achieve its fullness only in the freedom of consciences and values that structure lay identity.[46]

In his statement G. Coq raises the question of the value and credibility of a dualist and polarizing pattern of reading the situation of religion in society. He argues in favor of the creation of open spaces, of the construction of a secular society in order to overcome the paralysis of inauthentic and static Christian patterns. Surely a paralyzing educational structure is counterproductive and leads to pervasive outcomes. An open environment may stimulate moments of perplexity vital for the search for truth.[47] On the other hand, new boundaries are to be established in order to highlight the specific features of a Christian identity. The entire matter of different approaches to teaching in schools, including the religion class, can play an important role in this work of classification of the issues, particularly as regards religion.[48]

III. Perspectives for the Future

It is time now to imagine some characteristics of the teaching of religion(s) at school, taking into account the decisive changes on the European continent. We examine successively the importance of tolerance, dialectics, the search for truth, and the ethics of teaching of religion.

3.1 Tolerance

Charles Wackenheim insists on the importance of clarifying the meaning of tolerance.[49] The genesis of intolerance is strongly linked to the way religions and ideologies try to achieve certain objectives, which are in effect common to both (p. 120). The legitimate interest of a religion or of a particular ideology in imposing and maintaining its doctrine, in practicing its rites, involves protecting its borders and ensuring that its members are not distancing themselves from the center. Integration into a social context, which means linking oneself to the interests of an economic and political system, can result in less flexible collective awareness. Intolerance is an attitude that not only denies others the right to have their own opinions and different convictions, but that also tries to prevent, including by force, every manifestation of this right. Intolerance becomes further manifested when, because of the lack of appropriate means, the "acting out becomes impossible" (p. 117).

Facing the need for open-minded, respectful listening, for dialogue and common exploration of fundamental questions about values, ethics, and the uniqueness of a religious tradition, becomes obvious. Facing this task would be one of the priority objectives of a "religious culture." It would be essential to preserve spaces where individuals and communities express their ethical concerns and search for meaning. The community has the right to elaborate its cohesion and to situate itself in confrontation with a "different" environment, to search for salvation, to manage power, to search for the truth. These essential preoccupations, proper to each organization with confessional or ideological traditions, should be practiced in respect and with mutual interest. In this perspective "intolerance" loses its raison d'être.

3.2 Honest Dialectics

Clearly, one can misread the situation of religion today and become trapped in discussion of symptoms only. The deeper question is this: In what terms are we to utter the God question today? What discourse about faith will raise the deepest silent attention and committed response? These are core issues underlying many discussions.

Information proper to a tradition, exegesis of the sacred texts, and justification of an institutional ascetic all involve a social reality and a symbolic value. As one looks for information and investigates, one works on the objective material in interaction with one's personal curiosity. The search for factual information must lead to a personal interpretation of its meaning for the self. The interaction of information and interpretation is what in the end leads to personal decision, the yes or no that will appreciate and integrate what one has learned. In other words, persons interested in knowing a religion, an ethical or philosophical tradition, look for information that can build their identity and answer an existential need for solid roots, as inexhaustible sources of energy and inspiration.

Misunderstanding the hermeneutical link between objective, scientific, academic, ascetic information and an emotionally based curiosity—an irresistible perplexity—can actually lead to a regrettable break, a radical "indifference," in those whose questions are not met by official discourse. A better understanding of the dialectic between objective traditions and the deep personal quest of individuals could shed light on the future of the teaching of religion(s) in schools.

3.3 The Quest for Truth

In the negotiations between church and state concerning the status of religion in schools—especially taking into account the crisis, the insecurity, the disarray, and the absence of religious culture and practice—the churches can be tempted to take over the teaching of religion as a chance for the "new evangelization."[50] Here, to safeguard the unique character of the Christian and ecclesial tradition, it would seem important to reinforce the boundaries and to protect oneself against harmful influences of the environment. The ecclesial institution defends such a choice because of its responsibility for preserving the continuity of a collective identity.

However, here the institution risks misnaming as its foe what is actually an "other" who is different and whose difference causes anxiety. The major cultural areas today are filled with such differences. Science, for example, more than ever dominates, whereas religion, in spite of certain forms of awakening, seems to lose still more of its influence; philosophy, once at the core of science, seems more and more parochially limited, whereas the economy seems all-powerful to the point of commanding science itself (especially through budget allocations).

It seems to me that one may at least propose this: these very different areas testify in their diversity to an exploded culture. This explosion shows divisions within human persons themselves. These divisions characterize us: between reason and faith (this big separation at the beginning of modernity), between organizations and the mind, between the individual and the collective, between subjective and objective, between thinking and feeling, between the natural and the cultural, between tradition and progress, and so forth. Such divisions are, because of their style, foundational. An unexpected development is how the divisions allow each "branch" to become autonomous: organic medicine, for example, or techniques of production or individual aesthetic inventions, and so on. Such developments come at a cost: the exploded culture increasingly loses its specific human dimension. This culture is more and more incapable of offering persons human space and ways.[51]

M. Bellet highlights how the cultural changes occurring today and even the distortions of historically defined harmony are essential for the development of a new human maturity. The confrontation with "the other" offers opportunities for an institution to be transformed, purified, and forced to find new grounds for a solid identity. This process has implications for the teaching of religion. Religious education is called to commit itself to the emergence of unexpected newness in life. Such newness characterized every historical refoundation of religious identity.

The important task for the school is to create a space where the traps of a "perverted" dialectical reasoning are identified, where the students discover the value of a respectful dialogue shared by the different partners. The exploration of territory proper to a particular religious confession cannot but gain from it.

One cannot forget that, historically speaking, the Judeo-Christian tradition has often positioned itself in the antithesis as source of an irreducible originality, starting a fundamental transformation of the relation with the God of life. At several occasions and after a reversal of the relationship with political power, the antithesis has been transformed and hardened into a thesis, with the exclusive right to condemn every deviation, every effort to put forward an antithesis.[52]

Here again we find ourselves in the quest for truth. For religious believers this quest has at least three "moments": owning "what one believes"; trouble; and unbelief. In the second moment one meets "the test of truth": in the paradox that what I believe is not what I believe. What I believe becomes a matter of crisis from which emerges something new or different.

What happens here is such a failure of "God" that atheism, which struggles against it, has no longer any meaning. The substitute for atheism has neither name nor reference, obviously, because the so-called opponent is nowhere and everywhere.

Thus religion dies in itself, overwhelmed by the perversion its system blindly authorizes and by the oppressive unreality of its universal claims. Precisely in this death can become manifest what cannot die: the irreducible reality attested to by witness. The teaching of religion is confronted with conflicting choices between, on the one hand, the invitation to put itself at the service of doctrinal stances (which cannot support "the other") and, on the other hand, the ethical demand allowing the test of truth to be lived in complete honesty, that is, allowing everyone to reach the strongest possible affirmation of truth.[53]

The school can play an important role in establishing the space where the quest for truth can be lived in total honesty. It can help dismantle the misunderstanding between the demand of fidelity toward a traditional profession that does not recognize the subject in her or his originality and crucial experience, on the one hand, and the search for truth that leads subjects toward a different way of being, on the other hand. The school can help establish the fundamental condition of the credibility of all religious confessions.[54] It can allow things to be named for the first time and make way for a new understanding to replace fearful ignorance.

The teaching of religion cannot miss this great passage, this crossing from a world structured according to a false reasoning and marked by the explosion of a culture, toward a truth where "in my possibility to live concretely, and according to my limitation, the destiny of humanity will be decided in me."[55] The task is ever more fundamental than the transmission of the doctrinal knowledge, of a "neutral" information about world religions, of a particular tradition, or simply of personal testimony. The essential basis needs to be established, because what is at stake is the new question of God in all its truth. Thus, it will be possible to understand the code of what has been called a particular tradition and the meaning of "the word of God" in personal life.

[Religion is] a way profoundly one [that is, in harmony], which does not separate but unites. It lets itself be heard beyond death, not in order to flatter the imagination, but because its place does not belong to our mortality. Religion gives to each one the possibility to retain what he is, to return from one's deviations, and to give hope in darkness. It only desires respect, mutual care, and tender love among human beings.

Religion is, for those who discover it a total way to peace. It is active in everything but with extreme discretion. Its word is not overpowering and authoritative, but necessary and free.[56]

3.4 The Ethics of Teaching Religion

It is fashionable to argue in favor of maintaining the teaching of religion in schools as part of the curriculum. However, this discipline's rightful place in the school's curriculum must be proved by the status of its content, by its cognitive requirements, and by the complexity of its intellectual system. In adopting a solid program, in demanding that teachers be academically trained, and in using a pedagogy scientifically justified, the case is convincingly made.

In this reasoning, however, one does not take into account other factors that also decide the importance and the value of teaching of religion: parents and their motives in wanting religion in the curriculum; the students and their decoding of the subject and its intellectual demands; the teachers and their interpretation of the status of this discipline; the place of religion in society; and the educational policies of a government and its economic and political priorities that command the interpretation of all that is done in schools, including religion.

That the churches seek in an opportunistic way to anxiously evangelize the school world is unclear. Having the matter phrased this way underestimates the impact of the debate and does not respect sufficiently the issue of this confrontation for the implied actors. The key question is not about the conflict between the catechetical intention on the one hand and, on the other hand, the teaching of religion in schools to a pluralistic audience. The immediate and urgent issue concerns an ethics of the teaching of religion, the honest search for truth. When the opening toward non-Semitic religions or the ecumenical orientation favors a certain distance from the domination of a particular doctrine, that distance can foster a more objective examination of a tradition's credibility and of one's personal affiliation with that particular tradition.

Let us not underestimate the greater freedom children and young people have today in the family and in society. Because of the media and publicity, because of the differentiated open social life, they cannot but integrate a multitude of information and solve a good number of questions. They choose very soon and in a personal manner their proper "consumption" in a lot of fields. Every exclusive authority is put into question. This orientation is not against religion in itself. It enters into conflict with a certain way of managing the religious field, which seems inferior when compared with the sociocultural intelligence of our epoch.

An important step forward would be taken if the teaching of religion could be centered on the critical analysis of its ideological presuppositions and on the premises of its status within school and in society. Some institutional and ideological questions should not be kept in obscurity.

Moreover, inasmuch as young people can express themselves, communicate between themselves and with their teachers or their parents about their multiple perplexities and questions, the religion class can also contribute to the integration of a religious sense, indispensable in understanding and justifying a profession of faith.

The teacher of religion's competence does not stop at a good academic knowledge of different theological disciplines and of the human sciences. That isolated competence risks becoming an obstacle to creative perplexity and the search for truth, at least as young people perceive them. The primary competence concerns the dialogue about the religious and ethical conscience of the young—and the lack of conscience—given their social and cultural background. The contribution of a historical memory and the actual institutional consistency prove their value in the context of providing options or choices.

NOTES

1. E. Poulat, *Liberté, laïcité. La guerre des deux Frances et le principe de la Modernité* (Paris: Cerf, 1988).

2. In the second chapter of *Liberté, laïcité,* E. Poulat illustrates at which point "the Kingdom of God and its transformations" represent some big defects, before which the modest return to the essentials is unavoidable.

3. H. Lombaerts, "L'école chrétienne face à la société contemporaine," in *Lumen Vitae* (1987): 369–379.

4. D. Bloch, "Rapprocher l'école et l'économie," *Études,* 1987, 597–606; J. M. Berthelot, *Le piège scolaire* (Paris: P.U.F., 1983); S. Mollo-Bouvier, *La sélection implicite à l'école* (Paris: P.U.F., 1986).

5. E. Butturini, *La religione a scuola.* Dall' Unità ad oggi (Bresica, 1988); N. Galli, "Problemi generali e specifici aperti dal nuovo concordato," *Religione e scuola,* no. 15 (1987): 504–510; N. Galli, ed., *Quali valori nella scuola di stato* (Bresica, 1989): 233–277.

6. "Religionsunterricht an weiterführenden Schulen in Europa," *Materialien für den Religionsunterricht an Gymnasien,* no. 1, 1990.

7. R. Luneau, ed., *Le Rêve de Compostelle. Vers la restauration d'une Europe chrétienne?* (Paris: Le Centurion, 1989); J. Decornoy, "L'Europe sanctifiée par Jean Paul II," *Le Monde Diplomatique,* December 1990, 10.

8. J. Stoetzel, *Les valeurs du temps présent: une enquête européenne* (Paris: P.U.F.: 1983); J. Kerkhofs, "Between 'Christendom' and 'Christianity,'" *Journal of Empirical Theology* 1, no. 2 (1988): 88–101; L. Voye, B. Bawin-Legros, J. Kerkhofs, and K. Dobbelaere, *De versnelde ommekeer* (Tielt: Lannoo, 1992); F. Andres Orizo, *Los nuevos valores de los españoles* (Madrid, 1991).

9. P. M. Zulehner, "Ecclesiastical Atheism," *Journal of Empirical Theology* 1, no. 2 (1988): 5–20.

10. J. Maître et al., *Les Français sont-ils encore catholiques?* (Paris: Cerf, 1991).

11. C. Arends and G. Van Dartel, eds., *Katholieken in Oost-Europa. Opleving, getuigenis en engagement* (Kampen: Kok, 1989).

12. S. Abbruzzese, *Comunione e Liberazione. Identité catholique et disqualification du monde* (Paris: Cerf, 1989); "'Communion et libération' dans l'histoire du rapport église-monde en Italie," *Études* 374 (1991): 107–118.

13. K. Gabriel, "Die neuzeitliche Gesellschaftsentwicklung und der Katholizismus als Sozialform der Christentumsgeschichte," in K. Gabriel and F. X. Kaufmann, eds., *Zur Soziologie des Katholizismus* (Mainz: Grunewald, 1980): 201–225; F. X. Kaufmann, "Bewusstseins-Anpassung, Religiöse Indifferenz und Opportunismus," in F. X. Kaufmann, *Religion und Modernität. Sozialwissenschaftliche Perspektiven* (Tübingen: Mohr, 1989); see also the collective work edited by the Centre Thomas More, *Christianisme et Modernité* (Paris: Cerf, 1992).

14. A. Touraine, *La Crise de la Modernité* (Paris: Cerf, 1992).

15. F. Champion and D. Hervieu-Léger, *De l'émotion en religion. Renouveaux et traditions* (Paris: Le Centurion, 1990).

16. J. De Hart, "Impact of Religious Socialization in the Family," *Journal of Empirical Theology* 3, no. 1 (1990): 59–78; H. J. M. E. Vossen, "Family Religious Socialization: A View from Practical Theology," *Journal of Empirical Theology* 3, no. 1 (1990): 79–88.

17. R. L. Fetz and K. H. Reich, "World Views and Religious Development," *Journal of Empirical Theology* 2, no. 2 (1989): 46–61.

18. "Schulischer Religionsunterricht in einer säkularen Gesellschaft; Eine Erklärung des Zentralkomitees der deutschen Katholiken" (24–25 November 1989), *Herder Korrespondenz* 45 (1990): 31–36, 44.

19. F. X. Kaufmann, "Unbeabsichtigte Nebenfolgen kirchlicher Leitungsstrukturen. Vom Triumphalismus zur Tradierungskrise," in H. J. Pottmeyer et al., *Kirche im Kontext der modernen Gesellschaft* (Munich: Schnell und Steiner, 1989), 8–12.

20. U. Schneider, *Rollenkonflikte des Religionslehrers. Bedingungen ihrer Entstehung und Aspekte ihrer Bearbeitung* (Frankfurt, 1984); Y. Spiegel, "Beruf: Religionslehrer-Schwerpunkte der gegenwärtigen Diskussion," *Jahrbuch Religionspädagogik*, 1985; K. Kurten, *Der evangelische Religionslehrer im Spannungsfeld von Schule und Religion; Eine empirische Untersuchung* (Neukirchen: Neukirchener, 1987).

21. *Christifideles Laici*, Rome, 1988, nos. 3–6.

22. J. Ratzinger, *Die Krise der Katechese und ihre Überwindung* (Einsiedeln, 1983); cf. also U. Hemel, "Zur Katechetische Rede Kardinal Ratzingers in Frankreich," *Katechetische Blätter* 109 (1984): 35–42.

23. Kaufmann, "Unbeabsichtigte Nebenfolgen kirchlicher Leitungsstrukturen," 12.

24. F. X. Kaufmann and J. B. Metz, *Zukunftsfähigkeit. Suchbewegungen im Christentum* (Freiburg-Basel-Vienna: Herder, 1987), 37ff.

25. Kaufmann, "Unbeachtsichtigte Nebenfolgen kirchlicher Leitungsstrukturen," no. 19, 16ff; Kaufmann and Metz, *Zukunftsfähigkeit*, 37ff.

26. K. Gabriel underlines the ambiguous character of the term *secularization*. He favors a polarization, artificially introduced, capable of avoiding the confrontation with contemporary society: "Tradierungsprobleme einer 'bestimmten' Religion?" *Religionspädagogische Beiträge* 25 (1990): 20.

27. K. Gabriel, "Tradierungsprobleme einer 'bestimmten' Religion?" 22–23.

28. J. Delumeau, *La religion de ma mère* (Paris: Cerf, 1992).

29. Champion and Hervieu-Léger, eds., *De l'émotion en religion*, 243.

30. Ibid., 241–243.

31. Ibid., 244.

32. P. Valadier, *Inévitable morale* (Paris: Seuil, 1990), 20.

33. G. Lipovetsky, *Le crépuscule du devoir. L'éthique indolore des nouveaux temps démocratiques* (Paris: Gallimard, 1992).

34. See the analysis of the real functioning of the pastoral and catechetical infrastructure in a diocese, and of its probable efficacy, in N. Derksen, *Eigenlijk wisten we het wel, maar we waren het vergeten. Een onderzoek naar parochieontwikkeling en geloofscommunicatie in de parochies van het aartsbisdom Utrecht* (Kampen: Kok, 1989); M. F. M. Van Den Berk and R. G. Scholten, *De moeizame weg van beleren naar leren. Opzet van de Katechese in de parochies van de bisdommen Haarlem en Rotterdam* (Kampen: Kok, 1989).

35. Valadier, *Inévitable morale*, 24ff.

36. Kaufmann, "Unbeabsichtigte Nebenfolgen kirchlicher Leitungsstrukturen," 26–31.

37. Valadier, *Inévitable morale*, 34–35.

38. See the lucid analysis of J. Le Du, "L'économie des désirs et le désir, en économie," *Approches* 19 (1978): 53–91.

39. *L'Actualité Religieuse dans le monde*, 15 October 1988, 18–23.

40. F. Pajer, "L'insegnamento della religione in Europa all' inizio degli anni 90. Un Bilancio dell' esistente, un quadro dell' emergente," *L'insegnamento scolastico della religione nella nuova Europa* (Leumann [Turin]: Elle Di Ci, 1991): 425–463; F. Pajer, "Dieu au programme pour cent millions d'élèves," *Lumen Vitae* 47 (1992): 67–75; U. Hemel, "L'insegnamento religioso in Europa. Analisi del presente e speranze per il futuro," *Religione e scuola* 4 (1986): 162–169; U. Hemel, "Der Religionsunterricht im Europa von Morgen: Strukturen und Perspektiven," *Materialien für den Religionsunterricht an Gymnasien* 1 (1990): 81–88.

41. See, for example J. De Coulon, *Dieu à l'école. Les enjeux spirituels de l'éducation* (Lausanne: Faure, 1989).

42. G. Coq, "L'enseignement religieux à l'école?" *Esprit* 147 (1989): 45–49.

43. See the arguments presented by Maddy Noin Ledanois and by Danièle Hervieu-Léger in *La religion au lycée* (Paris: Cerf, 1990).

44. Coq, "L'enseignement religieux à l'école?" 48.

45. Ibid., 49.

46. Ibid. See also Poulat, *Liberté, laïcité*, 410.

47. *Creer en tiempos de increencia, Carta Pastoral de los obispos de Pamplona y Tudela* (Bilbao-San Sebastián-Vitoria: 1988).

48. See also P. Lamotte, *Guide pastoral de l'enseignement catholique* (Limoges: Droguet et Ardent, 1989), 181, 193, 240–241.

49. Charles Wackenheim, "Des religions aux idéologies: 'sécularisation' de l'intolérance," *Revue des sciences religieuses* 63 (1989): 117–135.

50. "Schulischer Religionsunterricht in einer säkularer Gesellschaft," 35–36.

51. M. Bellet, *Dire, ou la vérité improvisée* (Paris: Desclée de Brouwer, 1990), 53.

52. See Gabriel, "Die neuzeitliche Gesellschaftsentwicklung und der Katholizismus als Sozialform der Christentumsgeschichte."

53. M. Bellet, *Dire*, 122 and 21.

54. H. Lombaerts, "Texture culturelle et quête de vérité," *Lumen Vitae* 46 (1991): 261–275.

55. Bellet, *Dire*, 57. See also Poulat, *Liberté, laïcité*, 422.

56. Bellet, *Dire*, 122.

PART G
Ecclesial Documents

PART G. Ecclesial Documents

READING 19
Introduction

The title of the following document might cause it to be overlooked by catechetical leaders focused on the diocesan and parish levels. To do so would be a mistake. These guidelines merit close study for the way they tie "doctrine in catechetical materials" to the specific circumstances of catechesis. Worked out by a task force of the National Conference of Catholic Bishops headed by Bishop John Leibrecht of Springfield–Cape Girardeau, Missouri, the guidelines intend to offer catechetical wisdom to "theologians, biblical scholars, specialists in pastoral liturgy, professional educators, and catechetical experts," in preparing materials for various catechetical uses. They also have value for a much wider audience.

The wisdom of these directives comes from their familiarity with the principles of the key Roman Catholic catechetical documents since Vatican Council II. Readers may, for example, notice how these guidelines anticipate the kind of guidance offered by the *Catechism of the Catholic Church.* Written five years earlier, they spell out in greater detail the broad direction given by Cardinal Ratzinger and John Paul II in part E.

One of the first principles the guidelines offer is that church teaching should be clear and presented in a manner readily understood: "Language and images must be adapted to the capacity of the learners in accord with their age level and cultural background." Situating catechesis within the mission of the church and as a significant concern of the bishops, the guidelines (quoting *Catechesi Tradendae*) define it broadly as all "the efforts within the church to make disciples." Thus from beginning to end, this document highlights the communal dimension of all aspects of catechesis. Readers will prize the useful thumbnail sketches of the core of modern catechetics, especially their emphasis on practice, found in the brief sections on the dimensions of catechesis and on the principles and criteria for catechetical materials. Indeed, the set of guidelines for catechetical presentations in the final section offers a potential outline of several catechist training sessions.

READING 19

Guidelines on Doctrine
for Catechetical Materials

(UNITED STATES) NATIONAL CONFERENCE
OF CATHOLIC BISHOPS

*Guidelines for doctrinally sound catechetical materials were approved
by the U.S. bishops 14 November during their fall meeting in Washington. The guidelines, covering doctrinal content as well as its presentation, are "intended to present church teachings in a positive and
meaningful way" for authors, editors, and publishers. The guidelines
were developed by a task force headed by Bishop John Leibrecht of
Springfield–Cape Girardeau, Missouri. The first principle of doctrinal soundness "is that the Christian message be both authentic and
complete"; the second principle calls for "recognition that the mystery
of faith is incarnate and dynamic," the bishops state. Flowing from
those two principles are several criteria "that describe doctrinally
sound catechetical materials," the bishops state. According to one criterion, "catechesis reflects the progressive, step-by-step initiation of
the believer into the church community and the lifelong conversion
that is required of individuals and communities if they are to mature
in faith." Thus, "catechetical materials should relate to the age, ability, and experience of those being catechized," with the principal form
of catechesis being for adults. But, "catechesis for children and other
age groups is always necessary." The proper expression of faith "highlights the centrality of fundamental doctrines of the Christian tradition," and it "recognizes that Christian faith needs to be incarnated in
all cultures." Furthermore, the bishops say, "the fruit of effective catechesis is unity." The guidelines follow.*

Reprinted from *Origins* 20, no. 27 (13 December 1990): 429, 431–436. Copyright © 1990 by
the National Conference of Catholic Bishops.
    Note: The final title of the guidelines as published by the United States Catholic Con-
ference, 21 November 1990, is *Guidelines for Doctrinally Sound Catechetical Materials*.

Preface

As shepherds of the people of God and by reason of their unique teaching office, bishops have the responsibility of preserving the deposit of faith and ensuring that it is passed on so that the faith of individuals and the community becomes "living, conscious and active, through the light of instruction" (*Christus Dominus*, 14). According to the Decree on the Bishops' Pastoral Office in the Church of Vatican II, this responsibility implies the use of publications and "various other media of communication" that are helpful in proclaiming the Gospel of Christ (*Christus Dominus*, 13).

From time to time the National Conference of Catholic Bishops issues pastoral letters and statements on specific issues of national concern, but it is individual bishops who must provide guidance and oversee catechetical programs and materials in their dioceses. Diocesan bishops, acting alone, are not in a position, however, to influence publishers outside their jurisdiction. And for their part, publishers have on occasion asked for national norms and standard criteria that can help them in presenting the church's doctrine on faith and morals while taking into account "the natural disposition, ability, age and circumstances of life" of their audiences (*Christus Dominus*, 14).

Accordingly, the NCCB/U.S. Catholic Conference adopted as one of its objectives for the years 1988–1990, "to support the catechetical ministry of the church in the United States by developing policy guidelines for the creation of doctrinally sound textbooks and by providing for their implementation."

The Division of Catechesis/Religious Education of the USCC's Department of Education was given the assignment to implement this objective. The plan of action called for the formation of a task force chaired by Bishop John Leibrecht of Springfield-Cape Girardeau. The task force included as members Bishop Donald Wuerl of Pittsburgh and Bishop Robert Banks of Green Bay, Wisconsin. The 18 members who made up the task force brought varied professional and personal experiences to the work and were generally representative of the geographic, cultural and social profile of the church in the United States.

The task force met between June 1988 and May 1990. Evolving through several drafts, the guidelines benefited from consultations with publishers of catechetical materials, members of the NCCB Committee on Doctrine and the NCCB Committee on Liturgy. The task force submitted its work to the USCC Committee on Education, which after amending it presented it for adoption to the full body of bishops. The bishops, after making several recommendations to improve the text, approved the document at their meeting of 14 November 1990.

Introduction

Since the Second Vatican Council the church has experienced a remarkable renewal in catechesis. This renewal has been encouraged and guided by the *General Catechetical Directory* (1971), the third and the fourth general assemblies of the Synod of Bishops (1974, 1977), Pope Paul VI's apostolic exhortation "Evangelization in the Modern World" (1975), Pope John Paul II's "Catechesis in Our Time" (1979) and in the United States by the *National Catechetical Directory, Sharing the Light of Faith* (1979). In 1985 the extraordinary assembly of the Synod of Bishops proposed a Catechism for the Universal Church that will offer a presentation of doctrine, inspired by Scripture and the liturgy, and "suited to the present life of Christians" (II, B, 4).

In recent years the ongoing effort toward renewal of catechesis in the United States has been nowhere more evident than in the area of religion textbooks and catechetical materials. Each year many new materials for children, youth and adults appear on the market. Publishing companies, with admirable dedication and zeal, make significant investments in researching, testing, editing and marketing catechetical tools. They employ writers and editors with the finest credentials, and they seek the guidance of theologians, biblical scholars, specialists in pastoral liturgy, professional educators and catechetical experts. Most of these materials advance and enrich the church's catechetical mission, but their diversity and quantity present a new challenge. The faithful expect the bishops, and we recognize it as our responsibility, to assure them that these materials express the teaching of the church as faithfully as possible.

> The act of faith has two aspects that by their nature are inseparable: Faith includes both the firm adherence given by a person . . . and "the content of revelation."

The traditional way for bishops to exercise supervision in this ecclesial process is through the granting of an imprimatur to catechetical works. The 1983 Code of Canon Law directs that "catechisms and other writings dealing with catechetical formation or their translations need the approval of the local ordinary for their publication" (Canon 827.1). The code further states that it "is the responsibility of the diocesan bishop to issue norms concerning catechetics and to make provision that suitable instruments for catechesis are available" (Canon 775.I). It is with this latter directive in mind that the National Conference of Catholic Bishops, with due regard for the responsibility and prerogatives of the local ordinary, responding to the desire of publishers for guidance and concerns of the faithful, outlines a number of principles and offers a series of guidelines.

These guidelines are intended to provide direction to the publishers, particularly in the area of Catholic doctrine regarding both faith and morals. Based on the major catechetical documents of the church and the teachings of Vatican II, they highlight essential components of the documents which relate to doctrinal soundness in catechetical materials. Doctrinal soundness implies, first of all, a complete and correct presentation of church teaching with proper attention to its organic unity. In the context of catechesis, doctrinal soundness also requires that church teaching be presented clearly and in a manner that can be readily understood. Language and images must be adapted to the capacity of the learners in accord with their age level and cultural background.

Catechesis is a pastoral ministry "which leads both communities and individual members of the faithful to maturity of faith" (*General Catechetical Directory*, 21). Pope John Paul II reminds us that early in the church's history "the name catechesis was given to the whole of the efforts within the church to make disciples, to help people believe that Jesus is the Son of God, so that believing they might have life in his name, and to educate and instruct them in this life and thus build up the body of Christ" (*Catechesi Tradendae*, 1). Thus it is part of the mission of the church and a significant concern of the bishops that catechesis be provided for all members of the Catholic community.

The faith that the church seeks to strengthen is the free acceptance of the mystery of God and the divine plan of salvation offered in revelation to all peoples. The act of faith has two aspects that by their nature are inseparable: Faith includes both the firm adherence given by a person "under the influence of grace to God revealing himself (the faith by which one believes)," and "the content of revelation and of the Christian message (the faith which one believes)" (*GCD*, 36). This latter aspect has a communal dimension insofar as it is handed on by the church and shared by the Catholic faithful. These guidelines pertain chiefly to the Christian message as it is dealt with in catechetical materials.

Catechetical Materials

Catechetical materials are intended as effective instruments for teaching the fullness of the Christian message found in the word of God and the teachings of the church. They include many kinds of resources: printed and audiovisual materials, textbooks and programs that utilize such learning strategies as role playing, crafts and other supportive educational activities. They are prepared for groups and persons of diverse interests, needs, ages and abilities. Although the *National Catechetical Directory* recognizes that catechists are more important than their tools, it acknowledges that "good tools in the hands of skilled catechists can do much to foster growth in faith" (*NCD*, 249).

Dimensions of Catechesis

Catechesis nurtures the faith of individuals and communities by integrating four fundamental tasks, namely, proclaiming Christ's message, participating in efforts to develop community, leading people to worship and prayer, and motivating them to Christian living and service (*NCD*, 213). Catechetical materials aid this process.

First, catechesis, a form of ministry of the word, supposes that the hearer has embraced the Christian message as a salvific reality. It is the purpose of catechesis and, by extension, of catechetical materials to motivate the faithful to respond to the message in an informed way both personally and in community. Catechesis takes place within the church, and catechetical materials reflect the beliefs, values and practices of the Christian community.

Second, catechetical materials develop community by keeping traditions alive and recommending activities that build up the church, making it a community of believers striving to be "of one heart and one mind" (Acts 4:32).

Third, the church, from its earliest days, has recognized that liturgy and catechesis are supportive of one another. Catechetical materials can be expected, therefore, to explain how liturgical celebrations deepen the community's knowledge of the faith, and to "promote an active, conscious, genuine participation in the liturgy of the church" (*NCD*, 36). Sound catechetical materials provide examples of ways that the Christian community prays together, with particular emphasis on forms of devotional prayer inspired by and directed toward the liturgy itself (*Sacrosanctum Concilium*, 13).

Fourth, in calling upon Christians to serve others, catechetical materials should clearly explain the church's moral teaching. They should emphasize the twofold responsibility of individuals and communities to strive for holiness and to witness to Christian values. This includes respect for life, service to others and working to bring about peace and justice in society (*NCD*, 38).

In short, catechetical materials should present the story of salvation and the church's beliefs according to the principles of doctrinally sound catechesis that we describe below.

Principles and Criteria
of Doctrinally Sound Catechetical Materials

The first principle of doctrinal soundness is that the Christian message be both *authentic* and *complete*. For expressions of faith and moral teachings to be authentic they must be in harmony with the doctrine and traditions of the Catholic Church, which are safeguarded by the bishops, who teach with a unique authority. For completeness, the message of salvation, made up of several parts that are closely interrelated, must, in due course, be presented in its entirety, with an eye to leading individuals and communities to maturity of faith. Completeness also implies that individual parts be presented in a balanced way according to the capacity of the learners and in the context of a particular doctrine.

The second principle in determining the doctrinal soundness of catechetical materials is the recognition that the mystery of faith is *incarnate* and *dynamic*. The mystery of the divine plan for human salvation, revealed in the person of Jesus Christ and made known in the Sacred Scriptures, continues as a dynamic force in the world through the power of the Holy Spirit until finally all things are made subject to Christ and the kingdom is handed over to the Father "so that God may be all in all" (1 Cor. 15:29). God's creative power is mediated in the concrete experiences of life, in personal development, in human relationships, in culture, social life, science, technology and "signs of the times." The *National Catechetical Directory* refers to the Scriptures, the teaching, life and witness of the church, the church's liturgical life and life experiences of various kinds as "signs of God's saving activity" in the world (*NCD*, 42). These biblical, ecclesial, liturgical and natural signs should inform the content and spirit of all catechetical materials.

From these two basic principles flow several criteria that describe doctrinally sound catechetical materials.

First, a holistic approach to catechesis reflects the progressive, step-by-step initiation of the believer into the church community, and the lifelong conversion that is required of individuals and communities if they are to mature in faith. Catechetical materials should relate to the age, ability and experience of those being catechized. The principal form of catechesis is catechesis of adults, for adults are those "who have the greatest responsibilities and the capacity to live the Christian message in its fully developed form" (*Catechesi Tradendae*, 43). Catechesis for children and other age groups is always necessary and should in some way lay the foundation for adult catechesis (*GCD*, 20; *NCD*, 32).

Second, proper expression of our faith highlights the centrality of fundamental doctrines of the Christian tradition. Both the general and national catechetical directories offer valuable guidance in this regard, as will a Catechism for the Universal Church. The Trinitarian structure of the Apostles' Creed and the Nicene Creed is an example that offers helpful guidance in ordering the hierarchy of truths. In presenting the Christian message, catechetical materials take into account the developmental nature of the learner and the particular circumstances of the local church community, but they cannot be selective as to content and emphasis in ways that compromise the authentic and complete teaching of the church (*GCD*, 46; *NCD*, 47).

Third, authentic catechesis recognizes that Christian faith needs to be incarnated in all cultures; accordingly it is expressed in diverse ways that witness to the catholicity of the church without endangering its unity. Pope John Paul II has stated: "The Gospel of Christ is at home in every people. It enriches, uplifts and purifies every culture" (meeting with Native Americans, 14 September 1987). Catechetical materials not only alert the faithful to the full meaning of catholicity and the cultural dimensions of the Christian faith experience, but they also facilitate the assimilation of the Gospel message, using language, customs and symbols familiar to those being taught.

Fourth, the fruit of effective catechesis is unity "among all who hold and teach the Catholic faith that comes to us from the apostles" (Eucharistic Prayer 1). The common faith is shared and celebrated most perfectly in the Eucharist. Biblical, creedal and prayer formulas are also essential to the unity of the faith community. "There is one Lord, one faith, one baptism; one God and Father of all, who is over all, and works through all, and is in all" (Eph. 4:5). For believers to share their faith they must have common experiences and a shared language in which to express and celebrate it. Some common expression of faith is essential to the unity of the believing community. Without a shared language, the faithful cannot profess and celebrate their faith in communion with one another. Catechetical materials, taken as a whole, need to promote a healthy and vital Catholic identity in such a way that the believer hears the message clearly, lives it with conviction and shares it courageously with others.

In the document "Basic Teachings for Catholic Religious Education," the bishops of the United States expressed a desire for an informed laity, people of faith who know their religion and can give an account of it.[1] But now as then, this means a church transformed by the Gospel message, for Christians who bring the Gospel into their daily lives, for faithful men and women whose zeal for peace and justice, joy and simplicity, witnesses to Christ's continuing presence in the world while we await his return in glory when every tear will be wiped away and death will be no more. It is our hope that these guidelines for doctrinally sound catechetical materials will contribute to these goals.

> Catechesis nurtures the faith of individuals and communities by integrating four fundamental tasks, namely, proclaiming Christ's message, participating in efforts to develop community, leading people to worship and prayer, and motivating them to Christian living and service.

I. Guidelines for Doctrinally Sound Catechetical Materials

The following guidelines are based on major catechetical documents of the church, the constitutions, decrees and declarations of Vatican II, recent papal encyclicals and apostolic exhortations, and the pastoral letters of the U.S. bishops. The guidelines, even taken as a whole, are not a synthesis of the Gospel message nor an exhaustive list of Catholic beliefs. They are not intended to supplant, and in fact should be studied in conjunction with, the outline of the principal elements of the Christian message presented in the *National Catechetical Directory* (Chapter 5) and any exposition of doctrine found in a future Catechism for the Universal Church. The guidelines differ from the *National Catechetical Directory* and our earlier document "Basic Teachings for Catholic Religious Education" in two ways: First, they incorporate teachings and principles stated in recent papal encyclicals and in pastoral letters issued by the National Conference of Catholic Bishops; and second, they single out certain doctrines that seem to need particular emphasis in the life and culture of the United States at this time. The guidelines take into account a hierarchy of truths of faith insofar as they give priority to the foundational mysteries in the creed, but they do not prescribe a particular order in which the truths are to be presented (*GCD*, 46). The guidelines are intended to present church teachings in a positive and meaningful way so that authors, editors and publishers of catechelical materials can better assist the faithful to integrate the truth of Catholic doctrine and moral teachings into their lives.

General Doctrinal Content

Doctrinally sound catechetical materials:

1. Help the baptized, as members of the church founded by Christ, appreciate Catholic tradition, grounded in the Scriptures and celebrated in the divine liturgy, in such a personal way that it becomes part of their very identity.

2. Present the teaching of the church in a full and balanced way that includes everything necessary for an accurate understanding of a particular doctrine and express it in a manner appropriate to the audience and purpose of a given catechetical text.

3. Situate the teachings of the church in the context of God's saving plan and relate them to one another so that they can be seen as parts of an organic whole and not simply as isolated and fragmented truths (*GCD*, 39).

4. Describe the many ways that God has spoken and continues to speak in the lives of human beings and how the fullness of revelation is made known in Christ (Heb. 1:1–2; *Catechesi Tradendae*, 20, 52).

5. Explain the inspired Scriptures according to the mind of the church while not neglecting the contributions of modern biblical scholarship in the use of various methods of interpretation, including historical-critical and literary methods (1964 instruction of the biblical commission).

6. Are sensitive to distinctions between faith and theology, church doctrine and theological opinion, acknowledging that the same revealed truth can be explained in different ways. However, every explanation must be compatible with Catholic tradition (*NCD*, 16).

7. Reflect the wisdom and continuing relevance of the church fathers, and incorporate a sense of history that recognizes doctrinal development and provides background for understanding change in church policy and practice.

8. Explain the documents of the Second Vatican Council as an authoritative and valid expression of the deposit of faith as contained in Holy Scripture and the living tradition of the church (1985 extraordinary synod, the Final Report, 2).

9. Present the uniqueness and pre-eminence of the Christian message without rejecting anything that is true and holy in non-Christian religions, show a high regard for all religions that witness to the mystery of divine presence, the dignity of human beings and high moral standards (*Nostra Aetate*, 2).

Father, Son, and Holy Spirit

Doctrinally sound catechetical materials:

10. Are Trinitarian and Christocentric in scope and spirit, clearly presenting the mystery of creation, redemption, and sanctification in God's plan of salvation (*NCD*, 47).

11. Help Christians contemplate with eyes of faith the communal life of the Holy Trinity and know that through grace we share in God's divine nature (*GCD*, 47).

12. Arouse a sense of wonder and praise for God's world and providence by presenting creation, not as an abstract principle or as an event standing by itself, but as the origin of all things and the beginning of the mystery of salvation in Jesus Christ (*GCD*, 51; *NCD*, 85).

> Catechetical materials . . . need to promote a healthy and vital Catholic identity in such a way that the believer hears the message clearly, lives it with conviction and shares it courageously with others.

13. Focus on the heart of the Christian message: salvation from sin and death through the person and work of Jesus, with special emphasis on the paschal mystery—his passion, death, and resurrection.

14. Emphasize the work and person of Jesus Christ as the key and chief point of Christian reference in reading the Scriptures ("The Jews and Judaism in Preaching and Catechesis" [1985], II, 5, 6).

15. Present Jesus as true God, who came into the world for us and for our salvation, and as true man who thinks with a human mind, acts with a human will, loves with a human heart (*NCD*, 89), highlighting the uniqueness of his divine mission so that he appears as more than a great prophet and moral teacher.

16. Describe how the Holy Spirit continues Christ's work in the world, the church and in the lives of believers (*NCD*, 92).

17. Maintain the traditional language, grounded in the Scriptures, that speaks of the Holy Trinity as Father, Son, and Spirit, and apply, where appropriate, the principles of inclusive language approved by the NCCB. (See "Criteria for Implementation of Inclusive Language Translations of Scriptural Texts Proposed for Liturgical Usage.")

Church

Doctrinally sound catechetical materials:

18. Recognize that the church, a community of believers, is a mystery, a sign of the kingdom, a community of divine origin, that cannot be totally understood or fully defined in human terms (*NCD*, 63).

19. Teach that the church's unique relationship with Christ makes it both sign and instrument of God's union with humanity, the means for the forgiveness of sin as well as a means of unity for human beings among themselves (*NCD*, 63).

20. Emphasize the missionary nature of the church and the call of individual Christians to proclaim the Gospel wherever there are people to be evangelized, at home and abroad (*NCD*, 71; 74e).

21. Nourish and teach the faith and, because there is often a need for initial evangelization, aim at opening the heart and arousing the beginning of faith so that individuals will respond to the word of God and Jesus' call to discipleship (*Catechesi Tradendae*, 19).

22. Emphasize that Jesus Christ gave the apostles a special mission to teach and that today this teaching authority is exercised by the pope and bishops, who are successors of Peter and the apostles.

23. Highlight the history and distinctive tradition of the church of Rome and the special charism of the pope as successor of St. Peter in guiding and teaching the universal church and assuring the authentic teaching of the Gospel.

24. Explain what it means when the church professes to be "one, holy, Catholic and apostolic" (*NCD*, 72, 74i, ii).

25. Show how the church of Christ is manifest at the local level in the diocesan church and the parish, gathered in the Holy Spirit through the Gospel and the Eucharist (*Christus Dominus*, 11; *Lumen Gentium*, 26).

26. Present the church as a community with a legitimate diversity in expressing its shared faith according to different ages, cultures, gifts, and abilities.

27. Foster understanding and unity by accurately presenting the traditions and practices of the Catholic churches of the East (*NCD*, 73, 74g).

28. Are sensitive in dealing with other Christian churches and ecclesial communities, taking into account how they differ from the Catholic tradition while at the same time showing how much is held in common (*NCD*, 76).

29. Foster ecumenism as a means toward unity and communion among all Christians, and recognize that division in the church and among Christians is contrary to the will of Christ (*Unitatis Redintegratio*, 1).

30. Integrate the history of the Jews in the work of salvation so that, on the one hand, Judaism does not appear marginal and unimportant and, on the other hand, the church and Judaism do not appear as parallel ways of salvation ("The Jews and Judaism," 1985, 1, 7).

31. Explain the pastoral role and authority of the Magisterium—the bishops united with the pope—in defining and teaching religious truth.

32. Emphasize that individuals reach their full potential and work out their salvation only in community—the human community and the community which is the church ("Economic Justice for All," 63, 65 and passim).

33. Support the family as the basic unit of society and underline its role as "domestic church" in living the Gospel (*Familiaris Consortio*, 12).

Mary and the Saints

Doctrinally sound catechetical materials:

34. Explain the sacramental meaning of "communion of saints," linking it to the Eucharist, which bringing the faithful together to share the "holy gifts" is the primary source and sign of church unity.

35. Explain the biblical basis for the liturgical cult of Mary as mother of God and disciple par excellence; and describe her singular role in the life of Christ and the story of salvation (*Lumen Gentium*, 66, 67).

36. Foster Marian devotions and explain the church's particular beliefs about Mary (for example, the immaculate conception, virgin birth, and assumption) (*GCD*, 68; *NCD*, 106).

37. Explain the church's teaching on angels and its veneration of saints who intercede for us and are role models in following Christ (*GCD*, 68).

Liturgy and Sacraments

Doctrinally sound catechetical materials:

38. Present the sacraments as constitutive of Christian life and worship, as unique ways of meeting Christ and not simply as channels of grace.

39. Emphasize God's saving and transforming presence in the sacraments. In the Eucharist Christ is present not only in the person of the priest, but in the assembly and in the word, and uniquely in the eucharistic species of bread and wine which become the body and blood of Christ (*Sacrosanctum Concilium*, 7).

40. Link the Eucharist to Christ's sacrifice on the cross, explaining it as a sacrament of his presence in the church and as a meal of communal solidarity that is a sign of the heavenly banquet to which the faithful are called (*Sacrosanctum Concilium*, 7, 47; *Gaudium et Spes*, 38).

41. Call attention to the special significance of Sunday as the day of the Lord's resurrection, emphasizing active participation in Sunday Mass as an expression of community prayer and spiritual renewal.

42. Explain the liturgical year, with special attention to the seasons of Advent-Christmas, Lent-Easter (*NCD*, 144c).

43. Promote active participation in the liturgy of the church, not only by explaining the rites and symbols, but also by fostering a spirit of praise, thanksgiving and repentance, and nurturing a sense of community and reverence (*NCD*, 36).

44. Explain the Catholic heritage of popular devotions and sacramentals so that they can serve as a means "to help people advance toward knowledge of the mystery of Christ and his message" (*Catechesi Tradendae*, 54).

45. Embody the norms and guidelines for liturgy and sacramental practice found in the praenotanda of the revised rites, with special attention to those that preface the sacraments of initiation.

46. Assist pastors, parents and catechists to inaugurate children into the sacraments of penance and Eucharist by providing for their proper initial preparation according to Catholic pastoral practice as presented by the Magisterium.

47. Promote lifelong conversion and an understanding of the need for reconciliation that leads to a renewed appreciation of the sacrament of penance.

48. Establish the foundations for vocational choices—to the married life, the single life, priesthood, diaconate and to the vowed life of poverty, chastity, and obedience—in the framework of one's baptismal commitment and the call to serve.

49. Respect the essential difference between the ministerial priesthood and the common priesthood, between the ministries conferred by the sacrament of orders and the call to service derived from the sacraments of baptism and confirmation (*Christifideles Laici*, 22, 23).

50. Foster vocations to the priesthood and religious life in appropriate ways at every age level.

Life of Grace and the Moral Life

Doctrinally sound catechetical materials:

51. Teach that from the beginning God called human beings to holiness, but from the very dawn of history humans abused their freedom and set themselves against God so that "sin entered the world" (Rom. 5:12), and that this "original sin" is transmitted to every human being (*Gaudium et Spes*, 13).

52. Introduce prayer as a way of deepening one's relationship with God and explain the ends of prayer so that a spirit of adoration, thanksgiving, petition, and contrition permeates the daily lives of Christians (*NCD*, 140).

53. Promote the continual formation of right Catholic conscience based on Christ's role in one's life, his ideals, precepts and examples

found in Scripture and the magisterial teaching of the church (*NCD*, 190).

54. Cultivate the moral life of Christians by inculcating virtue and nurture a sense of responsibility that goes beyond external observance of laws and precepts.

55. Discuss the reality and effects of personal sins, whereby an individual, acting knowingly and deliberately, violates the moral law, harms one's self, one's neighbor, and offends God (*GCD*, 62).

56. Make it clear that the dignity of the human person and sanctity of life are grounded in one's relation to the triune God, and that individuals are valued not because of their status in society, their productivity, or as consumers, but in themselves as beings made in God's image ("Economic Justice for All," 28, 48).

57. Go beyond economic and political concerns in describing ecological and environmental issues, and define human accountability for the created universe in moral and spiritual terms (*Sollicitudo Rei Socialis*, 38).

58. Present a consistent ethic of life that, fostering respect for individual dignity and personal rights, highlights the rights of the unborn, the aged, and those with disabilities, and explains the evils of abortion and euthanasia.

59. Explain the specifics of Christian morality, as taught by the Magisterium of the church, in the framework of the universal call to holiness and discipleship, the Ten Commandments, the Sermon on the Mount, especially the Beatitudes, and Christ's discourse at the Last Supper (*NCD*, 105).

60. Include the responsibilities of Catholic living traditionally expressed in the precepts of the church.

61. Present Catholic teaching on justice, peace, mercy, and social issues as integral to the Gospel message and the church's prophetic mission (*NCD*, 170).

62. Explain that the church's teaching on the "option for the poor" means that while Christians are called to respond to the needs of everyone, they must give their greatest attention to individuals and communities with greatest needs ("Economic Justice for All," 86–87).

63. State the church's position on moral and social issues of urgent concern in contemporary society, for example, the developing role of women in the church and society, racism, and other forms of discrimination.

64. Present human sexuality in positive terms of life, love, and self-discipline, explain the responsibilities of a chaste Christian life and teach that love between husband and wife must be exclusive and open to new life (*Familiaris Consortio*, 29).

65. Link personal morality to social issues and professional ethics, and challenge the faithful to make responsible moral decisions guided by the church's teaching (*NCD*, 38, 170).

66. Teach that all legitimate authority comes from God and that governments exist to serve the people, to protect human rights and secure basic justice for all members of society ("Economic Justice for All," 122).

67. Teach that though sin abounds in the world, grace is even more abundant because of the salvific work of Christ (*NCD*, 98).

Death, Judgment, and Eternity

Doctrinally sound catechetical materials:

68. Explain the coming of Christ "in glory" in the context of the church's overall teaching on eschatology and final judgment (*NCD*, 110).

69. Teach, on the subject of the last things, that everyone has an awesome responsibility for his or her eternal destiny, and present, in the light of Christian hope, death, judgment, purgatory, heaven or hell (*NCD*, 109; *GCD*, 69).

II. Guidelines for Presenting Sound Doctrine

A second set of guidelines, no less important than the first if catechesis is to be effective, is based on pastoral principles and practical concerns. They are reminders that catechetical materials must take into account the community for whom they are intended, the conditions in which they live and the ways in which they learn (*GCD*, foreword). Publishers are encouraged to provide catechetical materials that take into consideration the needs of Hispanic communities and other ethnic and culturally diverse groups that make up the church in the United States. No single text or program can address the many cultures and social groups that make up society in the United States, but all catechetical materials must take this diversity into account. Effective catechesis, as we have noted above, requires that the church's teaching be presented correctly and in its entirety, and it is equally important to present it in ways that are attractive, appealing, and understandable by the individuals and communities to whom it is directed.

To present sound doctrine *effectively* catechetical materials:

70. Take into account the experience and background of those being catechized, and suggest ways that the Christian message illumines their life (*NCD*, 176e).

71. Must be based on accepted learning theory, established pedagogical principles and practical learning strategies (*NCD*, 175).

72. Use language and images appropriate to the age level and developmental stages and special needs of those being catechized (*NCD*, 177–188).

73. Integrate biblical themes and Scriptural references in the presentation of doctrine and moral teaching, and encourage a hands-on familiarity with the Bible (*NCD*, 60a).

74. Challenge Catholics to critique and transform contemporary values and behaviors in light of the Gospel and the church's teaching.

75. Maintain a judicious balance between personal expression and memorization, emphasizing that it is important both for the community and themselves that individuals commit to memory selected biblical passages, essential prayers, liturgical responses, key doctrinal ideas, and lists of moral responsibilities (*Catechesi Tradendae*, 55; *NCD*, 176e).

Catechetical materials must take into account the community for whom they are intended, the conditions in which they live and the ways in which they learn. Publishers are encouraged to provide catechetical materials that take into consideration the needs of Hispanic communities and other ethnic and culturally diverse groups.

76. Provide for a variety of shared prayer forms and experiences that lead to an active participation in the liturgical life of the church and private prayer (*NCD*, 145, 264).

77. Continually hold before their intended audience the ideal of living a life based on the teachings of the Gospel.

78. Include suggestions for service to the community that is appropriate to the age and abilities of the persons who are being catechized.

79. Stress the importance of the local church community for Christian living so that every Catholic contributes to building up the spirit of the parish family and sees its ministries as part of the church's universal mission.

80. Are sensitive to the appropriate use of inclusive language in the text and avoid racial, ethnic, and gender stereotypes in pictures (*NCD*, 264).

81. Reflect the catholicity of the church in art and graphics by presenting the diverse customs and religious practices of racial, ethnic, cultural, and family groups (*NCD*, 194, 264).

82. Assist catechists by including easy-to-understand instructions regarding scope, sequence, and use of texts.

83. Suggest a variety of strategies, activities, and auxiliary resources that can enrich instruction, deepen understanding, and facilitate the integration of doctrine and life.

84. Include material that can be used in the home to aid parents in communicating church teaching and nurturing the faith life of the family.

85. Instruct teachers and catechists on how to respond to the needs of persons with disabilities and individuals with special needs (*NCD*, 195, 196, 264).

86. Help teachers and catechists distinguish between church doctrine and the opinions and interpretations of theologians (*NCD*, 264).

87. Help develop the catechists' own faith life, experience of prayer and mature commitment to the church, and motivate them toward ongoing enrichment in catechist formation.

NOTE

1. United States Catholic Conference, "Basic Teachings for Catholic Religious Education" (Washington, DC: United States Catholic Conference, 1972), 2–3.

READING 20
Introduction

Some will be surprised to find in a catechetical sourcebook documents not dealing directly with catechesis. They find their place here because each, in a somewhat different way, deals with the twin questions of influence and communications.

If catechesis is a lifelong ecclesial strategy to draw members of the ecclesia ever deeper into the faithful living out of Jesus' Way, then it can be seen as a task of influencing, that is, of using the influence of the Gospel to direct people's lives. Using the category of influence can help us see the real difficulties encountered by catechesis in a time of electronic communications. Which zone of life has greater influence over people who call themselves Christians? Is it the imagination of what it means to be a human being proposed by Jesus, whom we name the Christ, or the myriad imaginations of what life is about offered us incessantly via film, TV, advertising in its electronic or print forms, and music? If the answer is both, one would then have to ask which influence is dominant in any particular human imagination. I am not suggesting that all electronically communicated imaginations are evil. Most readers will recognize that some secular narratives raise deeper questions about humanity than some religious statements, homilies, or rituals. My rhetorical either-or dichotomy is an attempt to name the religious dilemma today as, at least in part, the dilemma of how the world is imagined for us and how that imagination is communicated to us. This dilemma names what I consider the core catechetical problem of our time.

The first of the statements in this reading is an eloquent exhortation by John Paul II to those working with electronically communicated messages to consider their responsibility to children. Children notice behavior, follow carefully each gesture, and perceive quickly the sentiments being communicated. Whether on the small screen or large, these depictions "penetrate most deeply into the psychology of the human being and . . . condition, often in a lasting way, the successive relationship with [self], others and with . . . [the] environment."

John Paul II notes the common responsibility of "the parents, the educators, [and] the communications workers" to take seriously their duty to help children in their development toward maturity. In pointing out the dangers to the spirit of the children, he uses a telling word, to "poison," with its implicit metaphor of polluting the chain of human signification. Though his exhortation is to those in the communications media, catechists themselves may want to respond to his challenge by giving more systematic attention to what children watch and by helping parents ponder the influence of electronic communications on their children.

Further Reading

Auletta, Ken. "Annals of Communication: What Won't They Do?" *New Yorker* (17 May 1993): 45–53.

Bagdikian, Ben H. "The Lords of the Global Village." *Nation* (12 June 1989): 805–820.

Bogart, Leo. "The American Media System and Its Commercial Culture." Gannett Foundation Media Center, Fordham University, Bronx, NY, Occasional paper 8, March 1991.

Children and the Media

POPE JOHN PAUL II

With the same sentiments of sincere trust and living hope which have marked my pastoral service in the chair of Peter from its beginning, I turn to you, especially to those among you who are engaged in social communications, on the day which is consecrated to this important subject by the wish of the Second Vatican Council (cfr. Decree *Inter Mirifica*, 18).

The theme for which I wish to claim your attention contains, in fact, an implicit invitation to trust and hope because it deals with childhood, and I discuss it all the more willingly because it was already selected by my beloved predecessor Paul VI. It is opportune to reflect, in this year declared by the United Nations organization the "Year of the Child," on the particular needs of this vast band of "receivers"—the children—and on the consequent responsibilities of the adults, particularly those who work in communications and who can and do exercise such great influence on the formation—or unfortunately the malformation—of the young generations. Here is contained the seriousness and the complexity of the subject: "Social Communications; Protecting the Child and Promoting His Best Interests in the Family and in Society."

Without making any pretense of examining the subject, or much less, of exhausting the various aspects of it, I wish simply to recall briefly what children have a right to expect and to obtain from the communications media. Enchanted by the instruments of social communication and defenseless against the world and adult persons, they are naturally ready to accept whatever is offered to them, whether good or bad. You, communications professionals, and particularly those of you who work with the audiovisual media, are well aware of this. They are attracted by the "small screen" and by the "large screen"; they follow every gesture represented on them, and they perceive, quicker and better than anyone else, the emotions and sentiments which result.

Reprinted from *Origins* 9, no. 3 (7 June 1979): 45–47. Copyright © 1979 by the Catholic News Service.

Like soft wax on which every tiniest pressure leaves a mark, so the child is responsive to every stimulus that plays upon his imagination, his emotions, his instincts, and his ideas. Yet the impressions received at this age are the ones which are destined to penetrate most deeply into the psychology of the human being and to condition, often in a lasting way, the successive relationship with himself, with others, and with his environment. It was precisely out of an intuition regarding the extreme delicacy of this phase of life that pagan wisdom enunciated the well-known pedagogical guidelines which direct that *"maxima debetur puero reverentia"*; and it is in this same light that we must regard Christ's warning, with its reasoned severity: "Whoever causes one of these little ones who believe in me to sin, it would be better for him to have a great millstone fastened round his neck and to be drowned in the depth of the sea" (Mt. 18:6). And certainly among the "little ones" meant by the Gospel, the children especially are included.

For the believer who intends to base the conduct of his own life on the Gospel, the example of Christ has to be the norm. Now, it is as one who lovingly welcomes little children that Christ presents himself (cfr. Mk. 10:16), as one who defends them in their spontaneous desire to come close to him (cfr. Mk. 10:14), who praises their typical and trusting simplicity, as being worthy of the kingdom (cfr. Mt. 18:3–4), and who draws our attention to their interior transparency which disposes them so easily to experience God (cfr. Mt. 18:10). He does not hesitate to set down a surprising equation: "Whoever receives one such child in my name receives me" (Mt. 18:5). As I had occasion to write recently, "The Lord identifies himself with the world of young children. . . . Jesus does not condition children, he does not use children. He calls them, and brings them into his plan for the salvation of the world" (cfr. Message to the President of the Pontifical Society of Missionary Childhood, *L'Osservatore Romano*, April 21, 1979).

What then shall be the attitude of responsible Christians and especially of parents and mass-media workers conscious of their duties in regard to children? They ought, before all else, to take charge of the human growth of the child; any pretense of maintaining a "neutral" position in his regard and of letting him grow up in his own way merely disguises a dangerous lack of interest under the appearance of respect for the child's personality.

No such disengagement in relation to children can be accepted; for children really have a need for help in their development toward maturity. To be sure, there is a great richness and vitality in a child's heart; however, he is not capable, all by himself, of resolving the diverse mysteries and longings that assail him from within. It is on the adults that the duty falls—on the parents, the educators, the communications workers—and it is they also who have the capability of enabling the child to sort things out and find himself.

> Like soft wax on which every tiniest pressure leaves a mark, so the child is responsive to every stimulus that plays upon his imagination, his emotions, his instincts, and his ideas. Yet the impressions received at this age are the ones which are destined to penetrate most deeply. . . .

Does not every child in some way resemble the boy Samuel, of whom the sacred scripture speaks? Unable to interpret the call of God, he sought help from his master, who at first replied to him: "No, I did not call you; go back to sleep" (1 Sm. 3:5–6). Now, shall we adopt this kind of attitude and smother the inspirations that impel the child to higher things? Shall we not rather help him to understand and respond, as the priest Eli eventually did with Samuel: "If he calls you again, you shall say: Speak Lord, for your servant is listening" (ibid. 3:9).

There are enormous possibilities and means at the disposal of you adults in this connection. You are in a position to arouse the spirit of the children so that they will listen, or to lull it to sleep and—God forbid— poison it irremediably. What is required is that you should take such action as will cause the child to avail himself to the fullest of all the possibilities for personal realization and thus insert himself creatively into the stream of life in the world; and this thanks to the pains you take to give him an education which dulls none of his promise or talent but brings out the best in him.

You especially who are engaged in the mass media, stand by his side and help him in his search for knowledge, giving him cultural and recreational programs in which he may find an answer to his quest for his identity and for his gradual "entry" into the human community. Then, in your actual programs, it is important that the child actors should not appear merely in walk-on parts, a diversion to relieve the tired eyes or disenchanted ears of apathetic viewers or listeners, but that they should be allowed to represent characters that can serve as valid models for the younger generation.

I am well aware that in begging you to make this kind of human and "poetic" effort (I use "poetic" in its true meaning as the creative capacity proper to art), I am implicitly asking you to relinquish to some extent your adherence to program planning geared to instant success and closely tied to maximum audience "ratings." Is not the true work of art, perhaps, that which is born not from ambition to succeed, but from genuine ability and sure professional maturity? Do not exclude from your productions—I ask this of you as a brother—the opportunity to offer the heart of the children a spiritual and religious invitation; and you may take this as a trusting appeal for your collaboration in the spiritual task of the church.

Similarly I turn to you, parents and educators, and to you, catechists and officials of the various ecclesial associations, and I urge you to give very serious thought to the problem of the use of the social communications media by and for children, as a matter of capital importance; not only for their enlightened training which, as well as developing their critical sense and teaching them—as you might say—self-discipline in choosing their programs, helps them along on the human plane, but also for the evolution of the whole society along the lines of uprightness, of truth, and of brotherhood.

Dearest brothers and children, childhood is not just any period of human life, which can be isolated from the whole artificially; as a child is flesh of the flesh of his parents, so are all the children a living part of society. It is for this reason that what is at stake in childhood is the fate of the whole of life, of the child's life and of ours, that is, of the life of all. Let us therefore serve childhood, valuing life and choosing "for" life at every level, and let us help childhood, presenting before the eyes and to the vulnerable and sensitive hearts of the little ones the noblest and highest things in life.

Raising the eyes to this ideal, to me it seems that I meet the gaze of the most sweet mother of Jesus who, totally given to the service of her divine little son, "kept all these things in her heart" (Lk. 2:51). In the light of her example, I pay honor to the teaching mission which belongs to all of you and, in the confidence that you will carry it out with a love commensurate with its dignity, I bless you from my heart.

READING 21
Introduction

Catechists find themselves named as members of multiple interrelated groups: pastoral ministers, ministers of the Word, educators, liturgical ministers, theologians, and possibly, parents. In a radical way they are also communicators, and as such, they will want to know the quite radical principles set out by the Pontifical Social Communications Council in *Aetatis Novae.* Because of its implications, I propose that it is the most important catechetical document in this volume of the *Sourcebook.*

After originally reading the text, I thought to myself: "If this document were implemented, even in a beginning way, there would be an instant revolution in how the church works at all levels—in people's ability to speak their mind, in their sense of their right to have a say, in their approach to ministry (with more attention to ministry via the ear than the tongue), and in how they name core issues." It was only in a later reading that I noticed that the introduction actually uses this idea in its title: "A Revolution in Human Communication."

Written to commemorate the twentieth anniversary of *Communio et Progressio,* the famous 1971 Vatican instruction on social communications, *Aetatis Novae* brings the issues to a sharper edge. Beginning with the current contexts of social communications and the challenges they create for all people, *Aetatis Novae* moves to consider the work of social communications. Here—and this is the potentially revolutionary part—the church is to understand itself as a medium of communication, with everything said about communication needing to be mirrored in the church's own life. Thus, "where legal and political structures foster the domination of the media by elites, the church for its part must urge respect for the right to communicate, including its own right of access to media, while at the same time seeking alternative models of communications for its own members and for people at large."

Readers are reminded of the church's duty to provide "formation to communications professionals and to the public so that they will approach media with 'a critical sense which is animated by a passion for the truth.'" The final section dealing with pastoral responses and priorities has important implications for catechists and other pastoral workers. Most of the tasks outlined here are yet to be discussed in any depth, not to mention undertaken.

Catechetical leaders will sense the wisdom of the issues in this document, though they may find they have not been dealing with them explicitly. If so they will want to study the document's appendix for its outline of how a pastoral plan for social communications might be developed. In any such plan catechists and other pastoral ministers will join a very broad and creative work of collaboration.

Further Reading

Fuchs, Ottmar. "How the Churches Deal with the Media." In *Mass Media* Concilium Series, edited by John A. Coleman and Miklos Tomka. Maryknoll, NY: Orbis Books, 1993.

Staudenmaier, John M. "The Media: Technique and Culture." In *Mass Media* Concilium Series, edited by John A. Coleman and Miklos Tomka. Maryknoll, NY: Orbis Books, 1993.

Warren, Michael. "Judging the Electronic Communications Media." *The Living Light* 31, no. 2 (winter 1994–1995): 54–64.

White, Robert. "Mass Media and Culture." In *Vatican II: Assessment and Perspectives: Twenty-five Years After (1962–1987)*. Vol. 3, edited by Rene Latourelle, 580–611. Mahwah, NJ: Paulist Press, 1989.

Aetatis Novae: Pastoral Instruction on Social Communications

PONTIFICAL SOCIAL COMMUNICATIONS COUNCIL

Introduction: A Revolution in Human Communications

1. At the dawn of a new era, a vast expansion of human communications is profoundly influencing culture everywhere. Revolutionary technological changes are only part of what is happening. Nowhere today are people untouched by the impact of media upon religious and moral attitudes, political and social systems, and education.

It is impossible to ignore, for instance, that geographical and political boundaries were both of very little avail in view of the role played by communications during the "radical transformations" of 1989 and 1990, on whose historical significance the pope reflects in *Centesimus Annus*.[1]

It becomes equally evident that "the first Areopagus of the modern age is the world of communications which is unifying humanity and turning it into what is known as a 'global village.' The means of social communications have become so important as to be for many the chief means of information and education, of guidance and inspiration in their behavior as individuals, families and within society at large."[2]

More than a quarter century after the promulgation of the Second Vatican Council's decree on social communications, *Inter Mirifica*, and two decades after the pastoral instruction *Communio et Progressio*, the Pontifical Council for Social Communications wishes to reflect on the pastoral implications of this situation.

Reprinted from *Origins* 21, no. 42 (26 March 1992): 669, 671–677. Copyright © 1992 by the Pontifical Council for Social Communications. Used with permission.

We do so in the spirit expressed by the closing words of *Communio et Progressio:* "The people of God walk in history. As they . . . advance with their times, they look forward with confidence and even with enthusiasm to whatever the development of communications in a space age may have to offer."[3]

We encourage the pastors and people of the church to deepen their understanding of issues relating to communications and media, and to translate their understanding into practical policies and workable programs.

Taking for granted the continued validity of the principles and insights of these conciliar and post-conciliar documents, we wish to apply them to new and emerging realities. We do not pretend to say the final word on a complex, fluid, rapidly changing situation, but simply wish to provide a working tool and a measure of encouragement to those confronting the pastoral implications of the new realities.

2. In the years since *Inter Mirifica* and *Communio et Progressio* appeared, people have grown accustomed to expressions like *information society, mass-media culture,* and *media generation.* Terms like these underline a remarkable fact: Today, much that men and women know and think about life is conditioned by the media; to a considerable extent, human experience itself is an experience of media.

Recent decades also have witnessed remarkable developments in the technology of communicating. These include both the rapid evolution of previously existing technologies and the emergence of new telecommunications and media technologies: satellites, cable television, fiber optics, videocassettes, compact disks, computerized image making and other computer and digital technology, and much else. The use of new media gives rise to what some speak of as "new languages" and has given birth to new possibilities for the mission of the church as well as to new pastoral problems.

3. Against this background we encourage the pastors and people of the church to deepen their understanding of issues relating to communications and media, and to translate their understanding into practical policies and workable programs.

"As the council fathers looked to the future and tried to discern the context in which the church would be called upon to carry out her mission, they could clearly see that the progress of technology was already 'transforming the face of the earth' and even reaching out to conquer space. They recognized that developments in communications technology, in particular, were likely to set off chain reactions with unforeseen consequences."[4]

"Far from suggesting that the church should stand aloof or try to isolate herself from the mainstream of these events, the council fathers saw the church as being in the very midst of human progress, sharing the experiences of the rest of humanity, seeking to understand them and to interpret them in the light of faith. It was for God's faithful people to make creative use of the new discoveries and technologies for the benefit of humanity and the fulfillment of God's plan for the world . . . employing the full potential of the 'computer age' to serve the human and transcendent vocation of every person, and thus to give glory to the Father from whom all good things come."[5]

We express our gratitude to those responsible for the creative communications work under way in the church everywhere. Despite difficulties—arising from limited resources, from the obstacles sometimes placed in the way of the church's access to media, and from a constant reshaping of culture, values, and attitudes brought about by the pervasive presence of media—much has been and continues to be accomplished. The dedicated bishops, clergy, religious, and lay people engaged in this critically important apostolate deserve the thanks of all.

Also welcome are those positive ventures in media-related ecumenical cooperation involving Catholics and their brothers and sisters of other churches and ecclesial communities, as well as interreligious cooperation with those of other world religions. It is not only appropriate but "necessary for Christians to work together more effectively in their communications efforts and to act in more direct cooperation with other religions to ensure a united religious presence in the very heart of mass communications."[6]

I. The Context of Social Communications

A. Cultural and Social Context

4. As more than just a technological revolution, today's revolution in social communications involves a fundamental reshaping of the elements by which people comprehend the world about them and verify and express what they comprehend. The constant availability of images and ideas, and their rapid transmission even from continent to continent, have profound consequences, both positive and negative, for the psychological, moral and social development of persons, the structure and functioning of societies, intercultural communications, and the perception and transmission of values, worldviews, ideologies, and religious beliefs. The communications revolution affects perceptions even of the church, and has a significant impact on the church's own structures and modes of functioning.

All this has striking pastoral implications. The media can be used to proclaim the Gospel or to reduce it to silence in human hearts. As media become ever more intertwined with people's daily lives, they influence how people understand the meaning of life itself.

Indeed, the power of media extends to defining not only what people will think but even what they will think about. Reality, for many, is what the media recognize as real; what the media do not acknowledge seems of little importance. Thus de facto silence can be imposed upon individuals and groups whom the media ignore, and even the voice of the Gospel can be muted, though not entirely stilled, in this way.

It is important therefore that Christians find ways to furnish the missing information to those deprived of it and also to give a voice to the voiceless.

The power of media either to reinforce or to override the traditional reference points of religion, culture and family underlines the continued relevance of the council's words: "If the media are to be correctly employed, it is essential that all who use them know the principles of the moral order and apply them faithfully in this domain."[7]

B. Political and Economic Context

5. The economic structures of nations are inextricably linked to contemporary communications systems. National investment in an efficient communications infrastructure is widely regarded as necessary to economic and political development, and the growing cost of such investment has been a major factor leading governments in a number of countries to adopt policies aimed at increasing market competition. For this and other reasons, public telecommunications and broadcasting systems in many instances have been subject to policies of deregulation and privatization.

While public systems can clearly be misused for purposes of ideological and political manipulation, unregulated commercialization and privatization in broadcasting can also have far-reaching consequences. In practice, and often as a matter of public policy, public accountability for the use of the airwaves is devalued. Profit, not service, tends to become the most important measure of success. Profit motives and advertisers' interests exert undue influence on media content: Popularity is preferred over quality, and the lowest common denominator prevails. Advertisers move beyond their legitimate role of identifying genuine needs and responding to them, and, driven by profit motives, strive to create artificial needs and patterns of consumption.

Commercial pressures also operate across national boundaries at the expense of particular peoples and their cultures. Faced with increasing competition and the need to develop new markets, communications firms become ever more "multinational" in character; at the same time, lack of local production capabilities makes some countries increasingly dependent on foreign material. Thus, the products of the popular media of one culture spread into another, often to the detriment of established art forms and media and the values which they embody.

Even so, the solution to problems arising from unregulated commercialization and privatization does not lie in state control of media but in more regulation according to criteria of public service and in greater public accountability. It should be noted in this connection that, although the legal and political frameworks within which media operate in some countries are currently changing strikingly for the better, elsewhere government intervention remains an instrument of oppression and exclusion.

II. The Work of the Means of Social Communications

6. *Communio et Progressio* is rooted in a vision of communication as a way toward communion. For "more than the expression of ideas and the indication of emotion," it declares, communication is "the giving of self in love."[8] In this respect, communication mirrors the church's own communion and is capable of contributing to it.

Indeed, the communication of truth can have a redemptive power, which comes from the person of Christ. He is God's Word made flesh and the image of the invisible God. In and through him God's own life is communicated to humanity by the Spirit's action. "Since the creation of the world, invisible realities, God's eternal power and divinity have become visible, recognized through the things he has made";[9] and now "the Word has become flesh and made his dwelling among us, and we have seen his glory: the glory of an only Son coming from the Father, filled with enduring love."[10]

Here, in the Word made flesh, God's self-communication is definitive. In Jesus' words and deeds the Word is liberating, redemptive, for all humankind. This loving self-revelation of God, combined with humanity's response of faith, constitutes a profound dialogue.

Human history and all human relationships exist within the framework established by this self-communication of God in Christ. History itself is ordered toward becoming a kind of word of God, and it is part of the human vocation to contribute to bringing this about by living out the ongoing, unlimited communication of God's reconciling love in creative new ways. We are to do this through words of hope and deeds of love, that is, through our very way of life. Thus, communication must lie at the heart of the church community.

Christ is both the content and the dynamic source of the church's communications in proclaiming the Gospel. For the church itself is "Christ's mystical body—the hidden completion of Christ glorified—who 'fills the whole creation.'"[11] As a result we move, within the church and with the help of the word and the sacraments, toward the hope of that last unity where "God will be all in all."[12]

A. Media at the Service of Persons and Cultures

7. For all the good which they do and are capable of doing, mass media, "which can be such effective instruments of unity and" understanding, can also sometimes be the vehicles of a deformed outlook on life, on the family, on religion and on morality—an outlook that does not respect the true dignity and destiny of the human person."[13] It is imperative that media respect and contribute to that integral development of the person which embraces "the cultural, transcendent and religious dimensions of man and society."[14]

In seeking to enter into dialogue with the modern world, the church necessarily desires honest and respectful dialogue with those responsible for the communications media.

One also finds the source of certain individual and social problems in the replacement of human interaction by increased media use and intense attachment to fictitious media characters. Media, after all, cannot take the place of immediate personal contact and interaction among family members and friends. But the solution to this difficulty also may lie largely in the media: through their use in ways—dialogue groups, discussions of films and broadcasts—which stimulate interpersonal communication rather than substituting for it.

B. Media at the Service of Dialogue with the World

8. The Second Vatican Council underlined the awareness of the people of God that they are "truly and intimately linked with mankind and its history."[15] Those who proclaim God's word are obligated to heed and seek to understand the "words" of diverse peoples and cultures in order not only to learn from them but to help them recognize and accept the Word of God.[16] The church therefore must maintain an active, listening presence in relation to the world—a kind of presence which both nurtures community and supports people in seeking acceptable solutions to personal and social problems.

Moreover, as the church always must communicate its message in a manner suited to each age and to the cultures of particular nations and peoples, so today it must communicate in and to the emerging media culture.[17] This is a basic condition for responding to a crucial point made by the Second Vatican Council: The emergence of "social, technical and cultural bonds" linking people ever more closely lends "special urgency" to the church's task of bringing all to "full union with Christ."[18] Considering how important a contribution the media of social communications can make to its efforts to foster this unity, the church views them as means "devised under God's providence" for the promotion of communication and communion among human beings during their earthly pilgrimage.[19]

Thus, in seeking to enter into dialogue with the modern world, the church necessarily desires honest and respectful dialogue with those responsible for the communications media. On the church's side this dialogue involves efforts to understand the media—their purposes, procedures, forms and genres, internal structures and modalities—and to offer support and encouragement to those involved in media work. On the basis of this sympathetic understanding and support, it becomes possible to offer meaningful proposals for removing obstacles to human progress and the proclamation of the Gospel.

Such dialogue therefore requires that the church be actively concerned with the secular media and especially with the shaping of media policy. Christians have in effect a responsibility to make their voice heard in all the media, and their task is not confined merely to the giving out of church news. The dialogue also involves support for media artists; it requires the development of an anthropology and a theology of communication—not least so that theology itself may be more communicative, more successful in disclosing Gospel values and applying them to the contemporary realities of the human condition; it requires that church leaders and pastoral workers respond willingly and prudently to media when requested, while seeking to establish relationships of mutual confidence and respect, based on fundamental common values, with those who are not of our faith.

C. Media at the Service of Human Community and Progress

9. Communication in and by the church is essentially communication of the good news of Jesus Christ. It is the proclamation of the Gospel as a prophetic, liberating word to the men and women of our times;

it is testimony, in the face of radical secularization, to divine truth and to the transcendent destiny of the human person; it is the witness given in solidarity with all believers against conflict and division, to justice and communion among peoples, nations and cultures.

This understanding of communication on the part of the church sheds a unique light on social communications and on the role which, in the providential plan of God, the media are intended to play in promoting the integral development of human persons and societies.

D. Media at the Service of Ecclesial Communion

10. Along with all this, it is necessary constantly to recall the importance of the fundamental right of dialogue and information within the church, as described in *Communio et Progressio*,[20] and to continue to seek effective means, including a responsible use of media of social communications, for realizing and protecting this right. In this connection we also have in mind the affirmations of the Code of Canon Law that, besides showing obedience to the pastors of the church, the faithful "are at liberty to make known their needs, especially their spiritual needs, and their wishes" to these pastors,[21] and that the faithful, in keeping with their knowledge, competence and position, have "the right, indeed at times the duty," to express to the pastors their views on matters concerning the good of the church.[22]

Partly this is a matter of maintaining and enhancing the church's credibility and effectiveness. But more fundamentally, it is one of the ways of realizing in a concrete manner the church's character as *communio*, rooted in and mirroring the intimate communion of the Trinity. Among the members of the community of persons who make up the church, there is a radical equality in dignity and mission which arises from baptism and underlies hierarchical structure and diversity of office and function; and this equality necessarily will express itself in an honest and respectful sharing of information and opinions.

It will be well to bear in mind, however, in cases of dissent, that "it is not by seeking to exert the pressure of public opinion that one contributes to the clarification of doctrinal issues and renders service to the truth."[23] In fact, "not all ideas which circulate among the people of God" are to be "simply and purely identified with the 'sense of the faith.'"[24]

Why does the church insist that people have the right to receive correct information? Why does the church emphasize its right to proclaim authentic Gospel truth? Why does the church stress the responsibility of its pastors to communicate the truth and to form the faithful to do the same? It is because the whole understanding of what communication in the church means is based upon the realization that the Word of God communicates himself.

E. Media at the Service of a New Evangelization

11. Along with traditional means such as witness of life, catechetics, personal contact, popular piety, the liturgy and similar celebrations, the use of media is now essential in evangelization and catechesis. Indeed, "the church would feel guilty before the Lord if she did not utilize these powerful means that human skill is daily rendering more perfect."[25] The media of social communications can and should be instruments in the church's program of re-evangelization and new evangelization in the contemporary world. In view of the proven efficacy of the old principle "see, judge, act," the audiovisual aspect of media in evangelization should be given due attention.

But it will also be of great importance in the church's approach to media and the culture they do so much to shape always to bear in mind that: "It is not enough to use the media simply to spread the Christian message and the church's authentic teaching. It is also necessary to integrate that message into the 'new culture' created by modern communications . . . with new languages, new techniques and a new psychology."[26] Today's evangelization ought to well up from the church's active, sympathetic presence within the world of communications.

III. Current Challenges

A. Need for a Critical Evaluation

12. But even as the church takes a positive, sympathetic approach to media, seeking to enter into the culture created by modern communications in order to evangelize effectively, it is necessary at the very same time that the church offer a critical evaluation of mass media and their impact upon culture.

Where legal and political structures foster the domination of the media by elites, the church for its part must urge respect for the right to communicate, including its own right of access to media, while at the same time seeking alternative models of communications for its own members and for people at large.

As we have said repeatedly, communications technology is a marvelous expression of human genius, and the media confer innumerable benefits upon society. But as we have also pointed out the application of communications technology has been a mixed blessing, and its use for good purposes requires sound values and wise choices on the part of individuals, the private sector governments and society as a whole. The church does not presume to dictate these decisions and choices, but it does seek to be of help by indicating ethical and moral criteria which are relevant to the process—criteria which are to be found in both human and Christian values.

B. Solidarity and Integral Development

13. As matters stand, mass media at times exacerbate individual and social problems which stand in the way of human solidarity and the integral development of the human person. These obstacles include secularism, consumerism, materialism, dehumanization and lack of concern for the plight of the poor and neglected.[27]

It is against this background that the church, recognizing the media of social communications as "the privileged way" today for the creation and transmission of culture,[28] acknowledges its own duty to offer formation to communications professionals and to the public so that they will approach media with "a critical sense which is animated by a passion for the truth"; it likewise acknowledges its duty to engage in "a work of defense of liberty, respect for the dignity of individuals and the elevation of the authentic culture of peoples which occurs through a firm and courageous rejection of every form of monopoly and manipulation."[29]

C. Policies and Structures

14. Certain problems in this regard arise specifically from media policies and structures: for example, the unjust exclusion of some groups and classes from access to the means of communications, the systematic abridgment of the fundamental right to information, which is practiced in some places, the widespread domination of media by economic, social and political elites.

These things are contrary to the principal purposes and indeed to the very nature of the media, whose proper and essential social role consists in contributing to the realization of the human right to information, promoting justice in the pursuit of the common good and assisting individuals, groups and peoples in their search for truth. The media carry out these crucial tasks when they foster the exchange of ideas and information among all classes and sectors of society and offer to all responsible voices opportunities to be heard.

D. Defense of the Right
to Information and Communications

15. It is not acceptable that the exercise of the freedom of communication should depend upon wealth, education or political power. The right to communicate is the right of all.

This calls for special national and international efforts, not only to give those who are poor and less powerful access to the information which they need for their individual and social development, but to ensure that they are able to play an effective, responsible role in deciding media content and determining the structures and policies of their national institutions of social communications.

Where legal and political structures foster the domination of the media by elites, the church for its part must urge respect for the right to communicate, including its own right of access to media, while at the same time seeking alternative models of communications for its own members and for people at large. The right to communicate is part also of the right to religious freedom, which should not be confined to freedom of worship.

IV. Pastoral Priorities and Responses

A. Defense of Human Cultures

16. Considering the situation in many places, sensitivity to the rights and interests of individuals may often call for the church to promote alternative community media. Often, too, for the sake of evangelization and catechesis the church must take steps to preserve and promote folk media and other traditional forms of expression, recognizing that in particular societies these can be more effective than newer media in spreading the Gospel because they make possible greater personal participation and reach deeper levels of human feeling and motivation.

The overwhelming presence of mass media in the contemporary world by no means detracts from the importance of alternative media which are open to people's involvement and allow them to be active in production and even in designing the process of communications itself. Then, too, grassroots and traditional media not only provide an important forum for local cultural expression but develop competence for active participation in shaping and using mass media.

Similarly, we view with sympathy the desire of many peoples and groups for more just, equitable systems of communications and information which safeguard them against domination and manipulation, whether from abroad or at the hands of their fellow countrymen. This is a concern of developing nations in relation to developed ones, and often, too, it is a concern of minorities within particular nations, both developed and developing. In all cases people ought to be able to participate actively, autonomously and responsibly in the process of communications which in so many ways helps to shape the conditions of their lives.

B. Development and Promotion of the Church's Own Media of Social Communications

17. Along with its other commitments in the area of communications and media, the church must continue, in spite of the many difficulties involved, to develop, maintain and foster its own specifically Catholic instruments and programs for social communications. These include the Catholic press and Catholic publishing houses, Catholic radio and television, offices for public information and media relations, institutes and programs for training in and about media, media research and church-related organizations of communications professionals—including especially the international Catholic communications organizations—whose members are knowledgeable and competent collaborators with the Episcopal conferences as well as with the bishops individually.

Catholic media work is not simply one more program alongside all the rest of the church's activities: Social communications have a role to play in every aspect of the church's mission. Thus, not only should there be a pastoral plan for communications, but communications should be an integral part of every pastoral plan, for it has something to contribute to virtually every other apostolate, ministry and program.

> Church personnel require at least a working grasp of the impact which new information technologies and mass media are having upon individuals and society.

C. Formation of Christian Communicators

18. Education and training in communications should be an integral part of the formation of pastoral workers and priests.[30] There are several distinct elements and aspects to the education and training which are required. For example, in today's world, so strongly influenced by media, church personnel require at least a working grasp of the impact which new information technologies and mass media are having upon individuals and society. They must likewise be prepared to minister both to the "information-rich" and to the "information-poor." They

need to know how to invite others into dialogue, avoiding a style of communicating which suggests domination, manipulation or personal gain. As for those who will be actively engaged in media work for the church, they need to acquire professional skills in media along with doctrinal and spiritual formation.

D. Pastoral Care of Communications Personnel

19. Media work involves special psychological pressures and ethical dilemmas. Considering how important a role the media play in forming contemporary culture and shaping the lives of countless individuals and whole societies, it is essential that those professionally involved in secular media and the communications industries approach their responsibilities imbued with high ideals and a commitment to the service of humanity.

The church has a corresponding responsibility to develop and offer programs of pastoral care which are specifically responsive to the peculiar working conditions and moral challenges facing communications professionals. Typically, pastoral programs of this sort should include ongoing formation which will help these men and women—many of whom sincerely wish to know and do what is ethically and morally right—to integrate moral norms ever more fully into their professional work as well as their private lives.

V. The Need for Pastoral Planning

A. Responsibilities of Bishops

20. Recognizing the validity, and indeed the urgency, of the claims advanced by communications work, bishops and others responsible for decisions about allocating the church's limited human and material resources should assign it an appropriate high priority, taking into account the circumstances of their particular nations, regions and dioceses.

This need may be even greater now than previously, precisely because, to some degree at least, the great contemporary "Areopagus" of mass media has more or less been neglected by the church up to this time.[31] As the Holy Father remarks: "Generally, preference has been given to other means of preaching the Gospel and of Christian education, while the mass media are left to the initiative of individuals or small groups and enter into pastoral planning only in a secondary way."[32] This situation needs correcting.

B. Urgency of a Pastoral Plan for Social Communications

21. We therefore strongly recommend that dioceses and Episcopal conferences or assemblies include a communications component in every pastoral plan. We further recommend that they develop specific pastoral plans for social communications itself, or else review and bring up to date those plans which already exist, in this way fostering the desirable process of periodic re-examination and adaptation. In doing so, bishops should seek the collaboration of professionals in secular media and of the church's own media-related organizations, including especially the international and national organizations for film, radio-television, and the press.

Episcopal conferences in some regions already have been well served by pastoral plans which concretely identify needs and goals and encourage the coordination of efforts. The results of the study, assessment and consultation involved in preparing these documents can and should be shared at all levels in the church, as useful data for pastoral workers. Practical, realistic plans of this sort also can be adapted to the needs of local churches. They should of course be constantly open to revision and adaptation in light of changing needs.

This document itself concludes with elements of a pastoral plan, which also indicate issues for possible treatment in pastoral letters and Episcopal statements at the national and local levels. These elements reflect suggestions received from Episcopal conferences and media professionals.

Conclusion

22. We affirm once again that the church "sees these media as 'gifts of God,' which in accordance with his providential design unite men in brotherhood and so help them to cooperate with his plan for their salvation."[33] As the Spirit helped the prophets of old to see the divine plan in the signs of their times, so today the Spirit helps the church interpret the signs of our times and carry out its prophetic tasks, among which the study, evaluation and right use of communications technology and the media of social communications are now fundamental.

Appendix

Elements of a Pastoral Plan
for Social Communications

23. Media conditions and the opportunities presented to the church in the field of social communications differ from nation to nation and even from diocese to diocese within the same country. It naturally follows that the church's approach to media and the cultural environment they help to form will differ from place to place, and that its plans and participation will be tailored to local situations.

Every Episcopal conference and diocese should therefore develop an integrated pastoral plan for communications, preferably in consultation with representatives of international and national Catholic communications organizations and with local media professionals. Furthermore, communications ought to be taken into account in formulating and carrying out all other pastoral plans, including those concerning social service, education and evangelization. A number of Episcopal conferences and dioceses already have developed such plans in which communications needs are identified, goals are articulated, realistic provision is made for financing and a variety of communications efforts is coordinated.

The following guidelines are offered as assistance to those formulating such pastoral plans or engaged in reassessing plans which exist.

Guidelines for Designing Pastoral Plans
for Social Communications in a Diocese,
Episcopal Conference, or Patriarchal Assembly

24. A pastoral plan for social communications should include the following elements:

a) The statement of a vision, based on extensive consultation, which identifies communications strategies for all church ministries and responds to contemporary issues and conditions.

b) An inventory or assessment which describes the media environment in the territory under consideration, including audiences, public and commercial media producers and directors, financial and technical resources delivery systems, ecumenical and educational resources, and Catholic media organizations and communications personnel, including those of religious communities.

c) A proposed structure for church-related social communications in support of evangelization, catechesis and education, social service and ecumenical cooperation, and including, as far as possible, public relations, press, radio, television, cinema, cassettes, computer networks, facsimile services and related forms of telecommunications.

"A pastoral social communications plan should attempt . . . to identify new strategies for evangelization and catechesis through the application of communications technology and mass communications."

d) Media education, with special emphasis on the relationship of media and values.

e) Pastoral outreach to, and dialogue with, media professionals, with particular attention to their faith development and spiritual growth.

f) Means of obtaining and maintaining financial support adequate to the carrying out of the pastoral plan.

Process for Designing a Pastoral Plan for Social Communications

25. The plan should offer guidelines and suggestions helpful to church communicators in establishing realistic goals and priorities for their work. It is recommended that a planning team including church personnel and media professionals be involved in this process, whose two phases are: 1. research, and 2. design.

26. Research Phase. The elements of the research phase are needs assessment, information gathering and an exploration of alternative models of a pastoral plan. It includes an analysis of the internal communications environment, including the strengths and weaknesses of the church's current structures and programs for communications as well as the opportunities and challenges these face.

Three types of research will assist in gathering the required information: a needs assessment, a communications audit and a resource inventory. The first identifies areas of ministry requiring particular attention on the part of the Episcopal conference or diocese. The second considers what is now being done—including its effectiveness—so as to identify strengths and weaknesses of existing communications structures and procedures. The third identifies communications resources, technology and personnel available to the church—including not only the church's "own" resources but those to which it may have access in the business community, the media industries and ecumenical settings.

27. Design Phase. After gathering and studying these data, the planning team should identify conference or diocesan communications goals and priorities. This is the beginning of the design phase. The planning team should then proceed to address each of the following issues as it relates to local circumstances.

28. Education. Communications issues and mass communications are relevant to every level of pastoral ministry, including education. A pastoral social communications plan should attempt:

a) To offer educational opportunities in communications as essential components of the formation of all persons who are engaged in the work of the church: seminarians, priests, religious brothers and sisters, and lay leaders.

b) To encourage Catholic schools and universities to offer programs and courses related to the communications needs of the church and society.

c) To offer courses, workshops and seminars in technology, management and communication ethics and policy issues for church communicators, seminarians, religious and clergy.

d) To plan and carry out programs in media education and media literacy for teachers, parents and students.

e) To encourage creative artists and writers accurately to reflect Gospel values as they share their gifts through the written word, legitimate theater, radio, television and film for entertainment and education.

f) To identify new strategies for evangelization and catechesis through the application of communications technology and mass communications.

29. Spiritual formation and pastoral care. Lay Catholic professionals and others working in either the church apostolate of social communications or the secular media often look to the church for spiritual guidance and pastoral care. A pastoral plan for social communications therefore should seek:

a) To offer opportunities for professional enrichment to lay Catholic and other professional communicators through days of recollection, retreats, seminars and professional support groups.

b) To offer pastoral care which will provide the necessary support, nourish the communicators' faith, and keep alive their sense of dedication in the difficult task of communicating Gospel values and authentic human values to the world.

30. Cooperation. Cooperation involves sharing resources among conferences and/or dioceses and between dioceses and other institutions, such as religious communities, universities and health-care facilities. A pastoral plan for social communications should be designed:

a) To enhance relations and encourage mutual consultation between church representatives and media professionals, who have much to teach the church about the use of media.

b) To explore cooperative productions through regional and national centers and to encourage the development of joint promotion, marketing and distribution networks.

c) To promote cooperation with religious congregations working in social communications.

d) To collaborate with ecumenical organizations and with other churches and religious groups regarding ways of securing and guaranteeing access to the media by religion, and to collaborate in "the more recently developed media: especially in regard to the common use of satellites, data banks and cable networks, and in informatics generally, beginning with system compatibility."[34]

e) To cooperate with secular media, especially in regard to common concerns on religious, moral, ethical, cultural, educational and social issues.

31. Public relations. Public relations by the church means active communication with the community through both secular and religious media. Involving readiness to communicate Gospel values and to publicize the ministries and programs of the church, it requires that the church do all in its power to ensure that its own true image reflects Christ. A pastoral plan for social communications should seek:

a) To maintain public relations offices with adequate human and material resources to make possible effective communication between the church and the community as a whole.

b) To produce publications and radio, television and video programs of excellent quality which give high visibility to the message of the Gospel and the mission of the church.

c) To promote media awards and other means of recognition in order to encourage and support media professionals.

d) To celebrate World Communications Day as a means of fostering awareness of the importance of social communications and supporting the communications initiatives of the church.

32. Research. The church's strategies in the field of social communications must be based on the results of sound media research which have been subjected to informed analysis and evaluation. It is important that communications research include topics and issues of particular relevance to the mission of the church in the particular nation and region involved. A pastoral plan for social communications should be designed:

a) To encourage institutes of higher studies, research centers and universities to engage in both applied and fundamental research related to communications needs and concerns of the church and society.

b) To identify practical ways of interpreting current communication research and applying it to the mission of the church.

c) To support ongoing theological reflection upon the processes and instruments of social communication and their role in the church and society.

33. Communications and development of peoples. Accessible point-to-point communication and mass media offer many people a more adequate opportunity to participate in the modern world economy, to experience freedom of expression and to contribute to the emergence of peace and justice in the world. A pastoral plan for social communications should be designed:

a) To bring Gospel values to bear upon the broad range of contemporary media activities—from book publishing to satellite communications—so as to contribute to the growth of international solidarity.

b) To defend the public interest and to safeguard religious access to the media by taking informed, responsible positions on matters of communications law and policy, and on the development of communications systems.

c) To analyze the social impact of advanced communications technology and to help prevent undue social disruption and cultural destabilization.

d) To assist professional communicators in articulating and observing ethical standards, especially in regard to the issues of fairness, accuracy, justice, decency and respect for life.

e) To develop strategies for encouraging more widespread, representative, responsible access to the media.

f) To exercise a prophetic role by speaking out in timely fashion from a Gospel perspective concerning the moral dimensions of significant public issues.

NOTES

1. Cf. John Paul II *Centesimus Annus*, 12–13, in *Acta Apostolicae Sedis*, 1991, 807–821.

2. Ibid., *Redemptoris Missio*, 37, in *AAS*, 1991, 285.

3. *Communio et Progressio*, 187, in *AAS*, 1971, 655–656.

4. John Paul II, Message for 1990 World Communications Day, *L'Osservatore Romano*, 25 January 1990, 6; cf. *Gaudium et Spes*, 5.

5. Ibid.

6. Pontifical Council for Social Communications, "Criteria for Ecumenical and Interreligious Cooperation in Communications," Vatican City, 1989, 1.

7. *Inter Mirifica*, 4.

8. *Communio et Progressio*, 11.

9. Rom. 1:20.

10. Jn. 1:14.

11. Eph. 3:23; 4:10.

12. 1 Cor. 15:28; *Communio et Progressio*, 11.

13. Pontifical Council for Social Communications, "Pornography and Violence in the Media: A Pastoral Response," Vatican City, 1989, 7.

14. John Paul II, *Sollicitudo Rei Socialis*, 46, in *AAS*, 1988, 579.

15. *Gaudium et Spes*, 11.

16. Cf. Paul VI, *Evangelii Nuntiandi*, 20, in *AAS*, 1976, 18–19.

17. Cf. *Inter Mirifica*, 3.

18. *Lumen Gentium*, 1.

19. Cf. *Communio et Progressio*, 12.

20. Ibid., 114–121.

21. Cf. Canon 212.2.

22. Cf. Canon 212.3.

23. Congregation for the Doctrine of the Faith, "Instruction on the Ecclesial Vocation of the Theologian," 30, in *AAS*, 1990, 1562.

24. Cf. ibid., 35.

25. *Evangelii Nuntiandi*, 45.

26. *Redemptoris Missio*, 37.

27. *Centesimus Annus*, 41.

28. John Paul II, *Christifideles Laici*, in *AAS*, 1989, 480.

29. Ibid., 481.

30. Cf. Congregation for Catholic Education, "Guide to the Training of Future Priests Concerning the Instruments of Social Communications," Vatican City, 1986.

31. Cf. *Redemptoris Missio*, 37.

32. Ibid.

33. *Communio et Progressio*, 2.

34. "Criteria for Ecumenical and Interreligious Cooperation in Communications," 14.

READING 22
Introduction

I consider this document to have extraordinary significance for catechetical ministry in the near future. Though written under the direction of the Congregation for the Evangelization of Peoples specifically for catechists in "mission lands," embedded in it are many principles affecting the ministry of catechists anywhere. One could argue that it is a better focused statement about the mission of the laity than *Christifideles Laici,* John Paul II's 1988 apostolic exhortation on the vocation and mission of the lay faithful in the church and in the world.

By bringing together a treasure trove of Vatican statements prizing the key place in the church of the catechist's ministry, the document celebrates this ministry. It also emphasizes the place of formation in developing the Spirit-filled gifts of the catechist. At the document's beginning the catechist is identified as one marked by a specific Spirit-given call, a special charism recognized by the church. Throughout, the document's language underscores the importance of the catechist's mission: "distinctive," "indispensable," "decisive."

In both parts I and II, most of the space is given over to the formation of catechists. In part I the section on the catechist's spirituality stresses the catechist's life circumstances, openness to the word of God, coherence and authenticity of life, and zeal. The special stamp of authenticity can be found in how the catechist lives the spirit of the cross. This section is followed by another with a "formational" concern: the catechist's attitude toward contemporary issues, including a nuanced sense of inculturation and a commitment to the poor. Not all these emphases are found in the so-called established churches, a possible clue to the languishing condition of some of them.

Part II is more specifically about the choice and formation of catechists, and its wisdom deserves attention. For example, section 17 states:

> It should not be forgotten either that the community's esteem for this service will be directly proportional to the way in which pastors treat their catechists, giving them worthwhile tasks and respecting their responsibility. A fulfilled, responsible and dynamic catechist, working enthusiastically and joyfully in the tasks assigned, appreciated and properly remunerated, is the best promoter of other vocations.

Explicit in part II is the idea of levels of achievement, of advancement, and of the functioning of gifts. Charisms grow. Strong language is used to stress the need for quality training and continual updating, a principle appropriate for bishop, priest, and layperson alike, either in the church in general or in specific ministries. In fact, this document might be subtitled: "Concerning the ongoing formation of all those in ministry." In part II's section "Attitude to the Church," some will find it particularly interesting how the "attitude of apostolic obedience" receives fewer words than does the "ability to work with others."

Part III rounds off the *Guide for Catechists* by dealing with "The Responsibilities Toward Catechists," meaning, of course, the church's responsibilities. This section begins with a nuanced treatment of the "remuneration for catechists" in mission countries, an issue sometimes overlooked in some industrialized countries. Any bishops' conference would do well to adopt as policy markers the principles set forth here. In effect, these principles advocate supplementing foundational ideas with foundational funds.

The *Guide for Catechists* has another emphasis throughout that deserves comment here because it is not often emphasized in Vatican documents. Again and again, this guide calls its readers to be ever mindful of the varied social situations and actual practices of the different local churches. The writers of *The Guide* keep reminding their readers: remember that everything here must be adapted to the needs of particular churches. As the introduction states:

> Under each heading we will try to give the ideals to be aimed at, along with the essential considerations, while taking account of the difficulty, in certain missionary situations, of defining who exactly can be called a catechist. The directives are deliberately given in general terms, so as to be applicable to all catechists in the young Churches. It is up to the respective Pastors to make them more specific, in keeping with the requirements and possibilities of the individual Churches.

And a few pages later, the document states:

> Catechists in mission territories are not only different from those in older Churches, but among themselves vary greatly in characteristics and modes of action from one young Church to another, so that it is difficult to give a single description that would apply to all.

These two passages give the flavor of the reminder that occurs regularly throughout this document. Though one might call it the "missionary consciousness," it is surely a consciousness needed everywhere in a time more acutely attuned to "difference," "otherness," or "alterity." The local church of Rome is reminding the universal church of the important localness of all the churches, the foundation of the church's universality.

As one might expect of a document produced by committee, the *Guide for Catechists* is not without its flaws. One of them is overreliance (cited thirty-seven times) on John Paul II's 1990 encyclical, *Redemptoris Missio,* which itself seems flawed by a kind of religious imperialism. (I side with Aloysius Pieris in claiming the encyclical is a subtle regression to a pre-Conciliar approach to other religions.) The *Guide for Catechists,* while explicitly embracing the interreligious dialog, is tainted by *Redemptoris Missio*'s regressive stance toward non-Christian religions.[1]

However, my high regard for the positive accomplishments of the *Guide* makes me hope its well-thought-out principles will find their way into a revised

General Catechetical Directory. Its principles will be reliable guides for any local community.

1. Aloysius Pieris, "Interreligious Dialogue and Theology of Religions: An Asian Paradigm," *Horizons* 20, no. 1 (1993): 106–114, and "Does Christ Have a Place in Asia? A Panoramic View" in *Christ in Asia: Some Aspects of the Struggles,* Concilium Series, ed. Virgil Elizondo and Leonardo Boff (Maryknoll, NY: Orbis Books, 1993), 43–44. For a succinct treatment of the problem I am naming "religious imperialism," see Elizabeth Johnson, "Jesus and Salvation," *Catholic Theological Society of America (CTSA) Proceedings,* 1994, 15–17.

Further Reading

Johnson, Elizabeth. "Jesus and Salvation." *Catholic Theological Society of America (CTSA) Proceedings,* 1994, 15–17.
Pieris, Aloysius. "Interreligious Dialogue and Theology of Religions: An Asian Paradigm." *Horizons* 20, no. 1 (1993): 106–114.

Guide for Catechists: Document of Vocational, Formative, and Promotional Orientation of Catechists in the Territories Dependent on the Congregation for the Evangelization of Peoples

CONGREGATION FOR THE EVANGELIZATION OF PEOPLES

Vatican City 1993
Venerable Brothers in the Episcopacy,
Dearly beloved Priests,
Beloved Catechists,

In this historical period, which for various reasons is very sensitive and favorable to the influence of the Christian message, the Congregation for the Evangelization of Peoples has maintained a special interest in some categories of people, who play a decisive role in missionary activity. In fact, after having looked at formation in major seminaries (1986), considered the life and ministry of priests (1989), our Congregation directed its attention to lay catechists, in the Plenary Assembly of April 1992.

Catechists have always had a very important role in the secular journey of evangelization. Even today, they are considered to be irreplaceable evangelizers, as the encyclical *Redemptoris Missio* so rightly states. In his message to our Plenary Assembly, the Holy Father confirmed the uniqueness of their role: "During my apostolic journeys I have been able to observe personally what the catechists offer, especially in

---

mission territories, an 'outstanding and absolutely necessary contribution to the spread of the faith and the Church'" (AG 17).

The Congregation for the Evangelization of Peoples experiences directly the undisputed effectiveness of lay catechists. Under the direction of priests, in fact, they continue with frankness to announce the Good News to their brothers and sisters of other religions, preparing them for entry into the ecclesial community through baptism. Through religious instruction, preparation for the sacraments, animation of prayer and other works of charity, they help the baptized to grow in the fervor of the Christian life. Where there is a shortage of priests, the catechists are also entrusted with the pastoral guidance of the little community separated from the center. Often, they are called to witness to their faith by harsh trials and painful privations. The history of evangelization past and present attests to their constancy even to the giving of life itself. Catechists are truly the pride of the missionary Church!

The present Catechists' Guide, fruit of the last Plenary Assembly, expresses the concern of the missionary Dicastery on behalf of this "deserving band" of lay apostles. This Guide contains a vast and precise amount of material, which covers various topics: the identity of the catechist, his or her selection, formation and spirituality; basic apostolic tasks and finally, the economic situation.

With great hope I entrust this Guide to the Bishops, Priests and to the catechists themselves, inviting them to scrutinize it carefully and to carry out its directives. In particular, I ask Catechetical Centers and Schools for catechism to refer to this document for their formation and teaching programs, while for content they already have in their hands the Catechism of the Catholic Church, published after the Plenary Assembly.

The diligent and faithful use of this Catechists' Guide in all the Churches dependent on our missionary Dicastery will contribute not only to bringing about a renewed image of the catechist, but will also guarantee a concerted growth in this vital sector for the future of mission in the world.

This is my sincere wish confided in prayer to Mary, "Mother and Model of Catechists," so that she may become more and more a consoling reality in all the young Churches.

The Holy Father, informed of this commitment of our Dicastery and having seen the text of the Guide, greatly appreciated and encouraged the initiative, wholeheartedly giving his apostolic blessing, most particularly to the catechists.

Rome, Feast of Saint Francis Xavier, 3 December 1993
Jozef Card. Tomko, Prefect

Introduction

1. An Indispensable Service

The Congregation for the Evangelization of Peoples (CEP) has always had a special concern for catechists, convinced as it is that these are, under the direction of their Pastors, a factor of prime importance in evangelization. In April 1970 it published some practical directives for catechists,[1] and now, conscious of its responsibility and of radical changes in the missionary world, the CEP would like to call attention to the present situation, the problems that arise, and prospects for the development of this *"praiseworthy army"* of lay apostles.[2] It is encouraged in this project by the many pressing interventions of His Holiness Pope John Paul II, who, during his apostolic voyages, makes use of every opportunity to stress the importance and relevance of the work of catechists as a *"fundamental evangelical service."*[3] Our task is a demanding but also a necessary and an attractive one,[4] seeing that, from the very beginning of Christianity and wherever there has been missionary activity, catechists have made, and continue to make, *"an outstanding and indispensable contribution to the spread of the faith and of the Church."*[5]

And so, having examined, in its Plenary Assembly of 27–30 April 1992, the information and suggestions that came in from a wide-ranging consultation with bishops and catechetical centers in mission territories, the CEP has drawn up this *Guide for Catechists*, which treats in a doctrinal, existential and practical way the principal aspects of the catechists' vocation, identity, spirituality, selection and training, missionary and pastoral tasks, and remuneration, along with the responsibility of the People of God toward them, in today's conditions and those of the immediate future.

Under each heading we will try to give the ideals to be aimed at, along with the essential considerations, while taking account of the difficulty, in certain missionary situations, of defining who exactly can be called a catechist. The directives are deliberately given in general terms, so as to be applicable to all catechists in the young Churches. It is up to the respective pastors to make them more specific, in keeping with the requirements and possibilities of the individual Churches.

The Guide is addressed first of all to the lay catechists themselves, but also to the bishops, priests, religious, formators and the faithful, by reason of the strong links between the various components of the ecclesial community.

Before this Guide could see light, the Holy Father John Paul II had approved the *Catechism of the Catholic Church*[6] ordering its publication. The extraordinary importance, for the Church as well as for every man of good will, of this rich and synthetic "exposition of the faith of the Church and of Catholic doctrine, verified and enlightened by the sacred Scripture, by the apostolic Tradition and by the Magisterium"[7] is well known. Even though this is a document of different aim and content, it becomes immediately evident that the new catechism could offer some special enlightenment at different points of the Guide and, above all, that it could be a sure and authentic point of reference for the formation and for the activities of the catechists. In the final edition of the text, therefore, care has been taken to point out, particularly in the notes, the principal connections with the themes exposed in the catechism.

It is our hope that this Guide will be used as a reference book and will be a source of unity and encouragement for catechists and, through them, for their ecclesial communities. The CEP offers it, therefore, to the Episcopal Conferences and to individual bishops as an aid to the life and apostolate of their catechists and as a basis for the renewal of national and diocesan catechetical programs and directors.

Part I: An Apostle Ever Relevant

I. The Catechist in a Missionary Church

2. Vocation and Identity

Every baptized Catholic is personally called by the Holy Spirit to make his or her contribution to the coming of God's kingdom. Within the lay state there are various *vocations*, or different spiritual and apostolic roads to be followed by both individuals and groups. Within the general vocation of the laity there are particular ones.[8]

At the origin of the catechist's vocation, therefore, apart from the sacraments of baptism and confirmation, there is a specific call from the Holy Spirit, a *"special charism recognized by the Church"*[9] and made explicit by the bishop's mandate. It is important for the catechist candidate to recognize the supernatural and ecclesial significance of this call, so as to be able to respond, like the Son of God, *"Here I come"* (Heb 10:7), or, like the prophet, *"Here I am, send me"* (Isa 6:8).

In actual missionary practice, the catechist's vocation is both *specific*, that is, for the task of catechizing, and *general*, for collaborating in whatever apostolic services are useful for the building up of the Church.[10]

The CEP insists on the value and distinctiveness of the catechist's vocation. Each one, therefore, should try to discover, discern and foster his or her own particular vocation.[11]

From these premises it can be seen that catechists in mission territories have their own identity, which characterizes them in respect to those working in the older Churches, as the Church's Magisterium and legislation clearly recognize.[12]

In short, the catechist in mission territories is identified by four elements: a call from the Holy Spirit; an ecclesial mission; collaboration with the bishop's apostolic mandate; and a special link with missionary activity *ad gentes*.

3. Role

Closely linked to the question of identity is that of the role of the catechist in missionary activity, a role that is both important and many-sided. Apart from the explicit proclamation of the Christian message and the accompaniment of catechumens and newly baptized Christians on their road to full maturity in the faith and in sacramental life, the catechist's role comprises presence and witness, and involvement in human development, inculturation and dialogue.[13]

Thus the Church's Magisterium, when it speaks of catechists *"in mission lands,"*[14] treats the subject as an important one and gives space to it. The Encyclical *Redemptoris Missio*, for instance, describes catechists as *"specialized workers, direct witnesses, indispensable evangelizers, who represent the basic strength of Christian communities, especially in the young Churches."*[15] The *Code of Canon Law* has a canon on catechists involved in strictly missionary activity and describes them as *"lay members of Christ's faithful who have received proper formation and are outstanding in their living of the Christian life. Under the direction of missionaries, they are to present the Gospel teaching and engage in liturgical worship and in works of charity."*[16]

This description of the catechist corresponds with that of the CEP in its 1970 Plenary Assembly: *"The catechist is a lay person specially appointed by the Church, in accordance with local needs, to make Christ known, loved and followed by those who do not yet know Him and by the faithful themselves."*[17]

To the catechist, as indeed to other members of the faithful, may be entrusted, in accordance with the canonical norms, certain functions of the sacred ministry which do not require the character of Holy Orders. The execution of these functions, when a priest is not available, does not make a pastor of the catechist, inasmuch as he or she derives legitimation directly from the official permission granted by the pastors.[18] However, we may recall a clarification made in the past by the CEP itself: in his or her ordinary activity, *"the catechist is not a simple substitute for the priest, but is, by right, a witness of Christ in the community."*[19]

4. Categories and Tasks

Catechists in mission territories are not only different from those in older Churches, but among themselves vary greatly in characteristics and modes of action from one young Church to another, so that it is difficult to give a single description that would apply to all.

There are two main types of catechist: full-time catechists, who devote their life completely to this service and are officially recognized as such; and part-time catechists, who offer a more limited, but still precious, collaboration. The proportion between the two categories varies from place to place, but in general there are far more part-time than full-time catechists.

Various tasks are entrusted to both types of catechist, and it is in these tasks that one can see the great diversity that exists between different areas. The following outline would seem to give a realistic summary of the main functions entrusted to catechists in Churches dependent on the CEP:

—Catechists with the **specific task of catechizing,** which includes educating young people and adults in the faith, preparing candidates and their families for the sacraments of Christian initiation, and helping with retreats and other meetings connected with catechesis. Catechists with these functions are more numerous in Churches that have stressed the development of lay services.[20]

—Catechists who **collaborate in different forms of apostolate** with ordained ministers, whose direction they willingly accept. The tasks entrusted to them are multiple: preaching to non-Christians; catechizing catechumens and those already baptized; leading community prayer, especially at the Sunday liturgy in the absence of a priest; helping the sick and presiding at funerals; training other catechists in special centers or guiding volunteer catechists in their work; taking charge of pastoral initiatives and organizing parish functions; helping the poor and working for human development and justice. This type of catechist is more common in places where parishes cover a large area with scattered communities far from the center, or where, because of a shortage of clergy, parish priests select lay leaders to help them."[21]

The dynamism of the young Churches and their sociocultural situation give rise to other apostolic functions. For instance, there are *religion teachers* in schools, teaching both baptized and non-Christian students. These can be found in government schools, where the state allows religious instruction, as well as in Catholic schools. There are also *Sunday catechists,* who teach in Sunday schools organized by the parish, especially where the state does not allow religious instruction in its schools. And in large cities, especially in the poorer quarters, there are lay apostles doing excellent work among the destitute, immigrants, prisoners and others in need. Such functions are considered, according to the sensibilities and experience of the different Churches, as either proper to the catechist or as a general form of lay service to the Church and its mission. The CEP considers the multiplicity and variety of these tasks as an expression of the richness of the Spirit at work in the young Churches, and recommends them all to the attention of the bishops. It asks them to foster especially those that best respond to present needs and to the immediate future, insofar as this can be foreseen.

There is another consideration. Catechists may be old or young, male or female, married or single, and these factors should be taken into account in assigning tasks in the various cultural settings. Thus, a married man seems most indicated to be the community leader, especially in societies where men still have a dominant role. Women would seem to be the natural choice for educating the young and working for the Christian promotion of women. Married adults have greater stability and can give witness to the values of Christian marriage. The young, on the other hand, are to be preferred for contact with youth and for activities that take up more time.

Finally, one should bear in mind that, beside the lay catechists, there is a great number of religious men and women who carry out catechesis and, because of their special consecration, are able to bear a unique witness in the capacity of their mission and consequently are called to be available and prepared in their own way for this task. In practice they take on many of the tasks of the catechist and, because of their close cooperation with the priests, often play a directing role. The CEP, therefore, strongly recommends the involvement of religious men and women, as is already the practice in many places, in this important sector of ecclesial life, especially in the training and guidance of catechists.[22]

5. Prospects for Development in the Near Future

The tendency in general, and one which the CEP approves of and encourages, is for the figure of **the catechist as such to be armed and developed,** independently of the tasks he or she performs. The value of catechists and their influence on the apostolate are always decisive for the Church's mission.[23]

Basing itself on its own worldwide experience, the CEP offers the following suggestions to help promote reflection on this subject:

—**Absolute precedence must be given to quality.** A common problem is certainly the scarcity of properly trained candidates. The character of the catechist is of prime importance, and this must influence the criteria for selection and the program for training and guidance.

The words of the Holy Father are illuminating: *"For such a fundamental evangelical service a great number of workers are necessary. But, while striving for numbers, we must aim above all today at securing the quality of the catechist."*[24]

—In view of the present impetus toward a **renewed mission *ad gentes*,**[25] the future of the catechist in the young Churches will certainly be marked by missionary zeal. Catechists, therefore, should be ever more fully qualified as lay pioneers of the apostolate. In the future, as in the past, they should be distinguished by their indispensable contribution to missionary activity *ad gentes.*

—It is not enough to fix an objective, but **suitable means must be chosen** for attaining the goal, and this holds true also for the training of catechists. Concrete programs should be drawn up, adequate structures and financial support provided, and qualified formators secured, so as to provide the catechists with a solid formation. Obviously the scale of the facilities and the level of study will vary according to the real possibilities of each Church, but certain standards should be attained by all, without giving in to difficulties.

—**The cadres in charge need to be strengthened.** Everywhere there should be at least a few professional catechists who have been trained in suitable centers and who, placed in key posts of the catechetical organization under the direction of their pastors, see to the preparation of new candidates, introduce them to their functions and guide them in their work. These cadres should be found at all levels—parish, diocesan and national—and will be a guarantee of the good functioning of such an important sector of the Church's life.

—The CEP expects that in the near future the work of catechists will be still further developed, and we should try to see from now **how tomorrow's protagonists will act.**

Special encouragement will be given to catechists with **a marked missionary spirit,** who *"will themselves become missionary animators in their ecclesial communities and would be willing, if the Spirit so calls them and their pastors commission them, to go outside their own territory to preach the Gospel, prepare catechumens for baptism and build new ecclesial communities."*[26]

Catechists who are involved in the catechesis will have a developing future, because the young Churches are multiplying the services of the lay apostolate, which are distinct from those of the catechists.[27] Hence it will be of great use to have **specialized** catechists, for instance, those who promote Christian life where the majority of the people are already baptized but where the level of religious instruction and of the life of faith is not high. Catechists should also be trained for challenges which already face us today and will become even greater in the future:

urbanization, increasing numbers going on to third-level education, the world of youngsters, migrants and refugees, growing secularization, political changes, the influence of the mass media, and so on.

The CEP draws attention to these future prospects and the need to face up to them, while realizing that it is up to the local pastors to see how best to go about it. Episcopal Conferences and individual bishops should draw up a program for the preparation of catechists for the future, giving special attention to the missionary dimension in both their training and activity. These programs should not be vague, but specific and adapted to local conditions, so that each Church will have both the catechists it needs today and those that will be necessary in the near future.

II. The Catechist's Spirituality

6. Necessity and Nature of Spirituality for the Catechist

Catechists must have a deep spirituality, that is, they must live in the Spirit, who will help them to renew themselves continually in their specific identity.

The need for a spirituality proper to catechists springs from their vocation and mission. It includes, therefore, a new and special motivation, a call to sanctity. Pope John Paul II's saying: *"The true missionary is the saint,"*[28] can be applied without hesitation to the catechist. Like every member of the faithful, catechists are *"called to holiness and to mission,"*[29] that is, to live out their own vocation *"with the fervor of the saints."*[30] Their spirituality is closely bound up with their status as lay Christians, made participants, in their own degree, in Christ's prophetic, priestly and kingly offices. As members of the laity, they are involved in the secular world and have, *"according to the condition of each, the special obligation to permeate and perfect the temporal order of things with the spirit of the Gospel. In this way, particularly in conducting secular business and exercising secular functions, they are to give witness to Christ."*[31]

For **married catechists,** matrimonial life forms an integral part of their spirituality. As the Pope justly affirms, *"married catechists are expected to bear witness constantly to the Christian value of matrimony, living the sacrament in full fidelity and educating their children with a sense of responsibility."*[32] This matrimonial spirituality can have great impact on their activity, and it would be good for them to involve their spouse and children in the work, so that the whole family radiates apostolic witness.

Catechists' spirituality is also conditioned by their apostolic vocation, and therefore should bear the marks of: openness to God's word, to the Church and to the world; authenticity of life; missionary zeal; and devotion to Mary.

7. Openness to the Word

The office of catechist is basically that of communicating God's word, and so the fundamental spiritual attitude should be one of openness to this word, contained in revelation, preached by the Church, celebrated in the liturgy and lived out in the lives of saints.[33] This is always an encounter with Christ, hidden in his word, in the Eucharist and in our brothers and sisters. Openness to the word means openness to God, to the Church and to the world.

—**Openness to God** *Uno et Trino,* who is in the most intimate depths of each person and gives meaning to his or her life: convictions, criteria, scale of values, decisions, relationships, behavior etc. Catechists should allow themselves to be drawn into the circle of the Father, who communicates the word; of the Son, the incarnate Word, who speaks only the words He hears from the Father (cf. John 8:26; 12:49); and of the Holy Spirit, who enlightens the mind to help it understand God's words and opens the heart to receive them with love and put them into practice (cf. John 16:12–14).

It is a spirituality, therefore, that is rooted in the living word of God, with a Trinitarian dimension, like the universal mission itself with its offer of salvation. It requires a corresponding interior attitude which shares in the love of the Father, who wishes that all should come to the knowledge of the truth and be saved (cf. 1 Tim 2:4); which seeks communion with Christ, so as to share his own *"mind"* (Phil 2:5) and experience, like Paul, his comforting presence: *"Do not be afraid . . . because I am with you"* (Acts 18:9–10): which allows oneself to be molded by the Spirit and transformed into a courageous witness of Christ and enlightened preacher of the word.[34]

—**Openness to the Church,** of which catechists are living members, which they strive to build up, and from which they receive their mandate. The word is entrusted to the Church, so that it may keep it faithfully, deepen its understanding of it with the help of the Holy Spirit, and proclaim it to the whole world.[35]

As People of God and the Mystical Body of Christ, the Church requires from catechists a deep sense of belonging and responsibility, inasmuch as they are living and active members of it; as universal sacrament of salvation, it elicits the will to live its mystery and its manifold grace so as to be enriched by it and become a visible sign to the community. The catechist's service is never an individual or isolated act, but is always deeply ecclesial.

Openness to the Church expresses itself by filial love, dedication to its service and a willingness to suffer for its cause. In particular, it is expressed in the attachment and obedience to the Roman Pontiff, the center of unity and the bond of universal communion, so also to the bishop, the father and guide of the particular Church. Catechists should share responsibly in the earthly vicissitudes of the pilgrim Church, which is by nature missionary,[36] and aspire with it toward the final reunion with Christ the Spouse.

The ecclesial sense that is proper to the catechist's spirituality expresses itself, therefore, in sincere love of the Church, in imitation of Christ, who *"loved the Church and sacrificed himself for her."* It is an active and total love which becomes a sharing in the Church's mission of salvation to the point even of giving one's life for it if necessary.[37]

—**Missionary openness to the world,** finally—the world which is offered the salvation that springs from *"that fountain of love or charity within God the Father"*;[38] the world in which historically God's Word came to live among us to redeem us (cf. John 1:14), and in which the Holy Spirit was poured out to sanctify men and women and gather them into the Church, to have access to the Father through Christ in the one Spirit (cf. Eph 2:18).[39]

Catechists, therefore, will be open and attentive to the needs of the world, knowing that they are called to work in and for the world, without, however, belonging completely to it (cf. John 17:14–21). This means that they must be thoroughly involved in the life of the society about them, without pulling back from fear of difficulties or withdrawing through love of tranquillity. But they must keep a supernatural outlook on life and trust in the efficacy of God's word, which does not return to Him without *"succeeding in what it was sent to do"* (Isa 55:11).

Openness to the world is a characteristic of the catechist's spirituality in virtue of the apostolic love of Jesus the Good Shepherd, who came *"to gather together in unity the scattered children of God"* (John 11:52). Catechists must be filled with this love, bringing it to their brothers and sisters as they preach to them that God loves and offers his salvation to all.[40]

8. Coherence and Authenticity of Life

The work of catechists involves their whole being. Before they preach the word, they must make it their own and live by it.[41] *"The world . . . needs evangelizers who speak of a God that they know and who is familiar to them, as if they saw the Invisible."*[42]

What catechists teach should not be a purely human science nor the sum of their personal opinions but the Church's faith, which is the same throughout the world, which they themselves live and whose witnesses they are.[43]

Hence the need for coherence and authenticity of life. Before *doing* the catechesis one must first of all *be* a catechist. The *truth* of their lives confirms their message. It would be sad if they did not *"practice what they preached"* and spoke about a God of whom they had theoretical knowledge but with whom they had no contact. They should apply to themselves the words of Saint Mark concerning the vocation of the apostles: *"He appointed twelve, to be his companions and to be sent out to preach"* (Mark 3:14–15).

Authenticity of life means a life of prayer, experience of God and fidelity to the action of the Holy Spirit. It implies a certain intensity and an internal and external orderliness, adapted to the various personal and family situations of each. It might be objected that catechists, being members of the laity, cannot have a structured spiritual life like that of religious and that therefore they must content themselves with something less. But in every life situation, whether one is engaged in secular work or in the ministry, it is possible for everyone, priest, religious or layperson, to attain a high degree of communion with God and an ordered rhythm of prayer, including the finding of times of silence for entering more deeply into the contemplation of God. The more intense and real one's spiritual life is, the more convincing and efficacious will one's witness and activity be.

It is also important for catechists that they grow interiorly in the peace and joy of Christ, so that they may be examples of hope and courage (cf. Rom 12:12). For Christ *"is our peace"* (Eph 2:14) and he gives his apostles his joy that their *"joy may be full"* (John 15:11).

Catechists, therefore, should be bearers of paschal joy and hope, in the name of the Church. In fact, *"the most precious gift that the Church can offer to the bewildered and restless world of our time is to form within it Christians who are confirmed in what is essential and who are humbly joyful in their faith."*[44]

9. Missionary Zeal

In view of their baptism and special vocation, catechists who live in daily contact with large numbers of non-Christians, as is the case in mission territories, cannot but feel moved by Christ's words: *"Other sheep I have that are not of this fold, and these too I must lead"* (John 10:16); *"go out to the whole world and preach the gospel to every creature"* (Mark 16:15). To be able to affirm, like Peter and John before the Sanhedrin, *"we cannot but speak of what we have seen and heard"* (Acts 4:20), and to realize with Paul the ideal of apostolic ministry: *"the love of Christ overwhelms us"* (2 Cor 5:14), catechists should have a strong missionary spirit—a spirit that will be all the more effective if they are seen to be convinced of what they say and are enthusiastic and courageous, without ever being ashamed of the Gospel (cf. Rom 1:16). While the wise ones according to this world seek immediate gratification, the catechist will glory only in Christ, who gives strength (cf. Col 1:29), and will wish to know and preach only *"Christ the power of God and the wisdom of God"* (1 Cor 1:24). As the *Catechism of the Catholic Church* rightly affirms, from *"the loving knowledge of Christ springs out the irresistible desire to announce, to 'evangelize' and to lead others to the 'yes' of the faith in Jesus Christ. At the same time, one also feels the need to know this faith ever better."*[45]

Catechists will try to be like the shepherd who goes in search of the lost sheep *"until he finds it"* (Luke 15:4), or like the woman with the lost drachma who would *"search thoroughly until she had found it"* (Luke 15:8). Their convictions should be a source of **apostolic zeal:** *"I have made myself all things to all in order to save some at any cost. I do it all for the sake of the gospel"* (1 Cor 9:22–23; cf. 2 Cor 12:15). And again Saint Paul says: *"Woe to me if I do not preach the gospel"* (1 Cor 9:16). The burning zeal of Saint Paul should inspire catechists to stir up their own zeal, which should be the response to their vocation, and which will help them to preach Christ boldly and work actively for the growth of the ecclesial community.[46]

Finally, one should not forget that the stamp of authenticity on the missionary spirit is that of the cross. The Christ whom catechists have come to know is *"a crucified Christ"* (1 Cor 2:2): he whom they preach is *"Christ crucified, a stumbling block to Jews and folly to Gentiles"* (1 Cor 1:23), whom the Father raised from the dead on the third day (cf. Acts 10:40). They should be prepared, therefore, to live in hope the mystery of the death and resurrection of Christ in the midst of difficult situations, personal suffering, family problems and obstacles in their apostolic work, as they strive to follow the Lord on his own difficult road: *"in my own body I complete what is lacking in Christ's afflictions for the sake of his body, the Church"* (Col 1:24).[47]

10. Devotion to Mary

Through her own special vocation, Mary saw the Son of God *"grow in wisdom, in age and in grace"* (Luke 2:52). She was the teacher who *"trained Him in human knowledge of the Scriptures and of God's loving plan for his people, and in adoration of the Father."*[48] She was also *"the first of his disciples."*[49] As Saint Augustine boldly affirmed, to be his disciple was more important for Mary than to be his mother.[50] One can say with reason and joy that Mary is a *"living catechism,"* *"mother and model of catechists."*[51]

The spirituality of catechists, like that of every Christian and especially those involved in the apostolate, will be enriched by a deep devotion to the Mother of God. Before explaining to others the place of Mary in the mystery of Christ and the Church,[52] they should have her present in their own soul and should give evidence of a sincere Marian piety,[53] which they will communicate to the community. They will find in Mary a simple and effective model, for themselves and others: *"The Virgin Mary in her own life lived an example of that maternal love by which all should be fittingly animated who cooperate in the apostolic mission of the Church on behalf of the rebirth of humanity."*[54]

The preaching of the word is always connected with prayer, the celebration of the Eucharist and the building of community. The earliest Christian community was a model of this (cf. Acts 2–4), united around Mary the mother of Jesus (cf. Acts 1:14)

III. The Catechist's Attitude to Some Contemporary Issues

11. Service to the Community as a Whole and to Particular Groups

There are various groups in the community that may require the services of catechists: young people and adults, men and women students and workers, Catholics, other Christians and non-Christians. It is not the same thing to be a catechist for catechumens preparing for baptism as to be community leader for a village of Catholics, with responsibility for various pastoral activities, or to be a religion teacher in a school, or to be charged with preparing people for the sacraments, or to be assigned to pastoral work in an inner-city area, etc.

Catechists will try to promote communication and communion between the members of the community, and will devote themselves to the groups committed to their care, trying to understand their particular needs so as to help them as much as possible. As the needs differ from group to group, so the training of catechists will have to be adapted for the groups envisaged. It would be useful, therefore, for catechists to know in advance the sort of work they will be called to and make acquaintance with the groups concerned. Some useful suggestions in connection with this have already been offered by the Magisterium, especially in the *General Catechetical Directory*, nos. 77–97, and the Apostolic Exhortation *Catechesi Tradendae*, nos. 34–35.

Special attention should be paid to the **sick and aged,** because their physical and psychological weakness calls for greater charity and concern.[55]

The sick should be helped to understand the redemptive value of the cross,[56] in union with Jesus, who took upon himself the weight of our infirmities (cf. Matt 8:17; Isa 53:4). Catechists should visit them frequently, offering them the comfort of God's word and, when commissioned to do so, the Eucharist.

The aged too should be followed with special care, for they have an important role in the community, as Pope John Paul II recognizes when he calls them *"witnesses of the tradition of faith* (cf. Ps 44.1; Exod 12.26–27), *teachers of wisdom* (cf. Sir 6:34; 8:11–12), *workers of charity."*[57] Families should be encouraged to keep their elderly members with them, to *"bear witness to the past and instill wisdom in the young."*[58] The aged should feel the support of the whole community and should be helped to bear in faith their inevitable limitations and, in certain cases, their solitude. Catechists will prepare them for their meeting with the Lord and help them experience the joy that comes from our hope in eternal life.[59]

Catechists will also show sensitivity in dealing with people in difficult situations such as those in irregular marriages, the children of broken marriages, and so on. They must be able to share in and express the immense compassion of the heart of Jesus (cf. Matt 9:36; Mark 6:34; 8:2; Luke 7:13).

12. Need for Inculturation

Like all forms of evangelization, catechesis too is called to bring the Gospel into the heart of the different cultures.[60] The process of inculturation takes time, as it is a deep, gradual and all-embracing process. Through it, as Pope John Paul II explains,

> the Church makes the Gospel incarnate in different cultures and at the same time introduces peoples, together with their cultures, into her own community; she transmits to them her own values, at the same time taking the good elements that already exist in them and renewing them from within.[61]

Catechists, like all missionary personnel, will play an active part in this process. They should be specifically prepared for it, with courses on the elements of cultural anthropology and on their own culture, and should be aware of the guidelines that the Church has laid down on this matter[62] and which may be summarized as follows:

—The Gospel message, though it can never be identified with any one culture, is necessarily incarnated in cultures. From its very beginnings it was incarnated in certain specific cultures, and one must take account of this if one is not to deprive the new Churches of values which are now the patrimony of the universal Church.

—The Gospel is a force for renewal, and can rectify elements in cultures which do not conform to it.

—The local ecclesial communities, which are the primary subjects of inculturation, live out their daily experience of faith and charity in a particular culture, and the bishop should indicate the best ways to bring out the positive values in that culture. The experts give incentive and support.

—Inculturation is genuine when it is guided by two principles: it must be founded on the word of God, revealed in the Scriptures, and must follow the Church's Tradition and the guidance of the Magisterium; and it must never go against the Church unity that was willed by the Lord.

—Popular piety, understood as an expression of Catholic devotion colored by local values, traditions and attitudes, when purified of defects caused by ignorance and superstition, expresses the wisdom of God's people and is a privileged form of inculturation of the Gospel.[63]

Following the above directives, catechists should contribute to inculturation by fitting into the overall pastoral plan drawn up by the competent authorities and avoiding adventures into particular experiments that might upset the faithful. They should be convinced that the Gospel is strong enough to penetrate any culture and enrich and strengthen it from within.

13. Human Development and Option for the Poor

There is a *"close connection"* between the preaching of the Gospel and the promotion of human development.[64] They are both included in the Church's mission.

> *Through the Gospel message, the Church offers a force for liberation which promotes development precisely because it leads to conversion of heart and of ways of thinking, fosters the recognition of each person's dignity, encourages solidarity, commitment and service of one's neighbor, and gives everyone a place in God's plan, which is the building of his kingdom of peace and justice, beginning already in this life. This is the biblical perspective of the new heavens and a new earth (cf: Isa 65:17, 2 Pt 3:13, Rev 21:1), which has been the stimulus and goal for humanity's advancement in history.*[65]

It is well known that the Church claims for itself a mission of a *"religious"*[66] nature, but this has to take place, to be incarnated, in the real life and history of humanity.

To take the values of the Gospel into the economic, social and political fields is a task especially for the laity.[67] Catechists have an important role in the field of human development and the promotion of justice. Living as laypeople in society, they can well understand, interpret, and try to bring solutions to personal and social problems in the light of the Gospel. They should therefore be close to the people, help them to understand the realities of social life so as to try to improve it, and, when necessary, they should have the courage to speak out for the weak and defend their rights.

When it is necessary to take practical initiatives in this area, they should act in union with the community, in a program drawn up with the approval of the bishop.

Connected with human development is the question of the **preferential option for the poor.** Catechists, especially those engaged in the general apostolate, have a duty to make this ecclesial option, which does not mean that they are interested only in the poor, but that these should have a prior claim on their attention. The foundation of their interest in the poor must be love, for, as Pope John Paul II explicitly says, *"love has been and remains the driving force of mission."* [68]

By the poor should be understood especially the materially poor, who are so numerous in many mission territories. These brothers and sisters of Christ should be able to feel the Church's maternal love for them, even when they do not yet belong to it, so as to be encouraged to accept and overcome their difficulties with the help of Christian faith and themselves become agents of their own integral development. The Church's charitable activity, like all pastoral activity, *"brings light and an impulse toward true development"* to the poor. [69]

Apart from the financially deprived, catechists should pay special attention also to other groups in need: those who are oppressed, persecuted or marginalized, the handicapped, the unemployed, prisoners, refugees, drug addicts, those suffering from AIDS, etc. [70]

14. Spirit of Ecumenism

Discord among Christians *"openly contradicts the will of Christ, provides a stumbling block to the world, and inflicts damage on the most holy cause of proclaiming the good news to every creature."* [71]

All Christian communities should *"participate in ecumenical dialogue and in other initiatives designed to promote Christian unity."* [72] In mission territories this task assumes special urgency so that Jesus' prayer to his Father should not be in vain: *"may they be one in us . . . so that the world may believe it was you who sent me"* (John 17:21). [73]

Catechists, by their very mission, are necessarily involved in this aspect of the apostolate and should promote an ecumenical spirit in the community, beginning with the catechumens and newly baptized. [74] They should have a deep desire for Christian unity, should willingly engage in dialogue with Christians of other denominations, and should commit themselves generously to ecumenical initiatives,[75] keeping to their particular role and following the Church's directives as specified by the Episcopal Conference and the local bishop.[76] Their catechetical activity, therefore, and their teaching of religion in schools should instill an openness to ecumenical cooperation.[77]

Their activity will be truly ecumenical if they can both courageously *"teach that the fullness of the revealed truths and of the means of salvation instituted by Christ is found in the Catholic Church"*[78] and also *"give a correct and fair presentation of the other Churches and ecclesial communities that the Spirit of Christ does not refrain from using as means of salvation."*[79]

They should try to have good relations with catechists and leaders of other denominations, in accord with their Pastors and, when so charged, as their representatives. They should avoid stirring up useless rivalries; should help the faithful to live in harmony with and respect for Christians of other denominations, while fully maintaining their own Catholic identity; and should join other believers in working for peace.[80]

15. Dialogue with Those of Other Religions

Inter-religious dialogue forms part of the Church's evangelizing mission. Like preaching, it is also a way of making Christ known, and it is essential that the Catholic Church maintain good relations and contact with those of other faiths. It should be a **saving dialogue,** approached in the spirit of Christ himself.

Catechists, with their task of communicating the faith, should be open to this kind of dialogue and be trained to take part in it. They should be taught to realize its value and put it into practice in accordance with the guidelines of the Magisterium, especially those of *Redemptoris Missio,* of the subsequent document *Dialogue and Proclamation,* which was drawn up jointly by the Pontifical Council for Inter-religious Dialogue, and the CEP, and of the *Catechism of the Catholic Church.*[81] These guidelines include:

—**Listening to the Spirit,** who blows where He wills (cf. John 3:8); respecting his work in souls; and striving for inner purification, without which dialogue cannot bear fruit.[82]

—**Accurate knowledge** of the religions practiced in the area: their history and organization; the values in them which, like *"seeds of the Word,"* can be a *"preparation for the Gospel"*;[83] their limitations and errors which are not in conformity with the Gospel and which should be respectively completed and corrected.

—A **conviction** that salvation comes from Christ and that, therefore, dialogue does not dispense one from proclamation,[84] that the Church is the ordinary way of salvation and that only she possesses the fullness of revealed truth and salvific means.[85] As Pope John Paul II confirmed, while referring to *Redemptoris Missio:*

> *One cannot place on the same level God's revelation in Christ and the scriptures or traditions of other religions. A theocentrism which did not recognize Christ in his full identity would be unacceptable to the Catholic Faith. . . . Christ's missionary command remains permanently valid and is an explicit call to make disciples of all nations and to baptize them, in order to bring them the fullness of God's gift.*[86]

Dialogue should not, therefore, lead to religious relativism.

—**Practical cooperation** with non-Christian religious bodies in facing the great challenges to humanity such as the bringing about of peace, justice, development, etc.[87] There should always be an attitude of esteem and openness toward persons. God is the Father of all, and it is his love that should unite the human family in working for good.

In taking part in such dialogue, catechists should not be left on their own but should be integrated in the community. Initiatives in this area should be undertaken in the context of programs approved by the bishop and, when necessary, by the Episcopal Conference or the Holy See. Catechists should not act unilaterally, and especially should do nothing against the norms laid down. Finally, one should continue to believe in dialogue, even when it seems difficult or misunderstood. In certain conditions, it is indeed the only way to bear witness to Christ; it is always "*a path towards the Kingdom and will certainly bear fruit, even if the times and seasons are known only to the Father*" (cf. Acts 1:7).[88]

16. Attention to the Spread of Sects

The rapid spread of sects of both Christian and non-Christian origin presents a pastoral challenge for the Church throughout the world today. In mission territories they are a serious obstacle to the preaching of the Gospel and the orderly growth of the young Churches because they damage the integrity of faith and communion.[89]

Certain regions and persons are more vulnerable and more exposed to the influence of these sects. What the sects offer seems to work in their favor as they present apparently simple and immediate answers to the felt needs of the people, and the means they use are adapted to local sensibilities and cultures.[90]

As is well known, the Church's Magisterium has often given warnings about the dangers posed by sects, and called for "*serious reflection*" in view of their rapid spread.[91] Rather than a positive campaign against them, however, what is called for in mission territories is a renewal of mission itself.[92]

Catechists would seem to be particularly suitable for counteracting the influence of the sects. As they have the task of teaching the faith and of fostering the growth of Christian life, they can help both Christians and non-Christians understand what the real answers to their needs are, without having recourse to the pseudo-securities of the sects. Also, being members of the laity, they are closer to the people and can know their direct and lived situations.

The preferential work-lines for the catechists should be: to study first of all what exactly the sects teach and the points on which they particularly attack the Church, so as to be able to point out the inconsistencies in their position; to forestall their encroachment by giving positive instruction and encouraging the Christian community to greater fervor; and to proclaim clearly the Christian message. They should give personal attention to people and their problems, helping them to clarify doubts and to be wary of the specious promises of the sects.

It must not be forgotten that many of the sects are intolerant and are particularly hostile to Catholicism. Constructive dialogue is often not possible with them, even though here too one must have respect and understanding for persons. The Church's position must be made clear in this and also in an ecumenical way, for the spread of the sects poses a danger to the other Christian denominations as well.[93] Here, as in other areas, catechists should remain firmly within the common pastoral program approved by the Church authorities.[94]

Part II: Choice and Formation of Catechists

IV. Choice of Candidates

17. Importance of a Proper Choice

It is difficult to lay down rules as to the level of faith and the strength of motivation that a candidate should have in order to be accepted for training as a catechist. Among the reasons for this are: the varying levels of religious maturity in the different ecclesial communities, the scarcity of suitable and available personnel, sociopolitical conditions, poor educational standards and financial difficulties. But one should not give in to the difficulties and lower one's standards.

The CEP insists on the principle that a good choice of candidates is essential. Right from the beginning, a **high quality** must be set. Pastors should be convinced of this as the goal to be aimed at and, even though it may be achieved only gradually, they should not easily settle for less. They should also prepare the community, and especially the young, by explaining the role of catechists, so as to awaken an interest in this form of ecclesial service. It should not be forgotten either that the community's esteem for this service will be directly proportional to the way in which pastors treat their catechists, giving them worthwhile tasks and respecting their responsibility. A fulfilled, responsible and dynamic catechist, working enthusiastically and joyfully in the tasks assigned,[95] appreciated and properly remunerated, is the best promoter of other vocations.

18. Criteria for Selection

In choosing candidates, some criteria should be considered essential while others might be optional. It is useful to have a list of criteria for the whole Church, which could be referred to by those with the charge of choosing candidates. These criteria, which should be *sufficient, precise, realistic* and *controllable*, could be adapted to local conditions by the local authorities, who are the ones best able to judge the needs and possibilities of the community.

The following general considerations should be kept in mind, so that there may be a common policy in all mission areas while respecting inevitable differences.

—Some criteria concern the **catechist's person.** A basic rule is that no one should be accepted as a candidate unless he or she is positively motivated and is not seeking the post simply because another suitable job is not available. Positive qualities in candidates should be: faith that manifests itself in their piety and daily life; love for the Church and communion with its pastors; apostolic spirit and missionary zeal; love for their brothers and sisters and a willingness to give generous service; sufficient education; the respect of the community; the human, moral and technical qualities necessary for the work of a catechist, such as dynamism, good relations with others, and so on.

—Other criteria concern the actual **process of selection.** As it is a question of ecclesial service, the decision belongs to the pastor, which in this case usually means the parish priest, but the community should be involved in the proposal of candidates and their evaluation. At a later stage, the parish priest should present the candidates chosen to the bishop or his representative, to confirm the choice and eventually give them their official mandate.

—There should also be special criteria for the **acceptance of candidates in catechetical centers.** Apart from the general criteria, each center, in keeping with its character, will have its own requirements concerning the level of scholastic achievement needed for entry, its conditions for participation, its formation program, and so on.

These general guidelines will have to be made more specific for local conditions and applied to the particular circumstances in each area.

V. Process of Formation

19. Need for Proper Formation

In order to have a sufficient number of suitable catechists for the communities, besides a careful selection, it is indispensable to stress the training to which the quality is connected. This has often been stressed by the Magisterium, because every apostolic activity *"which is not supported by properly trained persons is condemned to failure."*[96]

The relevant documents of the Magisterium require both a general and a specific formation for catechists: general, in the sense that their whole character and personality should be developed; and specific, with a view to the particular tasks they will be charged with in a supplementary way: preaching the word to both Christians and non-Christians, leading the community, presiding when necessary at liturgical prayers, and helping in various ways those in spiritual or material need. As Pope John Paul II said:

> *To set high standards means both to provide a thorough basic training and to keep it constantly updated. This is a fundamental duty, in order to ensure qualified personnel for the Church's mission, with good training programs and adequate structures, providing for all aspects of formation—human, spiritual, doctrinal, apostolic and professional.*[97]

It will be a demanding training program therefore, both for the candidates and for those who have to provide it. The CEP entrusts its realization to the bishops as part of their pastoral task.[98]

20. Unity and Harmony in the Personality of Catechist

In living out their vocation, catechists, like all members of the Catholic laity, *"must be formed according to the union which exists from their being members of the Church and citizens of human society."*[99] There cannot be separate parallel lives: a *"spiritual"* life with its values and demands, a *"secular"* life with its various forms of expression, and an *"apostolic"* life with its own requirements.[100]

To bring about unity and harmony in one's personality, certain obstacles of a temperamental, intellectual or emotional nature must first of all be overcome, and an ordered lifestyle established. But what will be decisive will be the ability to reach into the depths of one's soul and find there the principle and source of the catechist's identity, namely, the person of Christ himself.

The first and essential object of catechesis is, of course, the person of Jesus of Nazareth, the only begotten of the Father, *"full of grace and truth"* (John 1:14), *"the way, the truth and the life"* (John 14:6). It is the *"mystery of Christ"* (Eph 3:4), in its integrity *"hidden for generations and generations"* (Col 1:26), which must be revealed. It follows that the catechists' concern should be to transmit, through their teaching and behavior, the doctrine and life of Christ. Their mode of being and of working should depend entirely on that of Christ. The unity and harmony in their personalities should be Christocentric, built upon *"a deep intimacy with Christ and with the Father,"* in the Spirit.[101] This cannot be too strongly insisted upon, when there is question of the catechist's role and importance in these decisive times for the Church's mission.

21. Human Maturity

From the beginning it should be clear that the candidate possesses basic human qualities that can be further developed. What is to be aimed at is a person with human maturity suitable for a responsible role in the community.

The following qualities should be taken into consideration: in the **purely human sphere:** psychophysical equilibrium: good health, a sense of responsibility, honesty, dynamism; good professional and family conduct; a spirit of sacrifice, strength, perseverance, and so on; with a view to the **functions of a catechist:** good human relations, ability to dialogue with those of other religions, grasp of one's own culture, ability to communicate, willingness to work with others, leadership qualities, balanced judgment, openness of mind, a sense of realism, a capacity to transmit consolation and hope, and so on; with a view to **particular situations or roles:** aptitudes for working in the fields of peacemaking, development, sociocultural promotion, justice, health care, and so on.

The aim of catechetical formation will be to build on the human qualities already present, to develop them and add the necessary skills for a fruitful ministry.

22. Deep Spiritual Life

To be able to educate others in the faith, catechists should themselves have a deep spiritual life. This is the most important aspect of their personality and therefore the one to be most stressed in formation. The real catechist is a saint.[102] Their spiritual life should be based on a communion of faith and love with the person of Jesus, who calls them and sends them on his mission.[103] Like Jesus, the only Master (cf. Matt

23:8),[104] catechists serve their brothers and sisters by their teaching and works (cf. Acts 1:1), which are manifestations of love. To do the will of their Father, which is an act of salvific love for others, is their food, as it was that of Jesus (cf. John 4:34). Sanctity of life, lived as a lay apostle,[105] is the ideal to be striven for. Spiritual formation should be a process of listening *"to Him who is the principle inspiring all catechetical work and all who do this work—the Spirit of the Father and of the Son, the Holy Spirit."*[106]

The best way to attain this interior maturity is an intense sacramental and prayer life.[107]

Basing itself on the actual experiences of catechists, the CEP proposes the following practices as key elements in the prayer life at least of the catechists who guide the community in a supplementary way, full-time catechists and those working closely with the parish priest, especially of the *cadres.*

—Regular, even daily, **reception of the Eucharist,** so as to nourish oneself with the *"bread of life"* (John 6:34), to form *"a single body"* with the community (cf. 1 Cor 10:17) and offer oneself to the Father along with the Lord's body and blood.[108]

—**Lived liturgy** in its various dimensions for the personal growth and for the help of the community.[109]

—Recital of part of the **Divine Office,** especially Lauds and Vespers, in union with the song of praise that the Church addresses to the Father *"from the rising of the sun to its setting"* (Ps 113:3).[110]

—Daily **meditation,** especially on the word of God, in an attitude of contemplation and response; experience shows that, even for laypeople, regular meditation and *lectio divina* bring order to one's life and guarantee spiritual growth.[111]

—**Personal prayer,** which ensures contact with God during one's daily occupations, with special attention to Marian prayer.

—Frequent reception of the **sacrament of penance,** to ask pardon for faults committed and renew one's fervor.[112]

—Participation in **spiritual retreats,** for personal and community renewal.

It is through such a life of prayer that catechists will enrich their interior life and attain the spiritual maturity required by their role. Prayer is also necessary for their ministry to be fruitful, for communication of the Christian faith depends less on the catechist's ability than on God's grace working in the hearts of those who hear the message.[113]

If a sufficient number of suitable candidates cannot be found, there may be a risk of settling for catechists who are not spiritual enough, but the CEP would not encourage such pragmatic solutions, for mission in the world today requires that the catechist hold a place of honor in the Church.

To help catechists in their spiritual life, **spiritual direction** should be made available. Dioceses are encouraged to name specific priests to interest themselves in the catechists and their work and provide spiritual guidance. But it is important that each catechist should choose a personal spiritual director from among the priests who are easily accessible. Parish priests in particular should be close to their catechists and help them even more in their spiritual growth than in their work.

Also to be encouraged are parish or diocesan initiatives for catechists, such as prayer groups, days of recollection together, or spiritual retreats, which will help them to share with each other on a spiritual level.

Catechists should also realize that the Christian community itself is a place where they can cultivate their own interior life. While they lead others in prayer, they will receive from them a stimulus and example to maintain their own fervor and grow in apostolic spirit.

23. Doctrinal Training

The need for doctrinal training is obvious, as catechists must first understand the essentials of Christian doctrine before they can communicate it to others in a clear and interesting way, without omissions or error.

All candidates should have attained a certain level of education, in keeping with the standards of the country. As mentioned above, there can be problems where the general standard is not high, but facile solutions should be resisted. On the contrary, standards for admission should be above average, as candidates should be able to follow a course of *"higher religious education."* Without this, they would feel inferior to those who have done higher studies and would be ill at ease in educated circles and unable to face certain issues.

As for the contents of the course, they should be based on the program for *"doctrinal, anthropological and methodological formation"* presented in the *General Catechetical Directory*, published by the Congregation for the Clergy in 1971.[114] For mission territories, however, there should be certain adaptations and additions, as the CEP had indicated in part at its 1970 Plenary Assembly and which it now summarizes and develops on the basis of the encyclical *Redemptoris Missio:*

—In view of the specific aims of missionary activity, the doctrinal formation of catechists will be based especially on theology of Trinity, Christology and Ecclesiology, presented in a systematic and progressive synthesis of the Christian message. As they have the task of making Christ known and loved, they will strive to know Him doctrinally and on a personal level; and in order to make the Church known and loved, they will study its tradition and history, and the witness of its great figures, the Church Fathers and the Saints.[115]

—The level of religious and theological training will vary from place to place and will also depend on whether it is given in a catechetical center or in short courses. A minimum standard, however, will be set by the Episcopal Conference or individual bishops, to ensure that the training will qualify as *higher* religious education.

Sacred Scripture will always be the main field of study and will be the soul of the program. Around it will be structured the other branches of theology. It should be borne in mind that the catechist must be qualified in the biblical pastoral, also in view of the comparison with the non-Catholic confessions and with the sects which often use the Bible in an incorrect way.

—The main elements of Missiology will also be studied, as this is an important subject for the mission.

—Liturgy must also, obviously, be given a prominent place, as catechists are to be leaders of community prayer.

—According to local circumstances, it may be necessary to study the beliefs and practices of other religions or Christian denominations in the area.

—Attention should also be given to other subjects connected with local conditions: the inculturation of Christianity in the country or region; the promotion of justice and human development in the local socioeconomic situation; the history of the country; the religious practices, language, problems and needs of the area in which the catechist is to work.

—Regarding the methodological training one should bear in mind that many catechists will be working in various pastoral fields, and almost all will be in contact with people of other religions; they will be taught not only how to teach the catechism but also how to go about the various tasks connected with the proclamation of the Christian message and the life of an ecclesial community.

—It will also be important to grant the catechist contents and materials connected to their new and emerging life situations. The programs of study, which have a starting point in the actual reality and from foresight, can also include subjects that help them to face the phenomena of urbanization, secularization, industrialization, emigration, sociopolitical changes, the world of youngsters, and so on.

—In spite of the diversity of subjects, one should aim at a global and not compartmentalized theological formation, that is, there should be an overall vision of faith that brings unity and harmony to the knowledge acquired, to the catechists' personalities and to their apostolic service. —At this point, it is necessary to emphasize the special importance the *Catechism of the Catholic Church* assumes for the doctrinal preparation of the catechists. In it, in fact, is contained an orderly synthesis of the Revelation and of the perennial Catholic faith, as the Church would propose to herself and to the community of men of our time. As the Holy Father John Paul II affirms in the Apostolic Constitution *Fidei Depositum,* in the catechism there are *"new things and old things (cf. Matt 13:52), since the faith is always the same and at the same time it is the source of the lights which are ever new."* The service which the catechism aims at pertains and is relevant to each catechist. The same Apostolic Constitution attests that it is offered to the pastors and to the faithful, so that it may help them to fulfill, inside and outside the ecclesial community, *"their mission to announce the faith and to call to the evangelical life."* Moreover, it *"is offered to each man who may ask us the reason for the hope in us (cf. 1 Pt 3:15) and who may desire to know what the Church believes."* There is no doubt that the catechists will find in the new catechism a source of inspiration and a mine of knowledge for their specific mission.

Training courses for catechists are best given in centers built for this purpose. Where these are not available, shorter courses may be provided in other locations by dioceses or parishes, and individual instruction could be given by a priest or an expert catechist. The courses should include lectures, group discussions and practical exercises, as well as personal study and research.

To provide adequate training is not easy and will require personnel, structures and financial support. But, in view of the importance of catechists, the challenge should be faced courageously, with realistic and intelligent planning.

Catechists should dedicate themselves to their studies so as to become lamps to light the way of their brothers and sisters (cf. Matt 5:14–16). They should be joyful in their faith and hope (cf. Phil 3:1; Rom 12:12), with the wisdom to transmit the authentic teaching of the Church, in fidelity to the Magisterium, without disturbing consciences, and especially those of the young, with theories that *"are only likely to raise irrelevant doubts instead of furthering the designs of God which are revealed in faith"* (1 Tim 1:4).[116]

They should submit their minds and hearts to Christ, who is the one Teacher, and be aware that *"anyone else teaches to the extent that he is Christ's spokesman, enabling Christ to teach with his lips."*[117]

24. Pastoral Spirit

The pastoral dimension of formation concerns the exercise of the prophetic, priestly and royal functions of the baptized layperson. Catechists will be taught, therefore, how to proclaim the Christian message and teach it, how to lead others in community and liturgical prayer, and how to carry out various other pastoral services.

Qualities to be developed for these tasks are: a spirit of pastoral responsibility and leadership; generosity, dynamism and creativity; ecclesial communion and obedience to pastors.

The **theoretical** part of the pastoral course will deal with the different types of pastoral work to be undertaken and also with the different groups of people to be addressed: children, adolescents, young people or adults; students or workers; baptized or unbaptized; healthy or sick; rich or poor; individuals or members of particular movements or groups, and so on.

The **practical** part of the course will include practical exercises especially at the beginning, under the direction of the teacher or a priest or an experienced catechist.

Special attention will be paid to the sacraments, so that catechists will learn how to help the faithful to understand the religious meaning of these signs and approach them with faith in their supernatural efficacy. The sacrament of the anointing of the sick should not be forgotten, as catechists will often have to help the sick and dying to accept their sufferings in a spirit of faith.

For training in the specific field of catechesis, it would be well to consult the General Catechetical Directory, particularly the section on *"elements of methodology."*[118]

25. Missionary Zeal

The missionary dimension is an essential part of a catechist's identity and work, and so should be given a prominent place in the formation program. Catechists should be taught, theoretically and practically, how to devote themselves as lay Christians to the missionary apostolate, which includes the following elements:

—Being **actively present** in society, offering true Christian witness, entering into sincere dialogue with others, and cooperating in charity to resolve common problems.[119]

—**Proclaiming boldly** (cf. Acts 4:13; 28:31) the truth about God and his Son Jesus Christ, whom He sent into the world for the salvation of all (cf. 2 Tim 1:9–10), so that those of other religions whose hearts are opened by the Holy Spirit (cf. Acts 16:14) may be able to believe and be freely converted.[120]

—**Meeting followers of other religions** in a spirit of openness and dialogue.

—**Introducing catechumens** to the mystery of salvation, the practice of evangelical norms and the religious, liturgical and community life of the People of God.[121]

—**Building community** and helping candidates prepare for the reception of baptism and the other sacraments of Christian initiation, as they become members of the Church of Christ, which is prophetic, priestly and royal.[122]

—With dependence on the Pastors and in collaboration with the faithful, **fulfilling those practices,** which according to the pastoral design are destined to the maturing of the particular Church. These services are connected with various necessities of each Church and mark the catechist of the mission territories. As a result the formative activity must help the catechist to improve his own missionary sensibility, enabling him to discover and be involved in all the favorable situations at the first proclamation.

We have already quoted words of Pope John Paul II concerning catechists who are well trained in a missionary spirit and who themselves become **missionary animators** in their community, work for the evangelization of non-Christians, and are willing to do so outside of their own region or nation when sent by their pastors. Pastors will make the most of these zealous apostles and encourage them in their missionary work.

26. Attitude to the Church

The fact that the Church is missionary by nature and is sent to evangelize the whole world means that apostolic activity is not something individual or isolated, but is always carried out in communion with the local and universal Church.

This remark was made by Pope Paul VI concerning evangelizers,[123] but it also can be applied fully to catechists, whose role is eminently ecclesial.[124] They are sent by their pastors and act in virtue of a mandate given them by the Church. Their activity is part of the Church's activity and shares in its grace.

The following points should he stressed when training catechists in this area:

—An **attitude of apostolic obedience** to one's pastors, in a spirit of faith, just as Jesus *"emptied himself, taking the form of a servant . . . and became obedient unto death"* (Phil 2:7–8: cf. Heb 5:8; Rom 5:19). Obedience should he accompanied by a sense of responsibility, as catechists in their ministry are called upon to respond to the grace of the Holy Spirit.[125]

In view of this, the **canonical mandate or mission** which is conferred in certain Churches is something to be encouraged, as it brings out the link between the catechist's mission and that of Christ and his Church. It should take place during a liturgical or liturgically inspired ceremony, at which the bishop or his delegate will confer the mandate, accompanied by some suitable sign, such as the presentation of a crucifix or a Bible. There could be different grades of solemnity for full-time and part-time catechists.

—An **ability to work with others** at all levels is essential. Catechists should work in harmony with the local priests and religious, and especially with other members of the laity involved in the apostolate. They should fit into the overall pastoral plan and should meet from time to time with the others to discuss matters of common interest and review the work. The bishops should promote this type of work in common.

Catechists will be prepared to suffer for the Church, accepting the difficulties of work in common and the imperfections of others, and imitating Christ, who *"loved the Church and gave himself up for her"* (Eph 5:25).[126]

Training in this community spirit will be part of the catechists' training course from the beginning, with practical exercises carried out in groups.

27. Agents of Formation

One of the problems of paramount importance in the field of formation of catechists is that of having suitable and sufficient formators. When we speak about the agents of formation, we should keep in mind all persons involved in formation.

The catechists should be convinced that: the most important formator is **Christ** himself, who forms them through the **Holy Spirit** (John 16:12–15). To hear God's voice requires a spirit of faith and an attitude of prayer and recollection. The education of apostles, in fact, is primarily a supernatural activity.

The **catechists** themselves can also be considered formators, in that they are responsible for their own interior growth through their response to God. They should be aware of this and should strive to listen always to the Divine Master so as to grow in wisdom and love.

Catechists work in communion with, at the service of and with the help of the **ecclesial community.** The community as a whole, therefore, is called to cooperate in the formation of its catechists, providing them with an atmosphere of acceptance and encouragement, welcoming them for what they are and offering them help. In the community, the **bishop and parish priests** hold a special place as formators. They will take an interest in the candidates, who in turn will be happy to learn from them.

Formators in the strict sense, that is, those designated by the Church to train the catechists, have a most important role entrusted to them. They may be directors and staff of catechetical centers or may be charged with providing initial or ongoing formation outside of these centers. They should be chosen with care, and should be good Christians, loyal to the Church, with proper intellectual qualifications and personal experience in the catechetical field. It would be good if they could work as a team, made up of priests, religious and lay men and women, chosen especially from among experienced catechists. Candidates should be able to trust their formators and respect them as guides offered by the Church to help them in their growth.

28. Initial Formation

The initial or basic training period that precedes the beginning of a catechist's ministry is not the same in every Church, on account of the varying local conditions, but, whether the training is given in a catechetical center or in other ways, it should meet certain requirements. The following criteria should be borne in mind:

—**Knowledge of the candidates:** they should be known personally and in their cultural milieu, not only so as to avoid making mistaken choices, but also for the formation to be personalized and adapted to the needs of each one.

—**Attention to the actual conditions** of the local Church and society. The training given should be not only theoretical but practical and rooted in the real-life situations of the people.

—A **step-by-step** approach. The program should be methodical and gradual, respecting each candidate's progress and growth. One should not pretend to have a perfect catechist from the beginning, but should assist him to grow without interruption and incompleteness.

—**Orderly and complete method:** taking into consideration the situations of mission and of the pedagogy, the training should be **based on experience;** should aim at developing the **whole personality;** should promote a continuous **dialogue** between the candidate and God, the formators and the community; should be **liberating,** freeing the catechist from conscious or unconscious obstacles to God's action; and should promote unity and **harmony.**

—The candidates should be helped to draw up a **life program,** with goals to be aimed at and means to achieve them, but in a realistic spirit. The goals should include identity and lifestyle, and also the qualities needed for the apostolate.

—There should be continual **personal dialogue** between the candidates and formators, who should be looked upon not merely as teachers but as friends and guides. As mentioned above, **spiritual direction** is very important, as it touches the depths of a person's soul and helps open it to God's grace.

—The **Christian community** in which the catechists live and work will also contribute to their formation, for no true apostolic education can take place outside of it. They will be constantly discovering how God's plan for salvation is being worked out in the community.

These guidelines should be taken into account where there are proper structures for initial formation, but even where these have not been established they can serve as a stimulus for both pastors and candidates. The training should not be improvised or left to the initiative of the candidates themselves.

29. Ongoing Formation

The fact that persons should never stop growing interiorly, the dynamic nature of the sacraments of Baptism and Confirmation, the process of continual conversion and growth in apostolic love, changes in culture, the evolution of society and constant updating of teaching methods all mean that catechists should keep themselves in a process of ongoing formation during the whole course of their service. It should include human, spiritual, doctrinal and apostolic formation, and they should be helped in this and not merely left to their own devices.[127]

In the **early period** of their apostolate, ongoing formation will be largely the reinforcement of the basic training and its application in practice. **Later** it will entail updating on various points, so as to keep in touch with developments in theology and changing circumstances. In this endeavor one can ensure the quality of catechists, avoiding the risk of wearing down. In **certain cases** of special difficulty, such as discouragement or a change of work, it will entail a process of renewal and revitalization.

Ongoing formation is not the responsibility of the pastoral centers only, but should be attended to in each local community, especially as needs differ from person to person and place to place.[128]

Besides, one should guarantee the use of the means of the ongoing formation. Obstacles to ongoing formation may come from lack of funds, of books and other teaching aids, of qualified personnel, of transport for distances that can often be considerable, etc. But, as with initial formation, every effort should be made to overcome such obstacles, as it is important that each catechist should be helped toward continual progress and growth. The catechetical centers are certainly the most suitable agencies for promoting ongoing formation. They should follow up their former students, especially soon after they graduate, through circulars and individual letters, teaching aids, visits from formators, refresher courses or meetings at the centers, etc.

Where there are no centers, the diocesan authorities will try to ensure ongoing formation by means of short courses or renewal days directed by qualified personnel. Likewise individual parishes, or groups of parishes cooperating with each other, should organize such courses.[129]

For proper ongoing formation, haphazard individual initiatives are not enough. There should be an organized program covering the various aspects of catechists' work, the development of their personalities and, above all, their spiritual growth.

In spite of going from time to time to catechetical centers or other meeting places, catechists will necessarily accomplish most of their ongoing formation in their local communities and will derive support from them. But wider horizons should also be opened, with opportunities for catechists to meet those of other local Churches.

Finally, ongoing formation will depend to a large extent on the catechists themselves. They should be aware of the need for constant renewal and updating, and should seek out the means for this in reading, prayer and contacts with others.

30. Means and Structures of Formation

Where possible, catechists should be trained in their own special **centers or schools.** Church documents from *Ad Gentes* to *Redemptoris Missio* stress the importance of making efforts *"to establish and support schools for catechists, which are to be approved by the Episcopal Conferences and confer diplomas officially recognized by them."*[130]

The centers are very different entities: some of them being large residential centers with a team of formators and well-organized training programs, while others are smaller centers for restricted groups or short courses. Most centers are diocesan or interdiocesan, some of them national or international.

There are **common elements** to these centers, such as a formative program, which makes the center a place of growth in faith, a possibility of residence, school teaching combined with pastoral experiences and, above all, the presence of the team of formators. There are also some **proper elements** which distinguish one center from the other: among them, for example, the minimum qualification and other conditions for entry, the length of the course, the methods employed, with a view to local conditions, and the categories of students: men or women or both; young people or adults: married or unmarried people or couples. Some centers will include training for the wife or husband of the candidate and issuing of diplomas.

It is important to promote contacts between catechetical centers, especially at a national level, under the guidance of the Episcopal Conference. Formators from the different centers should meet from time to time to exchange ideas and teaching methods and learn from the experiences of others.

Centers should aim not merely at training their students but at being places of research and reflection on themes connected with the apostolate, such as: catechesis itself, inculturation, interreligious dialogue, pastoral methods, etc.

Besides the centers or schools, there should also be **courses** and **encounters** of diverse duration and composition organized by the dioceses and parishes, particularly those in which the bishop and the parish priests participate. These are very significant means of training and, in certain zones and situations, they become the only way of formation. These courses do not counteract the programs of the centers, but help them keep on the impact or, as very often happens, compensate for deficiency.

Each diocese should make sure that it provides the books, audiovisual material and other teaching aids necessary for catechetical training, and it would be good if there could be a pooling of ideas, information and teaching aids between centers, dioceses and neighboring countries.

The CEP insists on the fact that it is not sufficient to propose high objectives in formation, but one should identify and use efficacious means. Therefore, besides confirming the absolute priority of formators, who must be well prepared and sustained, the CEP asks that a strengthening of centers should be at work everywhere. Here too, a healthy realism is essential in order to avoid a theoretical discourse. The objective is to do things in such a way that all the dioceses have the possibility to train a certain number of their catechists, at least the *cadres*, in a center. Besides this, fostering the initiatives on the post, particularly the guided and programmed meetings, because they are indispensable for the first training of those [who] were not able to frequent a center, and for the permanent formation of all.

Part III:
The Responsibilities Toward Catechists

VI. Remuneration for Catechists

31. The Financial Question in General

The question of proper remuneration for catechists is generally agreed to be one of the most difficult to solve. The problem, obviously, does not arise for religion teachers in schools where their salaries are paid by the state. But when catechists are paid by the Church, especially when they have a family to support, their salary must be adequate and must take full account of the cost of living. If the salary is not high enough, there will be several negative consequences: on the choice of candidates, because capable persons will prefer better-paid jobs; on commitment, because it might be necessary to take on other work to make up the deficit; on formation, because some might not be able to attend the training courses; on perseverance and on relations with the pastors. Also, in many cultures a job is respected only if it is a well-paid one, so if catechists are not well paid they risk being looked down upon.

32. Practical Solutions

Remuneration for catechists must be considered a matter of justice and not of benevolence. Both full-time and part-time catechists must be paid according to precise norms, drawn up at diocesan and parish levels, taking account of the local Church's financial situation, that of the catechist and his or her family, and the general economic conditions of the country. Special consideration has to be given to old, invalid and sick catechists.

The CEP, for its part, will continue, insofar as it can, to raise and distribute subsidies for catechists, but each diocese should try to arrive at a more stable solution of the problem.

Dioceses and parishes, therefore, should set aside a reasonable proportion of their budgets for catechists, and in particular for their formation.[131] The faithful too should contribute to their support, especially when it is a question of the village leader. The quality of persons, in particular those involved in direct apostolate, takes precedence over structures, and so funds earmarked for catechists should not be diverted to other purposes.

Money put into catechetical centers will be well spent, as these will certainly contribute to the *"active and effective catechesis"* of the community and therefore to its spiritual growth.[132]

The good will of voluntary catechists, who have another job but are willing to devote part of their free time to catechetical work, is certainly to be encouraged, and indeed many such generous workers are to be found in the more developed Churches. The faithful should be taught, in fact, to look upon the vocation of a catechist as a mission rather than a job. Further it may be necessary to rethink the organization and distribution of catechists. The problem of remuneration, therefore, is one that has to be solved basically by the local Church. Subsidies from abroad can help, but it is up to the local Church to find a place in its budget for this important apostolic work and to educate the faithful to contribute to its support.

VII. Responsibility of the People of God

33. Responsibility of the Community

The CEP would like to make a public declaration of gratitude to the bishops, priests and communities of faithful for the care and support they have given to catechists. Their attitude is a guarantee for the future of evangelization and the growth of the young Churches. For catechists are, indeed, frontline apostles without whom *"Churches that are flourishing today would not have been built up."*[133] They are essential to the Christian community and are rooted in it through their baptism, confirmation and special vocation. They should be given respect and responsibility in their work and should be able to achieve personal growth through it.

It is important to note that in his encyclical letter *Redemptoris Missio* Pope John Paul II says:

> *Among the laity who become evangelizers, catechists have a place of honor. . . . Even with the extension of the services rendered by laypeople both within and outside the Church, there is always need for the ministry of catechists, a ministry with its own characteristics.*[134]

And in his apostolic exhortation *Catechesi Tradendae* the same Pontiff remarked that *"the term 'catechists' belongs above all to the catechists in mission lands."*[135] Catechists are among those who have received Christ's command to *"go and teach all nations"* (Matt 28:19) and, according to Vatican II, they are *"legitimately active in the ministry of the word."*[136]

They should have a place of honor, therefore, in their communities and should be well represented in pastoral councils and other organizations of the parish and diocese. They are growing in number throughout the Church, and the future of Christian communities will depend on them to a considerable extent. In the secularized atmosphere of the modern world, as laypeople they will have a particular role to play in bringing the light of the Gospel to bear on various situations.[137] In any discussion on the theology of the laity, catechists will necessarily occupy a special place.

All these considerations converge on the urgency to strengthen the catechists with an adequate vocational promotion in number as well as, and above all, in quality, which calls for a careful and global formation program.

34. Responsibility of the Bishops in Particular

The bishops, as *"the ones primarily responsible for catechesis,"*[138] are also those primarily responsible for catechists. Recent documents of the Magisterium and the new Code of Canon Law stress this responsibility, based on the bishops' role as successors of the Apostles, both collegially and as pastors of local Churches.[139]

The CEP urges individual bishops and the Episcopal Conferences to continue and even increase their attention and care for catechists, making sure that there are definite criteria for selection, developing programs and structures for formation, seeing to questions of remuneration, and so on. They should take an interest in their catechists and, as far as possible, have a personal relationship with each of them. Where this is not possible, an episcopal vicar should be named for them.

From its own experience, the CEP suggests the following points for special attention:

—Making the faithful, and especially priests, aware of the **importance and role of catechists.**

—Drawing up or renewing **catechetical directories** on a national or diocesan level, so as to apply and adapt to local conditions the guidelines of the *General Catechetical Directory,* the Apostolic Exhortation *Catechesi Tradendae* and the present *Guide for Catechists.*

—Guaranteeing a minimum of **teaching aids and equipment** for the formation of catechists, so that they will be properly trained for their task; also, if possible, founding or improving catechetical centers.[140]

—Encouraging the preparation and selection of *cadres,* that is, catechists who have been well trained in a center and who have had a certain amount of experience, to work closely with the bishop and priests, to help in the training and guidance of volunteer catechists, and to take leading roles in the application of the catechetical program.

—Providing, with the help of the community, a **budget** for the training, activities and maintenance of catechists.

Above all, bishops will express their responsibility for catechists through paternal love, attention to their needs and personal acquaintance with them.

35. Responsibility of the Priests

Priests, and parish priests in particular, as teachers of the faith and immediate collaborators of the bishop, have a special responsibility for catechists. As pastors, who should recognize, promote and coordinate the various charisms in the community, they should have a particular interest in that of catechists, who share with them the task of instructing people in the faith. They should look on them as cooperators, responsible for the ministry entrusted to them, and not as subordinates carrying out instructions. They should encourage them to be creative and show initiative. They should also educate the community to respect their catechists, help them in their work and contribute to their support, especially if they have a family.

Future priests should be taught in the seminary to value and respect catechists as apostles and fellow workers in the Lord's vineyard.

36. Responsibility of the Formators

The training of catechists is usually entrusted to qualified persons, either in special centers or in the parishes. These formators have an important role and make a valuable contribution to the Church. They should be aware, therefore, of the responsibility that is theirs.

When a person accepts the mandate to train the catechists, he should consider the concrete expression of the care of pastors and should seriously follow their directives. In the same way, he should live the ecclesial dimension of this mandate, realizing it in a communitarian spirit and following the programs therein.

As was mentioned above, formators should be chosen for their spiritual, moral and pedagogical qualities. They should be exemplary Christians, able to educate others by the witness of their own lives. They should be close to their students and should communicate their own fervor and enthusiasm to them.

Every diocese will do its best to have a team of formators, made up possibly of priests, brothers, sisters and laypeople, who could be sent to parishes to help in the selection and training of catechists.

Conclusion

37. A Hope for the Mission of the Third Millennium

The directives contained in this *Guide* are proposed as a general model, to serve as an ideal and be adapted where necessary.

The catechists are held in great esteem for their participation in missionary activities and for their characteristics which are rarely found in the ecclesial communities outside the mission.

Their number continues to grow and in recent years has been between 250,000 and 350,000. For many missionaries they have been absolutely indispensable, serving as their close assistants and at times interpreters. They have often been able to keep the faith of a community alive during trying periods, and their families have given priestly and religious vocations.

We cannot but have the greatest respect for these *"fraternal animators of young communities,"*[141] and feel that we should place the highest ideals before them, while recognizing that, because of objective difficulties or personal limitations, ideals are not always attained.

By way of conclusion, we may quote the words of Pope John Paul II to the catechists of Angola during his visit to that country:

> *So many times it has fallen to you to strengthen and build up the young Christian communities, and even to found new ones through the first proclamation of the Gospel. If missionaries could not be there for this first proclamation or had to leave before it could be followed up, it was you, the catechists, who instructed the catechumens, prepared people for the sacraments, taught the faith and were leaders of the Christian community. . . . Give thanks to the Lord for the gift of your vocation, through which Christ has called you from among other men and women to be instruments of his salvation. Respond with generosity to your vocation and your names will be written in heaven (cf. Luke 10:20).*[142]

The CEP hopes that, with God's help and that of the Virgin Mary, this *Guide* will give new impulse to the promotion of catechists, so that their generous contribution will continue to bear fruit for the Church's mission in the third millennium.

The supreme Pontiff John Paul II, during the course of the Audience granted to the undersigned cardinal Prefect on June 16th, 1992, approved the present Guide for Catechists *and gave consent to its publication.*

Rome, from the Office of the Congregation for the Evangelization of Peoples, December 3rd, 1993, Feast of Saint Francis Xavier.
Jozef Card. Tomko, Prefect
Giuseppe Uhac, Arch. tit. of Tharros, Secretary

NOTES

1. Cf. Plenary Assembly of the Congregation for the Evangelization of Peoples, 14–16 April 1970, and its final report: *Bibliografia Missionaria* 34 (1970): 197–212, and *S. C. de Propaganda Fide Memoria Rerum* 111, no. 2 (1976): 821–831.

2. Cf. Vatican Ecumenical Council II. *Decree on the Church's Missionary Activity (Ad Gentes)*, 17.

3. Pope John Paul II, Address to the Plenary Assembly of the CEP 30 April 1992, or 1 May 1992, 4; cf. also the addresses to the catechists of Guinea at Conakry, 25 February 1992, and to those of Angola in the Benguela cathedral, 9 June 1992, or 11 June 1992, 6.

4. Cf. John Paul II Encyc. Letter *Redemptoris Missio (RM)*, 7 December 1990, 73: *AAS* 83 (1991): 320.

5. Vat. II, *Ad Gentes*, 17; 8.

6. *Catechism of the Catholic Church (CCC)* (Vatican City, 1992).

7. John Paul II, Apos. Exhort. *Fidei Depositum*, 11 October 1992, 4.

8. Cf. John Paul II, Apost. Exhort. *Christifideles Laici (CL)*, 30 December 1988, 56: *AAS* 81 (1989): 504–506.

9. Cf. Plenary Assembly cit., I.2.

10. Cf. Vat. II, *Ad Gentes*, 15.

11. John Paul II, *CL*, 58: loc. cit., 507–509.

12. Cf. *CIC* cc. 773–780 and c. 785.

13. Cf. *CCC*, 6.

14. John Paul II, Apost. Exhort. *Catechesi Tradendae (CT)*, 16 October 1979, 66: *AAS* 71 (1979): 1331.

15. No. 73, loc. cit., 321.

16. *CIC* c. 785, 1.

17. Plenary Assembly cit., 1.

18. John Paul II, *CL*, 23: loc. cit., 429–433; *CIC* c. 230, 2.

19. Plenary Assembly cit., I.4.

20. Cf. John Paul II, *RM*, 74: loc. cit., 322; *CCC*, 4–5; 7–8; 1697–1698.

21. Cf. John Paul II, Address to the Plenary Assembly cit., 2; *CCC*, 6.

22. Cf. John Paul II, *CT*, 65: loc. cit., 1330.

23. Cf. John Paul II, *RM*, 73: loc. cit., 321.

24. John Paul II, Address to the Plenary Assembly cit., 3; cf. S.C. for the Clergy, *General Catechetical Directory (GCD)*, 11 April 1971, 108: *AAS* 64 (1972): 161.

25. Cf. John Paul II, *RM*, 31ff.: loc. cit., 276ff.

26. John Paul II, Address to the Plenary Assembly cit., 4.

27. Cf. John Paul II, *RM*, 74: loc. cit., 322; *Angelus* 18 October 1987 or 19–20 October 1987, 5.

28. John Paul II, *RM*, 90: loc. cit., 337.

29. Ibid.

30. Paul VI, Apos. Exhort. *Evangelii Nuntiandi (EN)*, 8 December 1975, 80: *AAS* 68 (1976): 72–75.

31. *CIC* c. 225, 2.

32. John Paul II, Address to the Plenary Assembly cit., 2.

33. Cf. John Paul II, *CT*, 26–27; loc. cit., 1298–1299.

34. *CIC* 225, 2; John Paul II, *RM*, 87: loc. cit., 334; *CCC*, 2653–2654.

35. Cf. *CIC* c. 747, 1.

36. Cf. Vat. II, *Ad Gentes*, 2; 6; 9.

37. Cf. John Paul II, *RM*, 89: loc. cit., 335–336.

38. Cf. Vat. II, *Ad Gentes*, 2.

39. Cf. Vat. II, Dogm. Const. on the Church, *Lumen Gentium*, 4; *Ad Gentes*, 4.

40. Paul VI, *EN*, 76: loc. cit., 68; cf. John Paul II, *CT*, 57: loc. cit., 1323–1324.

41. Cf. John Paul II, *CT*, 27: loc. cit., 1298–1299.

42. Paul VI, *EN*, 75: loc. cit., 68; cf. John Paul II, *CT*, 57: loc. cit., 1323–1324.

43. Cf. Ireneaus, *Adv. Haer.* I, 10, 1–3; *PG* 550–554; John Paul II, *CT*, 60–61: loc. cit., 1325–1328; *RM*, 11: loc. cit., 259–260.

44. John Paul II, *CT*, 61: loc. cit., 1328.

45. *CCC*, 429.

46. Cf. John Paul II, *RM*, 89: loc. cit., 335–336; *CCC*, 849–851.

47. Cf. *CCC*, 853.

48. John Paul II, *CT*, 73: loc. cit., 1340.

49. Ibid.

50. Cf. *Sermo* 25, 7: *PL* 46, 937–938.

51. John Paul II, *CT*, 73: loc. cit., 1340; *RM*, 92: loc. cit., 339; cf. Paul VI, *EN*, 82: loc. cit., 76.

52. Cf. *CCC*, 487–507; 963–972.

53. Cf. *CCC*, 2673–2679.

54. Vat. II, *Lumen Gentium*, 65.

55. Cf. John Paul II, Address to the Third International Conference on Longevity and Quality of Life: *Dolentium Hominum:* Church and Health in the World, 10 (1989): 6–8.

56. Cf. John Paul II, Apos. Exhort. *Salvifici Doloris*, 11 February 1984, 19: *AAS* 19 (1984): 225–226.

57. Cf. John Paul II, *CL*, 48: loc. cit., 485–486.

58. John Paul II, Apos. Exhort., *Familiaris Consortio*, 22 November 1981, 27: *AAS* 73 (1981): 113.

59. Cf. S.C. for the Clergy, *GCD*, 95: loc. cit., 154–155.

60. Cf. John Paul II, *CT*, 53: loc. cit., 1319–1321.

61. John Paul II, *RM*, 52: loc. cit., 300.

62. Cf. Vat. II, *Ad Gentes*, 9, 16, 22; *Gaudium et Spes*, 44, 57ff.; Paul VI, Apos. Lett. *Ecclesiae Sanctae*, III, 18, 2; ID., *Address* at Kampala, 2 August 1969; *AAS* 61 (1969): 587–590; ID., *EN*, 62ff.: loc. cit., 52ff.; John Paul II, *Familiaris Consortio*, 10: loc. cit., 90–91; ID., *CL*, 44: loc. cit., 478–481; ID., *RM*, 52–54: loc. cit., 299–300; *CCC*, 854, 1204–1206; 1232.

63. Cf. *CCC*, 2628.

64. John Paul II, *RM*, 59: loc. cit., 307; cf. Paul VI, *EN*, 31: loc. cit., 26–27.

65. John Paul II, *RM*, 59: loc. cit., 307; cf. ID., Encyc. Letter *Centesimus Annus*, 1 May 1991; 53ff.: *AAS* 83 (1991): 859ff.; *CCC*, 1939–1942.

66. Cf. Vat. II, *Gaudium et Spes*, 42; Paul VI, *EN*, 25–28; 32–34; loc. cit., 23–25; 27–28; *CCC*, 2443–2449.

67. Cf. John Paul II, *CL*, 41–43: loc. cit., 470–478; *CCC*, 1908; 2442.

68. John Paul II, *RM*, 60: loc. cit., 309; cf. *CCC*, 2443–2449.

69. John Paul II, *RM*, 59; loc. cit., 308.

70. Cf. John Paul II, Encyc. Letter *Sollicitudo Rei Socialis*, 30 December 1987, 42: *AAS* 80 (1988): 572–574; ID., *CT*, 41; 45: loc. cit., 1311; 1314; *RM*, 60: loc. cit., 308–309; *Centesimus Annus*, 57: loc. cit., 862–863.

71. Vat. II, Decree on Ecumenism *Unitatis Redintegratio*, 1; cf. *Ad Gentes*, 6; John Paul II, *RM*, 36; 50: loc. cit., 281; 297–298; *CCC*, 817; 885.

72. Cf. Vat. II, *Unitatis Redintegratio*, cf. S.C. for the Clergy, *GCD*, 27: loc. cit., 115.

73. Cf. *CCC*, 820–822.

74. Cf. Vat. II, *Ad Gentes*, 15.

75. Cf. John Paul II, *RM*, 50: loc. cit., 297–298.

76. Cf. *CIC* c. 755.

77. Cf. John Paul II, *CT*, 33: loc. cit., 1305–1306.

78. Cf. John Paul II, *CT*, 32: loc. cit., 1304; cf. Vat. II, *Unitatis Redintegratio*, 3–4, 11; S.C. for the Clergy, *GCD*, 27: loc. cit., 115.

79. Cf. John Paul II, *CT*, 32: loc. cit., 1304; cf. S.C. for the Clergy, *GCD*, 27: loc. cit., 115.

80. Cf. John Paul II, *CT*, 32: loc. cit., 1304–1305; ID., *RM*, 50: loc. cit., 297–298.

81. Cf. John Paul II, *RM*, 55–56: loc. cit., 302–305; Pontifical Council for Inter-Religious Dialogue—Congregation for the Evangelization of Peoples, *Dialogue and Proclamation*, 19 May 1991; cf. Secretariat for Non-Christians, *The Church's Attitude to Followers of Other Religions*, 4 September 1984; *AAS* 76 (1984): 816–828; *CCC*, 839–845; 856; 1964.

82. Cf. John Paul II, *RM*, 56; loc. cit., 305–306; Pontifical Council for Interreligious Dialogue—Congregation for the Evangelization of Peoples, *Dialogue and Proclamation*, 40–41.

83. Cf. Eusebius of Caesarea, *Praeparatio Evangelica*, 1, 1: *PG* 21, 28 AB; Irenaeus, *Adv. Haer.* III, 18, 1: *PG* 7, 932; ID., III, 20, 2; ibid., 943; Saint Justinus, *1 Apol.* 46; *PG* 6, 395; Vat. II, *Ad Gentes*, 3; 11.

84. Cf. John Paul II, *RM*, 55: loc. cit., 302–304.

85. Cf. Vat. II, *Lumen Gentium*, 14; *Unitatis Redintegratio*, 3; *Ad Gentes*, 7.

86. Cf. John Paul II, Address to the Urban University, 11 April 1991 or 13 April 1991, 5; cf. *CCC*, 846–848.

87. Cf. Vat. II, *Ad Gentes*, 12; John Paul II, *Centesimus Annus*, 60: loc. cit., 865–866.

88. Cf. John Paul II, *RM*, 57: loc. cit., 305.

89. Ibid., 50: loc. cit., 297–298.

90. Cf. Secretariat for Christian Unity—Secretariat for Non-Christians—Pontifical Council for Culture, *The Phenomenon of Sects and New Religious Movements*, 7 May 1986 or 7 May 1986, tabloid supplement.

91. Cf. John Paul II, Address to the Bishops of Zaire; or 24 April 1988, 4.

92. Cf. John Paul II, *RM*, 50: loc. cit., 297–298.

93. Ibid.

94. Congregation for the Evangelization of Peoples, *Pastoral Guide for Diocesan Priests*, 1 October 1989, 17: *EV* 2579–2681.

95. Cf. Saint Augustine, *De catechizandis rudibus*, *PL* 40, 310–347.

96. S.C. for the Clergy, *GCD*, 108: loc. cit., 161.

97. John Paul II, Address to the Plenary Assembly cit., 3; also Vat. II, *Ad Gentes*, 17; *Christus Dominus*, 14; John Paul II, *RM*, 73: loc. cit., 320–321; *CL*, 60: loc. cit., 510–512; *CIC*, c. 785.

98. Cf. Vat. II, Decree on Bishops *Christus Dominus*, 40; S.C. for the Clergy, *GCD*, 108; 115: loc. cit., 161; 164–165.

99. John Paul II, *CL*, 59: loc. cit., 509.

100. Cf. ibid.

101. Cf. John Paul II, *CT*, 5–6; 9: loc. cit., 1280–1281; 1284.

102. Cf. John Paul II, *RM*, 90: loc. cit., 337.

103. Cf. *CCC*, 428.

104. Cf. Saint Ignatius of Antioch, *Epistula ad Magnesios*, IX, 1: Funk 1, 329.

105. Cf. Vat. II, *Lumen Gentium*, 41.

106. John Paul II, *CT*, 72: loc. cit., 1338; cf. Saint Augustinus, *In Joannis Evangelium Tractatus*, 97, 1: *PL* 35, 1887.

107. Cf. S.C. for the Clergy, *GCD*, 114: loc. cit., 164; *CCC*, 2742–2745.

108. Cf. Vat. II, *Lumen Gentium*, 34; *CCC*, 1324–1327; 1343; 1369; 1382ff.

109. Cf. *CCC*, 1071–1075; 1136ff.; 2655.

110. Cf. *CCC*, 1174–1178.

111. Cf. *CCC*, 2653–2654; 2705–2708.

112. Cf. *CCC*, 1446–1456.

113. Cf. S.C. for the Clergy, *GCD*, 71: loc. cit., 142.

114. Cf. *GCD*, 112–113: loc. cit., 163–164.

115. Cf. Plenary Assembly cit., II, 1–2.

116. Cf. Paul VI, *EN*, 78: loc. cit.; John Paul II, *CT*, 61: loc. cit., 1327–1328.

117. John Paul II, *CT*, 6: loc. cit., 1281.

118. S.C. for the Clergy, *GCD*, 70ff.: loc. cit., 141ff.

119. Cf. Vat. II, *Ad Gentes*, 12; John Paul II, *RM*, 44–45: loc. cit., 290–292; *CCC*, 854.

120. Cf. Vat. II, *Ad Gentes*, 13; John Paul II, *RM*, 44–45: loc. cit., 292–295; *CCC*, 854.

121. Cf. Vat. II, *Ad Gentes*, 14; John Paul II, *RM*, 46–47: loc. cit., 292–295; *Ordo Initiationis Christianae; CCC*, 854.

122. Cf. Vat. II, *Ad Gentes*, 15; John Paul II, *RM*, 48: loc. cit., 295; *CCC*, 854.

123. Cf. Paul VI, *EN*, 60: loc. cit., 50–51.

124. Cf. John Paul II, *CT*, 24: loc. cit., 1297.

125. Cf. Vat. II, *Lumen Gentium*, 12.

126. Cf. John Paul II, *RM*, 89: loc. cit., 335–336.

127. Cf. S.C. for the Clergy, *GCD*, 110: loc. cit., 162.

128. Cf. ibid.

129. Cf. Vat. II, *Ad Gentes*, 17.

130. Cf. John Paul II, *RM*, 73: loc. cit., 321; cf. Vat. II, *Ad Gentes*, 17; S.C. for the Clergy, *CT*, 71: loc. cit., 1337; *CIC* c. 785, 2.

131. Cf. John Paul II, *CT*, 63: loc. cit., 1329.

132. Cf. ibid.

133. John Paul II, *CT*, 66: loc. cit., 1331.

134. John Paul II, *RM*, 73: loc. cit., 320–321.

135. John Paul II, *CT*, 66: loc. cit., 1331; cf. *Angelus*, 18 October 1987 or 19–20 October 1987, 5.

136. Vat. II, *Dei Verbum*, 25.

137. Cf. John Paul II, Address to the Plenary Assembly cit. 2.

138. John Paul II, *CT*, 63: loc. cit., 1329.

139. Cf. Vat. II, *Christus Dominus*, 14; John Paul II, *CT*, 63: loc. cit., 1328–1329; S.C. for the Clergy, *GCD*, 108: loc. cit., 161; *CIC* cc. 773, 780.

140. Cf. John Paul II, *RM*, 71: loc. cit., 318–319.

141. John Paul II, Address to the catechists of Guinea cit.

142. John Paul II, Address to the catechists of Angola cit.